York S...
Fountains Learning Centre
Over.....

The study of sociolinguistic variation examines the relation between social identity and ways of speaking. The analysis of style in speech is central to this field because it varies not only between speakers, but in individual speakers as they move from one style to another. Studying these variations in language not only reveals a great deal about speakers' strategies with respect to variables such as social class, gender, ethnicity and age, it also affords us the opportunity to observe linguistic change in progress.

The volume brings together a team of leading experts from a range of disciplines to create a broad perspective on the study of style and variation. Beginning with an introduction to the broad theoretical issues, the book goes on to discuss key approaches to stylistic variation in spoken language, including such issues as attention paid to speech, audience design, identity construction, the corpus study of register, genre, distinctiveness and the anthropological study of style.

Rigorous and engaging, this book will become the standard work on stylistic variation. It will be welcomed by students and academics in sociolinguistics, English language, dialectology, anthropology and sociology.

PENELOPE ECKERT is Professor of Linguistics, Courtesy Professor in Anthropology, and co-Chair of the Program in Feminist Studies at Stanford University. She has published work in pure ethnography as well as ethnographically based sociolinguistics including *Jocks and Burnouts: Social Identity in the High School* (1989) and *Variation as Social Practices* (2000).

JOHN R. RICKFORD is the Martin Luther King, Jr., Centennial Professor of Linguistics at Stanford University. He is also Courtesy Professor in Education, and Director of the Program in African and African American Studies. He has published work on various aspects of sociolinguistic variation and change, including *Dimensions of a Creole Continuum* (1987), *African American Vernacular English* (1999) and *Spoken Soul* (2000, with Russell J. Rickford).

1 8 JUN 2024

WITHDRAWN

College of Ripon & York St. John

3 8025 00392716 0

Style and Sociolinguistic Variation

edited by

Penelope Eckert and John R. Rickford
Stanford University

YORK ST JOHN
COLLEGE LIBRARY

CAMBRIDGE
UNIVERSITY PRESS

PUBLISHED BY THE PRESS SYNDICATE OF THE UNIVERSITY OF CAMBRIDGE
The Pitt Building, Trumpington Street, Cambridge, United Kingdom

CAMBRIDGE UNIVERSITY PRESS
The Edinburgh Building, Cambridge CB2 2RU, UK
40 West 20th Street, New York, NY 10011–4211, USA
477 Williamstown Road, Port Melbourne, VIC 3207, Australia
Ruiz de Alarcón 13, 28014 Madrid, Spain
Dock House, The Waterfront, Cape Town 8001, South Africa

http://www.cambridge.org

© Cambridge University Press 2001

This book is in copyright. Subject to statutory exception
and to the provisions of relevant collective licensing agreements,
no reproduction of any part may take place without
the written permission of Cambridge University Press.

First published 2001

Printed in the United Kingdom at the University Press, Cambridge

Typeface 10/12pt Times NR MT   *System* QuarkXPress™   [SE]

A catalogue record for this book is available from the British Library

Library of Congress Cataloguing in Publication data

Style and sociolinguistic variation / edited by Penelope Eckert and John R. Rickford.
    p.   cm.
Includes bibliographical references and index.
ISBN 0 521 59191 0 (hbk.)   ISBN 0 521 59789 7 (pbk.)
1. Language and languages. – Variation.   2. Language and languages – Style.
3. Discourse analysis. 4. Sociolinguistics. I. Eckert, Penelope. II. Rickford,
John R., 1949–
P120.V37 S79   2001
417 – dc21   00-068947   CIP

ISBN 0 521 59191 0 hardback
ISBN 0 521 59789 7 paperback

The original idea for this volume was Malcah Yaeger-Dror's, and for her inspiration and engagement, we dedicate this book to her.

Contents

Part 3 Audience design and self-identification

Part 4 Functionally motivated situational variation

Figures

Tables

Contributors

JOHN BAUGH is Professor of Education and Linguistics at Stanford University. His publications include *Out of the Mouths of Slaves: African American Language and Educational Malpractice* (1999), and *Beyond Ebonics: Linguistic Pride and Racial Prejudice* (2000).

RICHARD BAUMAN is Distinguished Professor of Communication and Culture, Anthropology, and Folklore at Indiana University, Bloomington. He has served as President of the Society for Linguistic Anthropology, and as Editor of the *Journal of American Folklore*. The principal foci of his publications include the ethnography of speaking, oral poetics and performance, narrative, and genre.

ALLAN BELL is Professor of Language and Communication in the School of Languages, Auckland University of Technology. His paper "Language Style as Audience Design" (*Language in Society*, 1984) has been foundational in the sociolinguistic study of style. He is (with Nikolas Coupland) founding editor of the *Journal of Sociolinguistics*.

DOUGLAS BIBER is Regents' Professor of English (Applied Linguistics) at Northern Arizona University. His publications include *Variation across Speech and Writings* (1988), *Dimensions of Register Variation* (1995), *Corpus Linguistics* (with S. Conrad and R. Reppen, 1998), and *The Longman Grammar of Spoken and Written English* (co-edited, 1999).

NIKOLAS COUPLAND is Professor and Chair of the Centre for Language and Communication Research at Cardiff University, Wales. He is (with Allan Bell) founding editor of the *Journal of Sociolinguistics*. His principal research interests are: sociolinguistic variation, sociolinguistic theory, style and stylization in language, and the sociolinguistics of later life.

PENNY ECKERT is Professor of Linguistics and co-Chair of the Program in Feminist Studies at Stanford University. Her most recent work focuses on the role of variation in the co-construction of styles and identities.

Her publications include *Jocks and Burnouts: Social Identity in the High School* (1989); *Variation as Social Practice* (2000); she is co-author (with S. McConnell-Ginet) of a forthcoming textbook on language and gender.

SUSAN M. ERVIN-TRIPP is a Professor of Psychology Emeritus at the University of California in Berkeley, California. Her publications include *Child Discourse, Language Acquisition and Communicative Choice*, and articles on child language, bilingualism, and child and adult pragmatics, including extensive work on requests.

EDWARD FINEGAN is Professor of Linguistics and Law at the University of Southern California. He is author of *Language: its Structure and Use* (3rd edn., 1998) and *Attitudes toward English Usage* (1980), and co-editor of *Sociolinguistic Perspectives on Register* (1994). He has most recently contributed chapters on grammar and usage to two volumes of the Cambridge History of the English Language.

HOWARD GILES is Professor of Communication at the University of California, Santa Barbara with an affiliated position there in Psychology and Linguistics. His main research interests are in inter-group communication especially as it relates to inter-generational and police–citizen issues. He has published an array of books in these domains.

JUDITH T. IRVINE is Professor of Anthropology at the University of Michigan, Ann Arbor. Previously she was on the faculty at Brandeis University. Her publications include *Responsibility and Evidence in Oral Discourse* (co-edited with Jane Hill, 1993), *The Psychology of Culture* (1993), and many articles in linguistic anthropology and African studies.

WILLIAM LABOV is Professor of Linguistics and Director of the Linguistics Laboratory at the University of Pennsylvania. His publications include *The Social Stratification of English in New York City* (1966), *The Study of Non-Standard English* (1969), *Sociolinguistic Patterns* (1972), *What is a Linguistic Fact?* (1975), and *Principles of Linguistic Change 1* (1994).

RONALD MACAULAY is Emeritus Professor of Linguistics at Pitzer College in Claremont, California. His books include *Language, Social Class and Education* (1977), *Locating Dialect in Discourse* (1991), and *Standards and Variation in Urban Speech* (1997). He is the author of a forthcoming book on discourse sociolinguistics.

LESLEY MILROY is Hans Kurath Collegiate Professor of Linguistics at the University of Michigan. Her publications include: *Authority in Language* (with James Milroy, 1985; 3rd edn., 1998), *Observing and Analysing Natural Language* (1987), *Linguistics and Aphasia* (with Ruth Lesser, 1993), *Real English* (ed. with James Milroy, 1993), *One Speaker, Two Languages* (ed., 1995).

DENNIS R. PRESTON is Professor of Linguistics at Michigan State University and President-Elect of the American Dialect. He specializes in the interface between language variation and change and attitudes towards and perceptions of language variety. His publications include the *Handbook of Perceptual Dialectology* (ed., 1999) and *Folk Linguistics* (with Nancy Niedzielski, 1999).

JOHN RICKFORD is the Martin Luther King, Jr., Centennial Professor of Linguistics and Director of African and Afro-American Studies at Stanford University. His most recent publications include *African American English* (co-edited, 1998), *African American Vernacular English* (1999), *Creole Genesis, Attitudes and Discourse* (co-edited, 1999), and *Spoken Soul* (with R. J. Rickford, 2000).

ELIZABETH CLOSS TRAUGOTT is Professor of Linguistics and English at Stanford University. Her publications include *A History of English Syntax* (1972), *Linguistics for Students of Literature* (with Mary L. Pratt, 1980), *On Conditionals* (co-edited, 1986), *Grammaticalization* (with Paul Hopper, 1993), and *Regularity in Semantic Change* (with Richard Dasher, forthcoming).

MALCAH YAEGER-DROR is presently research scientist in the University of Arizona Cognitive Sciences Program. She has worked on sound change in real time, analyzing chain shifting in both English and Canadian French. Her publications include contributions to *Papers in Laboratory Phonology III* (ed. P. Keating, 1994), *Towards a Social Science of Language I* (ed. G. Guy et al.), *Language Variation and Change*, and *Speech Communication*.

Acknowledgments

The workshop that gave rise to this volume was funded by a grant from the National Science Foundation (no. SBR-9511724). (Any opinions, findings, and conclusions or recommendations expressed in this material are those of the authors and do not necessarily reflect the views of the National Science Federation.) We wish to acknowledge the support of the NSF, and particularly of Paul Chapin for his years of nurturing linguistics and linguists at NSF.

We also wish to thank a number of people at Stanford who helped make this workshop a success. Andrea Kortenhoven and Gina Wein, who arranged the workshop, made it a gracious and smooth event. We also wish to thank those who have helped us produce this volume: Andrew Wong, Julie Sweetland, and Admas Kanyagia.

Finally, we thank those who participated in the workshop, and who authored the papers that you are about to read.

Introduction

John R. Rickford and Penelope Eckert

1   The place of style in the study of variation

Style is a pivotal construct in the study of sociolinguistic variation. Stylistic variability in speech affords us the possibility of observing linguistic change in progress (Labov 1966). Moreover, since all individuals and social groups have stylistic repertoires, the styles in which they are recorded must be taken into account when comparing them (Rickford and McNair-Knox 1994:265). Finally, style is the locus of the individual's internalization of broader social distributions of variation (Eckert 2000).

In spite of the centrality of style, the concerted attention that has been paid to the relation of variation to social categorizations and configurations has not been equaled by any continuous focus on style. In other words, we have focused on the relation between variation and the speaker's place in the world, at the expense of the speaker's strategies with respect to this place. But as social theories of variation develop greater depth, they require a more sophisticated, integrative treatment of style that places variation within the wider range of linguistic practices with which speakers make social meaning. For this reason, the editors of this volume organized a two-day workshop on style at Stanford University in February 1996, funded by the National Science Foundation (no. SBR-9511724). Bringing together scholars who have worked on style in language from a variety of theoretical and methodological perspectives, the workshop had the goal of stimulating discussions that would set new directions for future work on style in variation. This volume is a product of that workshop.

2   The history of the study of style in variation

The study of sociolinguistic variation is commonly characterized (Bell 1984:145, Finegan and Biber 1994:316) as involving three principal components: *linguistic* or internal constraints, *social* or inter-speaker constraints, and *stylistic* or intra-speaker constraints.

The study of *linguistic* constraints is the area in which the concerns of

1

variationists articulate the most clearly with linguistic research in other areas, adding use data to intuited or experimental data, and bringing quantitative insights to an otherwise exclusively qualitative enterprise. The examination of linguistic constraints, both qualitative and quantitative, has been an active component of variationist work from the 1960s to the present. The quantitative study of large corpora of variable speech data has yielded detailed insights into several aspects of language, including constraints on variable speech output, sound change and syntactic change, the mechanisms of vowel shifts, and structural relations among regional dialects.

The study of *social* variation has also been continuous and productive over this period. The past thirty-five years have seen a flourishing of empirical studies of variation: studies not only in urban settings, but also in suburban and rural settings, in a range of societies outside the USA, and drawing on both survey and ethnographic methods. In these studies researchers have refined their understanding of the relation between variation and social parameters, including class, gender, ethnicity, social networks, identity, local categories, and ideology.

The study of *stylistic* variation, however, has been more uneven. The traditional delimitation of style in the variationist paradigm has been any intra-speaker variation that is not directly attributable to performance factors (in the strict sense) or to factors within the linguistic system. We will begin with this definition, partially to show that the next phase of stylistic studies will have to focus on the highly permeable boundaries among linguistic, social, and stylistic constraints.

William Labov's (1966) New York City study, which launched the current quantitative study of variation, gave central theoretical and methodological importance to style. This study established that stylistic variation constitutes a crucial nexus between the individual and the community – between the linguistic, the cognitive, and the social. Labov demonstrated that the use of sociolinguistic variables is socioeconomically stratified, and that each speaker's stylistic range covers a continuous subset of use within the socioeconomic matrix. Placing global prestige at the upper end of the socioeconomic hierarchy and global stigma at the lower, Labov characterized each speaker's stylistic continuum in relation to these two poles. He viewed the "prestigious" end of the speaker's range as the result of more formal, careful, speech, and the "stigmatized" end as the result of more casual, unmonitored speech. The speaker's stylistic activity, therefore, was directly connected to the speaker's place in, and strategies with respect to, the socioeconomic hierarchy.

While the notion of prestige plays an important role in Labov's work on style (e.g. 1972), it is attention paid to speech that he puts at the center of the theory, presumably because attention is the cognitive mechanism that links social to linguistic factors. Fundamental to his work, then, is the notion of the speaker's vernacular – that speech that is most natural, that is prior to an overlay of correction, and that emerges when the speaker is not monitoring their speech. And it is in the vernacular that Labov expects to find the most natural speech and the best evidence of the processes of change. With this theorizing of style came a focus on field methods, making the manipulation of informants' style central to the process of data extraction. Labov designed the sociolinguistic interview to elicit as wide a range of a speaker's style as possible, from the most careful to the most casual speech. Fundamental to the interview is what Labov called the "observer's paradox" (Labov 1975) – that the vernacular the linguist wishes to observe is unlikely to be produced in the relatively formal context in which speakers interact with interviewers who are strangers. Labov sought to elicit a broader range of interviewees' styles primarily by manipulating the topic, on the assumption that some topics will focus interviewees on their speech while others will focus them away from it. While topic is the parameter that Labov most consciously controls in the interview, the need for such a strategy, the observer's paradox, stems from the fact that audience is a fundamental influence in stylistic production. Labov showed some early recognition of this (1966:101–4) insofar as he defined speech to family members and friends rather than the interviewer as potential casual speech contexts within the interview.

Stylistic variation emerged from the New York City study as among the most important constructs in the field. Yet despite its importance, style became less of a focus of empirical research from the 1970s onward, at least in the influential American quantitative tradition. This was partly because people questioned Labov's focus on attention paid to speech (Milroy 1987:172–83), partly because of the operational difficulty of separating casual speech from careful speech via interview contexts and channel cues (Wolfram 1969:58–9), and partly because researchers became absorbed in the study of the linguistic and social constraints on variation. (See Rickford and McNair-Knox 1994:238–9 for further discussion.)

Social psychological work in accommodation theory (Giles and Powesland 1975, Giles 1984, Giles, Coupland, and Coupland 1991) ran parallel for some time to efforts in variation, showing among other things the important influence on language style of the speaker's orientation and attitude to addressees. Some early variation studies explicitly explored the effect on variation of the addressee (Van den Broeck 1977, Baugh 1979, Hindle 1979, Rickford 1979, Coupland 1980) and of audience more generally (Bell 1977). Bell (1984) followed up these early studies with focused research that put audience at the center of stylistic production. Specifically, he argued that stylistic variation can be explained as a response to the present audience: primarily the actual addressee, but also third persons (i.e. auditors and overhearers). He argued that the apparent influence of topic shift is actually due to the association of topics with audience types. Recognizing that not all stylistic shifts are obvious responses to present participants, he posited the effect of "referees" – absent reference groups – whose presence in the mind of the speaker could influence variability. This paper not only introduced a coherent view of style-shifting, it also integrated a wide range of previously disparate sociolinguistic findings, and posited a number of novel theoretical generalizations and testable predictions about the relation between social and stylistic variation.

In their (1994) paper on the relation between register and social dialect variation (first circulated in draft in 1990) Finegan and Biber credited Bell with explaining the parallel relation between stylistic and social variation, but not the internal systematicity of each category (why consonant cluster simplification *de*creases as formality *in*creases, for instance). Their own explanation for this systematicity was a functional one, which argued (p. 339) that "Social dialect variation . . . depends upon register variation, and register variation is largely shaped by communicative constraints inherent in particular situations." Where Bell focused on audience, Finegan and Biber focused on the broader *situation*, and sought to establish a link from the variables themselves to the situations in which they are used and finally to the socioeconomic hierarchy. They began with the argument that socially stratified variables tend to involve some kind of reduction or simplification, and that complexity of linguistic form correlates with socioeconomic status. They argue that more complex linguistic forms are called for in more "literate" situations, as a function both of the tasks being undertaken in these situations and of a relative lack of shared context. They then attribute the social stratification of language use to the stratification of access to these situation types.

With Coupland (1980), we come full circle, with a focus on the speakers themselves. Introducing an emphasis on the "identity dimensions" of style, Coupland treats stylistic variation as a dynamic presentation of the self. For this reason, rather than focusing on the cumulative use of variables by speakers or groups of speakers, he focuses on the strategic use of variables in discourse. This emphasis also led him to approach the selection of variables differently. Because of the structural focus in the field of variation, variables have been customarily selected not so much on the basis of their apparent social significance as on the basis of their interest to the study of linguistic structure and change. Coupland's focus on the speaker's identity led him to take seriously the participants' perceptions of style, and to argue that the tendency to focus on individual variables abstracts away from what speakers themselves perceive as style.

This emphasis on style as a set of co-occurring variables that are associated with the speaker's own persona was a major departure from the studies of style that preceded, and is becoming increasingly important in the study of variation. Rickford and McNair-Knox (1994:263–5) and Rickford and Rickford (2000:128) have raised the issue of performativity in style, suggesting that variability can play a role in the performance of the speaker's own social affiliations and identity. The California Style Collective (1993) and Eckert (2000) have explored the role of variation in the active construction of personal and group styles, viewing individual variables as resources that can be put to work in constructing new personae.

Some of these explorations are part of a movement in the field of variation away from the purely structural models of society that formed the original basis of variation theory, into a view of variation as social practice. An emerging focus on agency is bringing researchers to examine variation as part of a process of construction of identities and social meaning (California Style Collective 1993, Bucholtz 1996, Eckert 2000), and to view variation in terms of relations of linguistic production (Bourdieu 1982) rather than simply in terms of appropriateness to "social address" (Eckert and McConnell-Ginet 1992).

These explorations remain in the early stages, and are bringing variation studies into synch with work in anthropology. Roughly the same decades that have seen the development of modern variation theory have also seen the development of the anthropological study of communicative competence and the ethnography of speaking (e.g. Hymes 1964, 1972, Bauman and Sherzer 1974, Heath 1983, Briggs 1988). Researchers working on these topics, focusing on verbal performance, have developed perspectives on linguistic practice that are quite crucial and complementary to the explorations of style that have been developing in the field of variation. While in earlier years there was considerable interaction between people studying variation and people studying the ethnography of speaking, as variation emerged as a field in itself, this interaction dwindled. As a result, there has been little integration between the study of variation and the study of verbal genres as pursued in folklore and the ethnography of speaking.

The models of style discussed above that have arisen in the study of variation are not contradictory or mutually exclusive. One might think that, for example, Labov's view of style as a function of attention paid to speech is irreconcilable with the view of the use of variables in terms of "identity performances." A resolution between the views, however, may well lie in an examination of differences among variables, and also of the interaction among variants of a single variable, and of the situated use of variation.

As this volume will show, the very definition of style must expand. While the division into internal, social, and stylistic constraints has been heuristically important, as work progresses in the field, the areas of overlap are becoming increasingly interesting. It will become apparent in this volume that the division between social and stylistic constraints is a fine and highly permeable one indeed. Specifically, earlier models have viewed social categories and identities as given, and stylistic variation as the speaker's way of navigating with respect to the social. As we move toward viewing social life as a continual process of constructing these very categories and identities, style becomes in addition a resource for the process of construction. The view of variation is expanding, therefore, from marking categories to constituting a more fluid landscape of meaning; from a view of language as reflecting the social to a view of language as also creating the social.

We begin this volume with papers by the anthropologists Judith Irvine and Richard Bauman, with the purpose of setting a broader context for the study of stylistic variation. The variation papers follow, in roughly the chronological order of the development of the frameworks that they represent. The featured papers are followed by commentaries by people who have been engaged in related stylistic work.

3   Anthropological approaches to style

Judith Irvine's cross-cultural, ethnographic work on formality (1979) and status and style (1985) has directly addressed issues relevant to variationists, although the variationist literature has rarely taken it into consideration. Her chapter in this volume, "Style as distinctiveness: the culture and ideology of linguistic differentiation" (chapter 1), continues to bring the anthropological perspective to the study of variation. She begins by reminding us that style in language, as in other areas of everyday life, is essentially about *distinctiveness* within a system of possibilities, and that we need to explore the contrasts and boundaries among alternatives to appreciate their full significance.

Irvine's conception of style as a "social semiosis of distinctiveness" crucially involves attention to the language ideologies of native speakers and the principles of differentiation which "link language differences with social meanings." In particular, she identifies three semiotic processes – *iconization*, *recursivity*, and *erasure* – which have emerged from her joint work with Susan Gal (e.g. Gal and Irvine 1997), and she goes on to define and exemplify them with analyses of stylistic variation in a rural Wolof community in Senegal and a Hungarian/German speaking community in Southern Hungary. Although she is careful to emphasize that "language ideologies are to be investigated independently of the distribution of observable sociolinguistic facts, not as a substitute for them," it is clear that understanding them allows us to appreciate the workings of style in ways that might otherwise escape us.

Finally, Irvine's paper includes a useful discussion of the distinctions between *register*, *dialect,* and *style.* She suggests that although register (variety defined according to use) might in theory imply differentiation within a set more readily than dialect, the distinction is not as useful in practice, since speakers are often aware of a range of user-differentiated varieties, and dialects and registers are closely connected. (Indeed, awareness of social distinctions is a fundamental part of Bell's 1984 model of how styles come to be differentiated and deployed according to audience.) For Irvine, style is essentially a superordinate category which emphasizes processes of linguistic (as well as non-linguistic) distinction in general, while register is restricted more to relatively stable, often named, varieties like "sports announcer talk" within the larger category.

Susan Ervin-Tripp, well known in the study of style for her (1972) extension of the linguistic notions of "alternation" and "co-occurrence" to include different "ways of speaking," provides a commentary on Irvine's paper which extends its framework to include monolingual as well as multilingual situations (chapter 2). She suggests that Irvine's appeal to language ideologies is relevant to the acquisition of more than one language variety as well as its display in switching between codes or styles. She likens style-shifting within a single language using dialect features to code-switching between different languages insofar as both can be affected by changes in addressee and speech conditions, and both can be used to effect rhetorical shifts, to get attention, persuade, elaborate, personalize, mark identity, and perform a variety of other functions. One difference is that dialectal style-shifts are potentially accessible to a larger audience, since intelligibility is not usually an issue. Another is that co-occurrence restrictions are laxer, although speakers are very sensitive to shifts in the probabilities or frequencies of occurrence of specific features.

Most of Ervin-Tripp's paper is taken up with a detailed analysis of rhetorical shifting in recordings of two Black political leaders: Stokely Carmichael and Dick Gregory. The analysis of Carmichael is briefer, focusing on the use of one prosodic, one vowel height/length, and one lexical feature to rouse the audience at a Black Power rally in Oakland. The analysis of Gregory's speech is longer and more detailed, revealing the comedian/writer/politician's strategic use of phonological and morphosyntactic features of AAVE (African-American Vernacular English) and Standard English to incite, parody, amuse, and/or provoke serious political reflection. Her larger point is that Gregory's deft code-shifting exploits socially established ideologies about the relationship between speech styles and different social groups: Whites versus Blacks, old versus young, rioters versus sophisticated consumers and protesters, American colonists versus the British, and so on. The recurrent iconization of which Irvine speaks is not simple, but complex, revealed in the successive realigning of potential contrasts in Gregory's unfolding talk.

Richard Bauman's chapter (3) brings new insights from his work on genre and poetics (Bauman 1977, Briggs and Bauman 1992) to the understanding of how variation takes on social meaning. The papers that follow Bauman's in this volume focus on style as a function of situation, of speaker, of hearer, of text type – but always one at a time. As Bauman presents his analysis of market calls in San Miguel de Allende, he foregrounds the inseparability of speech styles, texts, situational contexts, and social categories.

Bauman's analysis of market sales genres focuses on "calls" and "spiels," genres that one could say have become thoroughly reified in the community. These have clear formal properties, and are used for the hawking of everyday items. Within the landscape of calls, Bauman argues, there is emerging a new genre called the "pitch," which builds on and elaborates properties of the simpler genre to produce a more elaborate genre appropriate to the hawking of luxury items. In other words, the currently existing genres present a discursive landscape within which new genres can develop and take on meaning.

Variationists have looked to discourse as a way to contextualize variation. An obvious relation between work on genre and work on variation lies in the potential for genre to define the situations within which variables are deployed, to circumscribe style and to establish stylistic equivalence. Labov's paper in this volume seeks to establish some kind of situational/interactional equivalence within which the differential use of variants can be said to reflect speaker differences. Genre, thus, is viewed as isolable and stable. Bauman's paper, however, focuses on genre as emerging, varying, and changing in practice. Rather than viewing genre as imposing constraint, he presents genre as the result of strategy, a reification to which community members can orient themselves in making meaning. Some genres are more reified than others, and the degree and nature of this reification leaves room for speaker and audience both to use convention and to change it. Bauman's paper thus embodies a shift of perspective from schema for the categorization of text to framework for the production and interpretation of text. He defines genre in terms of its affordances for change in discursive practice.

Most importantly for the variationist, this discursive practice is not abstracted from the day-to-day use of variation, but is a key element in the construction of social meaning in variation. Bauman points out that these texts are tied to a recurrent context, the market, to a category or categories of speakers, the hawkers. The subgenres, furthermore, are associated with different classes of wares, weaving ever more subtle social meaning into the styles. Bauman argues that as children grow up, hearing these calls must be an integral part of their sociolinguistic development. These calls foreground linguistic form, providing a stage for the performance of unusual linguistic variants, which is in turn enhanced by the poetic structuring of the calls – the lexical repetition and the phonological parallelism.

Ronald Macaulay's commentary on Bauman's chapter points out early on a theme that emerges in several of the papers in this volume, and that is at the heart of the problem of style (chapter 4). That is, while studies of variation focus on those variables that are relatively easy to define, measure and quantify, these variables exist in a much broader stylistic landscape that so far has not been subject to compatible treatment. Macaulay observes that the wider field of variables that characterize registers and genres may well be more interesting than classic sociolinguistic variables ". . . if we can find a way to deal with them." For this reason, much of Macaulay's commentary focuses on problems with the operationalization of the notion of genre, and particularly on problems of identifying genres and assigning linguistic features to them.

Observing that the market genres in Bauman's analysis form a continuum from categories that are clearly shared by analysts and speakers alike (calls) to those that may at this point only be an analyst's category (salestalks), he raises the issue of whether the speakers of San Miguel de Allende actually share Bauman's view of the discursive landscape, and how far the analyst can go in breaking genres down into subgenres, or grouping them into macro-genres. He goes on to point out similar problems elsewhere, most notably in the case of narrative, which is a fundamental genre for the analysis of variation yet quite variably defined across the literature.

4   Attention paid to speech

The first four sections of **William Labov's** chapter (5) emphasize the importance of stylistic variation to the understanding of language change, opposing the study of style-shifting in naturalistic contexts to its study within the sociolinguistic interview, and defending the value of the latter. Labov argues that both audience design and audio-monitoring (attention paid to speech) are factors in style-shifting, and recaps key findings in the study of style over the past two decades. For him, the central problem in stylistic analysis is separating casual and careful speech within the spontaneous sections of the sociolinguistic interview, and the mechanism that he and his students have found most useful for doing so is the "decision tree" and its eight contextual branches: Response, Narrative, Language, Group, Soapbox, Kids, Tangents, and Residual.

All of this is important groundwork by the sociolinguist most responsible for the attention paid to speech model. But it is with the fifth section that we really get down to new developments. Here Labov draws on a large data pool (184 speakers from the Language Variation and Change corpus at the University of Pennsylvania) to examine the nature of style-shifting in three stable sociolinguistic variables: (ING), (DH), and (NEG). The main point of this section is that although the various subgroups of the speech community (social classes, age-groups, and genders) are differentiated by their absolute uses of the variable, they are NOT differentiated by their relative use in casual and careful contexts. As Labov has noted earlier, shared patterns of style-shifting are one of the defining characteristics of membership in a speech community.

In the sixth and seventh sections, Labov explores the issue of whether the decision tree might be refined by eliminating individual subcategories which are less objectively identifiable and/or which contribute less to the differentiation of careful and casual styles. His overall conclusion is that the eight subcategories all contribute to the differentiation of styles and there is no motivation for discarding any of them, even when differentiation by social class and gender is considered.

While Labov skilfully deploys quantitative methodology to refine our understanding of the role of the various subcategories of the decision tree, his research raises a number of questions for future research. For instance, the style-shifting effects of the different variables Labov considered (DH, ING, NEG) were not uniform, and were we to consider others, the range of variation would undoubtedly increase. Bearing in mind that speech is an amalgam of variables, how do their differential effects contribute to the overall "styles" that speakers create and audiences interpret? Another question is whether style-shifting for variables undergoing change is different than it is for stable sociolinguistic variables. From other findings (for instance, the cross-over pattern for (r) in New York City, and the fact that the Philadelphia variables in change showed little style-shifting), this appears to be the case. But this makes the study of style-shifting through variables undergoing change even more compelling, especially given the centrality of style to the study of language change.

In his commentary on Labov's chapter, **John Baugh** emphasizes the development of Labov's approaches to the study of style between the 1960s and the present, isolating four areas in which improvement has already occurred or still seems necessary (chapter 6). The first is the use of reading passages and word lists, a central strategy for eliciting more careful styles in the framework of Labov's early New York City study. As Baugh points out, this strategy is inappropriate with illiterate subjects, a group which can include children and many adults in metropolitan societies, and virtually the entire population in oral, non-metropolitan communities, so other creative strategies for increasing attention to formal speech need to be explored. Secondly, the role of fieldworkers – their social attributes in relation to their interviewees, and their relative accommodation to their interviewees' speech – deserves further study, as a factor that could significantly affect the nature and range of styles elicited in an interview. Thirdly, the interviewer needs to maintain ethnographic sensitivity in trying to extend the interviewee's speech towards the formal or informal end of the stylistic continuum. Finally, in the analytical phase, it might be useful to classify speech within each branch of the decision tree as "formal/careful" or "informal/casual," in recognition of the fact that each cut invariably leaves on one side of the tree speech that really belongs on the other. To some extent, this final proposal runs counter to the decision tree, whose purpose is to provide a clear-cut formal procedure for classifying interview speech as careful or casual, but to the extent that clear-cut procedures can be developed for the additional classifications at the end of each branch, it is worth exploring.

Penelope Eckert, noting the centrality to Labov's analytic practice of the sociolinguistic interview as a constructed speech event, begins her commentary on Labov's chapter by critically considering the subevents in the interview that represent branches on his decision tree and their relation to the larger stylistic world in which interviews occur (chapter 7). *Response* versus *Tangent* speech, she suggests, might be defined more generally in terms of topic control, the latter bringing out the vernacular for a variety of reasons, including the interviewee's greater sense of enjoyment and comfort with self-selected topics. *Language* and *Kids* relate to topic and possibly genre; *Soapbox* and *Narrative* are definitely related to genre, the latter perhaps to an overarching category of reminiscence. *Group* speech is related to audience, but also involves topic control and other factors. Each of these subevents needs to be considered too in relation to the kind of population being interviewed, for instance, adolescents versus adults, whose style-shifting norms can be quite different, as Labov's paper shows.

Different variables might also have very different social-stylistic meanings in relation to specific subevents in the interview, Eckert notes. For instance, -*ing* is not stigmatized in itself, but negative concord is, associated with limited education and working- and under-class membership. The relation of attention-paid-to-speech to "ethnographic" and socially meaningful motives for style-shifting also requires further consideration. Like Bell and others, Eckert observes that the use of vernacular speech in an interview might result from *more* rather than less attention paid to speech and that the role of style in social meaning, particularly in the social construction of self, deserves closer attention. Named group styles – e.g. "Valley

Girl" or "New York Jew" – are very salient, and these provide part of the resources on which individuals draw to construct their personal styles.

Eckert suggests that not only do certain group styles and genres (e.g. market calls) provide "stages" for the construction of social meaning and personal style, but that certain individuals and groups of individuals do so too. She gives two examples. One is the high school "burned-out burnouts" she studied in a Detroit suburban high school, who represented the most extreme exemplars of the burnout style in dress, demeanor, and attitude, and also in the use of specific variants, like the raising of (ay) and the backing of (uh). The other is Trudy and her primarily Mexican American "home girls" in a San Jose, California, sixth grade. They are clear leaders in the heterosexual scene and in the construction of style; anything that Trudy does has "highlighted meaning because of her position in the age cohort as a cultural icon." Eckert urges us to study these larger processes of meaning and style construction to enrich and inform our collection and analysis of stylistically variable data in interviews.

Elizabeth Traugott notes the contributions that Labovian sociolinguistics has already made to our understanding of language change, and explores in her commentary on Labov's chapter the potential for contributions in the opposite direction – from research on grammaticalization to the sociolinguistic study of stylistic variation (chapter 8).

In grammaticalization, the transition of variants from open- to closed-class items is central, and studying it often involves attending carefully to the grammatical, semantic, and pragmatic functions of each form. Might a similar perspective advance the attention-paid-to-speech approach to style that Labov champions? Traugott's answer is yes, and she offers several illustrative examples. For instance, building on observations by Ellen Prince on variation in the Yiddish of Sarah Gorby, she suggests that open-class items might play a more significant role in conscious style-shift than closed-class items and morphophonemic variants. Even the latter might involve grammatical function – for instance, the (dh) variable that is so central in Labov's analysis might be more significant than other phonological variables because of its connection with definiteness and deixis (in words like *the*, *this*, *that*, and *there*).

More generally, Traugott suggests that "style can and should be related to different linguistic functions as well as to the different purposes of speakers using them" – a point she supports by noting semantic and pragmatic differences in the use of words like *obviously*, *in fact*, *actually*, and *anyway*. Many of these involve the speaker's subjective attitude to discourse, which she calls "*self-design*" ("I," paralleling Bell's *audience design* (*you*) and *referee design* (*they*, *we*). Her remarks focus on variables above the level of phonology, recalling but extending Lavandera's two-decades-old observa-

tion that morphosyntactic and lexical variants are polysemic while phonological variants are not, and pointing to one direction that the study of style
as attention paid to speech might fruitfully pursue.

5   Audience design and self-identification

Allan Bell, already well known in the variationist study of style for his
(1984) audience design model (conveniently summarized in his chapter of
this volume, chapter 9), proposes some theoretical and methodological
refinements and describes a new research project he has started in New
Zealand to test some of its key components. A key innovation is that the
referee design component of the model, involving initiative shift, is no
longer thought of as applying only after audience design, or only in occasional or exceptional cases. On the contrary, the two aspects of style-shift
are now conceptualized as potentially "concurrent, pervasive processes."
Bell believes that quantitative methods are likely to be most useful in the
analysis of audience design style-shift, and qualitative methods for referee
design style-shift, but the distinction is (thankfully) not absolute.
Additionally, Bell notes that the analysis of co-occurrence (and presumably
covariation) is important for understanding style-shift, but little is said
about this aspect of the model.

The new research project that Bell designed and conducted in New
Zealand – discussed in sections 3 and 4 of the chapter – represents a
clever attempt to control some of the key variables. Four interviewees –
one male and one female Maori, one male and one female Pakeha (white)
– are interviewed on different occasions over a three-week period, under
similar conditions and on similar topics, by three different interviewers
who vary in gender and/or ethnicity. We see clear evidence of stylistic
variation by audience in the male Maori interviewee's use of (eh), but
interviewers' use of this variable is harder to interpret in terms of audience design. More of the paper is devoted to the analysis of how speakers'
ethnic identities and attitudes are revealed through their pronunciation of
doublets (like *pane*) which can be read either as English monosyllables or
Maori disyllables, and of Maori place names which can be given English
or Maori pronunciations. The male Pakeha interviewee, least aware of
and sympathetic to Maori issues, read all the Maori/English doublets as
English words, while the male Maori interviewee appeared to mark his
pride in his ethnic heritage by providing the most consistently "Maori"
pronunciations of the Maori place names. Both quantitative and qualitative data are presented.

Bell's paper represents a welcome extension to the audience design
framework, but we will have to await later reports for fuller discussion of

audience design effects and for elaboration on how co-occurrence and covariation are to be integrated into the analysis. One other question that
remains relevant to the audience design framework, as to virtually all the
frameworks in this volume, is whether and how we can be sure that speakers
do have productive access to the full range of variants under discussion.
This is of course necessary for interpreting use or non-use as stylistically
significant.

Malcah Yaeger-Dror, in commenting on Bell's chapter, addresses a larger
concern about what are to be the primitives or basic units for the analysis of
style and how they should be studied (chapter 10). Finding little agreement
among the leading figures in the study of stylistic variation, including those
represented in this volume, she sets out to provide clarification as a basis for
future convergence. She agrees with Bell, for instance, that audience design
and referee design are worthy primitives for the study of style (see Bell's
paper for definitions), and notes their respective parallels with Coupland's
relational and identity variables. But she vigorously rejects the suggestion
that quantitative methods apply only to audience design, pointing to
several studies from the 1970s to the 1990s in which referee or identity variables were quantitatively measured. At the same time, she reminds us that
the determination of whether a shift is the former or the latter "can only be
made by careful qualitative analysis."

Yaeger-Dror also reminds us of a whole series of other parameters whose
effects on stylistic variation have been repeatedly demonstrated, but whose
status as stand-alone primitives or metaphorical subprimitives remains to
be determined. The list includes topic, purpose, setting, planning (=atten-
tion to speech/message), frame (=genre/key), footing, and stance (e.g. con-
frontational/supportive), and relatedness to informational versus interactional
parameters (nicely illustrated with her own analysis of negation). In her
conclusion, she urges us to consider a wider range of variables and cultural
and social situations as we try to determine the optimal primitives for the
analysis of style.

Like Judith Irvine, **Nikolas Coupland** focuses on style as distinctiveness
(chapter 11). While Irvine concentrates on community processes that create
distinctiveness, reifying particular personae and the relation between those
personae and semiotic resources, Coupland concentrates on the individual
speaker's use of linguistic resources to evoke these personae. To illustrate
his approach to style, Coupland provides the example of a Cardiff DJ who
is popularly known for his promotion of local Cardiff culture, and for his
use of non-standard dialect in so doing. Coupland shows how the DJ uses
standard and non-standard Cardiff features, as well as features from non-
local dialects such as Cockney and American English, to invoke a variety of
social meanings. These meanings are based in social characterizations asso-

ciated with stereotypic speakers of the source dialects, but they interact also, Coupland emphasizes, with specific content and contextual factors to produce all kinds of other meanings. He points out that these dynamics cannot be taken into consideration in correlational approaches, since they involve moment-to-moment expressive strategies that signal changes in such things as attitude or key. Coupland argues that because traditional analytic practice focuses on the relation between language use and social structural configurations, it does not engage with the social and interactive function of language variation.

Coupland emphasizes speaker agency, focusing on the speaker as performer, and viewing style as a situational achievement rather than simply conditioned by situational factors. The speaker thus is not simply a responder to context but a maker of context, defining situations and relationships. Thus he argues against analyses of variation that focus on one aspect of identity, or that begin with context as a condition for variation, arguing that style must be theorized within the realm of discursive social action.

Coupland's chapter argues against unidimensional models of style that predominate in the study of variation, arguing that any one of these dimensions (such as attention-paid-to-speech or formality) interacts with any number of other semiotic processes. He views the features that preoccupy the study of variation as a subset of stylistic features. These "dialect style" features, which tend to constitute regional dialect differentiation, are related in stylistic strategies primarily to identity and relational goals. As such, they constitute a subset of a wide range of stylistic features that serve not only identity and relational goals, but expressive and attitudinal roles as well.

In response to Coupland's claim that communication accommodation theory does not address issues of self-presentation, **Howard Giles** (chapter 12) brings recent research in social psychology to bear on a number of issues raised in Coupland's chapter. Supporting Coupland's general call for a multidimensional view of style, he provides a caution to what he views as an extreme deconstructive position, and argues for a focus on speakers' and hearers' intuitions to temper the analyst's constructs. He argues that inasmuch as people accommodate to "where they *believe* target others are," research needs to explore speakers' and hearers' own definitions of situations, identities, and styles. On the one hand, he suggests that participants may not perceive all of the style-shifts that Coupland identifies in the DJ's speech – that some of them may in fact be components of a larger style – and on the other hand, he points to findings that hearers may perceive style-shifts when in fact there has been no change in linguistic output, on the basis of non-linguistic factors. He concludes his commentary with a set of fundamental and challenging questions that he would pose to a study of style.

John Rickford's commentary on Coupland's chapter agrees with many of Coupland's critiques of unidimensional studies of style, but emphasizes the importance of expanding rather than replacing approaches to style (chapter 13). He argues that sociolinguistics has a multiplicity of goals, and that different approaches to style will suit different goals. Particularly, he notes that the goals and assumptions that underlie the "socially constituted sociolinguistics" of Hymes, make non-dialectal aspects of style (e.g. lexical variation, address terms, and types of speech events) of central concern, while these aspects of style are peripheral given the goals and assumptions that underlie the "socially realistic sociolinguistics" of Labov. While Rickford agrees that the study of style must recognize that style is an "active, motivated, symbolic process," he cautions against rejecting the more predictable, often automatic, aspects of stylistic variation that are the focus of quantitative studies of variation. He also cautions against discarding the empirical advantages of unidimensional models of style, and against discarding the social group or category in favor of focusing on individuals and their strategies, arguing that an understanding of style requires a multiplicity of approaches. Rickford embraces Coupland's focus on goals, but questions his distinction between dialect style and other ways of speaking. He argues that not only are features of dialect style capable of distinguishing ideational meanings, but that ways of speaking often figure in dialect differentiation.

In part 3 of his commentary, Rickford presents an example of a Guyanese radio personality, showing how he uses a variety of resources in ways similar to Coupland's DJ, reinforcing Coupland's observation of the moment-by-moment complexity of stylistic variation. But he then raises the question of whether the extent of this stylizing is not specific to public performances – whether the possibilities for the use of extreme stylization do not increase with the size of the audience. He speculates that these may be quite distinct kinds of performances, and questions the extent to which we can generalize from broadcast styles such as these to everyday spoken styles.

6   Functionally motivated situational variation

A fundamental fact of stylistic variation is that social and stylistic variation mirror each other, and **Edward Finegan** and **Douglas Biber's** chapter (14) offers an explanation for this fact that differs fundamentally from most work on variation. Bell has made explicit what has been taken for granted in variation studies, that is, that social variation is fundamental, and that stylistic variation is derivative. (Preston adopts this view, but subordinates both social and stylistic variation to linguistic constraints.) Finegan and Biber, however, offer a view in which situations are fundamental. They propose a "Register Axiom" that unites variables by their co-occurrence in registers, tying registers to the kinds of situations in which they are used, and explaining social groups' differential use of variants in terms of differential access to the situations in which their registers are used. This model extends to account for linguistic constraints on variation as well, and it is the interaction between linguistic constraint and situation that is at its heart.

Following a number of other analysts (Bernstein 1971, Kroch 1978, Heath 1983), Finegan and Biber argue that social and stylistic variables commonly fall along a continuum between simplification and elaboration. They tie these to a taxonomy of situations as more or less literate, hence more or less planned, more informational or more affective in purpose, and involving less or more shared context between interlocutors. More literate situations, then, require more elaborated language, while less literate situations call for greater economy. Against a background of previous analyses of corpus data that confirm this hypothesis, they go on to examine three socioeconomic groups of speakers from the British National Corpus, finding that much of the situational variation they have found is not mirrored in social differences.

Lesley Milroy's commentary on Finegan and Biber's paper presents several arguments against a single model that encompasses such a vast array of types and aspects of situational variability (chapter 15). She points to the heterogeneity of the variables that Finegan and Biber seek to account for, and the breadth and heterogeneity of the scholarship that must be brought to bear, questioning both the feasibility and the desirability of such an overarching account.

The core of Milroy's discussion lies in the distinction between literate and non-literate styles – a distinction that Finegan and Biber treat as somewhat continuous, and as spanning written and spoken genres. While Milroy agrees with Finegan and Biber that differential access to literary practice is central to an account of differentiated linguistic repertoires, she takes quite a different approach to the significance of literacy in this variability. Where Finegan and Biber focus on depersonalization, lack of shared context, and informational priority in literary genres, Milroy proposes that the key issue in the literate–non-literate distinction is collaborativity. Specifically, she points out the importance of distinguishing between conversation, which is fundamentally interactive, and monologic discourse, which is not. She argues that economy and elaboration are a collaborative enterprise in interactive discourse, and hence not to be found in the use of particular structures by individual speakers. In other words, the actual locus of the features that Finegan and Biber are concerned with is different in the two kinds of discourse.

Milroy also challenges more generally their claim that it is economy that characterizes social differences in speech, providing evidence of instances in which vernaculars are more "elaborate" than their standard equivalents, and suggesting that on the contrary, standard varieties in fact often exhibit the simplified characteristics of contact languages. Milroy also questions the grouping of heterogeneous variables, underscoring the importance of drawing a clear distinction between variables that are referentially equivalent and primarily indicators of identity (i.e. classic sociolinguistic variables), and those that have a non-social communicative function.

Dennis Preston's commentary (chapter 16) treats this latter point at length, drawing a contrast between Finegan and Biber's approach to variability and the approach taken by quantitative studies of variation. Preston focuses on Finegan and Biber's claim that it is situational factors that structure stylistic variation (and hence social variation), a direct contradiction of Bell's (1984:151) argument that stylistic variation is parasitic on social variation. He argues that this is an incorrect conclusion stemming from Finegan and Biber's failure to distinguish among types of variable. The classic sociolinguistic variable, which has been found to vary systematically according to style and socioeconomic status, consists of variants that are equivalent in every way except socially. Variants of classic sociolinguistic variables are interchangeable in the same discourse context, potentially yielding social inappropriateness but not awkward constructions. Preston argues that the few variables that Finegan and Biber found to show social as well as registral variation were of this type. The rest of Finegan and Biber's variables, Preston argues, are not of this type. Rather, in these cases, the choice of variants is constrained by the information structures characteristic of the texts in question rather than by the social situations themselves.

Part I

Anthropological approaches

1 "Style" as distinctiveness: the culture and ideology of linguistic differentiation[1]

Judith T. Irvine

1 Introduction: style as distinctiveness

"What gives a woman **style**?" asks a recent *New Yorker* advertisement for *The Power of Style*, a book in "the Condé Nast Collection" (the fall collection of fashionable books, perhaps?). The ad continues:

> "I'm nothing to look at," the Duchess of Windsor admitted. Rita de Acosta Lydig paid no attention to what was "in fashion." Jacqueline Kennedy Onassis had none of the attributes of the ideal American girl, and Diana Vreeland never had money. Yet each of these women had a personal magnetism and allure so strong that she could "dominate a room from a footstool." How did they do it? And what can you learn from them?

Whatever answers the advertised book may offer to these questions, they are likely to have more to do with the fashion industry's notions of style than with a sociolinguistic definition. Still, some aspects of the conception of "style" implicit in this ad are worth the sociolinguist's attention. We ignore the everyday meanings of terminology at our peril; and style in language should not be assumed *a priori* to be an utterly different matter from style in other realms of life. So, if the ad's discourse represents some popular conception of style, we might draw several inferences about that conception: "style" crucially concerns distinctiveness; though it may characterize an individual, it does so only within a social framework (of witnesses who pay attention); it thus depends upon social evaluation and, perhaps, aesthetics; and it interacts with ideologized representations (the "ideal American girl"; "in fashion"). In this particular ad the ideologized themes revolve around gender, and they implicitly contrast several visions of what female distinctiveness might be based upon.[2]

---

[1] This paper is heavily indebted to conversations with Susan Gal (University of Chicago) and to work we have conducted jointly. See Irvine and Gal 2000 and Gal and Irvine 1995.

[2] Thus the ad denies that money and position play a crucial role in female distinctiveness, instead proposing that distinctiveness lies in some mysterious "personal allure." The ad also suggests that the most widely available images of a female ideal ("the ideal American girl," "in fashion") are actually too common to provide the basis for true distinctiveness, which

The first lesson, then, that I would draw from this excursion into the world of advertising concerns *distinctiveness*. Whatever "styles" are, in language or elsewhere, they are part of a *system of distinction*, in which a style contrasts with other possible styles, and the social meaning signified by the style contrasts with other social meanings. Perhaps this point will seem obvious. Yet, its corollary has sometimes been overlooked: namely, that it is seldom useful to examine a single style in isolation. To describe a style's characteristics, examining the features that identify it, and to contemplate links between these features and the style's particular function, is to suppose that function suffices to explain form, without reference to system. The characteristics of a particular style cannot be explained independently of others. Instead, attention must be directed to relationships among styles – to their contrasts, boundaries, and commonalities. What is more important for a sociolinguistic view of style than a particular correlation between form and function – since correlations, as we know, are not explanations and do not identify causes – are the principles and processes of stylistic differentiation within a continuously evolving sociolinguistic system.

The second lesson is that the relationships among styles are ideologically mediated. It is a commonplace in sociolinguistics that ways of speaking index the social formations (groups, categories, personae, activity types, institutional practices, etc.) of which they are characteristic. But an index can only inform social action if it functions as a sign; and a sign requires an interpretant, as Peirce long ago pointed out. That is to say, it must be meaningful to, and at some level understood by, some persons whose actions are informed by it. So these indexes must partake in participants' understandings of their social world and the semiotic resources available in it. Those understandings are positioned, depending in some measure on the participant's social position and point of view. They are also culturally variable; that is, they are neither universal nor entirely predictable from social position (such as socioeconomic class) alone, without consideration of local history and tradition.

Finally, this notion of style is connected with aesthetics, an aspect of style some authors have emphasized (see, for example, many of the contributions to that foundational work, *Style in Language* [Sebeok 1960]. I interpret stylistic aesthetics as concerning (among other things) not only distinctiveness, but also the *consistency* of the linguistic features constituting a style. I have discussed this point with regard to Wolof registers (Irvine 1990); I broaden its relevance here. Consistency is hardly all there is to aesthetics, of course. Aesthetic systems are culturally variable and are orga-

footnote 2 (*cont.*)
    cannot be found in conformist behavior, even when the conformity is to an ideal. Implicitly, then, the ad identifies three different ideological perspectives – class-based, democratic, and individualist/aesthetic – on feminine "style" and its social setting.

nized around locally relevant principles of value, not all of which are conspicuously connected with sociological forces. Still, one of the things those principles of value do, whatever they may be in the particular case, is to motivate the consistency of stylistic forms.

This broad conception of style as a social semiosis of distinctiveness has some precedents in sociological works which, though they do not focus on language in detail, provide a framework that accommodates linguistic style among other semiotic forms. One such work is Dick Hebdige's (1979) *Subculture: the meaning of style*, a study of youth subcultures in Britain (Mods, Teddy Boys, punks, Rastas, etc.) and the history of their relationships, in which race relations are deeply embedded. "Style" in this work is broadly conceived: a subculture's "style" is something distinctive that appears in its members' dress, posture, argot, musical preferences, even in their focal concerns. "Style" crosscuts these communicative and behavioral modalities and integrates them thematically. Most importantly, Hebdige shows that these styles have a complex relationship. The styles that distinguish these subcultures cannot be understood in isolation from one another; they have a complex history of "dialectical interplay" (p. 57), drawing on portions of each other's symbolic resources while constructing contrast in other portions.

Influential at a more theoretical level is Pierre Bourdieu's work, including his (1984[1979]) book *Distinction*, a study of taste and lifestyle differences in France. Lifestyles, for Bourdieu – and this rubric includes aesthetic preferences and behavioral modalities of many kinds – are part of the "work of representation" in which social relationships are constructed, not just reflected. The "social space," as he calls it, is "constructed on the basis of principles of differentiation" (1985:196); it is a space of relationships, not of groups. (Bear in mind that socioeconomic classes, e.g., are relational categories, not real groups as social theory defines these; p. 198.) The organization of the social space is displayed in the relations among lifestyles, despite the fact that participants firmly believe many of their preferences are entirely personal (pp. 203–4). Writing on styles as practices of social representation, Bourdieu comments (1985: 204):

All practice is "conspicuous," visible, whether or not it is performed in order to be seen; it is distinctive, whether or not it springs from the intention of being "conspicuous," standing out, of distinguishing oneself or behaving with distinction. As such it inevitably functions as a *distinctive sign* . . . The pursuit of distinction – which may be expressed in ways of speaking or the refusal of misalliances – produces separations intended to be perceived or, more precisely, known and recognized, as legitimate differences.

Following these approaches to style, then, I take it that styles in speaking involve the ways speakers, as agents in social (and sociolinguistic) space, negotiate their positions and goals within a system of distinctions and possibilities. Their acts of speaking are ideologically mediated, since those acts necessarily involve the speaker's understandings of salient social groups, activities, and practices, including forms of talk. Such understandings incorporate evaluations and are weighted by the speaker's social position and interest. They are also affected by differences in speakers' access to relevant practices. Social acts, including acts of speaking, are informed by an ideologized system of representations, and no matter how instrumental they may be to some particular social goal, they also participate in the "work of representation."

A perspective that focuses on language ideology, and on how linguistic practices join in the "work of representation," is shared by a number of current authors (such as Silverstein 1979 and elsewhere, Kroskrity, Schieffelin, and Woolard 1992, Woolard and Schieffelin 1994, Kroskrity 2000, and others). Most sociolinguistic work, too, has appealed to some notion of social evaluation, attitudes, scales of prestige, or schemes of values, and/or has alluded to speakers' conceptions of social identity, and the like. Many sociolinguists, however, have placed those evaluative schemes in the background, as if they could be taken as obvious, or were but one "factor" among many, or, especially, as if they could be read off the distributions of sociolinguistic facts (i.e., as if they needed no independent investigation). By foregrounding ideology I emphasize the need to investigate ideas about language and speakers independently of empirical distributions, and the need to recognize that "attitudes" include participants' basic understandings of what the sociolinguistic system consists of, not just emotional dispositions. Moreover, the categories and behaviors toward which one has these attitudes cannot be assumed to have been established independently of anyone's perception of them.

Here some methodological comments may be in order. If I advocate foregrounding language ideology, am I merely recommending that the sociolinguist observer should ask participants (informants, consultants) what is going on, and rely on their analysis instead of his or her own? Not at all. Although participants are well placed in some respects to offer a sociolinguistic analysis (since participation means close acquaintance with the system), in other respects they are poorly placed to do so (since participation also means interestedness). The reason for calling participants' assumptions and analyses "ideologies" is that ideational schemes, whether about language or other things, have some relationship with point of view – the social position of the viewer, and the practices to which he/she differentially has access – and the viewer's baggage of history and partiality. Such schemes are *partial* in all senses of the word. Any one participant's ideational scheme is not likely to be shared by everyone else; nor is it likely to be identical with the distributions of behavioral forms which an outsider might observe (see Silverstein 1979). Although ideology cannot simply be considered "false consciousness" (see Eagleton 1991), there will always be some portions of an ideologically pervaded consciousness that would strike someone else, differently positioned, as false.

In short, participants in some community of discourse are not entirely objective observers of each other's behaviors. Yet, their own acts are deeply influenced by their perceptions and interpretations of those behaviors.[3] Language ideologies are therefore to be investigated independently of the distribution of observable sociolinguistic facts, not as a substitute for them. That investigation will require moving beyond the mere recording of informants' explicit statements of sociolinguistic norms, for beliefs and ideational schemes are not contained only in a person's explicit assertions of them. Instead, some of the most important and interesting aspects of ideology lie behind the scenes, in assumptions that are taken for granted – that are never explicitly stated in any format that would permit them also to be explicitly denied. As Silverstein (1979 and elsewhere) has suggested, the best place to look for language ideology may lie in the terms and presuppositions of metapragmatic discourse, not just in its assertions.

Applying these ideas to an understanding of "style," I focus on participants' ideologizing of sociolinguistic differentiation and distinctiveness, and the processes to which this gives rise.

2   Style, register, and dialect

How does this approach to "style" accord with, or differ from, what the term has meant in linguistics and sociolinguistics heretofore? A conception of style that has provided a starting-point for several other contributors to this volume comes from Labov's (1966 and other works) discussions of intra-speaker variation in the structured sociolinguistic interview.[4] Although this definition of style – as an individual speaker's shifts in details of usage within a very structured, monolingual situation – seems at first glance much narrower than mine, it actually opens a window onto an equally wide sociolinguistic scene. One of the most important findings of

---

[3] A conception such as this is crucial, I believe, if sociolinguistics is to avoid both the Scylla of methodological individualism (as found in extreme rational-actor models that ignore the configuration of inputs to the actor's choices) and the Charybdis of sociological determinism (as found in models that read individuals' motivation off observed social distributions of linguistic phenomena, and ignore individuals' agency).

[4] As other contributors have also noted, Labov's discussions of style in his early work went on to interpret intra-speaker variation in terms of degrees of formality in the interview situation – an interpretation that was to be contested, by the 1970s, on several grounds.

early variationist work was the discovery of relationships between intra-individual stylistic variation and inter-group variation, yielding two angles on one and the same sociolinguistic dynamic. There is some reason even within the variationist tradition, therefore, to look for the dynamics of style in this larger picture, as long as one does not lose sight of what individuals do.

Even in linguistics (and sociolinguistics) "style" has meant other things besides intra-speaker variation.[5] A great many of these are surveyed in a recent work by John Haynes (1995), *Style*, a "practical introduction" to the topic. Haynes avoids trying to define style, instead offering glimpses of the kinds of phenomena linguists have looked at under this rubric. If, as this approach implies, "style" is what students of style examine, it covers a very wide range of phenomena indeed. Apparently, "style" has meant almost anything within a language that could produce differences in and between monologic texts, apart from performance factors in the narrow sense (physical accident, for example), and apart from gross considerations of denotational adequacy.[6] The kinds of patterning Haynes discusses range from relatively institutionalized variation, at one pole, to kinds of patterning that have more to do with individuals' creativity and presentation of self, at the other.

Does the wide range of phenomena assignable to a notion of "style" just represent analytical chaos? On the contrary; I think these phenomena, though various, are interlinked. To sort out the links it is useful to return to basics, and look at some related concepts in our repertoire, particularly *register* and *dialect*.

These concepts come to mind because Haynes points "style" toward variation within the usage of a single speaker or author, and within a single "language" (itself a problematic conception, but space does not permit exploring it here). By excluding variation across users, his discussion of style implicitly reproduces the distinction, drawn decades ago, between

---

[5] See the many different definitions of style in the contributions to *Style in Language* (Sebeok 1960), also a conference volume. As Joseph Greenberg pointed out (1960:426) in the concluding discussion, participants in the conference "use the word 'style' in different ways . . . [initially] I came to certain pessimistic conclusions which might be stated in the following manner, that it was only the delightful ambiguity of the word 'style' that made this conference possible." Later, Greenberg felt that some higher synthesis might be possible after all: "Let us define style as that set of characteristics by which we distinguish members of one subclass from members of other subclasses, all of which are members of the same general class. This is simply a way of saying that style is diagnostic like a fingerprint" (1960:427). Meanwhile, Roman Jakobson's famous discussant comments in Sebeok 1960 ("Closing remarks: Linguistics and Poetics") do not focus on a definition of style at all, but rather assimilate it to a discussion of communicative function.

[6] That is to say, a change of topic does not necessarily require a change of style; and to some extent you can talk about the "same" thing in more than one style. Style is not the same thing as topic.

dialect and register: that is, between varieties according to users, and varieties according to uses (Halliday 1964; see also Gumperz 1968, on "dialectal" versus "superposed" varieties, for a somewhat similar conception). Styles, Haynes implies, would have something to do with registers. Indeed, *register* being a term originating in British schools of linguistics, some American authors have simply used the term "style" in its place, though "register" is gaining currency in American sociolinguistic parlance today.

In the usage of most linguists, registers are ways of speaking whose grammatical configurations overlap. That is, they are linguistically distinguishable, but only as varieties of one encompassing "language." Actually, the same could be said for dialects. The definitional difference between dialect and register is functional, rather than formal: which dialect you use indexes your social affiliation with a group of users (especially your locus of origin); which register you use indexes properties of your present situation and social activity (which may be a situation whose character has already been established prior to your speaking, or it may be a situation you are trying to create).

For Halliday, the principal proponent of this notion of "register" in the 1960s and 1970s, the functional distinction seemed to have consequences for registers' (and dialects') formal properties. According to him, the registers of a language tend to differ from one another primarily in semantics, whereas the dialects tend to differ from one another in phonetics, phonology, and "lexicogrammar" (Halliday 1978:35). Yet, even if such tendencies can be identified in some cases – perhaps most particularly in types of written texts, insofar as such types are conceived as registers (rather than, say, as genres) – they do not apply conveniently to all. The differences among registers are not actually limited to semantics, however broadly semantics is defined.[7] There can also be grammatical, phonological, and phonetic differences, and some registers may even be distinguished solely on those bases.

For example, varieties such as Pig Latin, or Cockney rhyming slang, or the many play languages worldwide that rely on syllable-inversions, are evidently *not* semantically distinguished from their ordinary-language counterparts. In these particular examples, what is most important in motivating the use of a special variety is the mere fact of difference – formal distinctiveness from everyday speech – not anything special about its treatment of reference. More than some intrinsic connection with semantics, then, a crucial aspect of the concept of register is that – like "style" – it implies differentiation

---

[7] When Halliday (1978:35) says that registers tend to differ in semantics, he adds "and hence in lexicogrammar, and sometimes phonology, as realization of this." But he does not tell us how this works or why phonological differences should be seen as the "realization" of semantic differences.

within a system. By definition, there must be a *set* of registers among which a speaker's usage alternates, and of which he/she is to some degree aware.

Linguists' conception of dialects, on the other hand, has not necessarily implied user-awareness of a system of alternative varieties. Classically, a dialect has been seen as a variety formed independently of others, under conditions of communicative isolation. A speech community might split, its offshoots migrating in opposite directions and entirely losing touch with one another; their forms of speech could drift apart without anyone's being aware that other dialects even existed. But while the conditions and dynamics of linguistic drift are not to be denied, their applicability may well have been overestimated. Equally relevant, if not more so, are the dynamics of social settings where there is widespread knowledge of a range of dialectal varieties associated with differentiated social groups, even subcommunities, and where such awareness is an inherent part of the mechanism of linguistic differentiation and change. This point is of course crucial to the social motivation of linguistic change as discussed within the Labovian sociolinguistic tradition.

A taxonomic distinction between dialect and register thus has fewer advantages than has sometimes been supposed; and this should come as no surprise, given the findings of Labov and his followers on speech variation and socioeconomic class. In the many cases where the varieties among which a speaker's usage alternates include those associated with other groups (multilingualism, multidialectism) – or echoes thereof, or exaggerated avoidances of them – the taxonomic distinction is necessarily blurred. I shall return to these matters in later pages. Ultimately more useful, however, than pursuing taxonomic concerns, which so often turn out to be chimerical, is an exploration of the principles of differentiation organizing the relationships and distinctiveness of varieties – principles I seek to capture in a conception of "style."

An advantage of focusing on these principles of sociolinguistic differentiation is that in them, and in their ideological matrix, we may look for the motivation of at least some of the particular linguistic features by which varieties are characterized.[8] Cockney rhyming-slang, and its relationship to "everyday" speech, provides a case in point. This is one of the examples Halliday drew upon in his (1976) discussion of "anti-languages" – linguistic varieties whose very existence is motivated by an ideology of opposition to a social establishment. Most often used in circumstances where that social opposition is salient, such as prison settings, or in conspiratorial communi-

---

[8] See Ervin-Tripp 1972 on the "co-occurrence rules" that describe linkages among linguistic devices in a register.

Table 1.1. *Javanese "language levels" or "speech styles" (Errington 1988:90–1)*

KRAMA:	1. *menapa*	*nandalem*	*mundhut*	*sekul*	*semanten*
	2. *menapa*	*panjenengan*	*mendhet*	*sekul*	*semanten*
MADYA:	3. *napa*	*sampéyan*	*mendhet*	*sekul*	*semonten*
	4. *napa*	*sampéyan*	*njupuk*	*sega*	*semonten*
NGOKO:	5. *apa*	*sliramu*	*mundhut*	*sega*	*semono*
	6. *apa*	*kowé*	*njupuk*	*sega*	*semono*
Gloss:	Question-marker	you	take	rice	that much
Translation:	Did you take that much rice?				

cation among members of underground groups, the "anti-language" itself is constructed via some sort of linguistic inversion, or antinomy, or other principle of opposition to a variety considered representative of the to-be-countered establishment.

In "anti-languages," as also in Pig Latin, the principles of differentiation which motivate the internal consistency of each variety are quite simple. In other cases, however, other kinds of principles and more complex relationships might be involved. Consider, for example, the so-called "language levels" in Javanese, registers among which speakers choose depending on their assessment of a situation. (Errington 1988, the main source on which I draw, calls them "speech styles.") The "levels" are illustrated primarily in sets of lexical alternants (see table 1.1), although their differences are actually not only lexical.[9]

The differences among these styles, and the rationales for choosing one or another style, are conceived (by users)[10] in terms of ideas about affectivity and social hierarchy. The "higher," more "refined" styles, called *krama*, are considered to be depersonalized, flat-affect, and regulated by an ethic of proper order, peace, and calm. In them one "does not express one's own feelings" (Wolff and Poedjosoedarmo 1982:41). The lower, "coarser" levels (called *ngoko*), in contrast, are the "language . . . one loses one's temper in" (Errington 1984:9). Actually, the point is considered to lie not so much in one's own feelings as in one's addressee's sensibilities. A high-ranking

---

[9] Although the Javanese "language levels" are often described as differing mainly in lexicon (sets of lexical alternants) and in some special affixes, Errington (1984:9) has pointed out that they also differ in prosody and morphophonemics, although these aspects have been little studied.

[10] The principal sources of information on the cultural background and the pragmatics of this Javanese system have been the Javanese traditional elite, the *priyayi*. It is *priyayi* understandings of their sociolinguistic system that are described by Errington (1988) and Geertz (1960), for instance. That these elite views, or some aspects of them, may be partial, in both senses of that term, is obvious.

addressee is supposed to be relatively disengaged from worldly concerns and to "need" protection from vulgarity and stormy emotion. Supposedly, it is because a speaker recognizes the importance of showing respect for those "needs," that he or she refrains from expressing strong feelings to exalted interlocutors.[11]

This principle of differentiation, conceived as concerning coarseness and refinement, organizes not only the prosodic differences among the styles, but, evidently, at least some of the differences among the lexical alternants. The more "refined" alternants tend to draw on loan words or loan morphemes taken from Sanskrit sacred texts, and they bring some of that aura of sacredness and learnedness along with them into the Javanese construction. Semantically, too, the more "refined" alternants reflect the ideology of "elevated" speech, in that they are relatively abstract and vague, less explicitly engaged with the messy details of worldly existence than are their low-style counterparts. Thus an ideological principle relating rank to refinement recruits at least some of the linguistic characteristics that differentiate the styles, and recruits them consistently, whether they be prosodic or lexical.

Now, notice that although the Javanese speaker's choice among language levels is governed by situational factors, in particular the relationships among a situation's personnel and the appropriateness of displaying affect in their presence and in the course of that situation's activities, there is also a sense in which the levels distinguish categories of speakers. It has been claimed (Geertz 1960) that the members of different Javanese social ranks also differ significantly in the range of varieties they control within the total repertoire, the traditional elite controlling a larger range, including the more "refined" levels especially associated with their high rank, while the "coarser" levels are associated with the peasantry. To speak in a "refined" manner is not only to show respect for an addressee's emotional delicacy; it is also to display one's own knowledgeability, pragmatic sensitivity, and refinement. As images of "refinement" and affective display, then, the language levels evoke both the situations characteristically connected with such responses and the persons characteristically manifesting them.

Finally, notice that Javanese "language levels" admit internal variation. As table 1.1 shows, there are sublevels distinguishable within the three major levels, according to similar principles of contrast. (The middle level, *madya*, is in fact a kind of compromise constructed on the basis of the principal opposition between *alus* "refined" and *kasar* "coarse" ingredients.) And there are also further subtleties of style admitted by the structure of the system, although complicated by a distinction between addressee and referent honorifics, among other things. Those participant-role complex-

---

[11] I owe this point to Michael Silverstein (p.c.).

ities aside, the principles of differentiation that organize this system provide several degrees of difference, with varieties distinguishing groups and situations as well as intra-speaker variation according to addressee and mood.

The Javanese case thus illustrates an ideologized, culture-specific principle of stylistic differentiation that motivates some of the linguistic characteristics of Javanese styles and provides various degrees of differentiation. The case also illustrates how the distinction between dialect and register, whether or not it offers a valuable analytical starting point, becomes more complicated as soon as one looks more closely at a particular speech community and repertoire. Some of the reasons for this have to do with the cultural structuring, and consequent creative deployment, of "voices" associated with social groups such as the Javanese elite and peasantry. Images of persons considered typical of those groups – and the personalities, moods, behavior, activities, and settings, characteristically associated with them – are rationalized and organized in a cultural/ideological system, so that those images become available as a frame of reference within which speakers create performances and within which audiences interpret them. This system informs the style-switching in which all speakers engage. To put this another way: one of the many methods people have for differentiating situations and displaying attitudes is to draw on (or carefully avoid) the "voices" of others, or what they assume those voices to be.

The concept of register, then, although initially defined in terms of situation rather than person or group, in fact draws on cultural images of persons as well as situations and activities. The reverse is also the case. Social dialects, no matter how they come into existence, may become imagined as connected with focal individuals and scenes, or with characteristic activities and ways of being; and in consequence they may be drawn upon (or imitated by persons outside the group-of-reference) to display attitudes or define situations. "Dialects" and "registers" are intimately connected.

Where does this leave style? With that term, I suggest, one places less emphasis on a variety as object-in-itself and more emphasis on processes of distinction, which operate on many levels, from the gross to the subtle. Research on "registers" has often concerned relatively stable, institutionalized patterns and varieties, perhaps having explicit names within their communities of use, and/or being connected with institutionalized situations, occupations, and the like ("sports announcer talk," for instance). Style includes these, but it also includes the more subtle ways individuals navigate among available varieties and try to perform a coherent representation of a distinctive self – a self that may be in turn subdividable into a differentiated system of aspects-of-self. Perhaps there is another difference too: whereas dialect and register, at least as sociolinguists ordinarily identify them, point to linguistic phenomena only, style involves principles of distinctiveness that may extend beyond the linguistic system to other aspects of comportment that are semiotically organized.

This notion of style rests on the possibility that the same, or at least similar, principles of distinctiveness may be invoked at the personal level as at the institutional. This is so, I suggest, because of the specific ways in which ideologies of linguistic differentiation systematize and rationalize relationships between linguistic phenomena and social formations.

The next section will elaborate and illustrate this point. Pursuing the specific semiotic processes through which ideologies of linguistic differentiation work, I propose a model of how social semiosis exploits available linguistic features (as differentiae), and how stylistic distinctiveness becomes available for creative deployment and interpretation.

3   Ideologies of differentiation: semiotic processes

In a 1992 paper on dialect variation in eastern Europe, Susan Gal suggested that to understand the variation and the linguistic changes occurring in the region she described, one must "pay close attention to a cultural system, to a set of ideas or ideologies about the nature of social value and the role of language in producing that value." Having done so, she noted, it turned out that "quite similar sociolinguistic processes can be found in village India, among the Wolof of Senegal . . . and in what Eric Wolf has called the really dark continent: Europe" (Gal 1992:2). The ethnographic research she had done in eastern Europe and I had done among Wolof in west Africa, though conducted in very different locales, language families, and social settings, revealed some interesting resemblances among the principles that organized the differentiation of linguistic varieties and subvarieties.

Comparing our observations, and focusing on the cultural ideas that interpret, rationalize, and locate – perhaps even generate – linguistic differences in a local social field, we found that in these two sociolinguistic systems the particular content of those ideas happened to be similar. In both systems, morally loaded notions opposing austerity to exuberant display served as an organizing principle linking linguistic differentiation with social distinctiveness at many levels, rationalizing (for participants) the differences between locally available ways of speaking (registers, subregisters, dialects, even whole languages). The point is not that an ideology of linguistic differentiation always operates with this particular axis of contrast. Indeed, the above-mentioned Javanese case is rather different. What the serendipitous similarity suggested to us was, instead, that it would be worthwhile to undertake a broader exploration of how linguistic ideologies organize and rationalize sociolinguistic distinctiveness.

We undertook to explore that question in a joint project, currently underway, on which I shall draw in the remainder of this paper. Though we have examined a large number of cases, historical as well as contemporary, I limit the present discussion to the two ethnographic cases we started with. It is important to note, however, that we believe we are looking at a very general kind of phenomenon.

In brief, the findings illustrated in these cases are the following. (1) The linguistic phenomena that constitute registers and styles, as forms of linguistic distinctiveness, have a consistency that derives, in some degree, from local ideologies of language – principles of distinctiveness that link language differences with social meanings. (2) Ideologies of linguistic differentiation interpret the sociolinguistic phenomena within their view via (we argue) three semiotic processes, which we have called iconization, recursivity, and erasure.[12]

Iconization is a semiotic process that transforms the sign relationship between linguistic features and the social images to which they are linked. Linguistic differences appear to be iconic representations of the social contrasts they index – as if a linguistic feature somehow depicted or displayed a social group's inherent nature or essence. The ideological representation – itself a sign – operates in terms of images; it picks out qualities supposedly shared by the social image and the linguistic features (or rather, an image of such features), binding these images together. Their connection thus appears to be necessary, perhaps even "natural," because of the supposedly shared qualities. In this way iconization entails the attribution of cause and necessity to a connection (between linguistic behaviors and social categories – of people or activities) that may be only historical, contingent, or conventional.

Recursivity involves the projection of an opposition, salient at one level of relationship, onto some other level. It is the process by which meaningful distinctions (between groups, or between linguistic varieties, etc.) are reproduced within each side of a dichotomy or partition, creating subcategories and subvarieties; or, conversely, by which intra-group oppositions may be projected outward onto inter-group relations, creating supercategories that include both sides but oppose them to something else. This is the process that links subtle forms of distinctiveness with broader contrasts and oppositions. Iconicity is involved here too, since the secondary, projected opposition stands in an iconic relationship to the original or primary one.

Erasure, meanwhile, is the process in which an ideology simplifies the sociolinguistic field. Attending to one dimension of distinctiveness, it ignores another, thereby rendering some sociolinguistic phenomena (or

---

[12] In earlier presentations we have called the first of these processes iconicity, but that word seems better suited to the result of the process than to the process itself.

persons or activities) invisible. So, for example, a social group, or a language, may be imagined as homogeneous, its internal variation disregarded or explained away. Again, iconization may be involved, since the aspects of the sociolinguistic scene not picked out in the iconizing process are precisely the ones most likely to seem to disappear.[13]

In the hope that examples will illustrate and clarify these points, I turn to our ethnographic cases, in which the three processes apply.

3.1   Speech varieties in a Wolof village (Senegal)

The first example comes from a rural Wolof community in Senegal, which I visited for ethnographic and linguistic research (most extensively in the 1970s).[14] There, villagers identified two salient styles of speaking which they associated with opposite social groups in Wolof society: the high-ranking *géér* ("nobles"), and the low-ranking *gewel* ("griots," a bardic caste). The system of ranks (known as "castes" in the ethnographic literature on the region) among Wolof includes many more categories than just these two; but, in these villagers' view, the contrast between (high) noble and (low) griot epitomized the principle of hierarchical differentiation as it relates to the activity of speaking.

My argument here (for more detail see Irvine 1989 and 1990) is that the linguistic differences between these ways of speaking are motivated by an ideology of language that connects social identity with verbal conduct – as if that conduct displayed social essences iconically. Moreover, the principles of stylistic differentiation operate on many different levels, from gross contrasts to subtle ones (recursivity).

In the traditions of Wolof village society, differences in rank are an acknowledged value that organizes all sorts of social activities and interactions, ranging from economic specializations and exchange, to the regulation of marriage, and including social contact and talk. Social organization, as conceived in this cultural framework, depends upon the differentiation of persons and their behavior. Wolof consultants drew a broad contrast between gravity and exuberance in behavior, and explained it in terms of a contrast between laconic and impulsive temperaments. The central idea is

---

[13] So although I have listed three semiotic processes, in a sense they are all aspects of the same one, iconization. Notice that most discussions of iconicity in language have focused solely on iconic relationships between the linguistic sign and its referent. Here, instead, iconicity concerns relationships between the sign and its conditions of production (i.e. its speakers, or the activities or scenes in which it is characteristically uttered). See Irvine and Gal 2000.

[14] Senegal today has been drawn more into a transnational sphere, with diasporan populations living in Paris and New York, than was the case at the time of my original fieldwork. Urban varieties of Wolof have changed and are probably more influential on the rural scene than they were at that time. The system I describe has been partially reconfigured.

that people are inherently dissimilar, having different constitutions (and physical ingredients, which were sometimes described in terms of the viscosity of bodily fluids). These different constitutions govern their possessors' feelings and motivations and make them behave in dissimilar ways. Thus villagers "explained" differences in caste-linked modes of conduct and rationalized caste inequality, since conduct has moral implications and the caste hierarchy is based on supposed moral distinctions.

Among the lower-ranking castes, the griots in particular have the image of high affectivity and excitability. They are seen – by themselves as well as by others – as somewhat volatile and theatrical personalities, endowed with energy and rhetorical skills, and most especially as people who excite others with whom they interact. The highest-ranking nobles, meanwhile, are conventionally associated with stability, but also with lethargy and blandness. Their restraint (*kersa*) may "make them reluctant to say bad things," as some villagers said, but (they continued) it also makes them reluctant to say or do much of anything. It takes a griot to make life interesting and attractive and to keep the high nobles awake. Once roused, kings and chiefs may be moved to great deeds – the greater because of the seriousness and weightiness of their personalities, and the many dependents whom they command – but griots are needed to stir them to that point. The griots' main services, therefore, lie in their ability to stir others, including their ability to convey a noble patron's ideas energetically and persuasively to his public (since he would be too torpid, or too removed, to convey them himself).

The ideology that contrasts these social images is, I have suggested (Irvine 1990), what motivates the particular linguistic contrasts distinguishing the two styles of speaking my consultants identified: "griot speech" and "noble speech." The "griot" style can be summarized as involving affectively charged, elaborated, aesthetically polished, supportive repetition (the idea of repetition deriving from the griot's role as "transmitter" of the high-ranking patron's ideas, which are sometimes initially whispered or conveyed to the griot in private, then repeated elaborately by the griot in public). The "noble" style, in contrast, is the style of the laconic, restrained, torpid or cautious speaker who lacks special rhetorical skills or fluency. Linguistically, the relevant contrasts are found in all aspects of verbal performance, from prosody, phonetics, morphology, and sentence structure to turn-taking and the management of conversational discourse. (See tables 1.2, 1.3, 1.4.)

The most extreme version of "griot talk" is displayed in the griot's public performances: loud, rapid oratory accompanied by emphatic gestures; pitch mostly high, but including sharp pitch contours; sentence constructions that contain many morphological and syntactic devices for emphasis, intensification, and repetitive parallelisms; and vivid vocabulary, especially

Table 1.2. *Wolof style contrasts in prosody (Irvine 1990)*

	waxu géér	*waxu gewel*
pitch	low	high
volume	soft	loud
tempo	slow	fast
voice	breathy	clear
contour	pitch nucleus last	pitch nucleus first
dynamic range	narrow	wide

Table 1.3. *Wolof style contrasts in phonology (Irvine 1990)*

Style:	"Noble speech"	"Griot speech"
Feature contrasts:	Contrasts in vowel length and consonant length not clearly maintained	Contrasts in vowel length and consonant length clearly maintained
	Non-nasal stops affricated and/or prenasalized, e.g.: [p] → [ɸ], [b] → [β], [mb], [mβ]	Stops in stressed syllables, and all "fortis" stops, energetically articulated
	"Breathy" or "creaky" (laryngealized) articulation of voiced stops	Voicing contrasts in syllable-initial consonants, and all "fortis" stops, clearly maintained
Stressed/ unstressed syllables and elisions:	Stresses not clearly marked (little difference between stressed and unstressed syllables)	Stressed syllables clearly articulated. Elisions in unstressed syllables: (1) "Lenis" final stop → 0 (2) Unstressed CV# → C# (3) Initial [k] → [ʔ]
Vowel height:	Some lowering of vowels?	Some fronting and raising of vowels, especially before palatal glides

regarding details of sound, motion, and feeling. The extreme of "noble talk," on the other hand – apart from silence – is represented by a laconic, slow, low-pitched drawl or mumbling, with simple or even incomplete sentence structures. Prosodic contrasts between the styles are conspicuous and salient to consultants, while phonological aspects of stylistic differentiation are less available to conscious contemplation. Yet the two kinds of contrast (prosodic and phonological) are closely linked. The "noble" style's mumbled drawl neutralizes features of vowel and consonant length and some distinctions between stops and continuants, as opposed to the "griot"

Table 1.4. *Wolof style contrasts in morphology and syntax (Irvine 1990)*

Style:	"Noble speech"	"Griot speech"
Emphatic devices:	Unmarked order of basic constituents (SVO); sparse use of markers	Left dislocations; cleft sentences; heavy use of focus markers (subject focus, object focus, and "explicative" verbal auxiliary)
	Sparse use of spatial deictics and determinants	Frequent use of spatial deictics, especially their "emphatic" forms
	Sparse use of modifiers	Heavier use of modifiers; ideophones (intensifiers); more use of verb–complement construction *né* ____, which often conveys details of sound and motion
Parallelism:	Little use of parallelism	Repetitive and parallel constructions (e.g., parallel clauses)
	Few reduplicated forms, especially in verbs; no novel constructions using morphological reduplication	Frequent use of morphological reduplication, especially in verbs, including novel word-formations
Disfluencies – morphology: (see Irvine 1978)	(1) choice of noun class marker "wrong" or semantically neutral (2) avoidance of class markers when possible (3) incomplete or inconsistent concord	(1) "Correct" class markers, following principles of consonant harmony and/or semantic subtlety (2) Inclusion of class markers, when optional (2) Complete and consistent concord
Disfluencies – syntax:	Incomplete sentence structures. False starts	Well-formed sentence structures

style's shotgun articulation that preserves those feature distinctions but highlights consonants at the expense of vowels. And so on.

Notice, first of all, the way in which an ideology of language "explains" the form of linguistic differentiation of these styles by associating it with essentialized social differences. The linguistic contrasts that differentiate the styles are not arbitrary; instead, they are motivated by a language ideology contrasting the laconic and austere with the impulsive and elaborated, and conceiving these qualities as deriving from the supposedly differentiated temperaments of their speakers. This is what I mean by iconization: in the rural Wolof-speakers' ideology, the contrasting linguistic behaviors are made to appear to be iconic representations – depicting the social relations they index. Linguistic features occurring at many levels of linguistic organization are vertically integrated along an ideological axis that contrasts them, along with their associated social images, according to the temperaments that supposedly "cause" the differentiation. And the linguistic differentiae themselves offer linguistic images that (iconically) share qualities with the social images they represent. Thus, for example, the linguistic image of the slow speaker coincides with the image of a person supposedly slow to act and slow to change allegiances, while the dynamic speaker is supposedly fast-moving, emotionally volatile, and changeable.

Second, we find here another common consequence of an ideology of contrasts: the fractal or segmentary replication of the same axis of contrast at different levels of inclusiveness. Despite the labels Wolof villagers assigned to these ways of speaking, actual speech in this Wolof community does not sort out into two utterly distinct types, but rather into a stylistic continuum. It is true that the poles of the continuum, i.e. the most extreme versions of the styles, are linked to the utterances of griots and high nobles on large-scale public occasions. Apart from those polarizing scenes, however, any speaker, no matter what his or her caste, may use either a noble-like or a griot-like style, depending on the circumstances. So while a local ideology of language links these styles with the social categories of noble and griot – caste categories whose membership is permanent, non-overlapping, and ranked on an absolute scale – in practice the styles are drawn upon by everyone. Two persons who belong to one and the same caste will differentiate their speech along the same stylistic axis that differentiates castes from each other, in order to represent subtler differences of rank (such as lineage seniority), or to define an activity, such as petitioning, that is reminiscent of inter-caste relations. The linguistic differentiae they deploy to do this echo the differentiae of caste-linked styles, but to a lesser degree, the differences of pitch, tempo, fluency, and so on being somewhat narrower (see Irvine 1990 for transcript examples). In short, there is not just one social boundary or distinction that is relevant here, but, instead, a scheme of sociolinguistic differentiation that semiotically organizes relationships at many levels. This is what I mean by recursivity. The recursive structure serves to organize many situations, and many aspects of talk, even when the stylistic contrasts are subtle.

Finally, notice that the ideology of these contrasts, in emphasizing a binary opposition and focusing on a particular level of social organization (here, the level of caste relations) ignores relationships and social categories that do not fit. The metapragmatic labels for these ways of speaking, in attributing them to permanent and exclusive social categories, disregard the (recursive) practices that distribute their use throughout Wolof society. Moreover, Wolof society includes not only nobles and griots, but also other "artisan" castes and, especially, the descendants of persons of slave status. Yet, the linguistic ideology described here erases slaves from the picture, ignoring their differences from griots (and nobles). There is no comparable notion of a "slave" style of talk co-ordinate with the other styles. These disregardings are what I mean by erasure. A linguistic ideology is a totalizing vision in which some groups (or activities, or varieties) become invisible and inaudible. The descendants of slaves, in rural Wolof society, are accorded no voice.[15]

The process of erasure is of course a crucial reason why a language ideology, whether discovered in informants' explicit statements and explanations or otherwise deduced, is not identical with an outside observer's analysis. The language ideology does not offer a complete picture (or explanation) of a sociolinguistic scene, in spite of motivating important portions of it.

3.2   Bóly: linguistic differentiation in eastern Europe

My second illustration, drawn from Gal's ethnographic and linguistic research (Gal 1992), concerns linguistic differences in Europe that have most often been called "geographic" or "social dialects." The site is a community in a region of southern Hungary that includes a sizeable population of German-speakers. In a context where Hungarian and standard German are also to be found, two named rural varieties of German are associated with different social categories. Although the epoch in which this system seems to have been most firmly established and elaborated is the inter-war years, families in the village today can still identify themselves with one or the other social category, and they still reproduce the relevant linguistic distinctions in the course of daily life.[16]

Though space does not permit more than the briefest sketch of these sociolinguistic distinctions, we shall see that they involve processes (axes) of distinction surprisingly similar to the Wolof case. Thus the semiotic processes discussed in this paper do not concern only exotic locales; nor do they concern only systems incorporating some traditionally ascriptive

---

[15] Many of them, not sharing the whole of the ideology described here, have moved away from communities like this one.

[16] Today it is the older generation (those who grew up in the inter-war years or earlier) for whom the system is most meaningful. It is they who are best able to assign everybody in town to one category or another, who reproduce the system most conspicuously in their own speech, and who remind others of its relevance and specifics.

Table 1.5. *Some lexical differences*

Handwerkerisch	Bäuerisch	
Kersche	Kirschen	"cherries"
Zimmer	Stube	"room"
zu Hause	Ham	"home"

social hierarchy. The German distinctions are not linked to some taken-for-granted system of social ranking. Although differences of status and rank are not irrelevant to the German case – the ideologies are not utterly egalitarian – the basis of rank is contested.

The two linguistic varieties in this German/Hungarian community are locally named Handwerkerisch and Bäuerisch (or, Schwäbisch). As their names indicate, members of the community conceive of them as associated with artisans and with farmers, respectively. The differences between the varieties are to be found in every part of the linguistic system (Gal 1992). Phonologically they involve different frequencies of variants within a shared set of variables (concerning, e.g., the raising of back vowels, as in *komm* versus *kumm*); different frequencies of use of patterns of verbal morphology and word order; different lexical sets, some items of which overlap with Standard German (see table 1.5); and contrasts in other aspects of discourse, such as in titles, greetings, and storytelling practices. There are also differences in the extent of overlap with other regional dialects, and in the frequency of borrowing: Handwerkerisch contains many more forms that overlap with other regions, especially with Viennese German; and it borrows forms from Viennese German, from Hungarian, and sometimes from Standard German, relatively freely (except if such forms happen to be found in Bäuerisch as well, for maintaining the distinctiveness of the Handwerkerisch style is paramount).

Though these varieties are locally conceived as characterizing distinct social groups, it turns out that in fact all speakers are bidialectal, and acquire both varieties in childhood. The two social categories, artisans and farmers, do not (and did not) occupy separate neighborhoods, nor have they been distinguishable in financial wealth, for each category includes relatively rich and poor families. Children's play groups are mixed, as are adult friendship networks. Yet, adults belong to formal organizations, established in Bóly at the end of the nineteenth century (on the model of *vereine* in Germany), that segregate the two categories; and until the postwar period, village politics maintained the distinction by guaranteeing equal representation on the village council, and strict alternation in the mayor's position. In family settings especially, but also elsewhere, discussion of the distinctive speech, behavior, and moral values proper to the two categories explicitly regiments children's affiliation and the contexts of adults' usage.

The difference between these varieties, especially for older people who remember the period when they were most elaborated and most socially relevant, is locally understood as a difference in basic values and lifestyle. The farmers, who based their conception of social status on agricultural real estate and its prudent management, valued restraint, conservatism, and austerity; the artisans, on the other hand, based their values on education, cosmopolitanism (especially oriented toward Vienna, long a source of professional expertise in their crafts), and the display of acquired skill. The farmers' principles of frugality and their sober aesthetic thus contrasted with the artisans' "refined," cosmopolitan, innovative orientation – their aesthetic of display, elaboration, elegance, and worldly sophistication. The two categories differed, therefore, not only in the predominant choice of styles but in the principle by which styles were chosen or produced, and which extended far beyond the linguistic into many other aspects of comportment and material surroundings, such as dress, housing and furniture styles, dance styles, investment choices, and so forth. Indeed, with respect to each other the two social groups practiced a stylistic differentiation, linguistically and otherwise, that (a few decades ago especially) exaggerated the opposition between them.

To members of both social categories, the linguistic differences between the two varieties of German are interpreted iconically as evidence of a difference in their speakers' values. For instance, the Handwerkers' more innovative linguistic forms, larger repertoire, and more frequent display of stylistic range (including code-switching with standard German and Hungarian) could be seen as evidence of their love of display and opulent decoration, and, when viewed from the farmers' perspective, revealed their failure to maintain frugality and tradition in language as elsewhere. Yet, just as in the Senegalese case, the contrast between groups also serves to contrast situations associated with the two categories respectively, or with their values. Talk in the village wine-cellars, for example – a local institution of long standing, and connected with tradition and farm products – favored Bäuerisch no matter who the speaker might be. And farmers occasionally shifted to the Handwerkerisch style to show, in argument perhaps, that they were actually just as *gebildet* ("educated") as any artisan.

Thus the two German dialects in Bóly reflect a principle of differentiation that provided not fixed linguistic practices, but a dichotomy that can be applied recursively at varying levels of contrast, or used as a frame to interpret difference. People in both categories have access to speech forms characteristic of both sides of the contrast. Even within the everyday inter-actions of a single speaker, the opposition of artisan and farmer – and the contrasts of activity and aesthetics that it summarized – could be called on and be recursively reproduced for social effect, distinguishing situations, moods, and aspects of the self. The recursive process even applies to a pro-jection of these local oppositions onto a broader regional and national opposition, when villagers in Bóly (and elsewhere in the south of Hungary) compared German and Hungarian as languages, and German-speakers and Hungarian-speakers as ethnic groups, along moral, aesthetic, and affective dimensions that were the same as those they had discussed in interpreting the local scene.

Finally, this case demonstrates as well the semiotic process of erasure. For by defining the major cultural opposition in the village as that between artisans and farmers, the ideology described here effectively elides the sub-stantial differences in wealth and position within each category. In the past especially, this erasure worked through institutions such as the voluntary associations, where the forms of membership evoked internal homogeneity, denying difference. But it worked as well through the everyday practice of linguistic differentiation, which provided no separate style of speaking for rich as opposed to poor; powerful as opposed to powerless. The ideology underlying this principle of distinctiveness helped create the illusion of homogeneity within the categories it defined.

4   Conclusion

My purpose in this paper has been to try to consider linguistic style as a truly sociolinguistic phenomenon, an organization of distinctiveness that operates on a linguistic plane yet is constitutive of social distinctiveness as it does so. It has now often been noted that linguistic differentiation is not a simple reflection of social differentiation (or vice versa), because linguistic and social oppositions are not separate orders of phenomena. As Ferguson (1994:19) writes, "language phenomena are themselves sociocultural phe-nomena and are in part constitutive of the very social groups recognized by the participants or identified by analysts." It is that mediating recognition and identification, together with its ideological frameworks and pressures, whose relationship with processes of stylistic differentiation I have sought to explore.

In consequence, I have found it important to place less emphasis on the specific features of a style (or register, or variety, etc.) and more on the con-trasts and relationships between styles. And I have found it helpful not to try to identify "style" with some particular level of differentiation, but to focus on the differentiating process – axes of distinctiveness that organize differentiation at many levels. "Style," as distinctiveness, is a creative process (recall the notion of style as connected with fashion, with which I began this paper); it will not be tied down to a predetermined structure. Yet its principles must be coherent if they are to be meaningful, as representations of social groups, activities, practices, and selves.

2   Variety, style-shifting, and ideology[1]

Susan Ervin-Tripp

Judith Irvine (this volume, chapter 1) has examined the role of ideology in the relation between social group language differences and the representation of those differences in each speaker's style contrasts. Her focus is on the social meanings signified by styles, which are primarily contrastive. She is interested, then, not in what Labov (Labov 1966) called *indicators*, which she calls "empirical distributions," but in ideas about language categories that represent social contrasts to participants.

Her paper makes some powerful and important integrative claims. The principle of *iconization* is a claim that the social contrasts that are imputed to groups or to situations are also represented by linguistic features. Wolof speakers have an account of language features that supports iconization, using the underlying trait explanation. That is, beliefs about contrasts in the traits of groups of people are consistent with contrasts in linguistic features, and these correspond to stylistic selections when traits are expressed by individuals. Iconization could create an arbitrary relation of trait to feature, "historical, contingent, or conventional," but in the Wolof case, the relation appears not to be arbitrary, but to have some naturalness, and the term "icon" implies a likeness.

Korean and Japanese politeness levels provide another example, besides the Javanese case scrutinized with care by Irvine. Here the higher the deference, the more the effort put into morphology, and the less rough the language is felt to be. A person ignorant of these two languages might still guess that the longer form is the more deferential.[2] Possibly there are a few universals in semiotic relations of sign to signified which would allow such prediction by non-members. For example, it might be hard to find that a style involving slower speech is associated with higher excitability.[3]

---

[1] This paper profited from comments of John McWhorter and Mary Bucholtz, but most of all from the tactful, creative, and detailed attention of John Rickford.

[2] This property of the status markers makes Koreans and Japanese in asymmetrical power encounters use styles which are, with respect to honorifics, the opposite from the register descriptions of Finegan and Biber (this volume, chapter 14), namely the higher-status speaker is more curt.

[3] There are some cross-cultural similarities in synaesthesia, suggesting non-random correspondences between sensory domains and imputed behavior, e.g. Osgood (1960).

The claim of *recursion* is that the same process of iconization occurs for different categories of language contrast in the same community – for inter-group contrasts, registers, and dialects. The effect is that iconization for one contrastive set is projected to another. I will examine a case of that below.

The last principle proposed by Irvine, *erasure*, is an ideological process in which the conception of contrasting categories or dimensions is partial and oversimplified. Of course erasure is very common in colonization or nation-building; an example is the Zionist slogan, "A land without people for a people without land," which erased Palestinians. Nationalism often erases minority linguistic varieties; factors in contrast may be entirely over-looked in the interest of dichotomizing. Irvine finds wealth and status differences were both institutionally and ideologically neutralized in Wolof. Currently in the United States social class is also commonly erased from popular views of immigrant or racially defined minorities. Erasure could have both a formal and a social explanation. For instance, it is possible that binary distinctions are preferred in ideologies of contrast, so that erasure arises for reasons of cognitive simplification, but the choice of what to erase is social.

1   Ideology and learning

Language ideologies have empirical manifestations in two forms that I will consider below. One is in acquiring skill in more than one variety; the other is in displaying that skill in code- or style-switching. There appear to be strong similarities in both acquisition and switching dynamics between bilinguals and skilled multidialect speakers. Ideologies affect both the prob-abilities of contact and motivation to speak like another, but it is not clear whether it is beliefs and attitudes accessible to interviewers, or underlying presuppositions and prejudices that are most powerful in affecting under-standing and speech. There are dramatic contrasts between reportable ideologies about groups in conflict situations such as in Quebec and in Israel and Palestine, and the more indirect, possibly unconscious meanings assessed by subjective reaction tests to speech guises[4] (Lambert, Anisfield, and Yeni-Komshian 1965, Woolard and Gahng 1990). Which is ideology?

We can expect that in contact situations, lexical, phonetic, and surface

---

[4] When voices were recorded reading in Arabic, and in Ashkenazic and Yemenite Hebrew, the conscious attitude measures gave very different results from subjective reaction measures. Yemeni had less education and more menial jobs than Ashkenazi, whereas many Arabs were known to be very well educated. Jewish adolescents reported more positive attitudes to Yemenite Jews on the attitude measures than in the guise measures (on honesty, intelligence, reliability) and more negative attitudes to Arabs in the conscious attitude tests than on the guise measures (on looks, intelligence, self-confidence, reliability, leadership). Overall, there was a significant negative correlation of the measures (Lambert, Anisfeld, and Yeni-Komshian 1965).

and deep grammatical features might have different trajectories of learning, for two reasons. One is that some features are perceived as membership markers more than others, that is, they are iconized as markers rather than indicators. The other is that some require more experience than others; in AAVE, the semantics of invariant *be*, for example, or the delicate distributional contrasts in narrative verb final -*s*. These could be reanalyzed by learners.

There is evidence that second dialect learning is alive and well; Carla, the child discussed by Labov (Labov 1980), spoke a variety of AAVE characteristic of some Black speakers; her casual speech was accepted by Black judges as that of a native speaker, and she was able in narrative quoting to use the level of deletions of copula and singular present verb affixes typical of more extreme forms of AAVE (Butters 1984).

2   Borrowing

We can separate isolated borrowing and mimicry of marked features, which Poplack (1980) has called *emblematic* from more extensive productive use. Emblematic use can be seen in switching proper-name phonology – during the conflicts over US–Central American relations in the 1980s the phonetics of *Nicaragua* or other Spanish proper names could be used to mark one's allegiances, and political leaders who otherwise could not speak Spanish could use such emblems or some borrowed words. There is also mockery in derogatory use (Hill 1995).

Ben Rampton's ethnographic research (1991) on Punjabi in British anglophone speech of teenagers is the most detailed study of the social functions of the deployment of isolated items and features without further learning. These included a few words and phrases, and mimicked phonetic features in nonsense words. Though the boys were good friends, they never learned Punjabi beyond use in taunts.

3   Switching

Those who study code-switching like to reserve the term for maximally bilingual speakers who are known to have parallel options in both codes. Gumperz (1982), McClure (1981), Myers-Scotton (1993), and many others have examined the functions of switching in stable bilingual populations.

Switching by bilingual individuals to different addressees is expected as an accommodation to other participants' abilities.[5] When the participants are all bilingual, code-switching can be induced by situational changes like entering a different setting or the arrival of a participant incompetent in

---

[5] Failure to switch can be evidence of anger or political ideology (Heller 1992).

that variety, or by choices of the speakers. A shift can itself be constitutive of situational change. Any of these can represent semiotic contrasts, as Irvine has proposed. The last is the type of switching referred to as metaphorical or conversational, since it is entirely within the semiotic control of the speakers. It appears to be a way to contextualize messages by allusion to a community of speakers and their values (Gumperz 1982).[6]

4 Types of style-shifts in monolinguals

Shifts of style appear to be like code-switching in invoking contrastive implications of the linguistic features.

4.1 Addressee

One shift is the change in language induced by a change in participants, because of the effect of speech accommodation (and divergence) on speech rates and speech variables. Dramatic examples of these changes can be heard when a speaker is overheard talking to a child or to a relative from another region on the telephone. Labov's analysis of Responses (chapter 5), shows that even brief accommodation alters style. Rickford and McNair-Knox (1994) have done the most detailed analysis of this issue, revealing statistically significant shifts in measurable features of AAVE when the conversational partner was changed. They were able to show that there was more than accommodation at work, since the changes were not finely tuned to the addressee's linguistic behavior so much as to the addressee's social attributes, as well as to topics that implicated past conversational partners. This is categorical or stereotyped shifting that implies iconization.

Shifts can be affected by stereotyped registers or norms for use, rather than feedback accommodation alone, as in cases of baby talk to children, or hypercorrection to interviewers, teachers, or government personnel. Such adjustments begin very early, in vocal shifts, and by four years old children can change syntax according to age of addressee (Shatz and Gelman 1973).

Some style-shifts to addressees involve not accommodation but contrast, as in the example of addressee honorific styles, where asymmetry of speaker and addressee rather than similarity is required when there is a status difference. Learning asymmetrical address styles requires seeing them modelled by others.[7] In performance they must be controlled by learned forms with imitation of the addressee resisted.

---

[6] In bilinguals, the relation of thoughts and values to language can be so close that constraining language choice can alter speech content (Ervin 1964).

[7] Koreans raised in the United States learn Korean honorifics best if they have heard their parents use them to older relatives and the family has an ideology promoting correct

4.2   Speech conditions

Circumstantial shifts can change features not because of addressee behavior or stereotypes about the addressee, but because the psycholinguistics of production and feedback are altered. The contrast between speech and writing, planned and unplanned speech, face-to-face conversation and speech to a crowd are examples. These changes do not necessarily bear on, for instance, dialectal features, but they can so deeply alter the possibilities to edit or monitor speech that the role of dominant norms or stereotypes in production can be affected. Biber and Finegan's studies showing syntactic shifts according to such mode contrasts may be in part due to these factors, which if they are due to production factors rather than custom should have similarities in different languages.

In code-switching studies these are usually considered situational shifts, for they may be accompanied by social norms constraining language type, for instance in writing and speaking, or in informal speech and planned courtroom testimony (Jacquemet 1996).

4.3   Rhetorical shifts

Even within fixed interlocutor and situation arrangements, speakers use register, language, or dialectal features as resources for conveying meaning (Blom and Gumperz 1972, Gumperz 1982), in courtrooms, for example (Fuller 1993). Switching has been used in literature for emotional effect,[8] much like literary use of second person pronominal variants in Shakespearean English and Russian. The capacity to make these shifts appears at least by four years, as Andersen has demonstrated with children's role play (Andersen 1990). In Andersen's research, the first features which children were able to shift in conveying different role voices were phonological. Later speech acts were shifted, as were lexical and syntactic choices, and eventually contrasts included even discourse markers. For example *well* was more often used when the child was enacting a powerful rather than subordinate role. Distributional contrasts in role playing provide vivid evidence that the iconization of linguistic contrasts begins in early childhood.

footnote 7 (*cont.*)

>   Korean speech. Such speakers are significantly more able to produce both roles in narrative dialogue than those from nuclear families without models (Jun 1992).

[8] Roger Shuy has drawn attention to D.H. Lawrence's use in *Lady Chatterley's Lover* of skilled dialect shifts by the gamekeeper for powerful social effects in redefining encounters. Lady Chatterley's awkward attempts to speak the gamekeeper's dialect in afterglow talk is a demonstration of Lawrence's belief in the emotional power of sexuality. There is iconization of dialect as naturalness, at least for Lady Chatterley.

The functions of dialect feature shifts are probably similar to those found in bilingual code-switches – change of domain or stance, emphasis, or emotion, for example. Functions identified in the many code-switching studies have included getting attention, persuasion, asides, elaboration, personalization, dialogue in a narrative, and marking identity. How each of these works to project oppositions in terms of the recurrence expected by Irvine remains to be studied.

Examining shifting in speakers of Hawaii creole English, Sato (1973) found that addressee, topic, audience, and emotion changes all were associated with shifts. The particular advantage that is afforded by creole or dialect forms was pointed out by Rampton (1991), comparing switches of youth groups in Britain which included Pakistanis and African Caribbean speakers of creoles. While shifts to Pakistani risked being unintelligible to listeners, shifts to creole could employ features which preserved interpretability.[9] In Hawaii speech the shifts can occur at any level, prosodic, phonological, lexical, syntactic, depending on who was among the participants and how important intelligibility might be.

There are two important differences between code-switching and style-shifting using dialectal features. One is that with the exception of situations or features where intelligibility doesn't matter, code-switching largely must be limited to use among bilinguals, whereas style-shifts are potentially available for any audience. The other is that dialects in contact have slippery boundaries and possibly weaker co-occurrence constraints between features.[10] It is not clear whether "violations" of the scaled features in creole continua are heard to be inappropriate, or by whom. Speakers are very sensitive to probabilities, so one does not need categorical contrasts to sustain semiotic difference.

4.4   AAVE rhetorical switching

To find style-switches in social dialects, I have examined data from two African-American college-educated leaders from the civil rights movement in the 1960s: Stokely Carmichael, chair of the Student Non-violent Coordinating Committee in the 1960s, and Dick Gregory, who in the same period was doing both political comedy and political protests. Carmichael

---

[9] "Although Punjabi might operate as a symbolic object around which youngsters could develop and display their understanding of group relations, it was never available to them as a vehicle in which ideas about society were acutely encoded. In contrast, because of its linguistic proximity to English, Creole could serve both as a social symbol *and* as a medium through which non-afro-Caribbeans could gain access to dissident political perspectives" (Rampton 1991:415).

[10] Mitchell-Kernan (1971:54; 1972) rejected the "two-systems" model for AAVE and Standard English because of the "absence of systematic co-occurrence relations, with or without social correlates."

immigrated from Trinidad to the United States at eleven years old; Gregory grew up in St. Louis.[11] Because of their education and their political experience they both had a wide acquaintance network.[12]

In the two texts Carmichael uses Standard English without any AAVE features except where he uses a shift to make his major point to a Black audience. The first sample is from a media interview with Charles Susskind to a general television audience. In this segment he explained some idioms from AAVE unknown to Susskind. He quoted and translated the idioms (e.g. *uptight*, *out of sight*), then made a general point about White ignorance of Black lexicon:

(1)   Stokely Carmichael interview with Charles Susskind
        1 it means it means that *white people ought to *realize
        2 that what *black people say to each other
        3 they cannot always *interpret from *their frame of *reference/

Not only was this segment entirely in Standard English, it included careful forms like *cannot*. The topic here is language, which Labov has noted (this volume) is the least vernacular of topics. However, when he was giving a speech at a Black Power rally and referring to the Vietnam War in which there were many Black servicemen, in the punch line he made a switch, which brought applause.

(2)   Stokely Carmichael at Oakland Black Power rally
        1 we will *not *allow them to make us *hired *killers/
        2 we will stand *pat/
        3 we will *not kill anybody that they say kill/[13]
        4 and if we *decide to *kill
        5 we're gon *decide {[slow, dropping] *who *we *gon *kiy::ll}
        6 Audience: [applause]

Three features marked the switch: *gon*, prosodic drop, and prolongation of the final clause, and vowel height and prolongation in *kiy::ll*. We will see similar features included in those used by Dick Gregory for marking punch lines that bring applause.[14]

---

[11] Gregory's childhood in desperate poverty in St. Louis, and his rise to national status are described in *Nigger* (1964) and *Up from Nigger* (1976).
[12] The transcriptions below use notations from Gumperz and Berenz (1993). These include * stressed word, : prolonged, [feature], {scope of feature}, . . . pauses, / terminal juncture, // emphatic terminal drop, = overlapped segment, ( ) not clearly audible. In addition, for ease of reading this publication, non-standard primary-stressed syllables are in capital letters, phonological deletions from Standard English forms are marked with apostrophe, and interpretive quotation marks have been added to identify representations of direct speech.
[13] A similar speech by Carmichael can be heard on the web at http://www.blackhistory.com/ Sounds/03.Stokely_Carmichael.aiff
[14] John Gumperz has analyzed switching in a Black Power speech of David Hilliard, showing special prosodic features (1982) similar to preaching styles.

Dick Gregory was a comedian and a political activist. After he ran for president in 1968, he went back to comedy in colleges and in nightclubs in Chicago and New York. By then he had participated in many political demonstrations and was well known for taking strong stands, including hunger strikes, on issues like civil rights and the Vietnam war. He was also a skilled professional comedian who began by drawing on stylistic features in vernacular wit, but also studied many traditional comedic techniques. In his autobiography (1964) he reports that he relied on quick relevant wit to survive in his early street experience.

In a recorded performance at Southampton College,[15] Gregory was in the midst of a political campaign, so his speech is both a political speech and an example of his skills as a comedian. His overall style contained certain AAVE features, such as -*in* verb suffixes and *de* as the dominant article, but variable *d/dh*- in other words such as demonstratives. Overall in the text examined, 33 percent of Standard English *dh* fricatives were realized as stops, post-vocalic or syllabic *r* deletion or non-constriction was 32 percent, and consonant cluster simplification was 54 percent (e.g., *send*, *post*). Copula and number agreement opportunities were few in this text, but there was 75 percent non-agreement and 47 percent copula deletion. Though these features are rare, their distribution is strategic.

Gregory was very situation-conscious, and refused some invitations so as not to tangle his political and entertainer worlds (1964). A 1978 formal interview on a California radio station gives us his most serious style, albeit at a later age. Here there is a dramatic difference in the level of the AAVE features,[16] with 6 percent of *dh* realized as stops, 5 percent *r* deletion, 26 percent cluster simplification, 21 percent verb non-agreement. One copula deletion occurred on a punch line.[17]

In the transcript below from the college performance, at several sites, Gregory moved from his normal unmarked style to the most Standard English features. One was a joke about why there was no rioting last year, with his usual slowing at the punch line where he referred to the *Consumer*

[15] "Black rioters" from *The dark side, the light side*, Poppy Records. The recording was made at Southampton College, Southampton, New York on March 6, 1969, two days after newspapers reported Gregory was "sworn into 'office' as president of the United States in exile" in a Washington, DC school (Gregory 1976:184). His rendition of the Declaration of Independence (lines 87–94) was on the television news. One can assume more than college students came to his performance.

[16] In the text samples examined, the sample Ns for each feature are given first for the college talk, second for the radio interview: 113/68 for initial voiced *dh*, 97/43 for post-vocalic *r*, 41/19 for final cluster simplification, 16/19 for number marking of verb, and 19/14 for copula deletion.

[17] January 22, 1978 interview on "the unheard-of hour" on KSAN, Oakland, California, with thanks to the Bancroft Library, University of California, and Alex Prisadsky of the Berkeley Language Laboratory.

Reports in carefully articulated middle class English with strong /r/ and final clusters. He combined allusion to White middle class behavior with speech features in contrast to Black rioters' behavior and speech.

(3)   Dick Gregory in "Black Rioters"[18]
        19 i'(ll) *tell you whe' we were las' *riot season/
        20 we got *tired a stealin all 'em ol' *bad an' *no-good products/
        21 so las' *july through *augus'
    → 22 we decided to go *underground and
    → 23 {-slow] study the con*su:mer repo:rts:/}..
        24 Audience: [light laughter]

In lines 22–3 he makes rioters sophisticated. In another passage we see in a ludicrous family scene the same contrast between parents (=old fools) and the politically up-to-date young protesters who can speak Standard English when drawing on political materials. The segment begins with directions to read the Declaration to parents while they are watching the television news of rioting. This "family talk" segment displays many AAVE features, including copula deletion and *gon*. This AAVE is not in quoted speech but in a description of a family setting that contrasts with the voice of the Declaration and the voice of the political youth. The quotation from the Declaration of Independence was intoned in a declamatory reading style. Here Standard English from a respected source is used to subvert, to promote revolution, to question American political consistency. Instead of politically sophisticated youth versus rioters, the contrast is now youth and the sacred texts of American history versus ignorant parents.

        66 pull out your *declaration of independence
        67 and wit de *soun' *turned *off so they cain't hear **nothin
        68 just look at dem *black folks *loot and *burn de *town down/
        69 at *that point i want you to move *way in de *back of your parents,
        70 and while they lookin at them cats *burn
        71 i want you to *read yo' declaration of independence
        72 as *loud as you can *read it, and maybe for the *first time
        73 dem *fools will understand what they lookin at//
        74 {[loud steady declamatory]
        75 "we *hold these *truths to be self-*evidint . . .
        76 that *all *men are *created *equal . . .
        77 and *endowed by the *creator . . .
        78 with *certain *inalienable *rights . . .
        79 that *when these *rights are *destroyed . . .
        80 over *lo:ng *periods of *time . . .
        81 it is your **du:{[lo] ty
        82 to *destroy or *abolish that *government//" } }
        83 Audience: [25 sec. applause]

---

[18] *The light side, the dark side.* Poppy Records.

84 Audience: =[5 sec. rhythmic applause]=
85 =now . . . now=
86 i know at firs' them old fools is gon *assume
87 that was some *message Malcolm *X lef' f'r *Rap Brown.

The response by this audience is usually applause to political messages and laughter to humor. The greatest laughter is to narrative segments involving quotations, where Gregory uses features like lack of number agreement for his depiction of George Wallace, the governor of Alabama.[19] Here he parodies a White racist view of Blacks that even failure to riot is a defect.[20] In his narrative lines, he uses standard past tense affixes so most of the AAVE marked features are in the representation of direct speech.

12 "where *were you-all ?
13 we had de *tanks waitin fa you/"
14 dey asked George *Wallace
15 {[loud] "why you think they didn't *riot las' season/"
16 he sid "ah, you *know dem niggers is *lazy and *shiftle'/.
17 =they jus' got **ti:re(d)/"}=
18 Audience: =[applause, laughter]=

He also gets humorous effects by putting AAVE features into the mouths of Whites as in the Wallace extract above (though this could be an allusion to White Southerner speech) and line 215 below. The violation of linguistic expectation is a regular source of humor, for example in *New Yorker* cartoons where cleaning personnel recite Kipling or children quote stockbrokers. In the segment below, Gregory, who later wrote a book analyzing the politics of American history books (1971),[21] complains about how Black violence is not seen in the same way as White violence in American history. The use of AAVE features for Paul Revere alludes to a shared political situation for colonists opposing the British and for Black Panthers opposing the police, made explicit in the next line by the term "White Panthers." Here, the contrast of AAVE and Standard English is turned to depict the revolutionary, Paul Revere, versus himself as modern, educated, commentator.

[19] "Marking" is an African-American folk term about a form of characterization used in narratives that reports "not only what was said, but the way it was said, in order to offer implicit comment on the speaker's background, personality, or intent" (Mitchell-Kernan 1971:137). Parodies may overdo features associated with a social group in the minds of listeners, so they depend on shared assumptions about the meaning of styles, and thus are an example of recursion. Skill in such parodies is honed in family and personal contexts.

[20] Woolard has a particularly nuanced examination of code-switching in humorous performances, based also on a recorded comedian. She found that during a period of tension about Catalan–Castilian linguistic issues, the Catalan comedian switched within every quote and never used single-variety quotes to make character types. She interprets this as a politically motivated move to peace-making by reducing boundaries (Woolard 1987).

[21] In his autobiographies he is Dick Gregory, in the history book he is Richard Claxton Gregory.

210 you didn't have no *respec for de *PO: lice
211 {[hi] yeah dat's in there!}
212 {[lo, slow] in the *early days, when the british *was the *PO:lice,
213 a *white boy, by the name of *Paul *Revere
214 rode through the *white *community and said
→ 215 "git a *gun, white folks, the *PO:lice is comin/"
216 Audience: =[laughter, applause]=
217 =you can understand the *white *panthas,=
218 can't you (smiling)
219 Audience: [laughter, applause]
220 but the *black *panthas make you forgit about your *history,
221 don't they,

He plays with stereotypes in "marking" his politically uninformed boyhood, using stereotypic AAVE features both for himself and the principal of his school. This is all done as a reality-defying parody.

141 i remember i was *back in the *ghet:to in *grade school,
142 *happy, jus' bein a *good nigger *singin ma blues
143 "{[hi singing] i *love mah *baby}
144 [lo, singing nonsense syllables] . . ."
145 Audience: [laughter]
146 n the principal *ran up *to us one day and *said
147 {[hi] "*boad of education say
148 you-all can't graduate from *grade school
149 till you *read and *learn de declaration of *independence/"
150 i said "[hi] **what, de decla-**who? . . .
151 Audience: [laughter]
152 man we ain't gon read that *old *white *stuff//}"
153 "{[fast] well you ain't gon *graduate/"
154 i said "*lay it *on me den/} . . ."
155 Audience: [laughter]
156 ="{[lo] as long as these (serious objections is xxx)=
157 =[light laughter]=
158 then you have the *duty to destroy or *abolish yo *govment}"
159 =i said "{[hi] baby you-all got some *more of this stuff man?} . . ."
160 Audience: [laughter]

At this point, Gregory makes a dramatic shift in key and begins a political statement that has the repetitious structures (lines 161, 164, and the conclusive 172) also found in political speeches like Carmichael's and is not intended to be taken as humorous. It seems to be what Labov (this volume) calls "soapbox" variety. While this segment is supposed to be directed to "white folks," there is consistent copula deletion. There are marked lexical items like *nigger* and *mammy*, *gon*, and *yo'* and *they* for the possessive, and AAVE monophthongization and cluster reduction of *mind*. On lines 163 and 172 there is the vowel prolongation, and in 172 the prosodic drop which typically marks punch line emphasis. This dense use of AAVE features in a serious political vein seems to be present to emphasize a stance that "we" are Black and "you" are White; the content is political implications drawn from the shared events which have politically educated Black soldiers. The applause given this segment, spoken to a mixed audience, suggests that the audience identifies itself as too radical to be aligned with the White establishment, the *you white folks* of line 161.

```
       161  {[slow, loud] you white folks really *sick enough to *believe
       162  you can put this *stuff in our *neighborhood,
→      163  and we're not gon *read it and *do what it say:s to::://
       164  you white folks *sick enough to *believe
       165  you can *stiyill *draf' *niggers into yo' army,
       166  and send 'em down to *Fort Benning Georgia,
       167  and teach 'em how to be *go: rillas,
       168  and send 'em to *Vietnam,
       169  {[accel] killin *foreigners to liberate *foreigners,
→      170  and think they not gon *come back to *America,
       171  and kill *you to liberate they *mammy}
→      172  then you *sick and *out yo [lo] *mi::n'// . . .
       173  Audience: right! [22 sec. applause]
```

In addition to growing up in a community that used linguistic marking as a narrative device, Gregory, who carefully observed other comedians, was certainly familiar with Jewish stand-up comics who exploited code-switching to get laughter. Jewish families relied on code-switching in humorous narratives (Kirshenblatt-Gimblett 1972), and, depending on the audience, Jewish comedians have drawn on both dialect features and language shifts (using Hebrew, Yiddish, and other languages) and even pseudo-Italian or other languages, with the punch line in English.[22] But what is striking about Gregory is the combined presence of switching for humor and switching for ideological impact.

Political comedy is a linguistic representation of ideology. What we see in Dick Gregory is a deft use of identity features at critical junctures to represent both the ideological message of White culture in the constitution and its interpretation by African-American citizens as indicated by AAVE features. This is no accident, as we see in his self-correction of *the* to *de*, although this feature is variable in his AAVE style, as we see in 139 and 141:

```
       137  and {[louder] git your *television set
→      138  and put it in the . . . de *middle a de *roo:m/
       139  and then turn on de *evenin *news
       140  cuz'ey're gon show dem niggers *riotin and *lootin
       141  and {[breathy] *sockin it to the *town/}}
```

[22] Mel Brooks, in a television interview with Charlie Rose October 9, 1997, speaking of Sid Caesar.

The AAVE and Standard English contrasts which are used for ideological goals in this performance convey a range of social contrasts, to indicate rioters versus sophisticated protesters, old versus young, colonists versus British, and in the most serious passages a dense use of AAVE features and the most radical political message are joined to evoke the most applause. This was the era of *The Student as Nigger* (Farber 1969), a perspective in which being African-American was to symbolize protest against the Vietnam war as well as against civil injustices. Yet the contrast shifts meaning in each segment. What never occurs, and thus indicates a kind of erasure, is any recognition of the social class range and political variety in each generation of African-Americans.

While we think of ideology as a powerful force in the societal processes involved in language planning, school curriculum decisions, and language maintenance and shift, such rich individual cases of shifting do not just represent higher and lower status, more and less educated, White and Black, or formality and informality, but allude to different aspects of the groupings and identities of speakers and their beliefs. If such style-switching exemplifies recurrent iconization, it is not necessarily simple. Here we see that it requires realigning a complex array of potential contrasts.

3   The ethnography of genre in a Mexican market: form, function, variation[1]

Richard Bauman

1   Introduction: genre in practice

Over the past several years, the concept of genre has made a hesitant entry onto the stage of style- and language-variation studies (e.g., Biber 1988, Biber and Finegan 1989, Ferguson 1994), though it has not as yet been granted anything more than a bit part. One apparent reason why genre has not graduated to a larger role in this line of inquiry is that its use in the computerized language corpora that have carried it onto the stage has been largely *ad hoc*, deriving for the most part from lay usage and lacking in analytical rigor. Another problem, in broader scope, is that the concept of genre resists disciplinary divisions of intellectual labor, which makes it difficult to domesticate to increasingly specialized scholarly theory and practice. But there is a deeper problem as well. To bring it to the fore, let me turn to one of the charter documents for the workshop on which this volume is based, Douglas Biber and Edward Finegan's recent collection of essays on *Sociolinguistic Perspectives on Register* (1994). In one of the framing essays of that collection, Charles Ferguson sets out the following "basic working assumption implicit in sociolinguistic study of genre variation":

A message type that recurs regularly in a community (in terms of semantic content, participants, occasions of use, and so on) *will tend over time to develop an identifying internal structure, differentiated from other message types in the repertoire of the community.* (1994; italics in the original)

[1] An earlier version of this paper was written while I was a Fellow at the Center for Advanced Studies in the Behavioral Sciences, with the support of funds from the Andrew W. Mellon Foundation. I am grateful to the Center and the Foundation for this support, and to Don Brenneis, Charles L. Briggs, John Haviland, and Deborah Kapchan for their valuable comments on that earlier draft, which was presented at the 1993 Spring Meeting of the American Ethnological Society in Santa Fe, NM, April 16, 1993. Ronald Macaulay, as respondent, and the other participants in the Stanford Workshop on Stylistic Variation helped me to clarify the arguments of the current version, and I am grateful as well for their contributions. Thanks also to Ana Maria Ochoa for invaluable assistance in transcription and to Josefina Vasques for help in untying some knots in translation.

In this formulation, genre represents a framework for discrimination among conventionalized message types on the basis of differential, mutually contrastive internal structures. But in the framing essay immediately following Ferguson's, Biber suggests that genres "are problematic in the same way that register distinctions are, in that they represent text categories at different levels of generality" (1994:52). And elsewhere, Biber observes that some genres include "well-defined sub-genres, and the variation within the genre is due in part to variation among the sub-genres" (1988:171). Biber's observations would suggest, then, that genre distinctions may not be so mutually exclusive after all, that genre discriminations operate at different levels of generality and that genres may incorporate other genres. We are faced, then, with an apparent tension: on the one hand, relatively clearcut and conventional types; on the other, categories that escape into the margins of classificatory ambiguity. What I would like to offer, based closely on a collaborative exploration that I have undertaken with Charles Briggs (Bauman and Briggs 1990, Briggs and Bauman 1992), is a perspective on genre that accommodates both possibilities within a unified frame of reference. This resolution requires a shift from the conception of genre as a framework for the classification of finished textual products with immanent formal properties to an understanding of genre as a framework for the comprehension of discursive practice.

We conceive of genre as one order of speech style, a constellation of systemically related, co-occurrent formal features and structures that contrasts with other such constellations (Ervin-Tripp 1972, Hymes 1989 [1974]) and provides a conventionalized orienting framework for the production and reception of discourse (cf. Hanks 1987). More specifically, a genre is a speech style oriented to the production and reception of particular kinds of texts. A text, as we use the term, is a bounded, formally regimented, internally cohesive stretch of discourse that may be lifted out from its immediate discursive environment and recontextualized in another. When an utterance is assimilated to a particular genre, the process by which it is produced and interpreted is mediated through its relationship with prior texts. The invocation of a generic framing device such as "Once upon a time" carries with it a set of expectations concerning the further unfolding of the discourse, indexing other texts initiated by this opening formula. These expectations constitute a textual model for creating cohesion and coherence, for producing and interpreting particular constellations of features and their formal and functional relations, that is, for generating textuality.

Now, while generic inter-textuality is a means of imbuing texts with order, unity, boundedness, and coherence, the same relational nexus also draws attention to the *lack* of self-sufficiency and autonomy of the formal–functional configuration of the utterance at hand. This is so because the fit between a particular text and the generic model – or other tokens of the generic type – is never perfect. Generic frameworks never provide fully sufficient means and bases for discursive production and reception. Emergent elements of contextualization inevitably enter into the process, forging links to the surrounding discourse, the ongoing social interaction, broader social relations, instrumental or strategic agendas, and other factors. In a word, other pragmatic and metapragmatic frameworks in addition to genre must be brought into play in shaping production and reception. These in turn will influence the ways in which the constituent features of the generic framework – formal and pragmatic – are variably mobilized, thus opening the way to generic reconfiguration. We suggest, then, that the process of orienting particular utterances to prior discourse in terms of generic expectations necessarily produces an inter-textual *gap*. While the creation of this hiatus is inevitable, the calibration of the gap – its relative suppression or amplification – has important correlates and effects. On the one hand, certain acts of entextualization may attempt to achieve generic transparency by minimizing the distance between the text and the generic model, thus rendering the utterance maximally intelligible in terms of generic precedent. This course assimilates an utterance to conventional practices for the accomplishment of routine ends under ordinary circumstances. On the other hand, manipulation of the inter-textual gap allows for the adaptation of generic frameworks to emergent circumstances and agendas. Such adaptive calibration may involve assimilation of a text to more than one generic framework, drawing upon and blending the formal and functional capacities of each of the genres thus invoked.

To conceptualize genre in the terms I have outlined is to shift the primary focus of attention from typology or classification of message forms – the dominant concern of most genre-oriented investigation – to discursive practice: how does the generic organization of linguistic means serve as a resource for the accomplishment of social ends in the conduct of social life? The problem is one of form–function inter-relationships as realized in communicative practice. As a linguistic anthropologist, I approach the solution of the problem as an ethnographic task.

In order to exemplify how the perspective I have offered in the preceding pages might shape an empirical investigation, let me turn now to a substantive case, the generic regimentation of vendors' speech in a Mexican market. Following this brief case study, I will suggest some implications of this approach for the investigation of speech styles more generally.

2   The language of selling in a Mexican market: the generic baseline

Open-air markets are display events par excellence in Roger Abrahams'
(1981:303) sense of the term, "public occasions . . . in which actions and
objects are invested with meaning and values are put 'on display.'" In
common with festivals, fairs, and spectacles – other display events to
which they may be attached – markets are characterized by qualities of
scale, heterogeneity, semiotic proliferation, abundance, and effervescence
that make for a special intensification and enhancement of experience and
social value. Small wonder, then, that markets have exercised an enduring
attraction to literary artists from Villon and Rabelais to Thackeray and
Proust, and to graphic artists as well, such as Marcellus Laroon, who
included the verbal elements of market language in his enormously
popular engravings of *The Criers and Hawkers of London* (Shesgreen
1990). The literary and other artistic attractions of market language point
up the expressive availability of language for the intensification of experience and the enhancement of value in market settings, not only on the
part of market vendors, but of other verbal performers as well, such as the
religious preachers and political orators who are drawn to markets to
work the crowds. Hence my own interest in market language, stimulated
first by my research on seventeenth-century Quakers (Bauman 1983), for
whom markets were a favored venue for preaching their religion, and
carried still further by my work with hunting-dog traders in Texas, invete-
rate story-tellers, and truth-stretchers (Bauman 1986).

In the marketplace, the verbal creation and enhancement of value is in
the service of value of a particular kind, namely, commodity value. There is
a small but growing and suggestive literature on such form–function inter-
relationships in the language of markets and related venues, from Mitchell's
pioneering article on the language of buying and selling in Cyrenaica
(1957) and Bakhtin's stimulating chapter on the language of the marketplace in Rabelais (1984[1965]) to the more recent work of Dargan and
Zeitlin on American commercial talkers (1983), my own writings on the discourse of dog-traders (1986), Kuiper on auctioneers (Kuiper 1992, Kuiper
and Haggo 1984), Lindenfeld on the performances of French market
vendors (1978, 1990), Kapchan on language, genre, and gender in
Moroccan markets (1993, 1995), and – especially relevant in the present
context – Flores Farfán's study of social interaction and power in Otomí
markets in Mexico (1984). This paper is intended as a contribution to that
line of inquiry. It is based upon a small field project I carried out in San
Miguel de Allende, in the state of Guanajuato, Mexico. On occasional
Tuesday mornings, I wandered through the weekly market in San Miguel
with a tape recorder running, yielding a small corpus of market-

soundscape recordings from which I have drawn the materials I will discuss in this chapter.[2] In addition to the market tapes, I gathered further data in the form of observational field notes, interviews with vendors and shoppers, and reflexive monitoring of my own participation in the market as a regular shopper.

Sound is one of the semiotic resources that is intensified and elaborated in the construction of the market ambience of abundance. The boom-boxes of cassette vendors blare out *ranchera* and rock, an aged man plays thin music by blowing on a piece of cellophane to coax coins from passers-by, the hammer blows of carpenters selling furniture punctuate the air. And a prominent feature of this market soundscape is the cacophony of calls and spiels of market vendors crying their wares. I borrow the terms "call" and "spiel" from Lindenfeld (1990). The local term for "call" in San Miguel is *grito*; older people also use the term *pregon*. These are relatively brief, formulaic, formally economical and condensed utterances designed to attract the attention of potential customers, inform them about the commodities for sale, and induce them to buy. Spiels perform some of the same general functions and employ some of the same formal elements and devices, but are longer, continuous rather than bounded, less stereotyped, and marked by more elaborate devices and structures of argumentation. While local people recognize the distinctiveness of spiels, there does not seem to be a commonly preferred name for this genre; the terms I was offered include *propaganda comercial*, *plática comercial*, or simply *comercial*, the latter by extension from radio and television commercials.

I should make clear here at the outset that the verbal genres I will examine in this paper constitute but one part of the overall repertoire of verbal forms employed in buying and selling in the marketplace. Functionally, they are preliminaries to the more dialogic interaction of vendors and customers in the actual conduct of the sale. The calls and spiels are intended to draw customers in to the point of negotiating the sale itself. I have data on this latter phase of buying and selling as well, but reserve the treatment of those materials for another paper.

The elementary forms of independent, free-standing calls feature either of two essential kinds of information, the identity of the commodity or the price, as in examples 1–4.[3]

(1)   Jícamas,   Jícamas,
        jícamas.   jícamas.

---

[2] These data were recorded on six occasions between December, 1985 and January, 1989.
[3] In transcribing the calls and spiels I have set them out into lines marked primarily by significant breath pauses, though with occasional attention as well to syntactic structures and intonation patterns.

| (2) | Nieve, nieve. | Ice, ice. |
| | Nieve, nieve. | Ice, ice. |

| (3) | Cien pesos, | One hundred pesos, |
| | cien pesos. | one hundred pesos. |

| (4) | A veinte, | At twenty, |
| | a veinte. | at twenty. |

Example 1 is an irreducible minimal form, for in calls that include only the name of the commodity for sale it is repeated at least twice. Example 2 doubles that, yielding two lines of two nominal repetitions each. Minimal calls of price only also require repetition, as in examples 3 and 4.

Note the extreme economy of these elementary forms. The goods are announced by a single noun (*jícama, nieve*; or, in more complex forms to be discussed later, article plus noun), and the prices by two-word combinations consisting either of a quantifier plus a unit of currency (e.g., *cien pesos*) or of a preposition plus a quantifier (e.g., *a veinte*). This expressive economy is characteristic of calls generally. The functional constituents of the calls – commodity, price, or the others to be identified in a moment – are all characteristically condensed, generally realized by one or two words and lean syntactic structures.

It is worth noting, however, that there is a significant non-verbal dimension to the vending of the commodities that adds a further semiotic component to the process, namely, the common resort to ostension, holding up or pointing to an example of the commodity being offered for sale. Thus, it should be borne in mind throughout that even the most condensed calls are part of a multisemiotic and multisensory process that combines verbal and visual appeal. I will come back again a bit later to the sensory dimension of market talk.

Returning, though, to the identification of verbal constituents, we may observe that both item and price may be elaborated, the former by proliferation of commodities for sale and/or syntactic extension in the form of declaratives, as in example 5, and the latter by multiple pricing of different objects, as in example 9 or again by syntactic extension as in example 6.

(5)	Hay aguacates,	There are avocados,
	hay las limas, aguacates,	there are limes, avocados,
	hay aguacates.	there are avocados.

| (6) | A doscientos, | At two hundred, |
| | valen a doscientos. | they cost two hundred. |

Again, the declaratives of examples 5 and 6 are consensed, syntactically lean: "there are avocados" or "they cost 200." Nevertheless, already in these elementary forms, the calls are marked by a degree of formal elaboration that draws the poetic function toward the foreground by means of such devices as repetition, phonological and grammatical parallelism, and prosodic patterning of pause and intonation. Such devices likewise serve as means for further expansion beyond the minimal forms, making for more complex poetic patterning, though still featuring a single factor, as in example 7.

(7)   A ciento cincuenta, a ciento cincuenta,
        a ciento cincuenta y a ciento cincuenta le valen 'ora.
        A ciento cincuenta, a ciento cincuenta, a ciento cincuenta,
        a ciento cincuenta, a ciento cincuenta.

        At one hundred fifty, at one hundred fifty,
        at one hundred fifty and at one hundred fifty they cost now.
        At one hundred fifty, at one hundred fifty, at one hundred fifty,
        at one hundred fifty, at one hundred fifty.

Here we have a parallelistic structure of

    aa
    a+ab
    aaa
    aa

The highly condensed formulaic language and poetic structuring that characterize even the simplest calls has at least three functional effects. For one thing, it enhances fluency, allowing for the rapid production and extension of calls. As the preceding example shows, it is a simple matter to extend a call building on a preposition plus a quantifier into a more extended, multiline compound by the use of relatively elementary parallel structures. Second, it endows the calls with a high degree of cohesion, an insistent tightness of textual organization. The lines are tied closely to each other in a textural web of formal and semantic inter-dependencies. In addition, as with the exploitation of the poetic function generally, its mobilization here sets up patterns of formal anticipation and fulfillment that elicit the participatory involvement of the passers-by, catching them up in the formal regimentation of the call (Burke 1968 [1931]:124).

Beyond the elementary forms, a range of other extensions is possible. For example, the two basic constituents, commodity and price, may be combined, as in example 8.

(8)   A cien la canela,   Cinnamon at one hundred,
        a cien.   at one hundred.

Now, in addition to the two free constituents of commodity and price, there are a number of "bound" ones that figure as part of the basic discursive and functional vocabulary of the calls. The inventory of bound elements includes: quality of the commodity, unit quantity in relation to price, directives, declaratives (introduced already in examples 5 and 6), questions, and terms of address. By "bound," I mean to indicate that they are not used by themselves to constitute fully free-standing calls, but occur only in combination with other constituents.

There are two ways that these constituents may be bound to others. Some can appear as complete turns in situations where more than one person is calling the same goods, but are always accompanied by other call-turns to which they are tied in these collaborations. Others lack even this degree of semi-independence, appearing only in combination with other constituents within free-standing calls or calls that constitute turns. The following examples, 9–12, illustrate combinatory possibilities in free-standing calls.

(9)   A trescientos, doscientos, y cien, mire.
       A trescientos, doscientos, y cien los globos, mire.
       A trescientos, doscientos, y cien los globos, mire.

       At three hundred, two hundred, and one hundred, look.
       At three hundred, two hundred, and one hundred the balloons, look.
       At three hundred, two hundred, and one hundred the balloons, look.

(10)   Piña fresca,   Fresh pineapple,
       piña fresca,   fresh pineapple,
       plátano maduro.   ripe banana.

(11)   Hay limas,   There are limes,
       lleve limas.   carry away limes.

(12)   A cien las bolsas,   At one hundred the bags,
       de a cien,   at one hundred,
       ciento cincuenta, señó,   one hundred fifty, Mr./Mrs./Miss,
       ciento cincuenta.   one hundred fifty.

Example 9 introduces one of the most common directives, *mire*; I will have more to say on this in a moment. Example 10 introduces qualities of the commodities, the adjectives *fresca* and *maduro*. And example 11 features the declarative *Hay limas* "There are limes" in combination with the directive *Lleve limas*. Finally, example 12 includes a term of address, *señó*, to a potential customer and a statement of unit quantity, *la bolsa* "the bag" or "per bag" (two sizes of bag are offered). Note the use of the omnibus term *señó* here and of *bara* for *barato* in the example 14 (lines 2 and 12), which condense the language of the calls still further. The vocative form *señó* is especially useful in neutralizing the gender and marital status of *señor*, *señora*, and *señorita*, thus targeting simultaneously customers of either gender, married or unmarried. This is address to everyone and to no one in particular. It could be addressed to you.

The next example, 13, is a collaborative co-performance between two men selling sewing materials.

(13) *Vendor 1*:

Hilos, agujas, cierres.	Threads, needles, snaps.

Vendor 2:

Escójale, oiga.	Choose, hear.
Hilos, aceite para máquina,	Threads, sewing machine oil,
cintas métricas.	metric measuring tape.
Escójale, oiga.	Choose, hear.

Vendor 1:

Acérquese, conózcalo, mire.	Come close, check it out, look.

Here, the first vendor cries out some of the principal commodities for sale: thread, needles, snaps. His partner continues the catalogue, tying his call to his partner's in terms of the first commodity, thread, but extending it to sewing machine oil and metric measuring tape and framing the catalogue with one-word directives. One type of directive, here represented by *oiga*, works to engage the sensory involvement of potential customers. The other directive in turn 2, *escójale*, elicits the participatory engagement of customers by inviting them to make a selection of the products in a way that suggests that the goods may become theirs. Then the first vendor comes back in the following turn with a set of additional one-word directives, *Acérquese, conózcalo, mire*, that extend the compulsive force of the calls. *Mire* is a companion directive to *oiga*, adding another dimension of sensory engagement. While *oiga* demands auditory engagement with the vendor's call, *mire* elicits visual engagement with the goods. *Mire* makes explicit what the ostensive display of commodities, mentioned earlier, leaves implicit: a demand for the gaze of the potential customer. To look ahead for a moment, *agárrele* in lines 1, 13, and 18 of the example 14 adds tactile engagement to the range of sensory modalities activated by the vendor. Finally, returning to the last turn of the current example, *acérquese* and *conózcalo* amplify *escójale* in drawing potential buyers into engaging with the commodities for sale, spatially and cognitively. Turns such as this last one, consisting only of directives, occur only in conjunction with other turns.

The following example, 14, is a stretch of call-collaboration among three vendors selling used clothing, to illustrate further how constituents may be bound up into turns that are tied to other turns.

(14) *Vendor 1*:

1 Agárrele, agárrele,	Take hold, take hold,
2 bara, bara, mire.	cheap, cheap, look.
3 Le doy barato, escójale,	I give it to you cheap, choose,
4 escójale si hay.	choose if it's here.

5 Sueter barato,	Cheap sweater,
6 pantalón barato,	cheap pants,
7 escójale.	choose.

Vendor 2:

8 Escójale, escójale,	Choose, choose,
9 todo barato, mire.	everything cheap, look.
10 De regalo y de remate,	Giving it away and finishing it up,
escójale.	choose.
11 Andele, escójale,	Go on, choose,
12 todo es bara, bara, mire.	everything is cheap, cheap, look.

Vendor 3:

13 Agárrele, agárrele,	Take hold, take hold,
14 baratos, ándele.	cheap, go on.
15 Que le damos?	What shall we give you?
16 Que le damos, oiga?	What shall we give you, hear?
17 (wd.?) por estos	(?) for these
pantalones.	pants.
18 Andele, agárrele, barato.	Go on, take hold, cheap.
19 Barato, ándele.	Cheap, go on.

Here, I want to call attention especially to lines 3, 15, and 16, which add the dimension of explicit social engagement with the vendors to the directives like *escójale, agárrele, conózcalo* that elicit engagement with the commodities being offered or the insistent *ándele* in lines 11, 14, and 19 that urge the customer to action. *Le doy barato* in line 3 sets up a relationship of giving and getting, of exchange, that is at the heart of the commercial transaction. *Que le damos?* in lines 15 and 16 builds upon the same dynamic of exchange, adding the compulsive power of the question, which has the pragmatic conversational force of demanding – if only tacitly – an answer. Terms of address, for their part, are phatic gestures toward potential customers, also drawing them into interaction.

Thus, we find built into these very highly condensed, stereotyped, and formulaic utterances an impressive range of functional capacities. The constituents or building blocks allow for the economical identification of the commodities, specification of their salient qualities and unit price, and elicitation of the participatory involvement of potential customers in terms of visual, auditory, tactile, spatial, cognitive, and behavioral engagement with goods and social engagement with the vendors in a relationship of exchange. The latter devices – directives and declaratives or questions concerning exchange – have a special rhetorical power in establishing in the potential customer's mind a virtual identification with the commodities and vendors that is a crucial prerequisite for accomplishing the sale that will make the virtual identification an actual one: "They are yours, if not yet yours." "You are in an exchange relationship with me, if not yet in an exchange relationship with me." And the poetic structuring of the calls enhances this rhetorical efficacy by building up patterns of formal expectation that again elicit the participatory energies of the customers. Note in the preceding example, for instance, the heavy use of lexical repetition, phonological parallelism (e.g., the saturation of the cries with /a/ in *agárrele, bara, barato, escójale, pantalón, regalo, remate, ándale, damos*), and syntactic parallelism. Yet all this functional business is accomplished in a highly economical way that allows for great fluency and cohesion that lends itself to smooth collaboration in the joint production of extended calls.

In fact, the production of these calls is so simple that even a child can do it. The team that produced the foregoing example, 14, was occasionally joined by a young boy of about ten who contributed calls like the one given in example 15.

(15)   Escójale doscientos lo que guste.   Choose two hundred what you like.
         Aquí está la barata, doscientos.   Here is the bargain, two hundred.

And just to take one other example, an even younger boy of about eight produced the call given as example 16:

(16)   Cincuenta el montón de brocoli,   Fifty the pile of broccoli,
            cincuenta.   fifty.
         Cincuenta el montón de brocoli,   Fifty the pile of broccoli,
            cincuenta.   fifty.

Acquisition of competence in the production of such calls does not require overt instruction. Children are exposed to the calls from babyhood, as they are carried through the market by parents or siblings or accompany parents who are vendors, and they pick up the formal patterns by observation and imitation.

Now, while my discussion thus far has emphasized the basic constituents, relatively elementary forms, and ease, simplicity, and fluency of production that characterizes the majority of calls in the San Miguel Tuesday market, as I suggested earlier there is a type of market cry, the spiel, that contrasts with these in interesting ways. Spiels are produced by selling specialists called *merolicos* in some areas, who, consistent with Santamaría's (1983:717–18) definition, tend to sell "artifacts of rare and marvellous properties, in loud voices and verbose language in order to call the attention of the passers-by." Unlike the general run of market vendors, who tend to stick to selling the same commodities, these *merolicos* purvey a variety of goods, principally medicine (such as *grasa de la iguana, sebo del coyote,* and *aceite de la víbora de cascabel* "iguana grease, coyote fat, and rattlesnake oil"), specialty items like jewelry, small appliances, or other items that require more considered purchasing decisions. They don't have to rely on the kind of aids to fluency or persuasiveness that characterize the economical calls I have described earlier, because they are practiced verbal virtuosi, true men of words. They also often put on a bit of a show to accompany the pitch: the snake oil man has a live rattlesnake in a wire cage with a live iguana tethered to the outside, an array of pickled parasites and vermin in bottles, and a set of biological charts to which he points to illustrate the afflictions cured by his products. The following example, 17, is a stretch of a spiel by a man selling a batch of Cannon Mills panty hose, certainly a specialty, luxury item in a market that caters principally to *campesinos* and laborers. His little performance involves running a hair-rake across the stockings stretched out between him and a young boy acting as his assistant; that is what is going on in lines 31–5.

(17)

1	Vale la pena.	It's worth it.
2	Vea usted las medias de categoría.	Examine the classy stockings.
3	Cannon Mills,	Cannon Mills,
4	Cannon Mills.	Cannon Mills.
5	How many? I got it.	[How many? I got it.
6	Too muche, too muche.	Too much, too much.
7	Panty hose.	Panty hose,]
8	la Cannon Mills,	the Cannon Mills,
9	Cannon Mills,	Cannon Mills,
10	para la (?) Cannon,	for the (?) Cannon,
11	calidad Cannon Mills.	Cannon Mills quality.
12	Sabemos de antemano	We know to begin with
13	que una mujer sin medias	that a woman without stockings
14	es como un hombre sin calzones.	is like a man without underpants.
15	Vea usted las medias de Cannon.	Examine the Cannon stockings.
16	[Customer]: Y esto?	And this?
17	Mil pesos, nada más, señora.	A thousand pesos, no more, ma'am.
18	Cannon Mills,	Cannon Mills,
19	la Cannon Mills.	the Cannon Mills.
20	Señora, vea usted,	Ma'am, examine,
21	que se atoró con la canasta,	whether it got snagged by the basket,
22	con la bolsa, no importa.	by the bag, it doesn't matter.
23	Fibra de vidrio Galilei,	Galileo fiberglass,
24	la versátil magia de la nueva ola,	the versatile magic of the new wave,
25	vea usted.	examine.
26	Más elástica y más resistente que cualquier media.	More elastic and more resistant than any stocking.
27	Vale la pena.	It's worth it.
28	Vea usted las medias de categoría.	Examine the classy stockings.
29	Vale la pena,	It's worth it,
30	vea usted.	examine.

31 Jálale ahí, niño.	Pull it there, son.
32 Jala más para allá,	Pull more over there,
33 eso ahí así.	right there.
36 Cannon Mills.	Cannon Mills.
37 Señora, vea usted.	Ma'am, examine.
38 Vale la pena.	It's worth it.
39 Vea usted las medias de categoría,	Examine the classy stockings,
40 unas medias mucho muy diferentes a todas las medias.	some stockings very much different from all the stockings.
. . .	. . .
41 . . . arboles,	. . .trees,
42 (?) unas tunas,	(?) some prickly pears,
43 y se atoraron allí con nopales,	and they got snagged there by nopales,
44 y a la media no le pasa nada.	and nothing happens to the stocking.
45 Ayer una mujer me dijo, me dice,	Yesterday a woman said to me, she says to me,
46 "Ay mire nomás que hoyote me hice ayer,	"Ay, only look at what a big puncture wound I got myself yesterday,
47 por ir al cerro,	going along the hill,
48 y me hice una llagota,	and I got a wound,
49 y a la media me quedó enterita.	and the stocking remained whole."
50 [Customer]: Sí.	Yes.
51 Nomás (?),	Only (?),
52 a ella le pasó,	it happened to her,
53 y a la media no le pasó nada.	and nothing happened to the stocking.
54 Calidad Cannon Mills.	Cannon Mills quality.
55 Señora, vea usted las medias.	Ma'am, examine the stockings.
56 Quiere clarita o quiere oscurita,	You want light or you want dark,
57 tengo cuatrocientos cincuenta mill colores.	have four hundred fifty thousand colors.
58 Calidad Cannon Mills.	Cannon Mills quality.
59 Que se atoró con la canasta,	Whether it got snagged by the basket,
60 con la bolsa, vea usted,	by the bag, you see,
61 a la media no la pasa nada,	nothing happens to the stocking,
62 porque está elaborada a base de acetato, rayón y nylon	because it is manufactured on a base of acetate, rayon and nylon
63 como las llantas Goodrich, Euzkadi.	like the Goodrich or Euzkadi tires.
64 Más elastica, más resistente	More elastic, more resistant
65 que cualquier media.	than any stocking.
66 Medias hay muchas,	There are many stockings,
67 cómprelas adonde usted quiera,	buy them where you like,

68 pero medias de estas	but these stockings
69 Nomás conmigo.	Only from me.

What I want to emphasize in the spiel of this vendor is that his pitch is in significant ways more elaborated than the calls we have examined in terms of syntactic structures, rhetorical constituents and structures, and formal devices. Certainly, we can identify in his spiel some of the elements now familiar to us from the cries of the vendors we have already analyzed, such as terms of address to potential customers (lines 17, 20, 37, 55), descriptions of the salient qualities of his merchandise (e.g., line 26: *mas elástica y más resistente que cualquier media*), or appeals to the senses (lines 2, 15, 20, 25, 28, 30, 37, 39, 55, 60: *vea usted*). Condensed and formulaically repetitious elements are prominent in his spiel, as witness his insistent repetition of *Cannon Mills, calidad Cannon Mills, vale la pena*, and *vea usted*. Lines 25–30 are especially dense in this regard, and by themselves might approximate closely to a call of the kind we examined earlier:

vea usted.	examine.
Más elástica y más resistente que cualquier media.	More elastic and more resistant than any stocking.
Vale la pena.	It's worth it.
Vea usted las medias de categoría.	Examine the classy stockings.
Vale la pena,	It's worth it,
vea usted.	examine.

Note, however, that the repeated elements in the spiel grow longer than those of the more condensed cries, which are notably lean. Take lines 21–2 and 59–60, for example: *que se atoró con la canasta, con la bolsa, no importa* and *Que se atoró con la canasta, con la bolsa, vea usted.* But look also at the closing lines of this extract (lines 66–9):

Medias hay muchas,	There are many stockings,
cómprelas adonde usted quiera,	buy them where you like,
pero medias de estas	but these stockings
nomás conmigo.	only from me.

This is a complex sentence, with multiple clauses, spanning four lines of the spiel, in marked contrast with the two- and three-word sentences of the calls.

With regard to the rhetoric of the spiel, recall that the rhetorical efficacy of the briefer calls resides especially strongly in a combination of directives eliciting sensory and cognitive engagement with the goods (e.g., *escójale, agárrele, mire, oiga, lleve limas*) and the evocation of a social relationship, especially a relationship of exchange, between vendor and customer (*que le damos? le doy barato*), as well as in the formal appeal of the utterance residing in its poetic form (e.g., repetition, parallelism). The spiel, as we have established, certainly depends upon a similar formal appeal, but we can see new and more complex rhetorical mechanisms at play as well. Among the rhetorical devices employed by the pantyhose pitchman is an epigrammatic statement, a *dicho*, syntactically complex and slightly risqué:

Sabemos de antemano	We know to begin with
que una mujer sin medias	that a woman without stockings
es como un hombre sin calzones.	is like a man without underpants.

This statement is framed as conventional, axiomatic knowledge, socially given, and takes the form of a parallel construction. Here, the central appeal is to identifications of class and respectability: the image of a man without underpants evokes associations of poverty, low-class status, unhygienic disrespectability. A respectable woman would want to avoid having such associations attached to her, and buying brand-name "classy" pantyhose, indices of modern bourgeois consumerism, offers the means to do so. But the *dicho* gains further efficacy from its risqué tone – pantyhose and underpants are intimate matters, all the more so by the rather prudish moral standards of the market's general clientele. This risqué tone carries through to the double entendre of the pitchman's admonition to the young boy assisting him in the demonstration of the stockings' durability by stretching them out while the vendor draws a sharp hair-rake across them (lines 31–5). Warning the boy to avoid tripping over a depression in the ground, he says,

Y mucho cuidado con caerse	And be very careful about falling in
al hoyo, porque ya saben que	the hole, because we already know
caerse al hoyo es muy	that to fall into a hole is very
delicado.	delicate.

The boy's footing takes on the overtone of sexual intercourse. Ultimately, to speak thus of intimate sexual matters is to evoke a relationship of seductive intimacy which can be consummated by making a purchase – buy my pantyhose. And, of course, the epigram derives still further weight from its purported axiomatic status and from the formal appeal of its parallel construction.

In addition to the *dicho*, the vendor also builds into his sales strategy a reported testimonial narrative, a *caso*,[4] in lines 45–9:

Ayer una mujer me dijo,	Yesterday a woman said to me, she
me dice,	says to me,

---

[4] Graham (1981:17) defines the *caso* as "a relatively brief prose narrative, focusing upon a single event, supernatural or natural, in which the protagonist or observer is the narrator or someone the narrator knows and vouches for, and which is normally used as evidence or as an example to illustrate that 'this kind of thing happens.'"

"Ay mire nomás que | "Ay, only look at what a big
  hoyote me | puncture wound
hice ayer, | I got myself yesterday,
por ir al cerro, | going along the hill,
y me hice una llagota, | and I got a wound,
y a la media me quedó enterita." | and the stocking remained whole."

The narrative is rendered in a different stylistic mode than the other portions of the vendor's spiel. Where the majority of the spiel is characterized by a declamatory mode of delivery that is louder and more rhythmic, with marked intonation contours and stress patterns and nasalized, lengthened vowels, the narrative is delivered in a more conversational, less measured style. It is directed not to the crowd at large, but to a specific individual, though intended to be overheard by the others in attendance. Notwithstanding the difference in delivery, which makes it more accessible to verbal response on the part of a customer than the relatively less permeable declamatory sections of the spiel, its rhetorical purpose is similar to that of the epigram, that is, it is intended to elicit identification. This time, however, what is elicited is not status identification, but experiential identification, a mapping of the experience of the woman whose narrative is reported onto those of the women in the market. Note how the narrative elicits an affirmative response from a woman in the crowd. Both dimensions of identification are virtual; they call upon the women to consider that a particular status or experience might be theirs if they wear Cannon Mills stockings.

In addition to the *dicho* and the *caso*, the pitchman indexes a third genre, the radio and television commercial, first in lines 23–4 and again in lines 62–5:

Fibra de vidrio Galilei, | Galileo fiberglass
la versátil magia de la nueva ola | the versatile magic of the new wave

and

porque está elaborada a base | because it is manufactured on a base
  de acetato, rayón y nylon | of acetate, rayon and nylon
como las llantas Goodrich, | like the Goodrich or Euzkadi
  Euzkadi. | tires.
Más elastica, más resistente | More elastic, more resistant
que cualquier media. | than any stocking.

These elements are significant in their invocation of brand-name products – Galileo fiberglass and Goodrich and Euzkadi tires – which complement the brand-name identification of Cannon Mills pantyhose. Note also that all of these products offer the wonders of modern technology – "the versatile magic of the new wave" – to the public: fiberglass, acetate, rayon, nylon.

These materials render the pantyhose more elastic and more resistant than any other, introducing the trope of "new and improved" that is so characteristic of contemporary marketing. The cumulative effect of these metonyms of media commercials is to convey elements of the modern economy of bourgeois consumerism into the traditional marketplace and thus within reach of its clientele, primarily laborers and peasants.

We may observe, then, that one of the distinctive features of the spiel, by contrast with the briefer calls, is generic incorporativeness: the spiel is a secondary genre that incorporates other primary genres and styles within it, exploiting their particular rhetorical capacities. And the spiel is stylistically heterogeneous in other respects as well. Beyond the incorporation of the *dicho*, the *caso*, and the commercial, the spiel is marked by switches in key (Goffman 1974) and even code. The vendor engages in speech play of various kinds, for example in his hyperbolic statement that whether you want light or dark he has four hundred fifty thousand colors (lines 56–7), and in his playful bit of code-switching into English (lines 5–7), directed at me:

> How many? I got it.
> Too muche, too muche.
> Panty hose.

I could go into still further detail about what this vendor is doing in this spiel, but this will have to suffice to establish the far greater formal and rhetorical complexity of his pitch as against the calls we have considered earlier in terms of constituent elements, formal structures, and rhetorical devices and strategies than those of the other vendors.

Now, to a significant degree, the contrast between calls and spiels is correlated with the kinds of commodities that are offered for sale and their cost. Calls are employed in the selling of basic necessities like food and ordinary clothing, the kinds of things for which people regularly come to the market. The customers for these commodities come with a predisposition to buy and there is little need to elaborate in the crying of these goods, as people are primarily concerned with locating the specific foodstuffs or clothing they need in a market whose spatial arrangements shift somewhat every week and with determining how much they cost in a market affected by the rapid inflation of the Mexican economy. These elements may be bolstered by a bit of poetically enhanced rhetoric to help impel people toward a purchase, but more would be unnecessary and even counterproductive. Likewise for small and inexpensive optional items like ices, a little treat to enhance the experience or to keep the kids quiet. But luxury and specialty items, like pantyhose or fitted sheets, require more persuasion. And while people are making up their minds on whether or not to splurge, it helps to keep them around with a good show. Accordingly, spiels are more adaptive in the vending of such special and more expensive goods.

3   Bridging the generic gap

Our considerations thus far have been devoted to establishing in terms of form–function inter-relationships the conventional organization of the two standard genres of market language, calls and spiels. Though only one of the two, the call, has a commonly used label, *grito*, the contrasts between them are recognized and oriented to by vendors and customers alike. Each is regimented toward the accomplishment of a routine marketplace task, calls toward the selling of nominally priced everyday goods and other small commodities for which consumers regularly come to the Tuesday market, and spiels toward the vending of more expensive commodities, luxury goods, and other items that require more considered consumer decisions. The conventional forms we have considered up to this point are generically transparent, closely related in inter-textual terms within each generic type.

Having established the generic configuration of the routinized genres, let us turn to the consideration of a further example that cannot be fully assimilated to either type. This is an extract from a longer stretch of sales-talk produced by a vendor of kitchenware: dishes, utensils, pots and pans, and the like. Here, he is hawking dishes, by means of a pitch in which he adds plates, one after another, to the stack to emphasize just how much the buyer will get for a thousand pesos:

(18) 1 Se lleva otro,   Take another,
      2 por mil.   for a thousand.
      3 Tenga otro,   Have another,
      4 por mil.   for a thousand.
      5 Otro,   Another,
      6 y otro por mil pesos.   and another for a thousand pesos.
      7 Deme mil,   Give me a thousand,
      8 y échales otro,   and choose another,
      9 y así todo el bonche por   and thus the whole bunch for a
        mil.   thousand.
     10 Aquí está el otro como regalo   Here is another as a New Year's
        de año nuevo.   present.
     11 Así todo el paquete,   Thus the whole package,
     12 mil pesos.   a thousand pesos.
     13 A ver, a ver, a ver   Let's see, let's see, let's see
        quién se los lleva,   who takes them away,
     14 quién se los gana.   who gains them.
     15 Nadie a la una,   No one at one,
     16 nadie a las dos,   no one at two,
     17 porque esto se lo está   because you are

	perdiendo este paquete	missing this package
	de platos.	of plates.
18	Así todo por mil.	Thus all for a thousand.
19	Son diez platos, mujeres,	They are ten plates, ladies,
	por mil pesos.	for a thousand pesos.
20	En la feria de allá de Celaya	At the fair over in Celaya,
21	se está cotizando a nada	it is priced at no
	menos,	less
22	que a mil quinientos.	than one thousand five hundred.
23	Y allá hasta las mujeres	And there the women almost tear
	se agarran del chongo	their hair out
24	para pagar los mil quinientos.	to pay one thousand five hundred.
25	Son mil quinientos,	They are one thousand five hundred
26	mil quinientos tienen	one thousand five hundred they
	que vender así.	have to sell them for thus.
27	Por todo el paquete de platos,	For the whole package of plates,
28	por diez platos,	for ten plates,
29	diez platos de lujo,	ten deluxe plates,
30	diez platos decorados,	ten decorated plates,
31	por solamente mil pesos.	for only a thousand pesos.
32	Nadie a la una, nadie a las dos,	No one at one, no one at two,
33	entonces la oferta va para	then the offer is going
	abajo.	down.
34	Todo por mil.	All for a thousand.
35	Nadie mil, nadie?	No one a thousand, no one?
36	Bueno, no ruegues,	OK, don't beg,
37	échalo para abajo este paquete	put down this package
	de platos.	of plates.
38	Vamos a vender las cubetas.	Let's sell the buckets.

At first glance, lines 1–19 might appear in formal terms to consist of a series of cries: condensed, formulaic, stereotyped, full of repetition and parallelism, with constituent elements that identify commodity and unit price and elicit the engagement of potential customers with directives and identificational elements such as *a ver quién se los lleva*. But note that lines 1–12 do not consist solely of a series of smaller cry units, but are in fact tied together sequentially by the cumulative device of including additional plates in the package, making for an overarching cohesive structure. Then, in lines 20–8, there is a stretch of syntactically more complex comparison pricing, reporting humorously how the women at the Celaya market would tear their hair out to buy an equivalent set of dishes for 1,500 pesos, followed by a return, in lines 29–34, to his own lower price in the manner of the earlier section. Finally, in lines 36–8, the vendor offers a nicely self-reflexive transition from pushing the dishes, for which he has attracted no immediate buyers, to hawking plastic buckets. These are all features that are more characteristic of spiels than calls: longer, more extended structures of cohesion, syntactic complexity, comparative references to other markets, reflexivity. Thus, in formal terms, this pitch emerges as a stylistic hybrid, blending features of call and spiel.

This stylistic calibration makes sense in functional terms as well. The dishes and other kitchen goods that make up this vendor's wares are not foodstuffs for daily consumption or nominally priced items like needles and snaps; nor are they specialty items of a bourgeois cast, like brand-name pantyhose. Rather, they are relatively durable household items of a kind that are purchased only occasionally. Every household needs these things, but purchases involve considered decisions, balancing utility against relative quality and cost. I am suggesting, then, that as consumer goods, these wares fall between the low-end necessities and high-end specialty items. A simple, terse call will not suffice to capture and hold the attention of potential buyers, but a more elaborately performed spiel is not necessary either. Hence a sales pitch that falls somewhere in between. Thus, this vendor, faced with the task of selling goods that differ in nature and cost from those for which standard calls and spiels are designed, draws upon the orienting frameworks of both routine genres to bridge the gap, producing an emergent hybrid adapted to his particular task. Though he was not immediately successful in this particular instance, which occurred late in the afternoon when only a few customers were left, he did manage to sell a fair number of dishes with a similar pitch earlier in the day.

4   Conclusion: speech styles in communicative practice

For the purposes of this paper, I have approached the sales pitches of market vendors as genres, orienting frameworks for the production and reception of texts, foregrounding modes of entextualization and inter-textual relationships. In practice-centered terms, to speak of inter-textuality is to focus on the ways in which the vendors fashion their sales pitches, as texts, by reference to other texts. Note, however, that by identifying the calls and spiels as the discourse of market vendors, I have also invoked their ties to a recurrent situational context, namely, the market, and to a social category of speakers, namely, vendors. That is to say that the texts I have examined, in addition to indexing other texts, also index contexts of use and categories of users.

Nor is this simply a matter of orienting the emergent production of calls and spiels to prior calls and spiels as overall generic frameworks. Recall, for example, the point at which the pantyhose vendor switches into English (lines 5–6 of the transcript):

> How many? I got it.
> Too muche, too muche.

This bit of speech play invokes and makes fun of the style of American tourists who frequent the market and whose attempts at the bargaining that they seem to feel obliged to do in Mexican markets often includes the protest, "Too much," when a price is quoted to them. Or consider *la versátil magia de la nueva ola*, which indexes the language and form of radio and television commercials. These are smaller indexical touches, brief metonyms of more complex speech styles – keyed to texts, situations, speakers – that add a bit of coloration to the spiel, whose incorporative capacities we have already observed, and contribute to the calibration of its social meaning.

But a speech style associated with recurrent situational contexts is what we usually identify as a register (Ferguson 1994:20); by the same token, a speech style associated with a social category of speakers is what we commonly designate a dialect (Ferguson 1994:18–19). Lest it appear that I am attempting to nullify the bases on which discriminations among orders of speech style are based, let me make clear that in pointing out that the sales pitches of market vendors appear to be simultaneously genre, register, and dialect in their overall configurations, and that spiels may also incorporate touches of other genres, registers, dialects, I do not mean to suggest that the distinctions we usually draw among these orders of speech style must inevitably dissolve into a single stylistic mass. Indeed, the examples I have considered make clear the operative salience of associational links between speech styles and texts, situational contexts, and social categories. What I do argue, rather, is that to isolate a single dimension of indexicality as *the* sole criterion for designating a speech style and to reify the resultant style in the process obscures the multiple indexical resonances that accrue to ways of speaking in social life. What is important from the vantage point of communicative practice is how the indexical ties of discourse to other texts, situations, or kinds of speakers serve as resources for the production and interpretation of social meaning. In the conduct of social life, there are no texts independent of contexts or speakers. Though one or another of these constituents of discursive practice may be metapragmatically foregrounded by practitioners or analysts as a means of invoking specific, conventional associational linkages – between style and text, style and situation, style and user – they are inevitably mutually implicated in actual practice. Moreover, the assimilation of an utterance to stylistic orienting frameworks, whatever their basis, is always a matter of inter-discursive calibration, negotiating the gap between the conventional and the emergent in communicative interaction. The dynamics of this negotiation can only be discovered through ethnographic investigation of form–function inter-relationships.

4   The question of genre

Ronald Macaulay

If you consult the *Oxford English Dictionary*, you will find that there are twenty-seven different headings for the word *style*, none of which corresponds to the way it has been used in recent sociolinguistic investigation. Accordingly, I looked elsewhere and I found two statements that seemed to me to provide a possibly fruitful starting-place for our discussion. The first is from notes of something Greg Guy said at an NWAVE meeting. This may not be what Greg said, but it is what I have written down:

> Style is a post-lexical effect of the output frequency of variable rules.

The second comes from Greg Urban's book *A Discourse-centered Approach to Culture*:

> As employed here, style means a form of language use characterizable independently of the content or semantic meaning that is communicated, which constitutes a sign vehicle that contrasts with others within a culture. (Urban 1991:106)

I interpret these statements to be near the extremes of what I will refer to as "The Greg Scale," with Guy at one end and Urban at the other. Another way of putting it, which may be a distortion of either Greg's position, is that the scale ranges from dealing with those variables that are relatively easy to identify, measure, and quantify to variables that it may be very hard to define operationally and quantify, but which may turn out to be more interesting, if we can find a way to deal with them. I believe that the papers for this conference can be ranged in order along the Greg Scale and while we may argue about some of the others, I am reasonably confident that we'll agree that Bauman's paper comes nearer the Urban end of the Greg Scale.

Urban claims that style shades into "register" which in turn shades into "genre." Bauman's chapter (3) deals with the shady side of style that is genre. There are probably just as many definitions of *genre* as there are of *style*, though the *OED* will not have recorded them all yet. What we understand by this term will come up again when we discuss Labov's chapter and the one by Finegan and Biber. One key issue here will be whether genres are named or lexicalized and, in Bauman's words, "represent locally salient elements in the speech economy" or whether they are categories of language use identified analytically by the researcher. This is important since, if all language use is to be identified as being assigned to one genre or another, it would be helpful to have agreement on the criteria for the assignment of a sample of language to a specific genre and also on the range of legitimate flexibility of the boundaries between genres. Another critical question is the extent to which, in Bauman's words, "genres represent conventional, recurrent frameworks for the organization of discourse and the production of textuality, with routinized structures that allow for comparability across contexts." There are two issues here. One is the degree to which all genres will display "routinized structures." The other is whether all routinized structures exemplify a genre. For example, do such varied speech events as greetings, insults, and compliments each constitute a genre? Bakhtin (1986) says so, but Bakhtin does not give us much help in operationalizing ways of identifying genres.

Bauman's chapter provides plenty of material for a discussion of these notions. It is clear that the "calls" are named as either *grito* or *pregon* and therefore can be considered "locally salient elements." It is also clear that the "spiels" are not as "locally salient" (by the criterion of naming) since "there does not seem to be a commonly preferred form for this genre," although when pushed, local people will suggest possible descriptive labels. Then there is the case of what Bauman calls *sales-talk*, which he claims is "a stylistic hybrid, blending features of call and spiel," but he doesn't say whether he asked local people for a name for this category. I presume he did not and that if he had, he might have had difficulty in explaining what he was asking about. These three examples seem to me to illustrate the problems with dealing with genre as an analytical category. The calls are a fairly clear example. Presumably, one could have a fairly coherent discussion with local people about differences in calls and why they take the form that they do. One would expect them to find the topic reasonable and not particularly odd, and they would presumably have their metalinguistic way of talking about calls, though they would be unlikely to discuss them in the terms and features that Bauman does. In dealing with the spiels there is a greater possibility of confusion. I imagine the local inhabitants would have greater difficulty focusing on the form and be more likely to stray off into comments about the character and motivation of the sellers. More importantly, would local people reject Bauman's example 18 as not a typical example of a spiel, or would they put it in the same category as example 17? Do the local people have a scale of "sales-talk" with snake oil salesmen at one end and vendors of kitchenware at the other? The local people will have some notion of how salespeople talk but is this enough to constitute a genre in the absence of a generally accepted name? This question will no doubt come up again later, for example, in the discussion of categories such as Labov's *soapbox*.

The second notion that I wish to discuss is the claim that "genres represent conventional, recurrent frameworks for the organization of discourse and the production of textuality, with routinized structures that allow for comparability across contexts." Here Bauman gives what seems to me an admirable analysis of the calls, showing their basic structure and possibilities of elaboration. This is an excellent illustration of finding the poetic in everyday discourse. We are also given sixteen examples to compare so that, with Bauman's help, we can see the pattern. In the case of spiels, however, we are given only one example. Again, I find the analysis of this example very impressive but I wonder how much of it represents "routinized structures" and I wonder how similar or different other examples would be. How common is it for spiels to contain a *dicho* or a *caso*? Is humor characteristic of spiels? Obviously, in a short chapter, there is not time to analyze several examples but I wish Bauman had mentioned how many spiels he had recorded and to what degree they show the same kind of structure. The same comment applies to the stylistic hybrid example 18. My suspicion is that there may be a relationship between the ability of local people to name a genre and the possibility of identifying "routinized structures that allow for comparability." Does this suggest that it is unprofitable to study "unnamed" genres (by "unnamed" I mean those genres for which there is no lay term that ordinary people would employ consistently with reference to the use of language)? I don't think so and I think Bauman's accounts of examples 17 and 18 show how profitably stylistic analysis can be done from a generic (if that is the correct adjective) perspective. I believe that the kind of analysis Bauman has presented here is very appropriate for a conference of this kind and that it is relevant to sociolinguistic investigation, broadly defined. I suspect, however, that those who wish to work closer to the Guy end of the Greg Scale will feel more comfortable dealing with genres that are clearly identifiable and have generally accepted names.

In his conclusion, Bauman deals with "the apparent tension" between "relatively clearcut and conventional types" of genres and "categories that escape into the margins of classificatory ambiguity" by summarizing the position put forward in his article with Charles Briggs (Briggs and Bauman 1992). I have looked at this article and I must confess that despite having taught the Language and Culture course with an anthropologist for many years, this kind of writing is tough-going for someone trained in English literature and linguistics. As I understand it, and I have taken the liberty of trying to translate the notion from their elegant but somewhat impenetrable anthropologese into ordinary English, they are saying that genres are real and help people to create and understand what develops dynamically in linguistic communication. Their position is obviously a lot more subtle than this but I see this as the essential point. I also believe that they are probably right, but my problem lies in trying to decide whether this is a brilliantly insightful observation or simply an elaborate way of stating something that most people have taken for granted. For our present purposes, however, this notion does not help in determining what a genre is. Bauman complicates the question by quoting Biber's reference to subgenres and then going on to talk about macro-genres. At this point, I find myself slipping a bit down the Greg Scale and wondering whether I ought to turn to Greg Guy for help. Anthropologists seem to be very fond of taxonomies but I wonder how easy it would be for the local people of San Miguel de Allende to deal with such notions. It is not clear, either, how much agreement there would be among Anglo-Americans as to which genres are salient in their communities.

However, even naming genres doesn't solve the problem. In his article in Biber and Finegan's book, Ferguson (1994) cites twenty-five examples of genres taken from Brown and Yule's (1983) textbook, ranging from such clearly defined entities as recipes and obituaries to such vaguer notions as interviews and conversation. There seems to me to be a problem in using a term so loosely and this becomes particularly problematic if we want to claim that separate instances of a genre are comparable. There is a test case in the same volume in Rickford and McNair-Knox's chapter. In contrasting Foxy's use of language in interview III and in interview IV, there is the assumption that the two speech events are equivalent. However, (without having heard either of the tapes) I believe that it is arguable that they are two very different kinds of speech events. Having conducted a large number of interviews myself and also listened to a number of oral history interviews, I am all too well aware of what different kinds of interaction they can be. In interview III Foxy participated in a three-way conversation with two people she knew, one of them her own age. In interview IV Foxy participated in a dyadic exchange with a stranger, ten years older and of very different background and education. It is clear from what Rickford and McNair-Knox say that the use of language by all three participants in interview III was very different from that of both in interview IV, and that Foxy was much more at her ease in interview III. To call these equivalent speech events just because they come under the name "interview" seems to me misleading. To say that the only difference between these two speech events lies in the nature of the addressee is to ignore what Hymes (1974a, b), Goffman (1981), Gumperz (1982), Bakhtin (1986), and others have tried to tell us. There is, however, one section of interview IV where Foxy apparently felt more at ease, that is the 12 percent of the transcript devoted to what Rickford and McNair-Knox call the topic "wives, slamming partners," a topic that also takes up 12 percent of interview III. If we treat these two sections as equivalent (instead of treating the interviews as a whole as the basis for comparison), then there is no style-shifting and no addressee effect. Contrary to supporting Bell's (1984) thesis, it is a counterexample. Foxy uses the same kind of language (in terms of the features tabulated by Rickford and McNair-Knox) in speaking to a complete stranger of different race as she does in speaking to Faye and Roberta. While it may be the topic that stimulates this use, it might also be possible to identify the use of language here in generic terms.

Labov's paper illustrates a way of classifying subsections of an interview into categories such as *narrative, soapbox, childhood*, etc., though it is not clear that they are all genres. *Childhood* is a topic and accounts of it may contain various genres; *soapbox* is an analyst's category that seems to be broader than what most people would understand by the expression "getting on his/her soapbox"; *narrative* is clearly a genre and Labov himself has been a pioneer in identifying important characteristics of oral narratives. However, even here there are problems and again there is a test case in Biber and Finegan's book. Ochs's (1993) use of the term "narrative" is very different from Labov's, since she is not concerned with personal accounts of remarkable events delivered essentially as monologues but rather with the co-construction of a "story" in which several participants have important, though unequal, roles. It would probably be misleading to treat Ochs's kind of narratives as the equivalent of Labov's, for comparative purposes. Schiffrin (1994) has an interesting article in which she deals with the notion of "lists." Some of these, e.g., examples 5 and 6 (1994:387), could also be classified as narratives, though different in kind from those analyzed by Labov or Ochs. Schiffrin observes that "it is also important not to dwell on the difference between genres, and their autonomy from one another, at the total expense of their similarities and interdependence" (1994:404). Multiple classification is not necessarily problematic provided the distinctions are clearly established and the extent of overlap recognized. It is all very well for Bakhtin to say that the study of style in language "will be correct and productive only if based on a constant awareness of the generic nature of language styles, and on a preliminary study of the subcategories of speech genres" (1986:64), but he didn't really show us how to go about doing this. Bauman has given us one example of how to do it and for this we are truly grateful.

Part 2

Attention paid to speech

5   The anatomy of style-shifting

William Labov

1   Taxonomies of style and their uses

The development of sociolinguistic methodology has witnessed a continual
tension between two approaches to contextual style: style-shifting as a naturalistic, ethnographic phenomenon, and style-shifting as a controlled
device for measuring the dynamics of sociolinguistic variation.[1] In many
ways, the naturalistic approach is the most immediately appealing and
satisfying. We would like to know as much as possible about the ways that
speakers shift forms and frequencies in the course of every-day life. Style-
shifting seems to be one of the keys to what we now see as the central
problem of the theory of language change: the transmission problem. In
the course of linguistic change, children learn to speak differently from
their parents, and in the same direction that their parents learned to talk
differently from their own parents. To trace this post-vernacular reorganization, we will need to record the dynamic inter-play between speakers and
their styles in the social setttings of most significance to their life chances.
The kinds of data needed are very exacting: high quality recordings with
minimum obtrusiveness of group interactions in which a well-known individual interacts with a variety of interlocutors and social situations (Hindle
1980, Cukor-Avila 1995, Coupland 1980, Bell 1984).

The difficulty of obtaining such data means that we cannot reasonably
expect to obtain a representative sample of style-shifting for an entire community by this means. The most solid and replicable findings of sociolinguistics so far rest on representative studies of communities through
comparable interviews, and in most cases, this involves the close study of
stylistic differences within the interview, that is, intra-speaker variation

[1] Throughout this paper, I have been drawing upon the work and the ideas of many students
in Linguistics 560, The Study of the Speech Community, one of the primary sites of innova-
tions in sociolinguistic methodology over the past few decades. I am equally indebted to my
associates in the Project on Linguistic Change and Variation in Philadelphia, supported by
NSF, and in particular to Anne Bower and Deborah Schiffrin, who did the analysis of the
stable sociolinguistic variables in Philadelphia which provides the primary data of this
study.

where the interlocutors and the social situation are roughly constant. Some community studies have exploited the differences between interviewers (Anshen 1969), and others have obtained a sizeable series of recordings involving group interaction (Gumperz 1964, Labov et al. 1968, Douglas-Cowie 1978, Labov and Harris 1986). But on the whole, the direct study of style-shifting in social groups has been an auxiliary undertaking, designed to throw light on the main findings of the community pattern. These findings in regard to style may be outlined under six headings:

(1) SOCIAL/STYLISTIC SYMMETRY. While previous studies (Kenyon 1948) had argued that cultural levels are distinct from functional varieties, in actual fact communities display both social stratification and stylistic stratification with the same variable. For a stable sociolinguistic variable, regular stratification is found for each contextual style; and conversely, all groups shift along the same stylistic dimension in the same direction with roughly slopes of style-shifting.

(2) BELL'S PRINCIPLE. In general, the range of social stratification is greater than the range of stylistic stratification, so that one may infer that speakers derive their stylistic parameters from observations of social differences in the use of language (Bell 1984; Preston 1989).

(3) THE CROSS-OVER PATTERN. The second highest status group will normally show a greater slope style-shifting than others (Labov 1966b). When change is in progress, this may actually reverse social stratification for the most extreme styles. This consideration applies to both the socio-economic and gender axes of social differentiation.

(4) STYLISTIC REINTERPRETATION. Groups of speakers who are in contact with the community but are still excluded from its main rights and privileges will often participate in the use of linguistic variables with altered stylistic patterns. This applies to minority ethnic groups (Poplack 1978, Labov 1963), children of the mainstream community, and geographic neighbors of smaller size (Modaressi-Tehrani 1978).

(5) STYLISTIC EVOLUTION. Style-shifting is not found in the earliest stages of linguistic change, but becomes stronger as the change matures and is maximized if the feature is assigned prestige or social stigma as the change reaches completion (Labov 1965).

(6) THE SOCIOLINGUISTIC INTERFACE. In general, style-shifting is related to the degrees of social awareness of a linguistic variable by members of the community, which in turn is based on the level of abstractness in the structures involved. Maximal style-shifting is characteristically found in the alternation of allophones and morphological stems. Differences in phonological inventory and abstract syntactic patterns are normally constant across contextual style, but exceptions can be found (Labov 1993).

These findings of the second half of the twentieth century were not predicted by earlier, intuitive writings on the subject of style (Kenyon 1948, Joos 1961). They have received strong support from convergent studies. Yet for each, there are areas of uncertainty and mystery that demand further exploration. For example, Bell's principle can be supported by a great many community studies; but Van den Broek's study of syntactic complexity in Maaseik shows the reverse relationship (1977); it remains to be determined what the limits of this principle are. Though in general, abstract structural patterns are not the topic of social evaluation, negative concord in English is a striking counterexample. How this syntactic variable came to be so highly evaluated is a matter of great interest. It does not seem likely that naturalistic individual studies of style-shifting will contribute to the resolution of these uncertainties, or uncover more large-scale community patterns of this type.

2   What is style after all?

Many discussions of style hope to unify all the phenomena within a single dimension. The organization of contextual styles along the axis of attention paid to speech (Labov 1966a) was not intended as a general description of how style-shifting is produced and organized in every-day speech, but rather as a way of organizing and using the intra-speaker variation that occurs in the interview. Bell's contention that all stylistic variation is a product of audience design can be extended by imaginatively treating intra-speaker variation as a form of metaphor: speakers speaking to the same audience *as if* they were a different audience.[2] However, this argument doesn't apply to the findings of Prince (1987), that stylistic variation in the Yiddish of Sarah Gorby was considerably greater for content words than for function words. Here it would seem clear that it is the difficulty of giving the same degree of attention to function words as to content words that is responsible for the effect.

Given the fact that both adaptation to different audiences and different degrees of audio-monitoring are involved in style-shifting, it becomes a major problem to apportion the variance among these two effects, and to derive the higher level generalization that will predict the result. A wide range of stylistic studies would be needed to explore this matter further; it will be necessary to track and compare both intra-speaker and inter-speaker variation across several different contexts. In any case, the study of intra-speaker variation must be pursued systematically. This report is intended as a contribution to that systematic study.

---

[2] Indeed, Gumperz's original term for inter-speaker variation was *metaphorical shifting*, as opposed to *transactional shifting* (Gumperz 1964).

3   Cues to the identification of style

Any sociolinguistic study that focuses upon linguistic variables should contain a section for formal elicitation and experiments on speech perception. In these areas of controlled speech, it is a simple matter to regulate the amount of attention paid to speech, and there are no real challenges to be met here. The main problem is to distinguish reliably levels of style-shifting in spontaneous speech, where the investigator has no experimental controls and in fact seeks to lower to the minimum the degree of control exercised over the flow of speech (Labov 1984). The major concern originally was to distinguish "Casual" from "Careful" speech. Again, there is no problem in defining Careful speech: it is defined as the main body of conversational exchanges between the interviewer and the subject. Here the social situation is defined as "an interview", a well-defined genre in which the interviewer asks questions and obtains answers from the subject's biography. The primary goal of all sociolinguistic interviewing is to alter this governing situation informally so that it approaches as closely as possible the format of a conversation between people who are well acquainted, if not friends. With varying degrees of success, the interviewer constructs a symmetrical exchange of ideas and reactions, defining himself or herself as the perfect and attentive listener, with no other goals and ambitions but to learn as much as possible from the subject's life experience. While the interviewer leads the conversation towards topics of maximal interest and emotional involvement, he or she is willing at the first opportunity to remit control over the direction of the conversation, and follow the subject's lead. The result of this effort is an hour or more of recorded spontaneous speech; the goal of stylistic analysis is to disengage those sections where the effects of observation and audio-monitoring are most clearly diminished, which come as close as possible to the vernacular speech that is used when the interviewer is absent.

The first approach that I took to this problem was to define five contexts in which the effects of observation were most likely to be diminished: (1) speech outside the interview format, (2) speech with a third person, (3) speech not in response to a question, (4) talk about kids' games, and (5) the danger of death question (Labov 1966a). Two of these contexts involve shifts in audience design, and three involve metaphorical shifts of topic and conversational genre. Shifts in the audience have been a major component of all the sociolinguistic studies in which I have been involved, and sometimes the primary means of controlling style-shifting. However, we cannot expect to gather such data in a large proportion of a community survey, and the main body of casual speech comes from the last three contexts.

In 1966, I tried to shrink the sections of casual speech by including only those where an actual style-shift occurred, rather than sections where style-shifting was likely to occur. This was done by the use of channel cues: changes in volume, pitch, tempo, breathing and laughter that are independent of the linguistic variables but signal overall shift of linguistic behavior and emotional involvement. With one or two exceptions, most other researchers have decided not to follow that route, since it was not easy to get reliable evidence that the same criteria were being followed. The general reaction was to prefer to use contextual criteria such as (1) to (5) alone, and this seems to be the clear consensus of the field.

4   The Decision Tree

The most vigorous development of stylistic analysis occurred in the early years of the course Linguistics 560, The Study of the Speech Community at Penn, in the 1970s. Here we developed eight contextual criteria as a decision tree for the analysis of spontaneous speech, and applied the tree to a large number of interviews (figure 5.1). Four of the contexts are categorized generally as *Casual speech* (on the right), and four define *Careful speech* (on the left). The decisions are arranged in the order of decreasing objectivity, so that the first four decisions can be made with the highest degree of reliability.

RESPONSE. The first cut is to separate the first sentence that follows speech of the interviewer as a *Response*. This includes the first sentence of a narrative, a tangent, or any other type of speech event. The sentence may not have a full finite verb, but a response will be more than a back channel feedback, or an echo.[3] In the examples which follow, the sections coded as Response are in square brackets.

NARRATIVE. The second step in the decision tree is to set aside all personal narratives as a separate category (after excluding the first sentence as a response). Since the interviewing techniques here place a high premium on the elicitation of personal narratives – dramatized accounts of events as perceived by the speaker – this has proved to be the single most important basis for a division of spontaneous speech. In the sixty-odd annual group reports completed by students in Linguistics 560, it is rare to find a linguistic variable that does not shift significantly towards the vernacular level in narrative as opposed to other speech styles.

Here personal narratives are distinguished from pseudo-narratives

---

[3] Some justification for this distinction can be found in the study of a Sydney high school by Eisikovits (1981). She distinguished all utterances where she was the previous speaker from those where another student was the previous speaker. For the majority of the linguistic variables, the girls shifted in her direction when she was the last speaker, while the boys moved in the other direction.

(accounts of sequences that are said to habitually occur, as in *we'd put up the 2x4's first...*), chronicles (undramatized accounts of extended events, all of about the same duration), and narratives of vicarious experience, where the speakers rehearse events that they did not actually witness.

The following example of narrative style, like the other examples to follow, is from an interview with a sixty-seven-year-old third generation Philadelphian of Irish descent interviewed in Kensington by Anne Bower in 1974. Tom McIntyre (T.M.) was a middle working class speaker who used a controlled and deliberate, easily paced style; the challenge of eliciting casual speech was a substantial one. The examples given are designed to illustrate and contrast the general level of vocabulary and grammar associated with each style, in this example, with a narrative style. Brackets delimit the Response portion of the excerpt. Parentheses show the remarks of the interviewer.

(1)

IVER: Did you have a favorite teacher?

T.M.: A favorite teacher? (A favorite nun). Favorite nun, Sister Ursula.
(Sister who?) [Ursula. She was an elderly sister and she was very, very nice]. Many a time she patted me and uh (you probably deserved it too). Yeah. Em – when I was older we were uh-well as uh – you know, in my teens yet I was uh, with my mother and father. Well she used to stop in our home, Sister Ursula, and uh – we were talking out there and uh, she was talking about me, you know, she taught me.
And I said, "When I was in your room I got good marks, didn't I, sister?"
She said, "You sure did."
I rolled up my sleeve and I said, "I still have some of them!" I said. (You got her). Well, she smacked me in the face then.

LANGUAGE. Towards the end of the interview, there were always questions about grammar, attitudes towards Philadelphia, Philadelphia dialect, and language in general, as well as minimal pairs. This or any other section where the topic was language, was set aside under the next decision.

(2)

IVER: What would it mean to you if someone said, "John drinks a lot anymore"?:

T.M.: [I think he drinks a lot anymore]. That means he's increased his drinking I would say, yeah.

IVER: Harry plays handball anymore?

T.M.: [Well, he never used to play that much before.] Now he's increasing his activity in the sport an – (It doesn't mean he doesn't like to play?) No, definitely not.

GROUP. The second portion assigned to the "Casual Speech" category was any speech addressed to third persons other than the interviewer. This corresponds to contexts (1) and (2) in the 1966 approach. Since this did not occur in the Tom McIntyre interview, no examples are given here.

SOAPBOX. This is the first of three decisions that are less objective than the preceding. The Soapbox style is characterized as an extended expression of generalized opinions, not spoken directly to the interviewer, but enunciated as if for a more general audience. The chief characteristics are an elevated volume level and a repetitive rhetoric. In many interviews, speakers discourse at length on such common topics as the prevalence of crime in the streets, the corrupt character of the police or local government, the behavior of minorities, and so on. Since this represents a large part of the interview time, it is important to distinguish it from tangents (see below). In this example, T.M. takes the Soapbox style to express a more liberal viewpoint, as indicated in italics.

(3)
IVER: How did your dad feel about it?
T.M.: [I don't think he was so much eh – to a bigoted quite, you know, but he was a strict on uh, livin' up to his religion.] He was a practical Catholic and ehh – but aah – I mean he wouldn't figure anyone was no good because they weren't Catholic, uh – like a lot of that went on in those days. *Today they're trying to dispel a lot of that which ehh- is a good thing, I think, because the only thing that keeps people separated is ignorance and if you dispel the ignorance your – your problem is licked. Uh. And then to prove that – uh – I don't care a lot for football, and people that go crazy over it, well I – the only reason I don't care for it is ignorance because I never went so deep into finding out about first down, second down, and what the rules of the game really are. And if I did this, uh – I would probably like it as much as anyone else, but the fact I don't know these things, and it makes me ignorant of the game, and the same with a person. If you don't know a person, you're ignorant of what type of person that person is, and rather than try to find out, you just ignore him because he's Protestant or he's Catholic or he's whatever, and if you would stop and talk to that person, and find out what – uh – what a beautiful person they are, and the religion has nothing to do with it.*

KIDS. It is a simple matter to identify the topics of kids' games, kids' experiences, and so on. But not all speech on this topic qualifies for this decision. An adult can talk about children's experience from an adult point of view, or from the kids' point of view. It is the latter that we want to set aside as a component of casual speech. The use of *we* rather than *they* is a useful clue, but it is the overall perspective which counts most. In the following example, T.M. begins with a general observation about parents, plainly taking the adult point of view. He then moves on to his children's experience, and then, in response to the interviewer's probe, shifts to his personal experience. The stylistic shift is a striking one.

(4)
T.M.: You don't see parents taking their children out so much like that, where they can have their own fun and pleasure, you know. I used to take them out, they'd go up the crick and we'd have a stick even with a line onto it . . . and they would

fish in the creek and maybe they wouldn't. (Could you eat what you caught?) *No, we – no – because you get these little sunfish and all that – and aaah when I was a boy we had – right up above Erie Avenue here was a little woods, and we had – a creek run under the rail road through there and had these crayfish, there were like little lobster, and we used to catch them for fun, and they had a big farm that we used to have to cross and the guy would shoot the rocks all at us, you know, and we'd run so, every once in a while you could steal a tomato, as you're on your way through . . .*

TANGENTS. The last of the categories to fall into the Casual rubric is the Tangent, defined as an extended body of speech that deviates plainly from the last topic introduced by the interviewer, and represents the strong interest of the speaker. In this example, the interviewer has been asking about other ethnic groups besides the Irish in North Philadelphia. T.M.'s response begins with an account of a Black ice-cream vendor, but then moves on to another vendor who had nothing to do with ethnic differences.

(5)
IVER: Was it hard for an Italian kid to join a group of guys?
T.M.: No. I wouldn't say so, no. Not when I was a kid.
IVER: How about Polish?
T.M.: [Nor Polish either, no.] And when I was a kid, I . . . I don't know when uh – the first time I saw a black person. Uh, maybe uh sometime on a wagon. On we did have – that's something I can tell you about when I was a little kid. *They had a man come around the street with a closed cart, you know, one of these long carts, and it had a top on it, like uh a rectangular, what you would say – (canvas?) – and uh he sold ice cream, little tiny blocks of ice cream, and they were two cents and they were called hokey pokies. Have you ever heard of hokey pokies? (Only the dance). And uh, he used to holler "Hokey, pokey, ice cream!" you know, and we were kids, we used to go out and we'd buy this little block of ice cream and uh – he was a colored man. And uh, they we had another one used to sell fish and crabs – mostly crabs he sold. He would come in with a cartload of crabs, you know, with ice on it and used to holler, "Maryland crabs!" you know. Supposed to have got them from Maryland, I suppose he did because he did a tremendous business, people – the crabs were very good that he had, so uh he did a tremendous business.*

We would expect the widest range of diverse responses in the identification of tangents. Yet it seems important to identify the long sections in which the speakers follow their own lead from those in which they are following the interviewers' lead. In fact, the concept of the Tangent as a stylistic category is a spin off from the Principle of Tangential Shifting, formulated by Ivan Sag in Group 3–73. This is perhaps the most basic guide for sociolinguistic interviewing. Whenever the interviewer recognizes that the speaker has moved in a different direction from the interview module, and has changed the subject, he or she pursues that topic without attempting to return to the previous one. The principle here is most widely recognized as originally stated by Ruth to Boas in the book of Ruth: *Whither thou goest, I go.*

The final category is simply the residual one. All speech that has not been marked under any of the preceding seven categories will be classed as Careful speech. That is not to say that all such residual material will have a common stylistic character. Undoubtedly much speech similar to the sections marked casual will escape classification by the four headings Narrative, Group, Kids, and Tangent. It is assumed that this will be so. The procedure of the decision tree is designed to filter out a subsection that is plainly distinct from the main body of speech by its topical and contextual character. We can summarize the operation of the decision tree in the following directions:

As you listen to speech, set aside the first utterance of every response to yourself; then take every personal narrative and put it into the Casual speech bin; otherwise, exclude any discussion of language. Any group discussion not about language is Casual. Look for extended, long-winded general pronouncements and exclude them as Careful. Mark any discussion of kids' affairs, from their own point of view as Casual, and include any sizeable excursion of the speaker into a different topic. Otherwise, interview speech is classed as Careful speech.

In most of the Linguistics 560 reports, the four components of Careful speech and the four components of Casual speech were merged in the final stylistic analysis, since there were not large enough bodies of data to justify an examination of the individual categories. The Project on Linguistic Change and Variation in Philadelphia used the decision tree on a much larger body of data, which will allow us to examine its effectiveness in distinguishing Casual speech from Careful speech.

5   The stylistic analysis of stable sociolinguistic variables

The Neighborhood Study of Philadelphia included research over several years in a series of representative neighborhoods which covered a wide geographic and social area. The analysis of style was not directed at the main target of the LVC project, the evolution of the Philadelphia vowel system, since there was no strong evidence of style-shifting within spontaneous speech for those variables. A stylistic analysis was carried out for three stable sociolinguistic variables:

(DH): the alternation of stops, fricatives, and affricates in initial position. The index was constructed by assigning a value of 0 to a fricative, 1 to an affricate or zero initial, and 2 to a stop; the mean value of these, multiplied by 100, gave the (DH) index, which varies from 0 to 200.

(ING): the alternation of apical and velar consonants for the unstressed syllable /iN/, where the index is the percent velar form. Proper nouns are excluded. The variable was subdivided

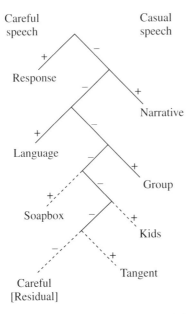

Figure 5.1 Decision Tree for stylistic analysis of spontaneous speech in the sociolinguistic interview

by grammatical category: progressives, participles, and nouns. The stylistic analysis was carried out on the largest subcategory with the highest percent of the apical variant, the progressives.

(NEG): the percent of negative concord in sentences where a negative precedes an indeterminate of the underlying form *ever*, *either*, or *any*.

A total of 184 speakers from the Neighborhood Study were studied for the distribution of these variables, a larger group than the 120 speakers whose vowel systems were analyzed, and including a sizeable number of younger speakers from eight to nineteen years old. In many cases, there were extended series of interviews, from two to eight; for comparability, only the initial interviews were analyzed here. All eight stylistic subcategories were used. In the first analysis to be presented here, these are combined into Careful speech and Casual speech as indicated in figure 5.1.

Figure 5.2 is a series of three histograms showing the differences between the combined Casual speech and Careful speech figures for the three variables. It is immediately evident that (DH) shows the greatest degree of style-shifting. Only 13 of the 168 speakers whose style-shifts were recorded had values below zero, while the great majority show strongly positive values. The modal value

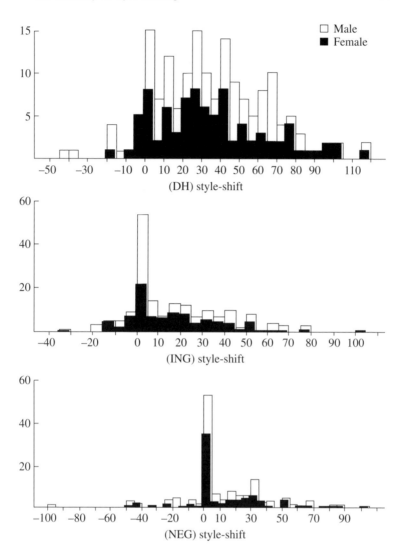

Figure 5.2 Style-shifting of stable sociolinguistic variables in Philadelphia
(index for Casual style minus index for Careful style)

is between 25 and 30. No strong difference by gender appears, though we do
find a concentration of women among the highest values, over 85 (7 out of 8),
and a concentration of males among those with negative values (6 out of 8).

Less pronounced style-shifting is shown for (ING), where the predominant modal value is close to zero. Again, a small number is found below zero,

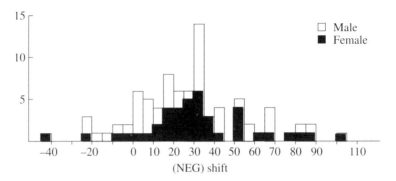

Figure 5.3 Style-shifting of (NEG) for Philadelphia speakers with (NEG) values greater than 10 in Casual speech (N = 84)

and the majority of the speakers have positive values for style-shifting. The same is true to an even larger degree for (NEG), but this is due to the fact that many middle-class speakers use no negative concord at all. Figure 5.3 corrects for this fact, showing the distribution of style-shifting only for the eighty-four speakers with values of (NEG) in Casual speech of 10 percent or higher. Here we see a pattern similar to that for (DH): only ten speakers with values below zero, only eleven with values close to zero, but with a wide range of large positive values. The modal value for the shift is between 30 and 35 percent. Again, there is little difference between men and women.

The style-shifting shown in figures 5.2 and 5.3 is a stable characteristic of the community. Though there is a wide range of individual variation, there is little differentiation by social characteristics. This is not the case for the individual variables themselves, which are very sensitive to age, social class, and gender. Table 5.1 shows significant factors emerging from the multiple regression of (DH) in Careful speech. The age groups here are not quantitative but qualitative categories: the equation assigns a value of 34 for membership in the eight-to-twelve-year-old group so that, all other things being equal, a speaker nine years old is expected to have a (DH) value that is 34 more than a speaker over fifty. The typical age profile for a stable sociolinguistic variable emerges. There is no significant effect of age for those over twenty (the residual group for comparison are those over fifty years of age). On the other hand, we find a sizeable adolescent spike, with a maximum of 82 points in the (DH) index for the sixteen year olds (figure 5.4a).

The socioeconomic profile for (DH) is the near-linear monotonic pattern to be expected for a stable stigmatized variable. The SEC measure is constructed from an equally weighted set of three indices: occupation, education, and house value. Figure 5.4b shows the steady decline from the base

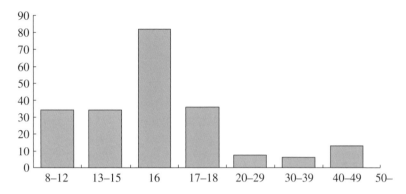

Figure 5.4a Age coefficients for (DH) in Careful speech

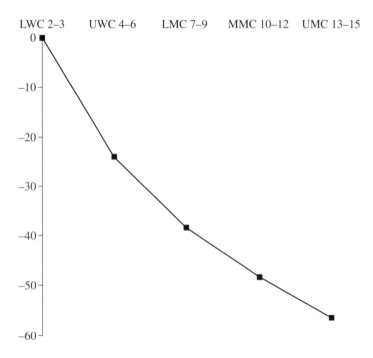

Figure 5.4b Social class coefficients for (DH) in Careful speech

Table 5.1. *Multiple regression coefficients for (DH) in Careful speech*

Variable	Coefficient	t-ratio	prob
Constant	86.95	5.96	≤0.0001
Age			
8–12	34	3.28	0.0013
13–15	35	3.52	0.0006
16	82	6.00	≤0.0001
17–18	36	2.54	0.0121
20–29	8	0.76	0.447
30–39	7	0.72	0.4703
40–49	14	1.37	0.1739
Social class			
UWC 4–6	−24	−1.77	0.0787
LMC 7–9	−38	−2.69	0.008
MMC10–12	−48	−3.22	0.0016
UMC13–15	−56	−3.09	0.0025
Upward mobility	−8	−2.26	0.0256
Gender			
Female	−24	−4.08	≤0.0001
Neighborhood			
South Philadelphia	27	4.14	≤0.0001

Note:
N = 168; r-squared (adjusted) = 48.1%.

level of the lower working class for each successively higher social class group. In addition, there is a small but significant disfavoring effect of upward mobility.

Table 5.1 also shows a sizeable and significant gender effect. Women are expected on the average to have a (DH) value twenty-four points lower than men. Finally, table 5.1 shows that being from any of the three South Philadelphia neighborhoods has about the same effect, but in the opposite direction.

If we take as our dependent variable the size of style-shifting for (DH), the resulting picture is quite different. Table 5.2 shows that there are only two significant coefficients to be derived from such an analysis. The sixteen-year-old group, which had the highest expected value for (DH) in Careful speech, is expected to show a reduced range of style-shifting: twenty-three points. It is clear that this group of adolescent speakers not only uses high

Table 5.2. *Multiple regression coefficients for style-shift of (DH)*

Variable	Coefficient	t-ratio	prob
Constant	31	10.6	≤ 0.0001
Age 16	− 23	− 2.36	0.0197
Social class UWC 4–6	11	2.26	0.0254

N = 168; r-squared (adjusted) = 4.0%.

values of (DH) in general, but also resists the normal tendency to correct downwards in Careful styles. Membership in the Upper Working Class group produces a small but significant expectation of a higher range. The total amount of variance explained by this regression as indicated by r-square is small: 4 percent, as compared to 48 percent for table 5.1.

Let us now examine the actual distribution of the (DH) style-shift in detail. Figure 5.5 is a scattergram that locates each individual on a two-dimensional field where the vertical axis is the size of the (DH) shift, and the horizontal axis is age; gender is indicated by solid circles (female) versus open squares (male). The straight solid line across the middle is the overall regression line; it is absolutely flat, indicating no overall age-effect. The two dotted lines indicate partial regressions for males and females; they are only slightly different, suggesting a small tendency for males to shift more as they grow older, females to shift less. But this is not to be taken seriously: the correlation of age with (DH) shift for males is only .08; and for females only − .03.

The scattergram of figure 5.5 does isolate a few local tendencies of interest for the study of style-shifting. Negative values of the (DH) shift, below zero in figure 5.5, represent speakers who are displaying behavior contrary to the dominant norm of the society, and they therefore demand a closer look. At the lower left of figure 5.5, there is a clump of six speakers with strongly negative (DH) shift among the youngest speakers, the cluster at the lower left, and point even lower, but no such point occurs among the older speakers. This is in line with earlier observations (Labov 1964) that although children begin to acquire the sociolinguistic norms of the community quite early, this is a gradual process controlled by both age and socio-economic class. Table 5.3 examines this tendency for all three variables by dividing speakers into younger (under thirty) and older (thirty and over) age groups. It gives the percentage who show shifting in a reverse direction,

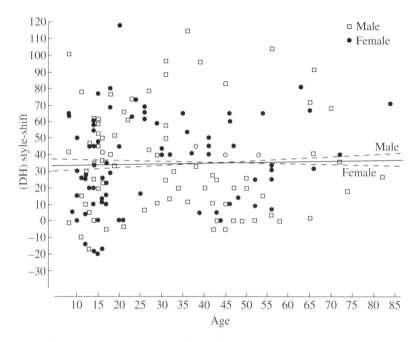

Figure 5.5 Distribution of (DH) style-shift by age and gender

with values less than zero, for (DH), (ING), and (NEG). It is clear that for both (DH) and (ING) the effect is a large one: three times as many younger speakers deviate from the community norm.

For (NEG), there is no significant difference, indicating that the stigmatization of this variable is more powerful, and controls behavior at an earlier age. This seems inconsistent with the fact that the actual percentage of reversals for (NEG) is in the same range as the other two, while we might expect it to be much smaller. This appears to be the result of the fact that the data for (NEG) is sparser. It has been generally established that sociolinguistic variables, like all other stochastic events, approach their limiting value as the frequency of data rise (Guy 1980, Roberts 1993).

To examine this question more closely we can display the style-shifts against the total frequency of data for each speaker. Figure 5.6a displays the (ING) shift data by total frequency: it shows that the difference between older and younger speakers is not the result of frequency for this variable. Speakers under thirty are shown by open squares; those thirty and over by solid circles. To the left of the zero value for the (ING) style-shift, we see eighteen empty squares which range across the whole frequency spectrum, but only four solid circles; in other respects, the distributions are not signif-

Table 5.3. *Percentage of speakers with*
reversed direction of style-shifting by age

Age	(DH)	(ING)	(NEG)	N
Under 30	17	9	12	105
Over 30	6	3	12	79

icantly different. Figure 5.6b is the corresponding diagram for (NEG). Again, the distributions for older and younger speakers are very similar. The younger speakers are concentrated at lower frequency levels, however, where they show a wider range of style-shifting. They do not show the heavier concentration of style reversal that we saw for (ING) (and for (DH) in table 5.4). The resistance of a small group of younger speakers to the norms for style-shifting of these two variables does not hold for (NEG).

It is this small concentration of younger speakers in the negative style-shift area that is responsible for the two significant regression effects of table 5.2. Other than this, the style-shift of stable sociolinguistic variables is uniform and compelling across the Philadelphia speech community. That is not to say that everyone behaves in the same way: there are widespread individual differences, as figures 5.6 and 5.7 show. But these differences in degrees of shifting are not socially organized, and do not correspond to social categories in the same way that the actual level of the variables do as exhibited in table 5.1. They may in fact correspond to the differences among the various subcategories in the style decision tree. If it turns out that some speakers had higher numbers of tokens in Tangent sections, and others in Narrative sections, and these subcategories vary in their efficiency in registering style, this might be responsible for the wide scatter of values in figures 5.6a and 5.6b, with standard deviations of 22 and 29.

6   The contribution of individual decisions to stylistic analysis

These results indicate that the method for distinguishing Careful from Casual speech has a solid basis in the speech practices of the speech community. At this point, however, we do not know which of the individual decisions of the style classification tree are contributing to the differentiation of styles. An analysis of the individual components of Careful and Casual speech might allow us to refine the measures further. It was pointed out above that the first four decisions are more objective than the others. As a result of a certain degree of uncertainty among students about concepts like *Soapbox*, *Kids*, and *Tangent*, more recent stylistic analyses carried out

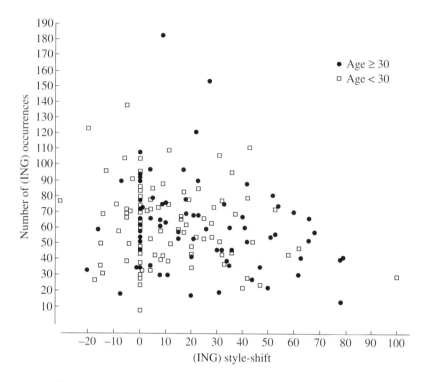

Figure 5.6a (ING) style-shift by size of data set and age

in Linguistics 560 have been confined to the objective subset, terminating at the identification of *Group* style in figure 5.1. It is possible that the less objective measures are actually diluting our view of style-shifting, and that the more objective measures will give a sharper and more accurate picture.

The data on the eight subcategories of the style decision tree have been preserved for a subsample of fifty-six speakers from the Philadelphia Neighborhood Study. This subsample covers the same social and age range as the main sample of 184 speakers that we have just considered. It includes twenty-eight male and twenty-eight female subjects, with speakers from all neighborhoods and age categories. We will consider the data for (DH) and (ING), but not (NEG), since there is not enough data to give meaningful results with this fine subdivision. Figure 5.7 shows the values for (ING) on the left, and (DH) on the right. The open circles and dashed lines show the mean (ING) values for the four Careful speech categories on the left, and the four Casual speech categories on the right. The solid squares and lines

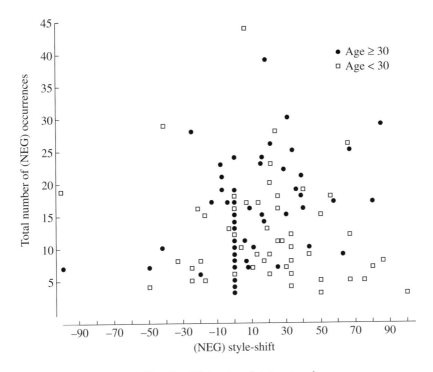

Figure 5.6b (NEG) style-shift by size of data set and age

show the corresponding values for (DH). The mean values for all styles for the two variables are shown by the two horizontal lines.

All four of the Careful speech subcategories of (ING) are below the (ING) mean, and there are not large differences among them. Three of the four Careful speech categories are above the mean, while Narrative lies at the mean level. The greatest difference from the mean is found in the least objective categories of Tangent. While this might at first lead us to think that this is in fact the most effective indicator of stylistic differences, a certain degree of caution is required: it is possible that the less objective character of the decision to call a passage a Tangent allows the realization of the linguistic variables to bias the decision more than with more objective categorizations. A certain amount of circularity might enter into the linguistic analysis of style.

The (DH) stylistic differences are considerably larger, even bearing in mind that the scale covers twice the range. The subjective category of Soapbox is the most differentiated from the mean in Careful speech, with no differences among the other three; in Casual speech, Narrative and Kids

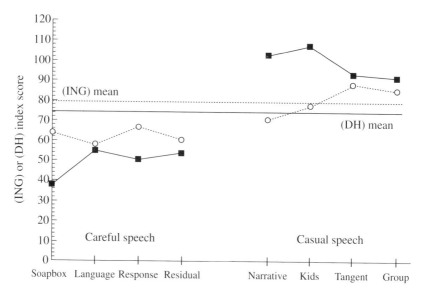

Figure 5.7 Stylistic differentiation of (DH) and (ING) for eight categories of the Style Decision Tree

are the highest, though all four subcategories are well above the mean level.

The overall view of the eight subcategories provided by figure 5.7 is that they all appear to contribute to the differentiation of style; no motivation is provided here for discarding any one of them.

7   Differentiation by gender and social class

Figure 5.8 separates the values for the twenty-eight men from the twenty-eight women for (ING). In general the (ING) values for men are higher than for women, as our regression analysis of the larger data set would predict. This difference is much more consistent in Casual speech, where the two sets follow parallel paths, than in Careful speech. In these subsets, Soapbox style is not differentiated from the Casual speech styles for women, while for men, it is. On the other hand, the Response category does not distinguish men's Careful speech from Narrative. The view of (DH) shows a sizeable overall differentiation of the four Careful subcategories from the four Casual subcategories.

A more severe test of the systematic character of the four subcategories is a correlation with three socioeconomic classes. Figure 5.9 displays this analysis for (ING). The three classes are well stratified, with the lowest values shown for the Middle Class group 9–14, intermediate values for the

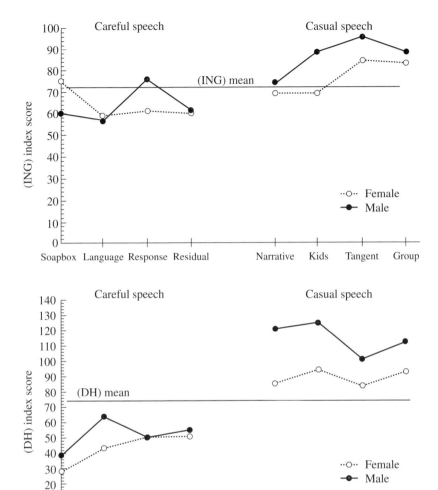

Figure 5.8 Stylistic differentiation of (ING) and (DH) by sex for eight categories of the Style Decision Tree

Upper Working Class 6–8, and the highest values for the Lower Working Class 2–5. There is considerable differentiation among the subcategories for 9–14, where the lowest (ING) values are found for Language, and the highest in Tangent and Group. For the 6–8 group, only Soapbox style is well below the mean, and Kids is well above it. For the 2–5 group, it is again

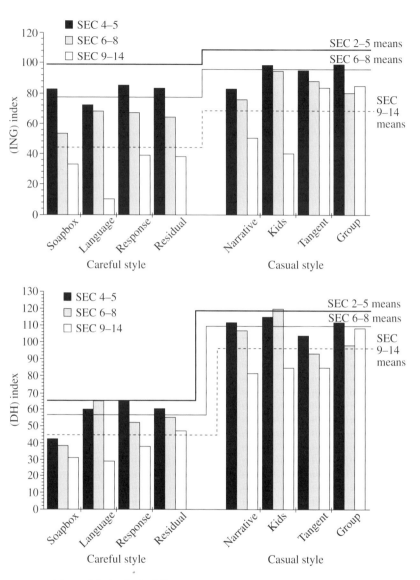

Figure 5.9 Stylistic differentiation of (ING) and (DH) for eight categories of the Style Decision Tree

Language which is the lowest subcategory. On the whole, we cannot point to any one subcategory that is not contributing to the overall categorization of style: there is no reason to think that dropping any one of them would enhance our view of stylistic differences. Indeed, the narrative category, which we have relied on as the most substantial and the most objective, is doing less work in this analysis than any other. This is contrary to my own initial expectation.

The (DH) data shows the most satisfactory deployment of the eight sub-categories. For each of the four classes, all four Careful speech styles are lower than all four Casual speech styles. No one subcategory appears to be exceptional on the whole, though there are minor fluctuations in the behavior of each. (DH) is the prototypical stable sociolinguistic variable in terms of the quantity of data and the clarity of community norms.

8   Conclusion

This report on the Style Decision Tree has led to a conclusion quite different from the one that I had originally anticipated. This data set held out the possibility of differentiating among the eight subcategories, refining and removing those that weakened the force of the stylistic analysis. However, it appears that the subcategories are all on a par: the four assigned to Careful speech are on the whole quite different in levels of the variables than the four assigned to Casual speech. The conclusion is that instead of pruning the Style Decision Tree, it might well be developed further. The fact that the Residual category is not the lowest for (DH) or (ING) makes it seem likely that there are many other Casual speech categories that can be extracted from it. But it is not very far from the lowest category, so that one would not expect any major additions of this type. The development that seems most promising is to give more analysts training in the recognition of such categories as Soapbox, Tangent, or Kids style, in workshops or other joint sessions where a confident consensus can be reached. Such a consensus should not be hard to achieve. The coding of the LVC project was done by three different analysts, and the agreement appears to be substantial.

Further exploration of intra-speaker variation in the interview situation, coupled with wider investigations of style-shifting outside the interview, should throw light on the unanswered questions raised in the first part of this paper. Even within the limited scope of this methodological study, substantive questions of considerable interest have emerged. The deviant behavior of a subsection of adolescent youth appears to be an intrinsic part of the structure of stable variables. Their resistance to the dominant norms, and their ultimate acquiescence in them, is a well-recognized part of the sociolinguistic ecology. What is new here is the possibility of measuring the orientation of speakers to these norms more accurately. We can go beyond the simple assessment of variables in speech production to the measurement of variation in style-shifting, and so register the dynamic component of sociolinguistic behavior.

6   A dissection of style-shifting

John Baugh

This review begins with a survey of Labov's contributions to stylistic and contextual research in sociolinguistics, including some observations about the evidence presented in chapter 5. After reinterpreting some of that data we pay brief tribute to Labov's sociolinguistic legacy. We then turn to some methodological considerations that are relevant to scholars who conduct linguistic analyses of style-shifting derived from combinations of recordings, experiments, questionnaires, and observations, all of which are ultimately intended to provide reliable and representative linguistic corpora that are amenable to rigorous scientific inquiry.

Labov begins his chapter by reviewing taxonomies of style and their uses. He acknowledges the desire "to know as much as possible about the ways that speakers shift forms and frequencies in the course of every-day life," and he confirms the complexity of this exceedingly difficult task. These remarks presume familiarity with Labov's discussion (chapter 5), and I hope to offer additional insights growing from some of Labov's earlier discussions about style. Various stylistic taxonomies, including most of those presented throughout this book, represent alternative heuristic approaches to alternative stylistic genres. The Labovian paradigm has largely been associated with quantitative studies of linguistic variation and change in progress. Evidence for these studies has been gathered in different contexts, and the definitions of those contexts have evolved during the past thirty years.

These opening remarks focus on four stylistic trends that can be traced in Labov's work: the first trend grows from his 1966 dissertation, "The Social Stratification of English in New York City." The second phase culminated in the publication of *Sociolinguistic Patterns* (1972a) and *Language in the Inner City: Studies in the Black English Vernacular* (1972b). The third trend explores his discussion of "Field Methods of the Project on Linguistic Change and Variation" (Labov 1984), and the fourth is reflected recently in "The Anatomy of Style-Shifting." When I was first introduced to these concepts, as a graduate student in Linguistics 560 during 1973 – within the same cohort of graduate students who witnessed Sag's formulation of the

"Tangential Shift" – I tried to integrate the contextual categories that Labov described in "The Isolation of Contextual Styles" into my own research (Baugh 1983). Labov (1972a:79) describes four experimentally controlled contexts, each providing increasing attention to speech: Context A, "for those situations which escape the social constraints of the interview situation"; Context B, the interview situation; Context C, reading style, and Contexts D and D'; that is, word lists and minimal pairs respectively.

During my own independent fieldwork in Los Angeles I ran into a problem with "Context C"; many of the African American informants whom I consulted were not confident readers, and several of my field interviews hit a snag at the first hint of any suggestion that I was planning to ask them to read. Eventually I stopped asking consultants to read, thereby eliminating Context C. I began to recreate alternative methods for Contexts D and D' that didn't require reading. For example, using two tape recorders, I would play recordings of word lists and minimal pairs as linguistic prompts; this procedure allowed each consultant to attend carefully to their own pronunciation of isolated words (i.e. they would pay greater attention to their speech), but it did so without the added embarrassment of exposing any limited reading proficiency.

Although Labov does not draw direct attention to the importance of literacy in "The Isolation of Contextual Styles," sociolinguistic subjects world wide can be divided into two major categories: those who are literate, and those who lack literacy. The early experimental formulations for contextual styles are well suited to literate consultants, but they can be counterproductive among consultants who would prefer to avoid recordings of themselves attempting to read.

Sociolinguistics, as a field, cannot hope to develop more fully before reconciling the fact that prospective informants fall into these two categories. Very young children, for example, will not know how to read for developmental reasons that have nothing whatsoever to do with access to various educational opportunities. Some languages of the world are written, while others reflect oral traditions; data collection among (il)literate informants may necessarily vary depending upon whether literacy is pervasive, or not, within the population under study.

I am perhaps especially sensitive to these matters because of my work with educators who are frustrated by the myriad of barriers that diminish educational prospects for many low-income and minority students in the United States and elsewhere. Some data collection procedures, such as recorded interviews, can be employed with any normal consultant who has the capacity to speak (sign language studies use video recordings for this purpose among the deaf). Experimental data collection that calls for reading can only be employed among the literate. Other cultural considerations come into play regarding the appropriateness of reading material, and this includes age appropriateness as well as topics that are considered to be acceptable to the consultants, or, in the case of minors, materials that are acceptable to their parents or guardians.

These cultural and ethnographic considerations do not diminish the primary data collection objective: "The primary goal of all sociolinguistic interviewing is to alter this governing situation informally so that it approaches as close as possible the format of a conversation between people who are well acquainted, if not friends." When prospective consultants have no "friends" from backgrounds similar to that of the fieldworker, the task of recording natural conversations, becomes more complicated (see Wolfson 1976), but with sufficient ethnographic sensitivity, sociolinguists can determine if they, or others with whom they collaborate, are sufficiently well suited to ensure successful interviews that provide representative samples of vernacular linguistic norms.

As Labov and his colleagues pursued these goals, field methods for the Philadelphia study of linguistic change and variation began to rely less on reading and more on recorded interviews containing interactive conversational speech. Labov's formulation of the decision tree represents an alternative stylistic diagnostic, one that is capable of providing considerable methodological utility. Before moving further, however, I should express a significant reservation. Labov states that "In these areas of controlled speech, it is a simple matter to regulate the amount of attention paid to speech, and there are no real challenges to be met here." I concede that I may not fully understand the preceding point, but I do not agree that "no real challenges" remain. These methods are not universally applicable in every speech community, and many fieldworkers will need to make on-the-spot adjustments to modify, adapt, or discard these procedures in favor of methods that will produce desired corpora.

The most essential point can be stated simply: fieldworkers must find ways to document and record the range of speech styles that occur naturally within the speech community being studied. Walters's (1987) studies of Tunisian diglossia within the context of Arabic/French bilingualism demonstrated that cultural norms play a tremendous role in the need for fieldworker adaptability. Walters, as an American man, could not interview Muslim women; had he done so it would have been highly disruptive to data collection. His research, and that of others, demonstrates the need for ethnographic sensitivity among fieldworkers.

Indeed, the original formulation of Sag's "tangential shift" resulted from the pragmatic observation that many informants enjoyed sociolinguistic interviews, but they enjoyed them even more when they had the freedom to wander from topic-to-topic, without strict adherence to a research questionnaire. Since sociolinguists, and Labovians in particular, seek to study ordinary speech in everyday life, it matters less to us that we constrain interview topics in a rigid or *a priori* manner. Rather, efforts to keep the conversation rolling, with ever-diminishing talk from the fieldworker, is the ultimate objective. This objective holds until one seeks to directly elicit linguistic judgments, linguistic attitudes, and other essential research information that must be gathered more directly.

Three decades ago, when Labov (1966) studied style "by the use of channel cues: changes in volume, pitch, tempo, breathing and laughter that are independent of the linguistic variables," he had not envisioned the formulation of "The Decision Tree," illustrated in Labov's figure 5.1 (this volume). Earlier renditions of LCV methods were somewhat more complicated, and relied on topical shifting through a "characteristic network of 20 modules," beginning with demography and concluding with overt discussion about language. Those modules are reproduced here in figure 6.1, and they first appeared in "Field Methods of the Project on Linguistic Change and Variation" (Labov 1984:35).

Each module, or potential interview topic, embodies variable combinations of Careful speech and Casual speech, often aligning with the branches of Labov's Decision Tree. It is important to recall his observation that the higher branches can be determined with greater objectivity than the lower branches. Another significant distinction is reflected by alternative orientations. Whereas Labov's tree involves procedures for stylistic analysis of completed sociolinguistic interviews, figure 6.1 provides a framework for the conduct of interviews themselves; that is, rather than for their ultimate analysis after the fact.

The Philadelphia research on linguistic change and variation also provided additional opportunities for Labov (1984:32) to portray sociolinguistic methods, which he specified in "Field Methods of the Project on Linguistic Change and Variation." Readers who are unfamiliar with that paper would be well advised to consult the original text, because the following abbreviated criteria could easily be misleading in the following decontextualized format. Labov presents ten principles governing sociolinguistic interviews. He further observed that "a number of these goals are complementary but others are contradictory":

1. to record with reasonable fidelity
2. to obtain the full range of demographic data necessary
3. to obtain comparable responses to questions
4. to elicit narratives of personal experience
5. to stimulate group interaction among the people present
6. to isolate topics of greatest interest
7. to trace patterns of communication among members

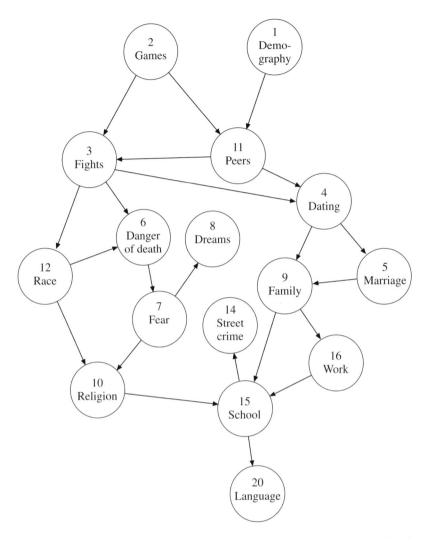

Figure 6.1 Field methods of the project on linguistic change and variation

 8. to obtain a record of overt attitudes toward language
 9. to obtain specific information on linguistic structures
10. to carry out field experiments on subjective linguistic reactions.
    In an effort to lend greater empirical flexibility to this enterprise, figure
6.1 offers an alternative formulation of the Decision Tree; one that is not
binary, but variable. Figure 6.2 is inspired by the same principles found in

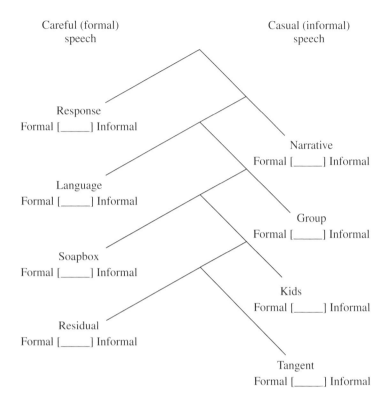

Figure 6.2 A variable adaptation of Labov's Decision Tree for stylistic analysis

Labov (1972b), when he redefined formal linguistic rules to account for variable optionality (see Chomsky and Halle 1968). Here we extend that principle to a reformulation for stylistic analysis of spontaneous speech in the sociolinguistic interview. We treat "formal speech" and "informal speech" as (synonymous?) alternatives to Labov's "Careful" speech and "Casual" speech respectively.

The most significant adaptations include the recognition that each branch of the tree reflects a tendency; that is, to either be formal or informal. However, figure 6.2 makes provisions to account for exceptions to these trends. Each node at the end of each branch can be evaluated in reference to combinations of (in)formality within the same, or different, sociolinguistic interviews. We also prefer a final "residual" category to a terminal "Careful" category; this avoids the redundant use of "Careful," and it may help to account for some of the unexpected results.

Whereas Labov's Decision Tree offers clear distinctions between Casual and Careful speech, the proposed modification presented in figure 6.2 does not do so. Any *a priori* designations regarding distinctions between Careful and Casual speech would be speculative at best, and researchers should be free to introduce the relevant evidence, including ethnographic data, that would lend greater empirical verification to ensuing analyses of the ratio of careful to casual speech, as well as the circumstances that may give rise to one form over the other during the course of sociolinguistic interviews. Finally, there may be a certain amount of variation or "noise" that does not lend itself to concise clarification, and instances of stylistic ambiguity can be described on a case-by-case basis.

Labov's definition of "the final category as the residual one," is described as follows: "All speech that has not been marked under any of the preceding seven categories will be classed as Careful speech. That is not to say that all such residual material will have a common stylistic character. Undoubtedly much speech similar to the sections marked Casual will escape classification by the four headings Narrative, Group, Kids, and Tangent." Figure 6.2 eliminates the catch-all "Careful" category in favor of a more general, or miscellaneous, residual category. Moreover, since each branch can be placed on a variable scale, rather than being locked into a binary category, it becomes possible to classify exceptions to the general trends that Labov observed in his findings.

Figure 6.2 is offered in support of Labov's analytic goals, and lends potential analytic refinement, since his

report on the Style Decision Tree has led to a conclusion quite different from the one originally anticipated . . . it appears that the subcategories are all on a par: the four assigned to Careful speech yield lower values of the variable than the four assigned to Casual speech. The conclusion is that instead or pruning the Style Decision Tree, it might well be developed further.

This further development has been one of my goals here.

For example, "The fact that the residual category of 'Careful speech' is not the lowest for (DH) or (ING) makes it seem likely that there are other Casual speech categories that might be extracted from it." In two words: I agree. Therefore, it is perhaps best to rename the residual category, since it is highly likely to include Casual speech. Indeed, the heuristic advantage of figure 6.2 is that provisions are made that allow for uncharacteristic linguistic behavior in each category that might otherwise fluctuate across the full range of Careful and Casual speech styles.

In closing I seek to make two additional observations that grow from my work with teachers and student teachers, many of whom are unfamiliar with sociolinguistics, or what our science can contribute to the educational enterprise; and these observations are directly relevant to the social stratification of test performance which shows striking correlations to the social stratification of English.

Returning to the importance of literacy, sociolinguistics should acknowledge that our consultants can all be divided into two groups: informants who can read and write, and other informants who have limited – or non-existent – literacy skills. Experimental sociolinguistic data collection is likely to differ among these populations. Very young children don't read or write, so studies of early child development shouldn't require reading; however, when normal adults lack reading proficiency it is for reasons other than normal language development, and sociolinguistics has always been in an exceptional position to lend scientific and empirical evidence to the alarming statistics reflected by many gross educational inequalities (Kozol 1991).

Labov mentions another concern in passing, that represents a potential weakness in sociolinguistic methodology: namely, "with varying degrees of success, the interviewer constructs a symmetrical exchange of ideas and reactions, defining himself or herself as the perfect and attentive listener, with no other goals and ambitions but to learn as much as possible from the subject's life experience." By what criteria should we judge the "varying degrees of success" among sociolinguistic interviews? And even if we could identify suitable evaluative measures, by what criteria should we then include or exclude (tainted?) evidence in our final analyses?

I have been fortunate: many of my best interviews resulted in "an hour or more of recorded spontaneous speech"; however, I doubt very much if I – an African American man – could have met with the same success as did Anne Bower among the working class Irish and Italian consultants whom she recorded as part of the LCV project. Similarly, she – as a white woman – might easily encounter difficulties in the minority speech communities where I felt most comfortable gathering interviews. The point exposes an essential limitation in sociolinguistic interviews; some of the best fieldworkers will be limited in the range of speech communities where they are most effective.

At the suggestion of several of my students who know me well, I have begun to look more closely at my own linguistic behavior during linguistic interviews among socially stratified populations of African American consultants in different regions of the country. I exhibit considerable linguistic variation, none of which was within my conscious control, nor have these data been the object of any of my own linguistic analyses, yet I strongly believe that my personal linguistic accommodations played a major role in the nature and quality of the African American corpora I have personally gathered.

What, then, do we do about experimenter or fieldworker effects; that is, how can we reduce the negative consequences of "the observer's paradox?" (Labov 1972a:121). One solution lies in more comprehensive analyses of the available linguistic evidence, such as that found in Gal (1979), Coupland (1980), and Trudgill (1981), each of whom strives to account for addressee accommodation or variation in interviewer speech. Their efforts expose limitations in my own work (Baugh 1983) accentuating the need for expanded analyses. By not accounting for fluctuations in my own linguistic behavior as a sociolinguistic fieldworker, based on the relative formality of the interview situation, or the relative personal or social importance of topics under discussion during an interview, I did not fully explore the extent to which my own linguistic accommodation (Giles and Powesland 1975) was influencing the attending audience (Bell 1984).

In an effort to overcome these limitations in our previous work we have begun to reanalyze our old African American corpus, focusing on analyses of the fieldworker (i.e., this author) as well as the consultants. Previous publications focused, quite understandably, on the speech of the most representative vernacular speakers of African American English – but my own style-shifting is likely to have influenced some of these results, and we can now consider conducting new experiments that control stylistic variation on my part as a fieldworker.

I suspect that I am not the first, nor last, fieldworker to realize significant degrees of linguistic variation in my own speech as I would accommodate toward the speech of various consultants, very much in an effort to help my subjects feel at ease, and to diminish any fear that I was attempting to record their speech with derogatory intent. But in order to convey that sense of linguistic respect to different people on different occasions I engaged in some of the co-occurrence behavior that Ervin-Tripp (1972) first outlined.

These remarks attempt to do more than offer a mere dissection of Labov's chapter. We have attempted to place this review within the larger arena of Labov's formidable contributions to the sociolinguistic studies of style. In so doing we offer an alternative, variable, configuration of "The Decision Tree," along with two major concerns regarding the relative utility of sociolinguistic procedures: (1) experimental sociolinguistic field methods may need to be varied depending upon alternative levels of literacy among consultants; those who can read and write may perform tasks that others may find more difficult – if not impossible; (2) future analyses may benefit from complementary analyses of fieldworkers' linguistic behavior, in an effort to identify any potential bias that might otherwise compromise, contaminate, or enrich, linguistic field evidence.

Finally, drawing inspiration from Rickford's (1997) call for positive contributions to the communities that provide the data that sustain our scholarly (and professional) livelihoods, I must affirm that the types of evidence that we sociolinguists routinely gather, including our acute awareness of variable thresholds of public (il)literacy, are essential to several important educational enterprises. One such example can be found in fields that employ standardized testing. For many years test developers have tried to devise nationally normed tests that can be administered nationally. A disproportionately high number of minority teachers have failed the California CBEST test, thereby threatening their careers at the same time that it reduces diversity among California's teachers. And the National Institute of Health has come to realize that many of the pathological speech tests that have been used by clinicians tend to over-identify African Americans and Latinos as having abnormal language development, when problems lie within the testing instruments themselves.

Several cases that are presently pending with the US Office of Civil Rights hinge on language, and the advancement of stylistic analyses may eventually play a substantially larger role than the advancement of sociolinguistic inquiry for its own sake. Labov, and other contributors to this volume, have made significant contributions beyond linguistics by challenging some of the established myths and stereotypes regarding language that prevail about the very minority populations that we sociolinguists have studied most extensively; that is, from various sociolinguistic perspectives. Most contributors to this volume, including this author and the editors, have built upon the sound scientific principles that have been the hallmark of Labov's contributions to linguistic inquiry, and the present observations are offered in harmony with the other contributions to this volume that seek to refine our collective understanding and future analyses of alternative styles of human linguistic behavior.

7 Style and social meaning

Penelope Eckert

Unlike the other papers in this volume, Labov's is not directly concerned with defining style, but with using style to control and identify intra-speaker variation. He does this, in his own words, as a means of "organizing and using the intra-speaker variation that occurs in the interview." Taking the analysis of variation as his point of departure, Labov's mission is primarily methodological: to operationalize style so as to elicit and extract chunks of speech in interviews that will show maximal and predictable intra-speaker differentiation in the patterning of variables.

Central to Labov's analytic practice is the sociolinguistic interview as a constructed speech event. The intention is, first of all, to maximize comparability of speech samples for multiple speakers. And within the interview, the intention is to elicit a predictable range of stylistic output from the interviewee, so that the analyst can systematically assign that output to stylistic categories. If the sociolinguistic interview constitutes the discourse universe within which Labov is operating, its validity as a methodological tool depends on the relation between the genres within the interview and similar genres in everyday linguistic practice. One could say, then, that the main connection between Labov's paper and the other papers in this volume is in the comparison between the constructed stylistic world of the interview and the larger stylistic world within which it is embedded and on which it draws.

If we approach variation in the traditional way, as a one-dimensional axis between standard and vernacular[1] extremes, we might see Labov's enterprise in this paper as a search for things that elicit the standard on the one hand, and things that elicit the vernacular on the other. This is specifically what he has constructed in his Decision Tree, arranging subevents of the sociolinguistic interview according to their potential for eliciting standard and vernacular variants. While he presents this tree as consisting of stylistic black boxes, much of his work in the past has gone into explaining

---

[1] I am using the term *vernacular* here to refer to a variety rather than to a portion of every speaker's repertoire. Specifically, I call vernacular those varieties that are the most locally differentiated, and associated with locally based populations.

what the boxes contain, and the other papers in this volume also focus on the contents. In comparing the predictions of his tree model with the actual data from his extended corpus of interviews, he shows that his predictions are correct in general, but that there remains more error than he is comfortable with. In order to understand the sources of this error, though, the black boxes need to be opened – and opened wider than Labov does in his discussion. It is to this opening that I will now turn.

Labov's Decision Tree shows us subevents in the interview that he has found to yield particularly standard or particularly vernacular variants. These subevents are heterogeneous and defined, in various combinations, by one or several of the stylistic parameters that are discussed in other papers in this volume. In addition, there is considerable potential for interaction of effects among them.

Response can be defined in terms of place in the discourse – immediately following the interviewer's question – or in terms of topic control. In this case, response could be directly opposed to a *tangent*, which is explicitly defined in terms of the interviewee's taking of control of the flow of the interview. Topic control, in turn, could be bringing out the vernacular for a number of reasons: because the interviewees are beginning to enjoy themselves, or to feel competent knowing that they are on comfortable ground for the moment, or because the topics they tend to introduce are those that in themselves tend to elicit the vernacular, and so on.

Two of Labov's subevents, *Language* and *Kids*, are defined in terms of topic, in these cases associated with opposite ends of the stylistic continuum. According to Labov, the salience of topic has more to do with point of view than with actual content – that is, the topic of language reminds interviewees of their potential inadequacies, while the topic of childhood games can bring speakers back to relive a time when they felt more relaxed. My own experience with the childhood games discussion, when Paul Cohen interviewed me in 1966 or so for his study of New Jersey (aeh), is that the language that goes with childhood games (e.g. jumprope or counting off rhymes) is fixed in the genre. While the discussion of the games did not bring me back to my childhood particularly, the rhymes themselves – which were obligatorily produced with vernacular Jersey phonology in childhood – retained the segmental phonology along with the rhyme, rhythm, and intonation. This, then, may well be a genre issue.

Soapbox and *Narrative* are both defined in terms of genre. I would argue that how casual the speech is when one is "on a soapbox" depends on what the speaker is getting on a soapbox about. An African American sixth grader who is participating in my current ethnographic study recently got on a very vernacular soapbox about racism in the classroom. In this case, I would say that her use of vernacular could be explained by a number of things, such as being "in your face" in relation to the non-African-American people in her audience (consisting of a number of her classmates), the association of AAVE with other (African American) situations in which she has witnessed soapboxing about racism, the establishment of authority with respect to the experience of racism, etc. etc. It is possible that the reason that narratives elicit more vernacular in Labov's interviews than soapboxing lies in the purpose and/or the content characteristic of the two genres. Narratives are frequently reminiscences that bring back a way of speaking associated with the situation about which the narrative is told. Viewed less passively, one might consider that a competently told narrative is done in a dialect appropriate to the situations portrayed in the narrative itself. In that case, the elicitation of vernacular in narrative and in talking about childhood and kids' games may be due to an overarching category like *reminiscence*.

Finally, *Group* speech is defined in terms of audience, but of course, the differences between a group conversation and an interview span the entire gamut of factors as the participants take control of topics, and as the nature of the interaction will determine a quite different use of such things as genre and point of view.

The reason I belabor these interactions is that if the subevents are to occupy a privileged analytical position without a solid basis for their relation to the production of standard and vernacular, we run the risk of circularity. For example, taking the decision tree as given leads to one kind of explanation of the speech of the adolescents who show negative style-shifting. We may believe that they have yet to learn the stylistic significance of the variables, or that they are flouting community norms in keeping with some kind of adolescent countercultural orientation. But who would flout norms by actually doing a stylistic flipflop? I would expect speakers who refuse to follow the norm to show no style-shifting at all. However, we might wonder if the stylistic tree, based as it is on assumptions about adult participation in interviews, simply doesn't work for younger people as well as it does for older ones. For example, talking about childhood games changes in significance as one gets older. Talking about childhood games could make an adolescent – particularly an early adolescent – very self-conscious, since this age group is at pains to separate itself from childhood. And kids may feel less certain of an unfamiliar adult interviewer's reception of their narratives, causing them to be less relaxed in their speech. In this case, then, I would say that the subevents need to be considered carefully in the light of the interviewed population.

Meanwhile, it is also possible that the difference in the degree and nature of the differentiation from variable to variable is an indication that each variable has different social–stylistic meaning that may be related to specific subevents. I would argue, for example, that the difference between -ING, DH and negative concord stems from quite different meanings. -ING is not stigmatized in itself, but is associated with formality and informality (which in itself may have different interpretations depending on the more general style in which they emerge). Negative concord, on the other hand, appears to be, in some circles, one of those variants for which, as Rickford mentions in this volume, one use is enough to stigmatize the speaker. It is associated with class, and toughness perhaps, but also quite specifically with lack of education. Fortition of (*th*) and (*dh*) has been found to be an ethnic as well as a class marker. This appears to be widespread in US urban areas as emphatic and connoting toughness, and its urban character most likely derives from its association with European immigrant groups. Fortition of (*th*) and (*dh*) has been found in New York (Labov 1966), Detroit, Northern California (Mendoza-Denton 1997), and Chicago (based on work done by my students at the University of Illinois at Chicago in 1986) to be used most by members of large local immigrant communities. In this case, it is quite probable that the substrate effect of Italian (in the case of New York and Chicago), Polish (in the case of Detroit), and Spanish (Northern California) introduced the fortis variants of these variables into the community, to be picked up and deployed by the native English speaking generations as markers of ethnic/class identity. In my own experience with New Jersey dialect, (*dh*) fortition signals "toughness," but the reduction of -ing signals informality or "homeyness" unless it co-occurs with other variables that signal toughness. This brings me to the relation between the variables we study and broader styles, and consideration of these broader styles raises the issue of the consciousness of style.

In the present paper, Labov opposes attention paid to speech to the "ethnographic," or what one might refer to as socially meaningful motives for style-shifting. While he mentions only audience design as such a motive, one could expand the list to include other aspects of style discussed in the other papers in this volume, such as genre, topic, audience, and persona management. He acknowledges that both kinds of motive are at work, and that separating their effects will be a major undertaking. It is important to point out, though, that attention paid to speech is related to socially meaningful motivations in heterogeneous ways: certain genres may tend to occur in situations that afford greater or lesser attention to one's performance, certain topics may remind people of how they are speaking, different interlocutors may make speakers nervous about their self-presentation, and so forth. But it is not clear how the issue of attention to speech will ever be separated from other issues – there is nothing to demonstrate that the emergence of the vernacular in a particular speech activity is due to lack of attention, and not other aspects of the activity. Indeed, audio-monitoring is likely to decrease when we're having fun being ourselves, when we take control of the discourse and talk about the things we care about, etc. But I don't think it's clear that it's the lack of monitoring or the act of being ourselves that is the most salient in our production of vernacular variants. More likely, it is both and a number of other things as well.

This is not to say that I disbelieve Labov's contention that decreased attention to speech will bring out vernacular variants. To date I have found only one variable in my own data in which emphasis favors the use of an innovative variant, and this is a variant that is a reaction to the primary, vernacular, direction of change (Eckert 1987). On the contrary, both secondary stress and de-emphasis of primary stressed syllables usually favor the use of vernacular variants. However, I do have many examples of vernacular variants being used quite consciously and emphatically, where speakers appear to step outside of their normal range of variation to express some kind of social meaning. (I will return to this issue below.) One key question I wish to address is the relation between the more and the less intentional uses of variables. And this is related to the issue of social meaning. While Labov prefers to abstract away from issues of social meaning in the interests of empiricism, the usefulness of the mechanical application of the decision tree to interview data ultimately depends on the predictability of the kinds of social meanings that get caught up in the subevents, and on the relation between the events within the interview and events that are embedded in everyday situations in which meaning gets made.

Let me begin with my own definition of linguistic style, as a clustering of linguistic resources, and an association of that clustering with social meaning. My major current preoccupation is with the kind of style discussed by Irvine and Coupland in this volume (chapters 1 and 11) – the stylistic construction of a self. A Stanford group, which called itself the California Style Collective (1993), assembled several years ago to examine the role of variation in what one might call "personal" or "group" style. Group style is the basis upon which people identify others as members of such categories as "Valley Girl" or "New York Jew" or, at a more local level, "burnout" or "hard rock." Such public naming of styles is a process of stereotyping – a reification of the named group as sufficiently constituting community to develop a joint style, and as sufficiently salient to public life to name and learn to recognize. These reifications then turn around and serve as resources for other styles – for those who may want to incorporate in their own style a bit of what they see as attractive, interesting, or striking about New York Jews or Valley Girls. In this way, group style stands at a level of sociolinguistic practice that allows us to examine the production and reproduction of social meaning in variation. But named styles are not the only resources – we are surrounded by stylistic material, and as long as we can position ourselves in relation to the sources of that material, and attribute meaning to it, we can use it.

The unanswered question, though, is how social meaning gets constructed in linguistic variation, which we are used to thinking of as a fairly low-level phenomenon, not amenable to the kind of conscious manipulation implied by a process of bricolage. One place to look for part of the explanation is among the emphatic uses of variables. This brings me to Bauman's discussion in this volume (chapter 3) of the importance of poetics in the study of style, and to his observation that poetics and performance bring the use of resources into the reflexive arena. Clearly certain genres such as the market calls discussed in Bauman's paper, function to highlight the relation between speech style and persona. The performances of the Okracoke "brogue" that Natalie Schilling-Estes (1998) has discussed constitute another such genre. I would agree, also, that not only do certain genres provide stages for the production of meaning, but certain individuals do as well. I will briefly present two examples.

(1) THE BURNED-OUT BURNOUTS. In my recent work (Eckert 2000) on variation and adolescent social categories in a Detroit suburban high school, I focused on two opposed categories, the *jocks*, an institutionally based corporate middle class culture, and the *burnouts*, a locally based working class culture. With strongly opposed practices and ideologies, the jocks and the burnouts develop their opposition through an elaborate stylistic complex that involves clothing, makeup, hair style, jewelry and other adornment, use and display of substances, territory, demeanor, body hexus, and so on and on – and, of course, language. The systematic differentiation of vocalic variables across the board results in quite distinct ways of speaking that embody both gender and class-based social categories. These variables, in turn, go with very different voice qualities, patterns of intonation, lexicon, and so on, and it is this combination that constitutes clearly distinct jock and burnout styles. The burnouts, an urban-oriented, working class culture, appropriate urban symbols of all kinds in their clothing style, and lead their age cohort in the use of urban linguistic variables. The jocks, an institutionally oriented, college-bound culture, lag in the use of urban variables, and lead in the use of what I will call suburban variables, which amount to reversals of urban variables. While the jocks tend to be fairly homogeneous in their use of language, the burnouts, particularly the burnout girls, show a considerable range of use of variables. This range corresponds to an important social division among the burnout girls between what are called the "regular" burnouts and the "burned-out burnouts" – two network clusters of girls who are quite different from each other, and who do not socialize with each other. The regular burnouts are a neighborhood-based crowd, whose identities as burnouts have to do with

Table 7.1. *Correlation of the raising of (ay) with combined sex and social category, separating two clusters of burnout girls.*

Input = .008	Female jocks	Male jocks	Main female burnouts	Burned-out burnouts	Male burnouts
Sig = .000	.248	.328	.357	.906	.664

such things as friendship loyalty, working class values, and opposition to the corporate culture of the school. The burned-out burnouts, on the other hand, became friends in junior high school and in the first year of high school, attracted to each other because of their "wildness." They consider themselves to be the "biggest burnouts" in the school, and they display the most extreme burnout style in dress and demeanor, looking upon the other burnouts as "a bunch of jocks." The burned-out burnout girls are in some sense local icons, defining for the entire community the quintessential burnout. As shown in table 7.1, their use of phonological variables is iconic as well. The vocalic variable that carries the clearest urban meaning in this community is the extreme raising and backing of the nucleus of (ay) (see Eckert 1996, 2000 for details). As shown in table 7.1, the burned-out burnout girls lead the entire cohort in the use of this variable, not just by a little but by a mile. This is typical of other variables as well, so that one might say that the burned-out burnout girls' very extreme speech, paired with their extreme behavior, is what defines the meanings of the style that lead to the more general correlations between vocalic variables and social category affiliation.

(2) TRUDY AND THE HOME GIRLS. In my current fieldwork with pre-adolescents in Northern California, I have been able to watch stylistic icons emerge. Sixth grade in US schools witnesses the emergence of a heterosexual marketplace in the age cohort. Kids come to see themselves as products on a market, and in the process of packaging themselves for this market they come to engage in the construction of style. There are clear leaders in the construction of style, and in this particular school, there is a primarily Latino crowd who dominate the center of the local heterosexual scene. At some point in sixth grade, the girls in this crowd dubbed themselves the "home girls." One day, as they were sitting on the edge of the area where the cool Latino boys were playing with a hackey sack, they began talking among themselves about how disappointing sixth grade was because there weren't any cute boys. They then moved on to a discussion of which boys in their class were cute, and then moved into taunting the boys, calling out individual boys' names, either in connection with girls' names or with

comments about the boy's looks. With each move, the girls called out in unison with a falsetto "woooo." The boys, unsure of what the girls were saying among themselves, began to shout back, telling them to shut up and flinging insults. Culminating the event, one of the girls, Trudy, stood up, stuck her butt out towards the boys and shouted, "Johnny, you give me a pain – you can kiss my ass, Johnny." The girls fell apart laughing, and the boys turned their attention elsewhere. The role that Trudy played in this interaction is typical of her general behavior in public – one could say that she herself is a stylistic icon. She represents the extreme in "home girl" style for this cohort: she engages energetically in the construction of a rebellious, carefree, gang-oriented persona, wearing baggy clothes, acting tough, throwing gang signs, kissing boys in the classroom, etc.

The combination of Trudy's actions with the actual nature of the genre that she and her friends are performing highlights, among other things, particular linguistic variants. For example, in Northern California in general, the variable (ae) is raised before nasals. In contrast with this Anglo pattern, this vowel tends not to be raised in Chicano English. In their calling out of cute boys' names, the name that comes to the fore is *Sam*. Several times, the girls call out "Sam" in unison, with a very prolonged and low realization of [ae]. I am not saying that they selected Sam because of the opportunity to use his name as a vehicle for the foregrounding of Chicano phonology, but that the coincidence of the possibility for this Chicano pronunciation and the cultural event provides an opportunity for the foregrounded co-construction of style and meaning.

It is this foregrounding that allows for a relatively conscious meaning-making process for sociolinguistic variables. Anything that Trudy does will have highlighted meaning because of her position in the age cohort as a cultural icon, and indeed as a cultural icon she also tends to participate in more of these iconic events than others. As a particular kind of public figure, she is in a position to make meaning for the rest of the community.

It is patterns like this that make me think that stylistic work is among the most important of all human endeavors: style is not just the product of the construction of social meaning, or even the locus of the construction of social meaning; it is what makes the negotiation of such meaning possible. And if we are going to call upon socially meaningful events to enable us to collect stylistically variable data in interviews, we do need to attend to this meaning.

8   Zeroing in on multifunctionality and style

Elizabeth Closs Traugott

1   Introduction

To a historical linguist like myself who works on grammaticalization and discourse analysis, William Labov's work has for several decades held out the prospect of developing a framework for a theory of language change that can illuminate the fundamental problems of conceptualizing and operationalizing differences between innovation and spread, whether within the linguistic system or within the community, and between structure and use (see especially the groundbreaking work in Weinreich, Labov, and Herzog 1968 and Labov 1974).[1] That only very little work has been done combining the insights of grammaticalization and sociolinguistics is regrettable. However, the projected volume 3 of Labov's *Principles of Linguistic Change* promises to address grammaticalization issues, while Bruyn (1995) and Baker and Syea (1996) directly take on the issues of the extent to which grammaticalization theory and the sociolinguistics of contact languages can inform each other.

Grammaticalization theory (see e.g. Heine and Reh 1984, Heine, Claudi, and Hünnemeyer 1991, Traugott and Heine 1991, Hopper and Traugott 1993, Pagliuca 1994, Lehmann 1995[1982]) has in the main not been directly concerned with "pure" phonological or semantic change (in so far as these exist, e.g. the Great Vowel Shift or recent changes in the meaning of *gay*). Like much "mainstream" historical linguistics (e.g. Lightfoot 1991, Roberts 1992/93), it privileges change in the individual over change in the community, and thus has not focused on social factors. But unlike much mainstream linguistics it focuses on the intersection of "internal" grammar (structure) and "external" grammar (use), and insists on gradience and process rather than

---

[1] Thanks to Scott Schwenter for discussing many of the issues with me, especially concerning discourse markers. Some of the views on grammaticalization and sociolinguistics were developed in a workshop given by Scott Schwenter and myself on the interface between the two theories at NWAV, Stanford University, October 1994; those on multifunctionality of adverbs and possible implications for style at a panel on "Embodied cognition or situated cognition? The testimony of oral languages," XVIth International Congress of Linguistics, Paris, July 1997.

product. The focus on the individual could have relevance for the study of intra-speaker variation that Labov calls for in his paper.

A theory of grammaticalization can provide a link between historical linguistics and sociolinguistics since it is speaker-oriented and concerned with speaker–hearer interaction. It uses tools from discourse analysis to uncover the pragmatic processes of inviting inferences and creative language use that push linguistic structures beyond the boundaries of their previous uses. The phenomenon of grammaticalization arises as speakers insert and shape external material within the internal grammar; it is the "harnessing of pragmatics" by language users. Grammaticalization theorists have a mainly "message-oriented" view of speech functions. Although changes occurring in one segment of the community can be consciously suppressed in others, as well as singled out in normative usage handbooks, the possibility of using a grammaticalizing construction for the marking of social identity has not been the subject of much research to date (see, however, Rickford 1992).

The crucial data for grammaticalization theory is evidence of the tendency over time (often several centuries) for open class items to develop variants that become closed class items. A standard example is the split starting in the later fifteenth century of motion verb *be going to* into the motion verb construction, as in *I am going (to Copenhagen) to give a lecture* and the "planned future" quasi-auxiliary, as in *I am going to like this!* (only the latter can be reduced to *gonna*) (see e.g. Bybee and Pagliuca 1987, Pérez 1990, Hopper and Traugott 1993: chapters 3 and 4). Alternatively put, the crucial data is evidence for a shift from lexical to functional category. In this research enterprise little, if any, attention is paid to how the resulting variation is used in style-shifting. On the other hand, the crucial data for Labov's study of style is morphological and phonological, material that, from the point of view of grammaticalization, is at the end or close to the end of the process.

Are there some areas of overlapping interest that might lead to fruitful results in future work on style-shifting? Two possibilities are touched on in Labov's paper, both pertaining to the issue of open versus closed class items. One is what the significance might be of Prince's (1987) findings with regard to Sarah Gorby's Yiddish. The other is whether there may be stylistic features other than those currently under investigation that would help distinguish among the styles already identified, especially the more careful ones.

2   Prince's findings: open- versus closed-class items

Prince's finding is that "the most-consciously aimed-at target is reached more successfully in open-class items, the items to which speakers are better able to attend" (than to closed-class items) (Prince 1987:110). Labov is particularly interested in this finding since it confirms his hypothesis that the axis of attention paid to speech is significant, even though the particulars are inconsistent with his finding that: "Maximal style-shifting is characteristically found in alternation of allophones and morphological stems" (this volume, p. 86). A significant difference between open- and closed-class items seems intuitively correct given what we know about tendencies in contact languages for lexical items to be derived more regularly than function words from the superstrate. It also seems generally correct when we think of grammaticalization as: "le passage d'un mot autonome au role d'élément grammatical . . . l'attribution du caractère grammatical à un mot jadis autonome"[2] (Meillet 1958[1912]:131), or, in more contemporary terms, of: "the process whereby lexical material in highly constrained pragmatic and morphosyntactic contexts becomes grammatical" (Traugott, in press). In keeping with the focus in grammaticalization theory on gradience and on clines and their functions (e.g. case, tense/aspect/mood), we may additionally ask whether a consideration of degrees of "openness" and "closedness" and of the functions of the closed classes might not lead to some potentials for the study of style.

For starters, we may note that Prince's closed-class items are selected by the criterion of being monosyllables or having monosyllabic stems (Prince 1987:114, note 14). They are therefore not yet grammatical items in the sense of being morphological affixes like -ing, or negative agreement, but rather independent words or clitics. Examples she cites are:

(1)   1. /u~I/: tsu "to," un "and," plutsem "suddenly"
        2. /o~U/: dos "the," do "here," tomed "always"
        3. /a~O/: ale "all," avade "of course," same "very"
        4. /ay~A/: mayn "my," dervayle "meanwhile," aykh "you" (Prince 1987:106)

Since these are examples only, it is difficult to assess whether there are significant differences according to grammatical function. But this may be the case (note that *of course* is an inter-personal or perhaps totally subjective marker of attitude, whereas *to* is not), and indeed some of the variation that is attributed to individual factors might be correlated with function. This is of course also a possibility with the DH variable which Labov cites: the voiced fricative /ð/ might have different effects from other fricatives and affricates considering its status not only as a stem, but also as an almost unique signal of definiteness and deixis.

A particular point of interest in Prince's examples is the fact that they include deictics (*do* "here," *mayn* "my," *aykh* "you"), intensifiers (*same* "very"), and what appears to be an epistemic evidential marker concerning

---

[2] "The passage of an autonomous word into the role of grammatical element . . . the attribution of grammatical character to a formerly autonomous word."

expectation (*avade* "of course"). Such items are subjective in so far as they encode speaker-based person and place reference, evaluations of degree, and epistemic values in terms of expectations. Prince suggests that particular variables may have more social value than others; she notes that Sarah Gorby "really wants to maintain /O/" (Prince 1987:109); this /O/ is precisely the variable illustrated by *avade* "of course," *same* "very" (and also *ale* "all"). It would be interesting to know whether this is a coincidence or not.

Although it is useful, at least as a starting point, to attempt to unify phenomena under a single dimension, as Labov says, it is also important to take a finely articulated view at more local levels, and to differentiate not only forms but functions. We may be obscuring important factors both for a theory of language change and for a theory of style when we treat linguistic categories as essentially the same. For example, we tend to treat *-ing*, present tense, past tense markers, multiple negation, etc., as functionally equal in the linguistic system, and then ask whether they have different socially symbolic or stylistic functions for speakers, rather than asking whether they have linguistically different functions because they do different grammatical work, and how that grammatical work interacts with socially symbolic or stylistic functions. Equally, in studies of grammaticalization we may try to shoe-horn the development of auxiliaries, case, discourse markers, etc., into one unidimensional model (autonomous item > bound item), and if historically a change does not fit the pattern, we say it is not grammaticalization, rather than asking ourselves whether developments that give rise to elements of grammar with different grammatical functions might not be expected to behave in different ways.

Lavandera (1978) suggested that there are problems with treating phonology and morphosyntax in the same way in variation studies because morphosyntactic elements involve meaning, in other words they have different linguistic design features. Similarly, I suggest we should not look at morphosyntax as a unidimensional thing – case is a design feature for event structure, auxiliaries for temporality, connectives for clause-combining, and discourse markers for metatextual[3] commentary on the discourse itself. Style can and should be related to different linguistic functions as well as to the different purposes of speakers using them. This may be more obvious to practitioners of linguistics in European traditions than to those in American traditions; for example, British linguistics takes as basic the Hallidayan distinctions between ideational, textual, and inter-personal functions of language, and recent work inspired by Bakhtin focuses on

---

[3] The term "metatextual," apparently first introduced into discourse analysis by Dancygier (1992), is more accurate than "metalinguistic," for reference to markers of attitude to the text being produced; "metalinguistic" can then be reserved for its original meaning: commentary on the form of linguistic expression, e.g. I said "rite," not "ripe" (see Horn 1985).

polyphony and "ventriloquism" (see especially Coupland's chapter of this volume). One further distinction that I propose we pay attention to is between inter-personal (*you and I*) and personal (*I*) functions.

It is standard in sociolinguistic theory to distinguish between the functions of the -*s* variable in English because they are semantically distinct (possessive, nominal plural, third person singular agreement on the verb), but less so to distinguish among functions of items like *anyway*, *actually*, or other words that belong to semi-closed classes and serve partially semantic and partially pragmatic functions. The basic observation is that many items can function in at least three different ways.[4] Sweetser (1990) has called attention to three different cognitive "worlds," the sociophysical, the epistemic, and the speech act worlds, and has suggested that the relationship among them is metaphorical, and also historical (her examples include modal verbs and connectives like *and, because*). Traugott (1995) has argued that many members of the class of "deictic discourse markers" (Schiffrin 1990), particularly the adverbs *anyway, besides, actually, in fact, indeed*, have historically developed from VP adverbs (where they serve as adverbs of manner and respect answering "in respect to what?") to sentential adverbs with epistemic function to discourse markers with metatextual function (see also Powell 1992). My original purposes were to show that the processes of change arose out of invited inferences in the on-line processing of utterances, i.e. were metonymic rather than metaphorical in nature (the apparent metaphorical motivation is a function of the result of change, not its process), and to suggest that although they become disjuncts syntactically, and therefore violate expectations of "discourse > syntax," "loose structure > tight structure" (cf. Givón 1979, Lehmann 1995[1982]) they are nevertheless cases of grammaticalization (see also Brinton 1996 for a similar point). I will not repeat these arguments here, but rather focus on the phenomenon of multifunctionality and why it might be important for the study of style.

3   Four examples of multifunctionality in semi-closed-class items

3.1   *Obviously*

First, some examples from writing. In a study of journalistic discourse, Lipari shows how, though "journalists are presumed to have no word, no voice, no conceptual system" (Lipari 1996:831) reporters do in fact use

---

[4] The syntactic and semantic multifunctionality of adverbs has been widely discussed in a variety of semantic and pragmatic traditions. Among particularly influential works are Greenbaum (1969), Jackendoff (1972), Ducrot (1980), Ernst (1984), Blakemore (1987), Schiffrin (1987), Fraser (1988), Blass (1990).

highly subjective linguistic markers, e.g. *obviously*. This analysis was made possible only because of the distinctions she draws between three modes of meaning:[5]

(A)   the manner adverb or empirical mode:
>   (2)   *Obviously* moved by the cheering Harlem crowd . . . Mandela thrust his right fist skyward. (UPI 6/22/90)

Here *obviously* marks the reporter's empirical, objective observation manifest to the reader.

(B)   the epistemic, inferential mode:
>   (3)   For President Bush, the stunning putdown of Saddam Hussein is *obviously* good political news. (UPI 3/3/91)

This *obviously* marks the reporter's conclusion; one that is presumably widely shared by the potential audience, and is therefore inter-personal.

(C)   the metatextual (Lipari calls it "metalinguistic") mode, functions to reorient the interpretation and information flow, particularly to smooth over a tenuous link between observed "fact" and reporter inference, and is primarily personal:
>   (4)   In his remarks, Bush, *obviously* taking a shot at Buchanan, said: "From some quarters, we hear the dim voice of defeatism, that tin trumpet sounding retreat." (UPI 2/19/92)

3.2   In fact

Likewise *in fact* has three senses (the data this time are from academic writing):

(A)   a verb phrase adverbial meaning answering the question "with respect to what":
>   (5)   Humanity, comfortably engaged elsewhere in the business of living, is absent *in fact* but everywhere present in feeling. (UA, May 1997)

Here *in fact* contrasts with *in feeling*.

(B)   an adversative epistemic sentential adverb:
>   (6)   Yet apart from some syntactic correlates of thematic roles, there is *in fact* a notable absence of consensus about what thematic roles are. (Dowty, p. 547)

This is dialogic both with other points of view expounded in the article, and with views that the author anticipates the reader will hold, i.e., it is inter-personal.

---

[5] Data in this paper are drawn from Boxer 1993, Dowty 1991, United Airlines, Hemisphere Magazine (UA), United Press International, Top Stories (UPI).

(C)   a discourse marker, confirming and specifying what preceded:
>   (7) But all is not negative for Bush and, *in fact*, there are signs that much of the public is willing to let the president back away from his 1988 vow. (UPI 6/26/90)

3.3   *Actually*

Similarly, we find at least three main meanings of *actually* in written data:

(A)   Concessive (favors right margin position):
>   (8) Trump himself seemed exhilarated by the marathon negotiations that preceded the bridge loan agreement.
>   "I enjoyed it, *actually*," said Trump, author of 'The Art of the Deal'." (UPI 6/27/90)

(B)   adversative, epistemic:
>   (9) [concerning military cutbacks in selected states] A council researcher said Hawaii and Idaho might *actually* benefit from the proposed changes, due to expected increases in military personnel or support services in the two states. (UPI 6/30/90)

(C)   discourse marker, signaling reformulation:
>   (10)   a. The British have the Tornado fighter and bomber in Saudi Arabia, and the Saudis fly US-built F-15s and the Tornado. And the F-117A stealth fighter, *actually* a bomber, was a likely participant in the raids. (UPI 1/17/91)
>   b. In the middle of the complaint I started to worry that maybe I shouldn't be saying anything. And *actually* I said to myself, "boy, I sound like a complainer." You know, when a person complains a lot, that bothers me. When I'm down I tend to complain more. But I said, "I'm really tired of working with these people." *Actually* I even embellished the complaint. (Boxer, p. 123; this is an interview transcript)

That these distinctions underestimate the range of possibilities is highlighted by Aijmer's (1986) study of uses of *actually* in the London–Lund and Lancaster–Oslo–Bergen corpora, in which she identifies ten syntactic positions, and a meaning which she characterizes as creating "contact with the listener" or "rapport", e.g. "I am telling you this in confidence" (Aijmer 1986:128). I have not found evidence of this use of *actually* in written data.

3.4   *Anyway*

My last example is *anyway*, this time from spoken language. This has been the subject of detailed sociolinguistic investigation of multifunctionality (though not for style reasons) in sociolinguistic interviews in Texas from

1992–95 by Ferrara (1997). She too distinguishes three types, according to syntactic position, and especially intonation contour:

(A)   additive *anyway*, semantically equivalent to *besides*:
>   (11) We didn't rent the apartment because it was too expensive. It was in a bad location *anyway*. (Ferrara 1997:347)

(B)   dismissive *anyway*, semantically equivalent to *nonetheless*:
>   (12) It was ugly but he wanted to buy the dog *anyway*. (Ferrara 1997: 348)

(C)   Resumptive *anyway*, "a discourse marker that reconnects utterances to chunks of discourse" (in other words, a topic-resumption marker):
>   (13) He drove to the dealership. He'd always wanted a Jag. I think I heard a noise. *Anyway*, he decided to buy one. (Ibid.)

Ferrara shows that these three *anyways* are distinct not only in syntax and intonational contour, but also in frequency: 4 percent of the tokens of *anyway* are additive, 7 percent are dismissive, and 89 percent are resumptive.

4   Implications of the examples

None of the polysemies above has been investigated in depth for evidence of whether one or other is used as a style marker.[6] It may be noted, however, that in their manner or respect function, these items are often thought to belong to relatively open classes (a VP adverb is a member of the set of all possible manner adverbs, and this in turn is a member of all the larger classes of adverbs that may occur in clause-final position in English, including temporal and spatial adverbs). In their concessive and epistemic uses, however, they belong to a smaller class, that of sentential adverbials like *probably* and *possibly*. And in their discourse marker use, they belong to a different set again, broadly speaking that of *well* (in its hedging function) (see Fraser 1988 for a typology). Therefore if Prince's findings regarding Sarah Gorby are to be generalized, degree of open- or closed-classedness may be worth attending to. I submit that we may not be able to answer the question whether *obviously*, *in fact*, or *anyway* are or are not style markers in one or more of their functions without paying attention to functional differences. Simply counting tokens of the word is not enough.

One possibility to explore is that strategic uses of discourse markers may signal a style-shift. In this case, the presence of a single marker may be what is significant. For example, it appears that the single token of *anyway* in line

---

[6] Aijmer (1986:129) does, however, point to differences between speech and writing in the use of *actually*; she says end-position is restricted to speech, whereas "[m]edial *actually* is associated with writing and with the function as a clause-emphasizer."

12 of Coupland's data has not only the function of topic management (it is used as a resumptive discourse marker), but also a style-shift back to the style used in connection with the topic. On the other hand, epistemic sentential uses may be characteristic of particular styles, but the first occurrence may not signal a shift; only the frequency with which they are used will do so. In this case, the pattern may be more important than the single instance.

For example, in narrative interview data collected in the 1970s in Ayr, Southwest Scotland, Macaulay (1995) finds that there is a marked difference in the use of *-ly* adverbs between middle class and lower class speakers, and has suggested that the differences may reflect an "authoritative" stance adopted by middle class speakers. He lists *obviously* along with *actually*, *certainly*, *possibly*, *probably* among evidential sentence adverbs that are used significantly more frequently by middle class speakers. For style, it would be important to know which of the several meanings of *obviously* were used twenty times by middle class speakers, which two times by lower class speakers, or which of the meanings of *actually* are among the fifty-two uses by middle class speakers as against only five used by lower class speakers (Macaulay 1995:44).[7]

Again, according to Biber and Finegan (1988:31) the use of modal stance adverbs expressing strong epistemic commitment to a position, e.g. *in fact*, *actually*, is primarily associated with spoken languages or writing that is inter-personal in orientation (editorials, essays, telephone conversations, spontaneous speeches). Press reports, and academic prose (and surprisingly, general fiction) are, by contrast, said to disfavor such adverbs and to be "faceless." However, they also note that: "more formal, more 'literate' situations typically exhibit a more frequent use of explicit and elaborated variants, and less formal, more 'oral' situations exhibit a more frequent use of economy variants" (Finegan and Biber 1994:317).[8] One wonders whether in the discussions of press and academic writing a failure to distinguish the different functions of the adverbs in question has not been reinforced by a failure to note how subjective many objective-seeming adverbs like *actually*, *in fact*, *obviously*, are. *Obviously* in its discourse marker use is "masquerading as evidence" (Lipari 1996:832). Writing is not autonomous, but the reader can of course only partially co-construct the argument. So the reader can easily be misled by the insistent epistemic certitudes of the

---

[7] Thanks to Ronald Macaulay for bringing this paper to my attention at the conference.

[8] See also Chafe on the tendency to make many more distinctions in writing than in speech: "academic writing, especially, is sprinkled with words like *basically*, *by definition*, *essentially*, *exactly*, *generally*, *in some sense*, *invariably*, *literally*, *normally*, *particularly*, *primarily*, *specifically*, and *virtually* . . . In other words, writers are prone to worry about HOW true something is" (1986: 165).

author. So too can the analyst, including the linguist, who is, after all (at least in the role of academic), a member of the middle class and therefore likely, if Macaulay's findings can be generalized, to automatically adopt an authoritative stance.

It is precisely these kinds of fine-grained distinctions that might lead to insights into the "Careful" styles that Labov rightly suggests deserve more articulation. I note that the "Soapbox" style excerpt he cites is characterized by a remarkable number of epistemic modal markers, whether parentheticals like *I think* (see Thompson and Mulac 1991), conditionals (*if you dispel... If I did this...*), and the counterfactual modal *would*. The speaker refers to objective *reason* and *fact*, but these have to do with his own subjective opinions about what is a good thing, why he doesn't care for football, etc., rather than with any sociophysical or even inter-personally verifiable entities. Greater attention to the kinds of open and semi-closed-class items discussed in these comments might help identify Soapbox style.

5   Conclusion

In conclusion, an elaborated theory of style would benefit from attention not only to phonological and morphological variables, but also to lexical items, whether in open classes or semi-closed classes.[9] It would also benefit from fine-grained consideration of linguistic cues correlated not only with degree of attention to speech, but also, as Bell suggests, to design. Beyond audience design, which focuses on the addressee (*you*), and referee design (*they, we*), there is also the subjective attitude to discourse task (*I*) to consider. This is metatextual, what might be called "self-design," though often only covertly so, much of the time.

[9] I am using the term "lexical item" broadly here. The discourse marker function, being more frequent, and involving relatively greater class-closedness, suggests these are strictly speaking grammatical items (Traugott 1995, Brinton 1996). Note also that the manner and concessive meanings are conceptual and semantic, whereas the discourse marker meanings are primarily procedural and pragmatic (Blakemore 1987).

Part 3

Audience design and self-identification

9 Back in style: reworking audience design[1]

Allan Bell

1 Introduction

I take the sociolinguist's core question about language style to be this:

Why did *this speaker* say it *this way* on *this occasion*?

There are three points to be made about such a catchline: first, the sociolinguist's ultimate interest in examining style is the *why* question – a search for explanations. The search for explanation presupposes a search for – and the existence of – regularities, of patterns. Secondly, the question implies an alternative, a choice – a "*that* way" which could have been chosen instead of a "this way." It locates linguistic style in language difference (see Irvine, this volume). Thirdly, the context of style is a *speaker* – a first person, an I, an ego, an identity or identities – together with the *situation* she or he is in – however we may believe that situation subsists or is defined, either theoretically or specifically.

The audience design framework (Bell 1984) had its genesis twenty-something years ago when I looked for an explanation for the style-shift I was finding in my doctoral research on the language of radio news in Auckland, New Zealand (Bell 1977). As so often, serendipity played its part in what I was able to find: I turned up an unexpected situation which proved to be tailored to describing and explaining a particular style-shift. The organization of New Zealand public broadcasting[2] meant that two of the radio

[1] This chapter represents my thinking at the time of the workshop where it was presented (1996). I acknowledge the support of the New Zealand Foundation for Research, Science and Technology in funding this study as part of the New Zealand English Programme in the Department of Linguistics, Victoria University of Wellington. I am grateful to the Department for its hospitality over several years. I appreciate the work of Gary Johnson in undertaking and writing up the analyses presented here, and in contributing to the project as a whole (e.g. Bell and Johnson 1997). I also acknowledge the contribution of Nikolas Coupland (e.g. 1996, chapter 11 of this volume) to my thinking about style. Lastly, I wish to recognize John Rickford for putting style back on the agenda of North American sociolinguistics, for applying audience design (Rickford and McNair-Knox 1994), and for encouraging me back into style after I had been some years away.
[2] This structure has only been demolished in the late 1990s with the sale of Radio New Zealand's commercial stations (such as ZB) into private (foreign) ownership. National Radio remains as a network funded by the levied "broadcasting fee."

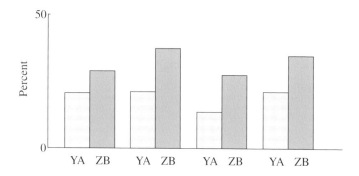

Figure 9.1 Percentage of intervocalic /t/ voicing by four newsreaders on two New Zealand radio stations, YA and ZB (from Bell 1984)

stations I was recording originated in the same suite of studios, with the same individual newsreaders heard on both radio networks. It was in effect a natural matched guise situation (Lambert 1967). Station YA was New Zealand's "National Radio," which has a higher status audience than the local community station ZB (see Bell 1991 for detail).

I examined a number of phonological and syntactic variables, including intervocalic /t/ voicing. In NZ English, intervocalic /t/ can be realized as an alveolar voiced flap or stop instead of as a voiceless stop, making words such as *writer* and *better* sound like *rider* and *bedder*. In American English this rule is semi-categorical, but in New Zealand it is a genuinely variable rule. Figure 9.1 shows the percentage of intervocalic /t/ voicing for four newsreaders I recorded on both these stations.

The newsreaders shifted on average 20 percent in each linguistic environment between stations YA and ZB. Single newsreaders heard on two different stations showed a consistent ability to make considerable style-shifts to suit the audience. These switches between stations were at times made in a very short space of time. At off-peak hours a single newsreader might alternate between YA and ZB news with as little as ten minutes between bulletins on the different stations.

Why then the shifts? There is after all just one individual speaker producing two divergent styles. The institution is the same in both cases. The topic mix of the news is similar (in some cases, even the same scripted news items are read out on both stations). The studio setting is identical. And there is no reason to suppose that the amount of attention paid to speech is being systematically varied. Of all the factors we might suggest as possible influences on these shifts in news language style, only the audience correlated with the shifts evident here.

Looking beyond my study, I began to see that the same regularities which were writ large in my own media-originated data were operating in face-to-face communication. Later I discovered that outside sociolinguistics this idea was not quite new, when in the closing stages of the doctoral work I encountered speech accommodation theory (Giles and Powesland 1975) and benefited from the insights Howard Giles had recently been drawing about style from a social psychological perspective. Later I came to call my approach "audience design." The label was of course not new either – it derived from Sacks, Schegloff, and Jefferson's "recipient design" (1974) by way of Clark (e.g. Clark and Carlson 1982).

2   The gist of audience design

I will summarize what I take to be the main points of the audience design framework – I have until now deliberately tended to avoid both "model" and "theory" as labels, but perhaps we are now far enough forward that these terms are less of an exaggeration than they would have been a decade ago. By and large, I summarize what was in the original published exposition of audience design (Bell 1984), with some minor updating and citing of supporting evidence gathered since the paper appeared. At this stage I will not critique the framework, but will flag the points to which I will return for later reworking.[3]

Rereading my own paper again, I was, like Rickford and McNair-Knox (1994:241), struck by the "bold hypotheses and predictions" it puts forward. Some of these were consciously stretching the boundaries at the time, and some seem to me now to be questionable. However, over a dozen years down the track, I find myself still in substantial agreement with what I wrote then – with one main exception, which I shall return to below. Certainly I think that the interest the paper generated derives in large measure from its attempt to generalize and hypothesize – to draw conclusions across a wealth of data which might remain valid when tested against much more data. In short, from its attempt to do sociolinguistic theory. The gist of audience design can be summarized in the following points.

1:   *Style is what an individual speaker does with a language in relation to other people.*

This is the basic tenet of audience design – that style is oriented to people rather than to mechanisms or functions. Style focuses on the person. It is

---

[3] Again, I have avoided both modification and elaboration of the framework until now, partly cautioned by the example of accommodation theory which has, to my mind, overelaborated itself and so risked both losing touch with its core insights and becoming impracticably complex.

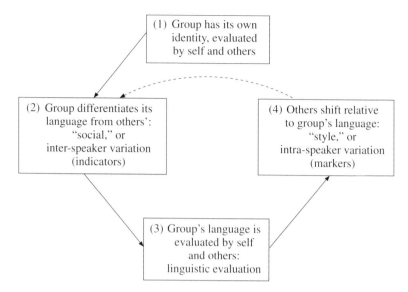

Figure 9.2 The derivation of intra-speaker from inter-speaker variation, by way of evaluation (from Bell 1984)

essentially a social thing. It marks inter-personal and inter-group relations. It is interactive – and active. Although audience design and its hypotheses are based on evidence behind this proposition, this is really a premise rather than a hypothesis. Our view of style is ultimately derived from our view of the nature of personhood. Behind audience design lies a strong, general claim that the character of (intra-speaker) style-shift derives at an underlying level from the nature of (inter-speaker) language differences between people. It is a reflex of inter-speaker variation.

2:      *Style derives its meaning from the association of linguistic features with particular social groups.*

The social evaluation of the group is transferred to the linguistic features associated with the group. So style derives from inter-group language variation by way of social evaluation, as diagrammed in figure 9.2. This has been noted at least since Ferguson and Gumperz (1960). Evaluation of a linguistic variable and style-shift of that variable are reciprocal, as Labov (1972) demonstrated. Evaluation is always associated with style-shift, and style-shift with evaluation. These findings must be accounted for in a theory of style.

Stylistic meaning therefore has a normative basis. A particular style is normally associated with a particular group or situation, and therefore carries with it the flavor of those associations (cf. Myers-Scotton's 1993 "markedness model" of inter-lingual code-switching). As supporting evidence, we can turn to a source who may seem surprising, but who has some claim to be acknowledged as a herald of modern sociolinguistics – the Soviet literary theorist Bakhtin writing in 1934/35: "All words have the 'taste' of a profession, a genre, a tendency, a party, a particular work, a particular person, a generation, an age group, the day and hour. Each word tastes of the context and contexts in which it has lived its socially charged life" (Bakhtin 1981:293). Note that Bakhtin is using "the word" as a shorthand for language as a whole. Irvine's commentary (this volume, chapter 1) on Javanese lexical alternates and the "voices" and "auras" they bring with them offers a specific example of this phenomenon.

There is a fundamental divergence on the origin and basis of style here between my view and that advanced by Finegan and Biber in their major theoretical paper (1994) and their chapter in this volume. I have critiqued this briefly elsewhere (Bell 1995) and at greater length in an unpublished paper (Bell 1994). If I understand Finegan and Biber correctly, the difference between the two positions may be symbolized succinctly by reversing the direction of the arrows in figure 9.2, so that stylistic significance (4) leads to inter-group language differences (2) rather than vice versa. The evaluation component (3) however has a central role in the processes described above (cf. Irvine, this volume), and it is unclear to me what are its place and function in Finegan and Biber's approach.

3:   *Speakers design their style primarily for and in response to their audience.*

This is the heart of audience design. Style shift occurs primarily in response to a change in the speaker's audience. Audience design is generally manifested in a speaker shifting her style to be more like that of the person she is talking to – this is "convergence" in the terms of the Speech/Communication Accommodation Theory developed by Giles and associates (e.g. Giles and Powesland 1975, Coupland et al. 1988). Rickford and McNair-Knox's exemplary study of "Foxy" (1994) provides good supporting sociolinguistic evidence for this assertion.

Response is the primary mode of style-shift (figure 9.3). Style is a responsive phenomenon, but it is actively, so not passively. Responsiveness to the audience is an active role of speakers. Again, we can compare with Bakhtin (1981:280) on the essentially dialogic nature of language: "Discourse . . . is oriented toward an understanding that is 'responsive' . . . Responsive understanding is a fundamental force . . . and it is moreover an *active* understanding."

Bakhtin's theories are founded on the dialogic nature of language: "For the word (and, consequently, for a human being) nothing is more terrible

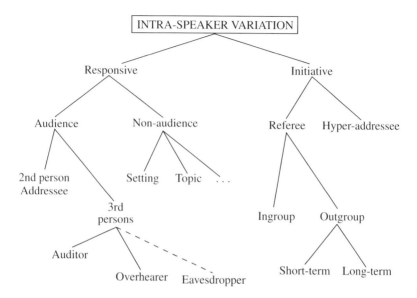

Figure 9.3 Style as response and initiative: audience design and referee design (from Bell 1984)

than a *lack of response*" (Bakhtin 1986:127). For someone to speak is to respond and be responded to: "An essential (constitutive) marker of the utterance is its quality of being directed to someone, its *addressivity*" (1986:95).

I regard audience design, then, as part of a dialogic theory of language. That is, hearers as well as speakers are essential to and constitutive of the nature of language not just of its somehow abstracted production. This is why it is entirely natural that there should be a link between stylistic and inter-speaker differences. Dialogue is the natural instantiation of language. We should no more conceive of language without audience than of language without speaker.

4:       *Audience design applies to all codes and levels of a language repertoire, monolingual and multilingual.*

Audience design does not refer only to style-shift. Within a language, it involves features such as choice of personal pronouns or address terms (Brown and Gilman 1960, Ervin-Tripp 1972), politeness strategies (Brown and Levinson 1987), use of pragmatic particles (Holmes 1995), as well as quantitative style-shift (Coupland 1980, 1984).

Audience design applies to all codes and repertoires within a speech community, including the switch from one complete language to another in bilingual situations (Gal 1979, Dorian 1981). It has long been recognized that the processes which make a monolingual shift styles are the same as those which make a bilingual switch languages (e.g. Gumperz 1967). Any theory of style needs to encompass both monolingual and multilingual repertoires – that is, all the shifts a speaker may make within her linguistic repertoire.

5:     *Variation on the style dimension within the speech of a single speaker derives from and echoes the variation which exists between speakers on the "social" dimension.*

This is the Style Axiom (Bell 1984:151). It claims that the inter-relation between intra-speaker style-shift and inter-speaker dialect differences is a derivation. The axiom is meant to apply both diachronically and synchronically. That is, it refers both to the historical origins of styles, and to the ongoing basis on which styles may be said to carry social meaning. Just as first person (speaker) differences underlie "social" differences in language, so stylistic differences are underlain by second person (and to a lesser extent third person) differences in the communicative situation. The relationship is captured well in Coupland's exposition in this volume.

The Style Axiom encapsulates the now often-noted fact that the same linguistic variables operate simultaneously on both social and stylistic dimensions, so that for one isolated variable it may be difficult to distinguish a "casual salesman from a careful pipefitter," in Labov's well-turned phrase (1972:240). It also reflects the quantitative relationship of the social and stylistic dimensions – that the range of style variation is less than the range of inter-speaker variation (cf. Preston 1991). But this is not just a quantitative relation without independent, causal motivation (as is Preston's social/status axiom; cf. Coupland, chapter 11 of this volume). Social evaluation is the engine which links the two.

Audience design is therefore a strategy by which speakers draw on the range of linguistic resources available in their speech community to respond to different kinds of audiences. The monolingual relies on the differential use and evaluation of linguistic forms to make them available as a resource for style-shift. The bilingual relies on the presence of the two languages in the community and in the interlocutor's (passive) repertoire. This does not downgrade the creativity of speakers or imply that they are passive. They are very active in exploiting the resources of their speech community, as I shall argue below.

These differences are not just in terms of social class, but also of gender, ethnicity, age, etc. If a linguistic feature or pattern is used differently by speakers of different gender or ethnicity, then it will usually be used differently *to* those people as listeners. We can see this in the morphological and syntactic variables analyzed in Rickford and McNair-Knox (1994), and at the pragmatic level of language in the fact that the same groups both receive and give most compliments and apologies (Holmes 1995).

6:     *Speakers have a fine-grained ability to design their style for a range of different addressees, as well as for other audience members.*

These are the classic findings of the accommodation model. At its essence, speech accommodation theory proposed that speakers accommodate their speech style to their hearers in order to win approval (Giles and Powesland 1975). The theory was extensively developed, expanded, and revised during the 1980s (e.g. Thakerar, Giles, and Cheshire 1982, Coupland et al. 1988). But we should not lose sight of its principal insight – that speakers respond primarily to their audience in designing their talk. Rickford and McNair-Knox's study shows what this means for the addressee, and we can compare with Youssef's study (1993) on the role of auditors and overhearers in affecting a speaker's style.

7:     *Style-shifting according to topic or setting derives its meaning and direction of shift from the underlying association of topics or settings with typical audience members.*

The hypothesis that shifts according to topic echo shifts according to audience was one of the "bolder" ones put forward in Bell (1984). This kind of association is however the foundation of Fishman's proposal (e.g. 1972) of domains as an integrative concept for style-shift or language switch, and Rickford and McNair-Knox (1994) found some supporting data in their study. The evidence is, however, not clear, nor is it obvious whether the appeal to an audience association is helpful or necessary. However, this kind of association between topic types and audience types has been widely noted, including for example by Finegan and Biber (1994, chapter 14 of this volume). The common character of the shifts invites a common explanation in terms of either audience or discoursal function.

8:     *As well as the "responsive" dimension of style, there is the "initiative" dimension (figure 9.3) where the style-shift itself* initiates *a change in the situation rather than* resulting from *such a change.*

Sociolinguists have drawn attention to this distinction at least since Blom and Gumperz (1972) coined the terms "situational" and "metaphorical" switching.[4] In situational switching there is a regular association between

---

[4] Blom and Gumperz's definitions and exemplifications of their distinction seem to me, however, after repeated attempts at interpretation, to be inconsistent. Myers-Scotton (1993:52) notes the same problem.

language and social situation. These situational switches reflect the speech community's norms of what is appropriate speech for certain audiences. Initiative style trades on such regular associations, infusing the flavor of one setting into a different context. Here language becomes an independent variable which itself shapes the situation.

In initiative style-shift, the individual speaker creatively uses language resources often from beyond the immediate speech community, such as distant dialects, or stretches those resources in novel directions. Bakhtin (1981) uses the apt term "stylization" for such usages. While not diminishing the role of linguistic creativity in initiative shift, it is worth noting that such creativity is rarely *ex nihilo*. Whether literary or conversational, it usually draws on existing if distant resources and remakes them – for instance using other dialects, whether social or geographic, other languages, or earlier forms of the user's own language.

The relationship between the responsive and initiative modes of style-shift is, however, one of the principles I will rework below.

9:      *Initiative style-shifts are in essence "referee design," by which the linguistic features associated with a reference group can be used to express identification with that group.*

Initiative style-shifts derive their force and their direction of shift from their underlying association with classes of persons or groups. They focus on an often-absent reference group – for example by adopting a non-native accent – rather than the present addressee. Referees are third persons not usually present at an interaction but possessing such salience for a speaker that they influence style even in their absence.

Initiative style-shift is essentially a redefinition by speakers of their own identity in relation to their audience. The baseline from which initiative shifts operate is the style normally designed for a particular kind of addressee. Examples of referee design include the use of non-native dialects in television commercials (Bell 1990, 1992); Yaeger-Dror's studies (1991, 1993) of variation in the language of Israeli singers; Rampton's research (1995) on "crossing" – the use of Panjabi, Creole, and Indian English by British youth of other ethnicities; Schilling-Estes' investigation (1998) of the hyper-use of local dialect variants.

Referee design can involve a speaker shifting to identify more strongly with their own ingroup, or to an outgroup with which they wish to identify. It can even involve simultaneous identification with two groups at once, as Yaeger-Dror's (1993) study of a coarticulated variant of (r) shows. Referee design may be short term, or long term as in diglossia.

This is the area where I assess audience design to be in most need of serious rethinking, and I will return to this task below.

10:   Style research requires its own designs and methodology.

To progress beyond our current level of knowledge, research on style needs to be tailored to that end, not just grafted on to a study with other main aims. The speakers we sample, what we record them saying, and even the kinds of analysis we carry out, are specific to our concern with style rather than, for instance, with dialect differences. I report now on one project which has aimed to investigate style in its own right and test many of the audience design hypotheses.

3   Designing research on style

The focus of this project is on issues of sociolinguistic accommodation, the linguistic presentation of self in response to others, and the effect of gender and ethnicity on these. It examines and seeks to explain the ways speakers talk to each other differently depending on the characteristics of their interlocutors, their own self-presentation, and other factors in the speech situation. Specifically, it tests certain of the hypotheses about style from Bell (1984) and, for example, aims to:

1. Investigate how speakers vary their style in response to a systematically varied range of addressees
2. Make aspects of the informants' identities salient, especially gender and ethnicity, and investigate how these identities are expressed in stylistic choices, particularly in cross-gender and cross-ethnic interviews
3. Investigate how speakers vary their style in response to a systematically varied range of topics, from the formal to the informal, and in relation to referee personas (e.g. talking about teachers when discussing education, and about bosses when discussing work)
4. Elicit the standard Labovian interview "styles" and calibrate these against style-shifts according to audience and topic

I present some detail on the design of the study because it is an example of how one can specifically design a project on style, and is also of a kind which has not to my knowledge been undertaken before.

3.1   Speaker sample

The language sample consists of three interviews conducted with each of four speakers. A set of four informants aged in their twenties were interviewed in succession by a set of four interviewers (table 9.1). The informant and interviewer samples were each structured by gender and ethnicity, so that each contained a Maori woman, Maori man, Pakeha woman and

Table 9.1. *Structure of style project
sample: four informants each talk to
three different interviewers*

	Informants			
Interviewers	MF	MM	PF	PM
MF	1st	2nd	3rd	—
MM	2nd	1st	—	3rd
PF	3rd	—	1st	2nd
PM	—	3rd	2nd	1st

Notes:
Ethnicity: Maori (M); Pakeha (P)
Gender: Female (F); Male (M).

Pakeha man.[5] Thus, for example, the Maori man was interviewed first by the Maori male interviewer, then by the Maori woman, and lastly by the Pakeha man. The fourth possible combination of interviewers and informants was intentionally excluded (the practicalities of a fourth successive interview with each informant being prohibitive).

While gender and ethnicity were varied, other factors were held as constant as possible:

• Age: all four speakers were in their early to mid twenties.
• Class: all were middle class, had either done and/or were currently undertaking further education, and were employed in or currently training for professional occupations.
• Origins: all were New Zealanders of (at least) several generations' standing.
• Familiarity: all informants and interviewers were strangers to each other.

The demographic and other assessments were all done through a preliminary interview by the project's Research Manager.

In addition, we tried to keep aspects of the setting constant. Interviews were conducted in the informants' own homes. No third parties were present. Interviewers were asked to dress in a neutral fashion (neither too formal nor too untidy), and similarly both to each other and for each of the three interviews they were to conduct.

---

[5] Maori are the indigenous Polynesian inhabitants of New Zealand/Aotearoa, and now make up some 15 percent of the population. "Pakeha" is the term for New Zealanders of European (mainly British) origin who colonized the country from the nineteenth century. They make up some 80 percent of the population.

3.2   *Interview design*

The attempt to hold factors constant extended to interview design as well as personal characteristics and setting. This meant that we could not use just two naive speakers chatting to each other. An interview situation was inevitable in order to structure the content in a comparable way across the encounters. So the attempt to elicit maximally informal speech was sacrificed to some extent by the need to ensure comparability across the interviews, e.g. by topic, and even by framing of topic. This is one example of the different methodology needed for style research, and paid dividends in enabling us to compare how different informants presented their opinions and identities in response to the same questions.

Three standardized questionnaires were designed, one for each of the interviews conducted with each informant. Each interview consisted of four components:

1. Free conversation
   e.g. holidays, living in Wellington, danger of death.
2. Set topics
   Work, education, issues of gender and ethnicity.
3. Reading tasks
   e.g. word lists, minimal pairs, Maori placenames.
4. Other tasks
   e.g. British/American lexical alternates, use of Ms. versus Miss/Mrs.

In general there was an initial language-related task to begin the interview, settling the two participants in. Then it proceeded into free conversation (with certain topics offered for discussion by the interviewer), and on to one or more set topics of discussion, concluding with another task. The free conversation was intended to achieve some level of "casual" speech, without expecting to elicit truly "vernacular" talk.

An obvious issue for the study was what rationale could be given to the informants for recording them three times in as many weeks. The justification given was twofold – and genuine: that we had a range of topics to explore with them, too much for a single interview. And in particular, that people say different things to different people, which was why there was to be a series of interviews involving different interviewers.

The first interview was designed as a baseline. Although all the demographic information had been obtained in the Research Manager's pre-interview, there were certain things which needed to be accomplished in this first interview, where the informant was talking to their most-like interviewer – same ethnicity, same gender. So Interview 1 contained a reading passage, a word list, and a minimal pairs list to enable calibration of the conventional sociolinguistic style elicitation techniques against the style variation anticipated across the suite of interviews to be conducted. The "free conversation" topics in this interview were:

- Danger of death.
- Family history was explored as a means of focusing part of the interview on the informant's identity – particularly their ethnic identity, which in this interview they shared with the interviewer.
- What it was like at school. The telling of childhood experiences is a means of eliciting maximally informal speech from speakers (cf. Labov 1972, 1984). These questions focused on the non-classroom life of school – what the other kids were like, friends and enemies, playground games.

Set topic sections followed more of a question-and-answer format than did the free conversation. Set topics were kept till last mainly because the topics in the second and third interviews (gender and ethnic relations) were potentially contentious, and the rest of the interview content needed to be done first in case the interview either stranded or exploded when it reached these topics. Given the size of the sample, it was not possible to test for differing ordering effects, although we know that such interviews tend to become less formal as participants grow more familiar with each other (e.g. Douglas-Cowie 1978).

The first interview contained two set topics: education and work. These were chosen as being the archetypal "formal" topics, as used for instance in Fishman's domain model (1972). The education topic concentrated on the content of the informant's formal schooling and subsequent education. It was intended to contrast with the earlier more casual discussion of school life from the viewpoint of the students. There was a set of questions about teachers, good and bad. This was deliberately to make the association between topic and referent, which bears upon the hypothesis that one talks about the topic of education in a similar style to how one might talk to an educationalist. Talking about the teacher is the closest simulation of this situation in this interview design. Thus the referee associations here were to be with teachers, whereas the reference group of the earlier discussion on school life was to be "other kids." (In practice, of course, the "free" and "set" topics did not divide so neatly.)

A basic principle of the interview design was to make gender salient in the cross-gender interviews, and ethnicity salient in the cross-ethnic interviews. So the set topic for the second interview – the cross-gender combination – was gender, focusing the informants on their own gender identity and its contrast with the interviewer's. Similarly, the primary topic of discussion in the third, cross-ethnic interview was the issue of ethnic relations and identity in New Zealand.

Some of the tasks were designed to relate to the set topic under discussion in the interview. In Interview 2, two of the set tasks related directly to the gender issue, for example a reading passage about gender and language. The tasks in Interview 3 included reading Maori placenames and a list of English/Maori doublets – spellings which could be pronounced either as English or Maori words.

3.3   Accomplishing the data collection

This was an ambitious research design, particularly in its use of repeated interviews involving the same set of informants and interviewers. Recording failure or speaker withdrawal could have jeopardized the whole project, requiring location of fresh speakers and rerecording interviews in order to maintain the integrity of the design.

However, all twelve interviews were completed despite this potential for disaster – perhaps because the interviewers spent much more time interviewing by way of training than doing the final interviews themselves. The interviews averaged over one hour long. Their content was logged in detail – chunked under topic headings and timed – and the interviews were transcribed in their entirety. The sample amounts to some 14 hours of taped interviews, with about 700 pages of transcripts, and a total count of about 150,000 words. The findings presented below are from three analyses that focus on the reflection and representation of ethnicity in this speech sample.

4   Some findings

4.1   Discourse particle eh

The pragmatic particle *eh* is a salient sociolinguistic marker in NZ English, as it is also in Canadian English (although the function and prosody associated with the form are not necessarily the same). The main study of New Zealand *eh* is by Meyerhoff (1994) using the Porirua sample of NZ English (Holmes, Bell, and Boyce 1991). Linguistically *eh* is a tag. Its chief discourse function seems to be to invite the interlocutor's participation: to seek reassurance of the listener's continuing attention to and empathy with what is being said; establishment of shared experiences, knowledge or belief; and introduction of information that is new and often surprising. Even then, it conveys a meaning like "you know the kind of thing I mean."

I quantify this and other pragmatic features in this study using an index of the number of tokens per amount of speech (Bell and Johnson 1997). The index counts the occurrences of *eh*, divides by the number of words produced by the speaker, then multiplies by a factor of 10,000. This gives a normalized base of tokens per 10,000 words, which is in fact close to the average interview length in this database.

Table 9.2. eh *index in speech by*
informants to interviewers

By informants	To interviewers			
	MM	MF	PM	PF
MM	46	26	19	—
MF	2	4	—	0
PM	0	—	0	1
PF	—	0	0	0

Notes:
Ethnicity: Maori (M); Pakeha (P)
Gender: Female (F); Male (M).

Informants' usage According to both the findings of our previous research and popular stereotype, the discourse particle *eh* is a marker of the English of Maori people, especially men. This pattern is confirmed here (table 9.2). There is high *eh* usage by the Maori male with indexes of 46, 26, and 19. The Maori woman uses some *eh*, but at a much lower frequency – indexes of 4, 2, and 0. The marker *eh* is all but absent from the speech of the Pakeha informants. The Pakeha woman uses none at all, and the Pakeha man just one token in nearly four hours of interview. So *eh* is functioning here mainly as a marker of group identity – foremost of ethnicity (Maori), and secondarily of gender (Maori men). This fits the association between linguistic features and group usage outlined above as point 2 of the summary of audience design.

Further, as hypothesized in points 3 and 6 in that summary, the speakers use different amounts of *eh* with different interlocutors. The Maori man uses *eh* more with the Maori male interviewer (46), less with the Maori woman (26), and least with the Pakeha man (19). This is parallelled by the Maori woman informant, albeit at a much lower level of frequency. She also uses some *eh* with her most-like interlocutor (4 to the Maori woman), less with the Maori man (2), and none with Pakeha woman. These patterns conform with an interpretation of *eh* as a marker of Maori identity particularly for men. It is also the sort of precisely graded style-shift which is predicted by audience design. We can note that the Pakeha man does not attempt to use *eh* to the Maori male interviewer. His one token occurs with the Pakeha female interviewer (perhaps because this was the most relaxed of his three interviews, and therefore gave more scope for the use of this solidarity marker).

We can also assess how these findings bear on other audience design

Table 9.3. eh *index in speech by*
interviewers to informants

To informants	By interviewers			
	MM	MF	PM	PF
MM	6	28	29	—
MF	10	25	—	5
PM	0	—	0	3
PF	—	35	14	9

Notes:
Ethnicity: Maori (M); Pakeha (P)
Gender: Female (F); Male (M).

hypotheses sketched earlier. The Style Axiom (point 5 above) proposes that the range of style-shift by any one speaker will be less than the range of usage between different speakers. The difference in *eh* usage across these four speakers with all interviewers ranges from an index of 0 for the Pakeha woman to 46 for the Maori man. This range of 46 indeed considerably exceeds the amount of style-shift for any one speaker – the maximum style-shift is 27 (from 46 to 19) by the Maori man.

This is just one sample analysis, and these patterns could equally be represented by some of the other variables I have analyzed in this data set (cf. Bell and Johnson 1997). In sum, these data offer good support for the central audience design generalizations presented earlier.

Interviewers' usage Moving from this comparative orderliness, we now examine the interviewers' level of *eh* in the same interviews. Interviewers of course had a very different role in these encounters from the informants. Their job was to encourage the informants to talk, so they provided much less speech. By quantifying their *eh* usage only over the amount of their own speech we can distinguish their usage from that of the informants. Nevertheless their role differentiation needs to be kept in mind as a potential influence on their speech.

In table 9.3 we see that the lowest usage of *eh* is by the Pakeha female interviewer – but also by the Maori male with indexes of 6, 10, 0! This is against the identity pattern we have been led to expect by the informant analysis. Its explanation seems to lie in the way in which the Maori male interviewer conducted his interviews, producing a minimum of speech himself, but with an easy, comfortable presence that encouraged his inter-locutors to talk. His three interviews yielded the lowest ratios of interviewer-to-informant speech out of all twelve interviews. He therefore literally gave himself little chance to use *eh* at all (or any other pragmatic feature).

The highest interviewer usage is by the Maori woman and Pakeha man. The Pakeha female interviewer's usage of some *eh* (5, 3, 9) also contrasts with the Pakeha female informant's total non-usage, even though all interviewers used some *eh* to the latter.

Probably the clearest pattern in interviewer usage is that the Pakeha male interviewer does a lot of accommodating to his audience. He reciprocates the zero *eh* usage of the Pakeha male informant in his baseline interview. As the demographics of his informant get more distant, he uses more *eh* – an index of 14 to the Pakeha woman, and 29 to the Maori man. We can also note mutual accommodation in his interview with the Maori man, with the Maori man shifting from his high baseline of 46 (table 9.2) to a much lower *eh* level (19), and the Pakeha male interviewer shifting from a zero base to a rather high usage of 29 (table 9.3). This is exactly the kind of pattern we see in quantifying the degree of accommodation in other data sets – e.g. Coupland's (1980, 1984) travel agent study. Speakers often seem to go more or less half way to meet their interlocutor. In this case both shift, and they in effect overshoot each other.

The main remaining puzzle is that usage of *eh* to the Pakeha woman is almost as high as to the Maori man, with interviewer indexes in speech to her of 35, 14, and 9 (table 9.3). This seems to go against what one would expect from audience design: the interviewers are using a feature which is absent from their interlocutor's own speech. It is indeed counter to that principle, although I think there is an explanation: the Pakeha female informant was a quite hesitant speaker, and I suspect that interviewers wanted to encourage her to talk. So they used *eh* as the solidary, interactive device available to them in the NZ English speech community. It is noteworthy that the level of *eh* from the interviewers also increases with the demographic distance here, so that the Pakeha woman interviewer uses least (9) to her, the Pakeha man next (14), and the Maori woman most (35).

The interpretations offered in this section are clearly much more *post hoc* than in my discussion of the informants' patterns. This may be in part due to the small amount of speech produced by interviewers and to their role in the interaction. But the need to seek such explanations seems to me one of the main issues for *any* attempt at a framework for regularizing style-shift, including audience design. Just as the regularities I found for the informants on the *eh* variable could be paralleled by other regular variables, so the lesser regularity shown for interviewers is paralleled elsewhere in this data set. This is of course the common lot of our research: some things pattern as we hypothesized they would. Others do not pattern in that way but we can offer a plausible, congruent *post hoc* explanation. Still others follow no pattern at all that we can discern or explain. Should we expect this to be any different for style? Should we expect our frameworks in this area to do anything more than offer a best achievable generalization as the basis for hypothesizing? I will return to this question below.

4.2   Maori language usage

The second data set concerns the usage of the Maori language in the context of NZ English. Maori is a minority language in New Zealand, under considerable threat from English. New Zealand is one of the world's most monolingual nations. English is the first language of at least 90 percent of the 3.5 million population – and the only language of 85 percent, most of whom are of British descent. Only a small proportion of Maori people – and still fewer younger Maori – can speak the Maori language fluently (Te Taura Whiri 1996). Maori has therefore followed the typical pattern of an indigenous tongue overwhelmed by an imperial language.

However, the language has gained increasing official recognition over the past decade, and is undergoing a renaissance along with a revival in Maori cultural, social, and political identity and power. Immersion pre-school and school programs aim to produce a new generation of speakers. Although it remains to be seen whether this will be able to reverse over a century of neglect and opposition by Pakeha, the Maori language is unquestionably having a renewed impact on New Zealand life – to the extent of increasing use of the Maori name "Aotearoa" for the country itself.

In this kind of situation, where biculturalism is an important social and political matter, the usage of Maori words and the way in which Maori words are pronounced within the flow of English-language talk, have become salient, culturally and politically charged issues. There is quite frequent borrowing within our interviews of Maori words and phrases into English, particularly to refer to specifically Maori cultural and social phenomena. Maori words are also in constant usage in NZ English in that most of the names for places, flora, and fauna are Maori. How Maori placenames are pronounced is increasingly an issue in its own right.

Maori/English doublets In the third interview conducted with each informant – that is, the cross-ethnic interview – a number of the tasks related to Maori language. In earlier interviews informants had been asked to read out several lists of English words. Early in the third interview, they read a list of New Zealand placenames, half of them Maori. Then to close the third interview, they read aloud another list containing fifty-seven words. The first forty-four of these were mainly English words but with a scattering of (six) Maori words which are well-established borrowings into English. The list then ended with the following thirteen words:

marae	kiwi	mana
one	hoe	toe
take	ate	pane
pure	nuke	
hope	no	

The first line contains three Maori words which are well established in English. The remaining ten words are English–Maori "doublets" – spellings which represent legitimate words in either language, but are syllabified differently, being pronounced as monosyllables in English but disyllables in Maori (except *no* of course, which is distinguished by vowel quality).[6]

This list came at the end of Interview 3, after a – usually lengthy – conversation on the set topic of "ethnic relations in New Zealand," which included a discussion of the place of the Maori language in New Zealand. Maori versus Pakeha ethnicity would therefore have been at its most salient as a dimension of identity. In addition, the three Maori words *marae*, *kiwi*, and *mana* were placed to cue the informants in to a Maori-language frame. However, the interviewer introduced the word list in the same way as earlier lists, with no explicit indication that any of these words might be of a different kind.

The Pakeha man read straight through the list of doublets as English monosyllables. He gave no indication of being aware of any alternative reading, and was the only one of the four informants not to make some comment after the reading. He had also been the least aware of, and the least sympathetic to, Maori language and culture when those topics were under discussion earlier in the interview.

The Pakeha woman read seven of the ten doublets as English, but part way through the list began to attempt Maori pronunciations for *ate*, *pane*, and *nuke*. Her intonations when reading this list indicate that she was aware that alternative readings were possible, but unsure of what the pronunciation ought to have been. In a brief exchange after she finished reading the list, she made the self-deprecating comment "useless." In her

---

[6] The phonetics of most of the vowel and consonant phonemes also differ between Maori and English, but the present analysis looks only at syllabification (cf. the analysis of Maori placename pronunciations below). Glosses of Maori words: *marae* "meeting house"; *kiwi* "kiwi" (a bird); *mana* "standing"; *one* "sand"; *hoe* "paddle"; *toe* "be left"; *take* "root"; *ate* "heart"; *pane* "head"; *pure* "ceremony to remove tapu"; *nuke* "crooked"; *hope* "waist"; *no* "from."

earlier discussion, she had expressed a sense of inadequacy in Maori language and pronunciation, and intentions of trying to change that.[7]

Both Maori informants had a moderate second-language level of fluency in Maori, and both were very conscious of the use and standing of the *reo* (the "language"). The Maori woman gave the most Maori readings of the items, and was the only informant to flag alternative readings as she went (for *hoe, toe, take,* and *no*). For *hoe* she gives the Maori reading first, for *toe, take,* and *no* the English reading first. Her rereadings and her comment to the interviewer show she was very aware of the alternative readings, though she favored the Maori version in her responses.

The Maori man mixed his readings, with six out of ten words as English and four as Maori (*hoe, toe, take, pane*). From his comments at the end of the word list (that he had had to decide whether to say the doublet in Maori or English), it is clear he was aware of the alternative readings.

Maori placenames Most New Zealand placenames are Maori, and pronunciation according to a Maori or English model is a very obvious indicator of ethnic orientation or sensitivity. The pronunciation of the twenty Maori placenames from the list of English and Maori names read at the beginning of this interview was analyzed to identify whether informants used a pronunciation closer to English or to Maori. The features analyzed were (with the Maori pronunciation first):

- realization of *r* as a flap or an approximant (e.g. in *Kerikeri, Waitarere*)
- non-aspiration versus aspiration of *p, t,* and *k* (*Karekare, Piripiri*)
- realization of grapheme *wh* as voiceless bilabial or labiodental fricative versus voiced bilabial [w] (*Whakatane, Te Kauwhata*)
- realization of grapheme *ng* as velar nasal only versus velar nasal + stop (*Whangarei*)
- retention versus deletion of *h* (e.g. *Ohakune*)
- Maori versus English realizations of vowels and diphthongs
- pronunciation of full number of syllables versus reducing syllables through elision, especially apocope (specifically in *Paraparaumu* versus *Paraparam*).

In each word the relevant sounds were marked 0 for a Maori pronunciation or 1 for an English pronunciation. These were tallied as scores, aver-

---

[7] Non-use of Maori syllabification by these two speakers cannot be attributed to lack of knowledge of, or ability in, this aspect of Maori. Although some Maori placenames are resyllabified by some Pakeha speakers, all Pakeha remain aware of Maori syllabification and can produce it (see discussion of placenames in the next section). In addition, many of the orthographies in this list also occur within well-known placenames, where Pakeha unreflectingly use the Maori syllabification – e.g. *Onehunga, Ohope*. Wrong syllabification is the subject of (Pakeha) jokes about overseas visitors' pronunciation attempts on New Zealand placenames, e.g. *One-hunga* and *O-ne Tree Hill.*

Table 9.4 *Scores for possible pronunciations of* Kerikeri

Pronunciation	Alignment	Raw score	Normalized score
[kerikeri]	fully Maori	0	0
[kerikeri]	largely Maori	2	1
[keri:keri:]	midway	4	2
[kʰeri:kʰeri:]	largely anglicized	6	3
[kʰiri:kʰiri:]	fully anglicized	8	4

Table 9.5. *Four informants' pronunciations of twenty Maori placenames according to Maori or norms (score 0 = fully Maori; 4 = fully anglicized)*

		Informants			
	Score	MM	MF	PM	PF
Fully	0	8	4	0	0
Maori	1	7	8	0	0
	2	3	5	2	0
	3	2	2	5	8
Fully English	4	0	1	13	12
Total placenames		20	20	20	20
Mean score (0–4)		0.9	1.4	3.5	3.5

aged, and normalized to a five-point scale, with 0 representing purely Maori pronunciation and 4 representing purely English pronunciation (at least for the sounds analyzed). By way of example, some of the possible pronunciations of *Kerikeri* would be coded and scored as in table 9.4 (there are of course other possible combinations of the variant pronunciations). Table 9.5 shows where the pronunciation of the twenty words fell on the scale for each informant, and the informant's average rating for Maori versus English pronunciation. Against these criteria, the pronunciation of the Maori man was closest to Maori at 0.9 on the 0–4 scale, followed by the Maori woman (1.4). The pronunciations of the Pakeha man and woman were both close to the English end of the scale (3.5).

The Maori man consistently had the most features identified as Maori. The Maori woman had one pronunciation fully anglicized (*Tikitiki*), but overall had a Maori-oriented rendering of the placenames. The Pakeha informants gave English pronunciations for half or more of the twenty tokens, on the basis of the features analyzed. The Maori man semi-categorically gave a flap realization for *r* (in names like *Kerikeri*), pronounced the vowels as monophthongs not diphthongs, and tended not to reduce vowels in unstressed syllables, following the rhythm of Maori. The Maori woman generally gave a flap realization for *r*. Though she was more inclined to use an English vowel than the Maori man, she still produced fewer diphthongal realizations of monophthongs than the two Pakeha informants did.

For the Pakeha man *r* was nearly always realized as an approximant, *p*, *t*, and *k* were nearly always aspirated, and vowel values were as for English. However, he did pronounce the *ng* in *Whangarei* as a velar nasal rather than a nasal + stop sequence, and said *Paraparaumu* with the full number of Maori syllables.

The Pakeha woman gave an approximant realization for *r*, aspirated *p*, *t*, and *k* to a greater extent than the Maori informants, and frequently reduced the vowels in unstressed syllables. However, she did consistently pronounce *wh* as [f], whereas the Pakeha man said *wh* as [w] in *Te Kauwhata*.

5   Language as identity marker

In these analyses, we find encapsulated the essence of how linguistic features operate as identity markers which is the basis of how style *means* in the audience design framework. The choice of a Maori-identified particle, a more Maori pronunciation of a placename, or a Maori-language reading of a word versus an English-language reading, marks ethnic identity.

For the two Maori speakers their pronunciation registers their identification with their own Maori heritage. For the Pakeha speakers, it marks their degree of sensitivity to Maori pronunciation as an important ethnic and cultural matter – remembering that Maori–Pakeha relations were the explicit set topic of discussion in Interview 3. We can compare how the informants understand and present their views on ethnicity at the discourse level with their expression of ethnic identity through specific linguistic features. The Pakeha man showed little overt sympathy with Maori language or culture, either in his discussion of ethnic relations or in his linguistic performance. For example, a salient marker of such awareness is the use of the Maori zero plural on Maori words used in English, a practice which has become common though not dominant in NZ English in the past decade. Thus, *Maori* would be used as the plural for the Maori people rather than *Maoris*. The Pakeha man is the only one of the four informants to use plural -*s* on the word *Maori*.

The Pakeha woman, by contrast, showed awareness of the issue both in discussion and in her recognition of the Maori potential of the doublet words. We can construe her attempted pronunciations as audience design. She is speaking to a Maori, and therefore tries – within her limited knowledge of Maori language – to accommodate towards native-like pronunciation of Maori words. The Pakeha man accommodates much less. He may – in line with some of his argumentation about the issue – even be diverging from such a pronunciation as a sociopolitical statement.[8] For example, the use of the label *Pakeha* is itself an issue, and more conservative white New Zealanders reject it as a self-description. Our Pakeha man uses *European* fifty times and *Pakeha* only once, despite explicitly declaring his self-identification with New Zealand not Europe, and despite his Maori interviewer's invariant use of *Pakeha*.

The two word lists also show in a nutshell the identical nature of the process which produces inter-language shifts for a bilingual and style-shift for a monolingual (point 4 of the audience design outline). The choice of reading the doublets as Maori or English is driven by the same identification process as is the pronunciation of Maori words used in English, which – at least for monolingual Pakeha – is a style choice. An adequate theory must encompass both the monolingual and multilingual manifestations of intra-speaker shift.

For all speakers, then, Maori language usage is a means of declaring either their own ethnic identity, or their sensitivity to another's identity. It parallels some speakers' use of Maori words within the conversational sections of the interviews, and the overt expression of opinions on ethnic relations during the set-topic discussion. So we can talk in terms of accommodation or non-accommodation, for the Pakeha speakers, and this fits passably with an audience design approach.

But in what terms do we explain the Maori informants' pronunciations? They are not accommodating to the interviewers through convergence. However, nor are they necessarily intentionally dissociating themselves from the individual interviewer through divergence. The Maori man and the Pakeha male interviewer had an amicable, jointly constructed exchange about the exercise after its completion. The Maori woman, however, passed the comment "I'd like to hear some of the others read these," indicating she recognized the pronunciation alternatives as a site of ethnic distinction. This also is in line with her more confrontational approach to the ethnicity discussion compared with the Maori man. In this interview her delayed and

---

[8] A related factor here, at least for the Pakeha man, could be a preference for staying with a straight Pakeha pronunciation rather than risk producing a misfired Maori imitation in front of a Maori listener. However, his unhesitating production of anglicized pronunciations seems to indicate unconsciousness of the options rather than deliberate choice of the Pakeha one.

cryptic answers to questions related to Maori language and culture come across as reluctance to discuss these matters with a non-Maori interviewer. She fails to respond to her Pakeha female interviewer's attempts to find common ground for conversation and opts instead to keep herself separate on ethnic grounds. At one point this becomes overt when she defines her identity as primarily Maori and only secondarily female:

MF: but that's sort of my thing you know when I've been involved in stuff at Teachers College it's been from a Maori perspective rather than a woman's or a Pacific Island whatever you know that's my sort of (that) women can look out for themselves if they want to form a women's group and stand up staunchly or and same with Pacific Islanders
INT: and you don't think Maori can?
MF: yeah: but that's the one that I want to be involved in
INT: yeah (oh I see)
MF: just picking your bandwagon I think

What the Maori informants seem to be doing is expressing and affirming their own ethnic identity as Maori, to which divergence from the interviewer is incidental. This can be explained as referee design, specifically what I have called hyper-speaker shift (Bell 1984:201) – a short-term shift towards a heightened form of one's own group's speech. The situation matches precisely the characteristics spelled out for this particular kind of shift in Bell (1984:187):

a speaker talking to members of an outgroup, and reacting with a shift towards the style of the speaker's own (absent) ingroup. Such a speaker takes the initiative to deliberately reject identification with the immediate addressee, and identifies instead with an external referee. Ingroup referee design seems to require a general sociopolitical situation in which in- and outgroups and their linguistic codes are in conflict, and a set of social psychological circumstances which bring that conflict to the surface in a specific situation.

This is undoubtedly going on here. But I am no longer sure that it can be considered the exceptional, marked case which I treated it as in 1984. The question is not whether the above description is accurate – it seems to fit the case well – but whether referee design is secondary as implied. This leads me on to my primary modification to the audience design framework as originally proposed.

6   Conclusion

6.1   Integrating audience and referee design

To my mind, the greatest problem for the audience design framework as outlined – and indeed the main challenge for any theory of style – is to take account of the dynamic, initiative use of style by individual speakers to express aspects of their identity (points 8 and 9 in the summary of audience design above), while retaining a worthwhile level of generalization. One main critique made of frameworks such as audience design which attempt to systematize style is that they are reductionist. They run the risk of minimizing or discounting the complexity of speakers' moment-by-moment, self-expressive use of language (although one could argue that an approach which is as richly person-oriented as audience design is by definition not reductionist). This is indeed an issue for audience design, but it is equally one that *any* style model will face, because any attempt to discern patterns or regularities in people's style will be open to the same critique.

Individual speakers use style – and other aspects of their language repertoire – to represent their identity or to lay claim to other identities. They may do this in ways and on occasions which are certainly unpredictable beforehand, and sometimes uninterpretable *post hoc*. This is what I have classed as referee design – the linguistic expression of identification with a reference group who are important to the speaker, usually in response to a change in some aspect of the audience. This reference group may be the speaker's own ingroup, as evidenced earlier in analysis of the Maori/English examples.

Another criticism (see Finegan and Biber, chapter 14 of this volume) is that audience design predetermines what factors may influence style. This is contrasted with a multidimensional approach which is supposedly free of *a priori* categorization. Such a criticism of course would apply to all variationist sociolinguistics, and variationists must indeed beware of taking even the most apparently obvious social variables such as gender or age for granted. But there is no particular methodological virtue in declining to examine how some factor may affect language use in favor of deducing *post hoc* what factors may have been operating in a particular situation, especially when the same small set of parameters are repeatedly found to be operating (Biber and Finegan 1994, Finegan and Biber, this volume). There is no way to falsify such a framework.

I share concerns (Finegan and Biber, this volume) that the concept of "audience" may be in danger of being overextended to encompass a wide range of imagined or possible reference personas. The strength of audience design as proposed in 1984 is its falsifiability. It is possible for its predictions to be proved wrong. So I remain wary of widening its scope to become a catch-all, while convinced of the need for some extension. It is notable that extensions of the notion of audience as an explanatory concept are often very natural ones. That is, we come across a pattern in our data that puzzles us, and search for an explanation of why it is so. What is the reason that this speaker chose to say it this way on this occasion? That explanation may go beyond strict accommodation to the present audience, but what is very obviously going on in the situation may be the design of talk in relation to some person or group in a way that is a natural extension of the audience approach. Moreover, this is precisely the form of explanation that *any* framework finds itself reaching for when faced by such patterns.

What lies at the base of these debates is our view of the nature of personhood. Such views of course are not a provable hypothesis of sociolinguistics or any other academic discipline. They are a premise, a prime based on our own belief system. My belief is that a person is indeed more than a static bundle of sociological categories – although to say that someone is male, or Pakeha, or middle class does tell us something about that person. A part of our behavior is a reflection of the social characteristics of groups we are associated with. However, categories such as ethnicity have fluid boundaries, and people's definition of their own ethnicity may even change in different situations. Language itself is an active factor in the presentation of one's own ethnicity or gender.

But I also believe that a person is more than an ever-shifting kaleidoscope of personas created in and by different situations, with no stable core – although to say that we appear as child to our parents, employee to our boss, partner to our partner does tell us something about the person. We do not recreate ourselves moment by moment out of nothing. We are not a *tabula rasa*. We bring to the present the shapings of our past, of our relationships, of our environment. Yet we are more than the sum of those things.

The view that persons are not static entities has validity and is paralleled by a view that situation or context cannot be regarded as a fixed, external given (see in particular Duranti and Goodwin 1992). Contexts are not (or at least, not wholly) extralinguistic. They are in part created by the language used. In some situations, language may be virtually the sole determinant of context. That is, the context is constituted linguistically. Coupland (this volume, chapter 11) has shown this in the speech of a Cardiff radio presenter who adopts a range of personas during his show, and it is also evident in my own analyses of television commercials (Bell 1992).

Nevertheless, I do not believe we need to give up the use of such extralinguistic factors, although we must recognize that it is an idealization to call them "extralinguistic." There are norms for different situations and groups. An analyst wishing to cut loose from all such categorization must provide an explanation for the pervasive if partial regularities which we find in speakers' style choices – just as those who wish to establish generalizations must make allowance for that significant chunk of style which even their best theories refuse to account for. If a particular style can be used to create a situation, how does it get to have the meaning that makes it usable for that purpose? I maintain it gets that force from its normative use in response to certain kinds of situation. There is a sense (*pace* Coupland, this volume) in which we are *not* enacting a persona in producing our own native dialect – although we may do so in producing a hyper-version of that variety, and distinguishing the "natural" from the intentional may be no easy task. When we talk our vernacular (however we may define that), we are in some sense "being ourselves."

Therefore we need a *bothland*. We need a framework which acknowledges that much of our inter-personal linguistic behavior displays a pattern which can be discerned. I call that pattern audience design, and hold that it is largely guided by our response to our audience. We also need a framework which acknowledges that we are continually making creative, dynamic choices on the linguistic representation of our identities, particularly in relation to those others we are interacting with or who are salient to us. This I have called referee design.

I think the basis of such a dynamic view of style is present in my concept of referee design. However, as originally presented in Bell (1984) it had the character of an add-on – in two senses. First, quite literally, the origin and basis of my generalizations in that paper was audience design, and the concept of referee design was added to cater for what could not be handled by audience design. Secondly, I treated referee design as a secondary dimension, which could kick in, as it were, when audience design failed. This left the problem of knowing what was the boundary between the two dimensions: where did audience design end, and referee design begin? When did speakers shift from responsive to initiative mode?

I now tend to think that we have to acknowledge referee design as an ever-present part of individuals' use of language. We are always positioning ourselves in relation to our own ingroup and other groups, and our interlocutors. This was expressed in Bell (1984:184), but was not worked through far enough: "The responsive–initiative distinction is a continuum rather than a dichotomy. Response always has an element of speaker initiative; initiative invariably is in part a response to one's audience." What I now suggest is that these may be two complementary and coexistent dimensions of style, which operate simultaneously in all speech events. Yes, we are designing our talk for our audience. But we are also concurrently designing it in relation to other referee groups, including our own ingroup.

I think there is still merit in regarding referee design as in some sense derived from audience design, because the normative use of style in one situation still defines the force of style as used in referee design. However, I now wish to suggest that the two may be concurrent, pervasive processes, rather than necessarily treating referee design as occasional or exceptional.

Catering for the dynamic and the referee is not in fact a new proposal. Referee design under another name is the core of Le Page's approach to style, treating every utterance as "an act of identity towards an audience"

Table 9.6. *Various approaches to style*

Responsive	Initiative	Source
Style	Stylization	Bakhtin (1981) [1934/35]
Situational	Metaphorical	Blom and Gumperz (1972)
Audience design	Referee design	Bell (1984, this volume)
Unmarked	Marked	Myers-Scotton (1993)
—	Crossing	Rampton (1995)
Relational	Identity	Coupland (this volume, chapter 11)

(1980:13). He formulates it as a general sociolinguistic principle (McEntegart and Le Page 1982:105): "Each individual creates for himself patterns of linguistic behaviour so as to resemble those of the group or groups with which from time to time he wishes to be identified." Similarly, Traugott and Romaine (1985) propose that style should be considered as primarily "strategic." They emphasize speakers' active participation and give a central role to the individual's meaningful choice: "It is not meant to imply the speaker's conscious intention in all cases, but rather to focus on style as an interactive and dynamic process involving both speaker and hearer, both symmetrically and asymmetrically." What we are now finding in the study of monolingual style-shift, inter-lingual code switching and multilingual language use is a wide recognition of the pervasiveness of both the responsive and the initiative facets of language use. There is a smorgasbord of frameworks and labelings for what are manifestations of basically the same phenomena – whether in a bilingual's code-switching, the adoption of an outgroup's language, or the manipulation of dialects to present different personas. Table 9.6 schematizes these approaches. They include Blom and Gumperz's situational and metaphorical switching (1972), Myers-Scotton's Markedness Model of code switching (1993), Coupland's relational–identity distinction (this volume), Bakhtin's Style and Stylization (1981), and Rampton's concept of Crossing (1995), as well as my own audience/referee design (1984).

6.2   *Integrating quantitative and qualitative analyses*

This complementarity of audience and referee has a correlate in the kind of linguistic analysis we do. Audience design will often, though not always, be able to deal in quantification – that is, a speaker's style will be amenable to counting the relative frequency of certain variants. To this extent we can see the justification for this statement by Labov on style quantification (1972:109):

Whether or not we consider style to be a continuum of expressive behavior, or a subtle type of discrete alternation, it is clear that it must be approached through quantitative methods. We are in no position to predict exactly when a given speaker will produce a fricative, or when he will produce a stop [for the (dh) variable]. A complex of many factors operates to obscure stylistic regularities at the level of the individual instance. The remarkable fact is that the basic unit of stylistic contrast is a frequency set up by as few as ten occurrences of a particular variable.

However, this is not to say that such quantification tells us everything there is to know about a speaker's style in a certain stretch of language, although it does tell us a proportion of what is going on. It seems to me undeniable that quantitative style-shift can be correlated with differences in audience. It is equally undeniable that this does not exhaust the account we are to give of style – even of that particular variable. Individual tokens of the variable may have heightened significance in the flow of the interaction, or they may cluster together with each other or with other variables in a way which is significant. Referee design will often deal in the qualitative, the one-off, the single salient token which represents an identity. Not always, of course: referee design also has its quantifiable aspects, particularly when it is long term. However, my analyses of television commercials (Bell 1990, 1992), where referee design is rife, show how a single token of a salient variable can be enough to stake a stylistic claim.

Our stylistic analysis should consist of a complementary identification of both audience and referee design in the stretch of language we may be analyzing, and complementary quantitative and qualitative analysis. I believe that generally audience design will be manifested quantitatively in a stretch of talk, not just qualitatively, and this regularity contributes to my sense that it is a more basic dimension than referee design. Referee design, on the other hand, may be manifested entirely qualitatively, at a minimum in just one occurrence of a salient feature. So we will look for regular patterns which may be interpretable as audience design, and expect that departures from such regularity may be attributable to referee design. But we will apply both frames of reference to all our analyses, no longer treating referee design as just the backstop option.

My analysis above of Maori pronunciation in fact shows on a small-scale the combination of quantitative and qualitative approaches. The basic analysis of the Maori/English doublets was a quantitative one – how many doublets does this speaker pronounce as Maori, how many as English. But our interpretation of that behavior is illuminated by qualitative analysis – the pronunciation of individual tokens, together with the voluntary remarks that three out of the four speakers offered about the exercise, their own performance, and the sociocultural implications of it.

In addition to quantitative and qualitative approaches, however, we will need a third level of analysis – co-occurrence. This level has rather dropped out of sight since Ervin-Tripp's classic paper (1972). Sociolinguists have concentrated on the alternation she identified, focusing on single variables, and ignored the co-occurrence of a range of variables and features in a stretch of talk. The stress on co-occurrence is a hallmark of Biber's approach to style (Biber and Finegan 1994, this volume), but there is no reason why it should not also inform variationist or qualitative approaches to language use. A main issue, however, for such analyses is to ensure that they do not become remote from the individual language features which they bring together, just as quantification of a sociolinguistic variable must ensure it is not entirely removed from the on-line qualitative occurrence of the individual tokens which are being counted.

So my proposal is for a three-layered approach to stylistic analysis of language:

- Quantification of particular stylistic features. This will be partly in standard variationist terms, of relative frequency, of counting actual over potential occurrences. But *absolute* frequency also plays a part – the frequency with which a *variable* occurs, not just the relative frequency of its different variants.

- Qualitative analysis of the individual tokens of a stylistic feature – while recognizing that not all (or even most) individual occurrences will be explicable. Such information illuminates or even alters the interpretation we might offer solely on the basis of quantification (as shown in Bell and Johnson 1997).

- Analysis of the co-occurrence of different features in stretches of language. My own study of the use of non-native accents in New Zealand television commercials (Bell 1990, 1992) is grounded in analysis of co-occurring features, as is Coupland's work on the performance of a Cardiff radio presenter (1996, this volume).

Co-occurrence analysis concentrates on the patterning of two or more linguistic features in the flow of speech. While qualitative analysis of on-line talk enables us to see how a single feature is distributed in a stretch of talk, co-occurrence analysis combines the patterns for more than one feature. It builds a picture of where, for instance, certain kinds of features cluster together or are entirely absent. We will seek to interpret these patterns in terms of the identities and relationships which participants are representing at different points of their interaction. Bell and Johnson (1997) develop in more detail this kind of on-line analysis and a means of displaying it for the interviews discussed in the present paper. This analysis reveals for the *eh* variable that the Maori man clusters his tokens of *eh* in stretches of speech where Maori identity is most in focus – discussions of family, Maori culture, and Maori language.

We will seek in the first instance to interpret the patterns we find in relation to audience design. We will expect this to be most evident in the quantitative analysis, but it will also inform the qualitative and the co-occurrent approaches. Rickford and McNair-Knox's study (1994), and my own findings introduced above, show that such an approach can take us a good way to understanding speaker style. We will then interpret those same patterns in relation to referee design, seeking to understand how the speaker may be positioning herself in relation to different referee groups, including her own ingroup. We will anticipate that this will be most evident in the qualitative analysis. The analysis of co-occurrence is likely to be informed more equally by both audience and referee design.

I believe such an approach can take us a good way to understanding why "this speaker said it this way on this occasion." Nevertheless, I still expect the creativity of individual speakers to leave some things unpredictable, and I for one think that such an element of the mysterious and unfathomable about persons will – and should – remain.

10 Primitives of a system for "style" and "register"

Malcah Yaeger-Dror

1 Introduction

In the course of reading papers for the workshop, it became clear that we do not all share the same terminology. This may appear to be a very minor concern, manageable (as stated by many) by each of us clearly defining our terminology, but on closer examination, it seems that it is not merely an issue of terminology, but a lack of agreement on what I will be referring to as the underlying **primitives**, the variables used for the analysis. Consequently, this discussion will be shaped by the need to agree on some finite number of primitives for the analysis of what I prefer to refer to (following Biber and Finegan, 1994) as "register," but which is discussed in Bell's chapter under the cover term "style."

To the degree that terminology alone is at issue, careful definitions may permit inter-researcher communication ("I say [tomeitow]; you say [tomatow].") but to the degree that we do not share our theoretical analytical primitives, our work may not be comparable no matter how carefully we define our terms. It is not sufficient for us to each define carefully what we are looking at, if we do not reach an understanding that will permit us to all follow a research design that would make our work mutually intelligible.

The present paper will attempt to evaluate the primitives advanced by Allan Bell, whose seminal paper (1984) launched the research focus that is being discussed here. One question addressed by Bell's and Coupland's papers was "What are the research primitives which can be isolated in the analysis of 'style' or 'register' variation?" I think we would all agree with both of these researchers that "style" would have as one of its subordinate units "audience design." However, even by the end of the workshop, it was not clear to me whether or not we are all ready to include under that definition all the issues of gender and ethnicity (as Bell did), as well as other foci of power and solidarity (Brown and Gilman 1960). While that issue was simply not addressed by many of the speakers, Bell appears to have evaluated gender and ethnicity as subcategories of audience design, although I would categorize them as referee design.

I believe it is important to acknowledge the importance of gender and ethnicity (among other variables) in some formal way, because those of us who have worked with more "marked" ethnic groups or gender know that attention to "marked" social groups (e.g., female, "ethnic," etc.) radically complicates research design – so many estimable corpora are limited by a research design in which interlocutor combinations of gender, ethnicity, and power were NOT taken into consideration. Bell's Pakeha–Maori study (in chapter 9 of this volume) shows how central such issues can be, but if we do not follow his lead, and clarify the importance of these "style" primitives, they will be presumed unimportant, and ignored in the research design, as they have been in the past. As he pointed out, the financial constraints imposed on our research require that we jettison all but the most critical primitive variables from a study.

2   Comparison of "register" primitives in different systems

2.1   Bell's conceptual definition of "style" and its primitives

Bell's "framework" includes "relational" (or audience design) and "identity" (or referee design) parameters. Indeed, the definitions he uses are respectively – "what a speaker does with a language in relation to other people" and "association of linguistic features with particular social groups." These appear to be two main subdivisions in his framework (or "design") as now discussed. In his earlier studies, audience design pertained to inter-personal relations, and it has now been expanded to clarify the importance of ethnicity and gender as inter-personal variables. However, the relationship of these to some overarching understanding of the inter-personal vectors of power and solidarity is assumed rather than expressed in his discussion. In addition, identity or referee design, while considered only tangentially in Bell (1984), is now more central to his theory, providing an important expansion.

"Responsive"/audience design is now understood to refer to all inter-personal forces influencing a speaker's use of language, whether they are convergent or divergent. "Initiative"/referee design is understood to refer to those internal self-defining forces, also related to a speaker's understanding of who s/he is, but less concerned with who some given hearer is.

Although over the years several researchers have analyzed audience design, focusing on overtly accommodative variables, few linguists have analyzed referee design variables in detail in recent years. Bell's paper permits us to renew our focus on initiative or "self identificatory" variables. However, we should be wary of following Bell's lead and assuming that while audience design is quantitatively analyzable, referee design can only be studied qualitatively (Bell, chapter 9 of this volume). In fact, I will claim that both audience design and referee design are quantitatively measurable, but whether a specific case of variation is one or the other must be determined qualitatively.

Even in very early sociolinguistic studies, evidence of referee design surfaced, and was quantitatively measured. Examples of some of these studies follow.

Labov's (1972) work on Martha's Vineyard makes the point that holding steady the relationship between the ingroup member and a marginal outgroup member there are still two distinct sets of Islanders – those who emphasize their (linguistic as well as economic) stakes in their own community, and who maintain their native phonology, and those who converge more or less radically toward the larger outgroup community; this latter group of speakers is seen not as converging toward an outgroup, but as defining themselves as belonging to a larger (unmarked) community of citizens. The two groups are distinguished primarily along a continuum of "referee design." The determination of the speakers' motivation is qualitative, but the differences in (ai) and other variables are quantitatively measurable.

Trudgill's (1972) discussion of overt and covert prestige also (in effect) incorporates self-identification/referee design as a primitive without distinguishing between the two motives: his claim was that women **accommodate** to the prestige/prescriptive norm of the culture, while men accommodate to their referee design concept of macho-language, not because all the other guys are doing it (audience design), but because their reference group is "macho" (referee design). Assuming that analysis for the moment, we find both the women's (audience design) and the men's (referee design) variation is quantitatively measurable.

Yaeger (1974) analyzed speech from Word List Style, and found that while for some speakers the referee effect is relevant, for others the audience effect is relevant: Labov (1972) had already shown that Leon A. chose to identify himself with the Standard (and merged his (æh) with (æ)). Given the interviewer's working class persona, Labov's qualitative analysis had determined this shift to be referee designed rather than audience designed, but the evidence is quantitatively measurable. Another interviewer is a lifelong neighbor of the teenaged interviewee, and their joint goal appears to be to demonstrate that Fishtown is on the Philadelphia phonological vanguard: even so, the interviewee accommodates her (æh) toward the interviewer's (somewhat more conservative, male) phonology. Jane's word list style (æhN) is consistent with her conversational tokens, but her word list (æhF) is less raised than in conversation. Here again, the quantitative evidence reveals major stylistic shifts for the speaker, but the source of that variation can only be determined qualitatively. In either case, *pace* Biber and Finegan (1994), register varies more radically than change within the community, at least when the difference in attention paid to speech is at issue.

Cheshire (1982) took a slightly different tack, showing that boys and girls follow different dialect models because they expect to become members of non-overlapping linguistic marketplaces (women needing the more prestigeful speech, and men needing a less prestigeful dialect), and here the understanding of dialect choice reflects both referee design ("I will be a hairdresser/truckdriver.") as well as audience design ("I will adapt my dialect to the linguistic marketplace as defined by my future boss."). But how does one distinguish referee and audience design factors? Not by whether or not they are quantitatively analyzable.

Both Prince's study of Sara Gorby (1987) and my own work on Israeli *Mizraḥi*-ethnic singers (1988, 1993, 1994) showed that the self-identificatory component is divergent, and the convergent component is audience-designed for the larger "Standard" community, and I found that even if interviewer and audience are held constant there is still a large difference among singers based on their own self-definition along a continuum from ethnic to koiné group membership.

Recent work by Eckert (1989) and Mendoza-Denton (1994) also traces speech distinctions among the teenagers they study (at least partly) to referee design. Undoubtedly, part of the quantitatively measurable difference in phonology between "jocks" and "burnouts," or between members of different Chicana gangs is traceable to inter-personal convergence among members of one group, but their point is well taken that the bulk of such convergence is toward a platonic ideal of group membership (referee design), rather than specifically to those members of the group who provide the immediate audience, although the line between the two is ill-defined.

A look at a range of data relevant to the primitives may help us to quantitatively verify their relative importance and how they interact, but while the quantitative analysis is useful to measure variation, qualitative analysis is often necessary to determine which of the primitives is causing the variation, especially within a given primitive node. Jakoby in a 1996 internet discussion, now unavailable, cited Ochs as having pointed out that

if any one person has multiple social identities . . . on what grounds can any one of these membership labels be said to be operative in a discourse or any particular part of a discourse? To flag everyone as Turks or females or whatever is just to select a label and presume its relevance. One could then use statistics . . . to explore label significance, but then one is engaged in some other enterprise.

Table 10.1. *Comparing Bell's parameters (this volume) with Coupland's (this volume)*

Coupland:			
	+ Instrumental	+ Identity	+ Relational
	• discourse	• self-identification	• social relations
Bell:			
	Initiative		Responsive
	• initiative	• referee design	• audience design

Now, while most sociolinguists do systematically make use of statistics, Jakoby is aware that it is a qualitative question which of a given set of social identities are relevant for a given speaker in a given social situation, and, in addition, which of a given set of potential audience design scenarios are situationally relevant.

Bell's analysis of dyads of Pakeha–Maori pairs of men and women (this volume) qualitatively determined that while convergence was primarily traceable to audience design, much of the divergence is traceable to what Giles refers to as "group maintenance" (Bell's referee design) rather than to (audience design) divergence from the immediate audience: "Language itself is an active factor in the presentation of one's own ethnicity or gender." However, as with the earlier studies mentioned, the distinction between the two designs must be qualitatively determined, although both are quantitatively measurable. Like Bell, I would like to see a rule-governed method for distinguishing reliably between referee and audience design. Unfortunately, the distinction between qualitative and quantitative analysis will not help do that.

Both of the variables proposed by Bell have clear antecedents in Giles' Communication Accommodation Theory model (Coupland and Giles 1988, Giles and Coupland 1991). Both are usable as primitives for the analysis of register variation. To the degree that audience and referee design may be difficult to distinguish from each other, perhaps Giles has hints to give us as to how to manipulate research design to more easily distinguish one from the other. I interpret the studies in this paradigm (e.g., Coupland and Giles 1988, Giles, Coupland, and Coupland 1991) to have shown that while divergence and convergence are both quantitatively measurable, the determination of whether a given shift is referee design or audience design can only be made by careful qualitative analysis.

2.2   One dichotomy, two emphases

Comparison of Bell's and Coupland's primitives (this volume) reveals their consensus on the importance of the dichotomy between audience-driven and self-identificatory motivations for variation. It is clear that Coupland's "self-identity" can be interpreted as referee design, and his social relations "+relational" can be interpreted as audience design, while "instrumental" has yet to be clearly explained, and will not be discussed further here.[1] Table 10.1 reveals the overlap in the two systems.

Coupland permits a loose interpretation of a tridimensional "framework," which favors analyzing both relational and self-identity through a "persona management" prism. This is consistent with his travel agent corpus data (1988), and his radio moderator data (1985, this volume), while analysis of Bell's multistation news announcers (1984) requires the audience design mode, and my own multigenre singers (1991, 1993, 1994) and Bell's interviewees (this volume) vary their speech for both referee design and audience design. In short, there appears to be mutual interpretability between the two contributors, with a referee design/self-identification primitive and an audience design/social relations primitive. Both are important, and can be used to explore the register universe.

Coupland appears to suggest that some linguistic variables have greater affinity with one primitive: he points out that "dialect style," which is what most sociolinguistic analysis of style variation has discussed, can be contrasted with "ideational selection," used for expressive variation. Dialect style concerns phonetic, phonological, morphological, and lexical variables, while "ideational selection" influences pragmatic and paralinguistic variables (e.g., address terms, disagreement, overlap). Dialect style maintains semantic equivalence while expressive style does not. I interpret his discussion as claiming that it is possible that different linguistic variables have greater affinity with one node than with another, with, say, dialect style reflecting audience design, while ideational selection is tied to self-identification. If that were the case, distinguishing between audience design and referee design would be greatly simplified. Unfortunately, the evidence does not support this theory.

Mendoza-Denton's (1994) work shows the degree to which dress style and linguistic variables co-vary; each factor (dress, shoes, lipstick, choice of (ŋ) or (I) realization) serves multiple functions. As Coupland writes, even "dialect style usage is . . . metaphorical and creative, but we sometimes opt to invoke personas whose . . . associations are predictable and so appropriate to particular social circumstances" (this volume, chapter 11). Unfortunately, just as dressing patterns are simultaneously referee- and audience-designed, so are phonological and pragmatic choices.

Mizraḥi singers vary (r) for a variety of reasons, and their ideational selection varies in tandem with it. Two other dialect style variables, (ḥ) and

---

[1] Coupland's instrumental variable is related to Accommodation Theorists' focus on intelligibility as a primitive (Coupland, p.c.).

(ʕ), (and choice of apparel) shift for other reasons; the fact that referee design and audience design influence all three phonological variables quantitatively not only contradicts Bell's claim that referee design is not quantitatively measurable, but in addition refutes Coupland's claim that "ideational selection" will not be revealed in phonological variation.

2.3   Additional parameters to consider

Both Bell and Coupland also specifically consider topic, purpose, setting, and perhaps planning as well, as metaphorical extensions of audience or referee design. Blom and Gumperz 1972, Hindle 1979, and Rickford and McNair-Knox 1994, all have shown the influence of **topic**, which is dependent on context as well as message. It may well be (as Bell says) that topic is metaphorically bound to the audience you expect to discuss that topic with, and is "metaphorical." This is a hypothetical, falsifiable claim; the data reported in Yaeger-Dror (1993, 1994) were gathered specifically to test that hypothesis. Unfortunately, neither the results of that analysis, nor the results of Bell's present analysis, prove his claim. Only further data, gathered with this claim in mind, will help us to determine the truth of the claim.

Similarly, the "Style Axiom" needs further study. If "the relation between intra-speaker style-shift and inter-speaker dialect differences is a derivation," and the "axiom is meant to apply both diachronically and synchronically," then one could assume (with Bell) that dialect differences will be more extreme than style variation. Certainly work by Bell (1984) and Coupland (this volume) support the synchronic version of this claim. Yet, Yaeger-Dror (1993, 1994) found that style variation for one group of singers exceeded dialect variation within the group. Certainly, when we consider prosodic stylistic variation (Yaeger-Dror 1996a, 1997) individual variation can far exceed group variation. Further study is needed, and the "axiom" is more realistically termed a "hypothesis."

We should not equate style (the influence of culturally defined social context on speech) with interactional dynamics (the influence of interactive variables between speaker and addressee at a given moment). There are other variables to be considered, and more work must be done to determine which of these effects are secondary, much less parasitic/metaphorical.

The question is, can quantitative or qualitative analysis determine whether topic, purpose, and setting are stand-alone primitives, or whether they are metaphorical subprimitives? Whichever is the case, there is already ample quantitative evidence that topic is an important variable (Hindle 1979, Rickford and McNair-Knox 1994), as is purpose (cf. also "frame" or "footing": Schilling-Estes 1998); planning (cf. Labov (1972), "attention paid to speech") is also quantitatively demonstrable, while the importance of setting has yet to be quantitatively clarified, although some of the evidence from Rickford and McNair-Knox (1994) may be reinterpretable to demonstrate its importance. Bell considers these as metaphorical extensions of the basic audience design influence; Biber and Finegan consider them as stand-alone primitives. The evidence is not yet all in, and more studies are needed to resolve the issue.

Performance "frame" is also relevant: *Mizrahi* singers are caught between shifting toward the vernacular-stereotype (for self-identification) and shifting toward the "standard" (for accommodation to the audience). The frame (which kind of song they are singing, and what the expectations are for that song register, or where and with whom they are being interviewed) influences the realization of (r), without helping disambiguate referee from audience design. The variation in musical registers is partially referee design, partially audience design, partially "instrumental," partially "*genre*"-frame related. Should frame be made a primitive as well?[2] Or, as Bell suggests, is it a parameter parasitic on either referee or audience design? Hopefully, further studies can help answer this question.

Schilling-Estes (1998) has recently completed analysis of Ocracoke, SC, (ay) nucleus variation: the nucleus is low-front, and unglided when the speaker accommodates to a Southern model, low-front and gliding when the speaker accommodates to a Northern model, and raised, with a glide, when the speaker accommodates to a local model. The (ay) nuclei of Schilling-Estes' speaker RO are lowest when he is accommodating to, and talking with, the non-local interviewer, but it is not clear to what degree accommodation toward the interviewer's phonology is referee-designed or truly accommodative (1998). RO's nuclei are slightly higher when he is talking to his siblings and higher yet when he's performing his dialect for Northern outgroup members (both audience and ratified overhearers, in Bell's sense) than when he is talking to his siblings. Would his performance register be considered accommodation? Perhaps it would reveal accommodation to the perceived interests of his interviewers, but certainly not self-identification with the local phonology.

RO "performs" "hoi toider" speech for visiting dialectologists, Coupland's talk-show host "performs" Cardiff (this volume), *Mizrahi* singers "perform" different dialects depending on the musical frame in which the song is set (Yaeger-Dror 1994). Like Word List Style, performance frame is going to shift in different directions depending on what kind of frame it is: self-identificatory, referee- or audience-designed. Coupland's Cardiff

---

[2] In fact, frame is statistically very significant in the (r) analysis, while the factor group topic had no effect. This does not imply that topic is not a useful primitive, but does show that frame is a strong candidate.

vernacular performance (this volume) may well be self-identificatory; Schilling-Estes' (1998) vernacular performance was in all likelihood accommodative to the perceived desires of the interlocutors;[3] the *Mizrahi* singers' (and politicians')[4] vernacular performance (Yaeger-Dror 1993, 1994) modes are primarily referee-designed and self-identificatory, with an audience-designed accommodative component more pronounced in interview than in song, and more pronounced for politicians than for singers. Both the Israeli data and Shilling-Estes' Ocracoke data show that speakers converge toward their audience more radically when they are interacting with the audience than when performing a role for that audience. Both studies reflect the difficulty of distinguishing between referee [who-I-want-to-appear-to-be-to-an-outside-observer] and audience [how-I-want-you-to-see-me] as the prime motivator. Performance itself is not a primitive, since, as was shown by the study of *Mizrahi* singers, a given speaker [or singer] can perform different personae, or distinct performance varieties determined by the culture or by the present context. I project that performance frame is a good candidate for one of Bell's parasitic variables, and that Coupland's radio performer data should be interpreted in this light.

2.4   Elaboration of style primitives by other researchers

"Style" is of interest to students of other research domains, and I would contend that we should take advantage of their insights. Contextual dynamics – such as topics and genres – have been analyzed primarily by literary theorists and anthropologists; setting, frame, and footing have been discussed primarily by sociologists and anthropologists. Hindle (1979), Bell (1984, 1991a, b), Coupland (1984), Trudgill (1986), Rickford and McNair-Knox (1994), and Yaeger-Dror (1991) have all analyzed quantitative variation which can be traced to addressee and other audience effects, specifically from an accommodation perspective. Variationist studies concerned with addressee effects from this accommodative perspective have followed Bell's lead, in referring to the parameter as audience design. But those linguists who have looked closely at gender effects (that cross-cut

---

[3] In actuality, the distinction between Bell's and Coupland's terminology is relevant here: RO wants to frame his performance of Ocracoke dialect as very authentic, so the frame is referee-designed. On the other hand, the transcript shows that he himself does not want to be considered to be identified with the dialect, since he says "I say h[ay] t[ay]d," although in the performance he says [hoy toyd]. Thus, while the performance could not be called self-identification, it can be called referee-designed.

[4] Politicians' speechifying is also a complex mixture of audience-designed and referee-designed phonology, morphology, prosody, and costume, varied for different specific occasions providing an elaborate demonstration of dialect style of performance, within which regional and/or ethnic markers are politically advantageous in some (but not all) situations.

Bell's Pakeha/Maori work, as well as Trudgill's, Cheshire's, and other data cited here) or the power vector (that generally is correlated both with gender [Eckert 1989, Ochs 1992] and ethnicity [Giles and Coupland 1991, Ben Rafael 1994, Bell this volume]) are rarely clear as to the relative importance of audience and referee effects, since both are often simultaneously involved.

Interactional dynamics have been discussed by accommodation theorists (Giles and Coupland 1991) and conversation analysts (Sacks 1992), as well as by sociolinguists (Brown and Gilman 1960, Brown and Levinson 1978) and sociologists (Goffman 1971). However, the bulk of sociolinguistic research has ignored many ways in which interactional dynamics should be taken into consideration. Whether our research design specifically incorporates variations in power and solidarity vectors, or whether a more indirect system is used (cf. Bell's reference to those who use more apologies), it is important that these factors be "unpacked." The solidarity vector probably is incorporable within our understanding of audience design, but the power vector, like gender, ethnicity, and age characteristics, influences both audience design and referee design. Bell's chapter has made a good beginning by incorporating two of these parameters (gender and ethnicity) directly into this analysis.

Another interactional parameter which feeds into the analysis of audience design is the designation of a turn as supportive, neutral, or remedial (Goffman 1971, expanded on in Brown and Levinson 1978); this parameter interacts with the social position (or "face") of the addressee(s) relative to each other, and therefore is mediated by power and solidarity vectors. As in Bell's initial presentation (1984), the critical primitive is audience design. If an addressee is not assumed to have a specific position relative to a given statement, then the conversational dynamic ascribed to the statement is said to be "neutral," and informational considerations take precedence. If a speaker assumes a statement will be supportive of the addressee's position, the turn will be termed "supportive," while, on the other hand, if a statement is remedial (Goffman 1971) or face-threatening (Brown and Levinson 1978) to the addressee, this will be referred to as "confrontational."[5] The accommodative dynamics and conversational dynamics can be distinguished from each other in theory, but an individual's choice of confrontational or supportive conversational stance is often mediated by (among other things) the (macro)accommodative position, vis à vis a given addressee. Even given a particular choice of conversational stance, the turn

[5] Of course, CONFRONTATION and SUPPORT on the "micro," or conversational level reflect Giles' DIVERGENCE and CONVERGENCE on the larger level of inter-personal dynamics. Similarly, topic can be viewed as the micro/conversational counterpart of register. The discussion of the patterned parallel is beyond the bounds of this paper.

will be made more or less forceful – 'aggravated' or 'mitigated' (Goffman 1971) – at least prosodically, depending partly on the accommodative dynamics between the speakers.

Another distinction, which Bell's proposal does not incorporate, but which both Biber (1988) and Yaeger-Dror (1985, 1996a, b) have found to be a useful primitive is the continuum from interactive to informational presentation. To the degree that a speaker varies speech relative to his audience, the speech can be interpreted as interactional; but it is necessary to consider the "style" primitive which focuses on the informational content. Perhaps Coupland's "instrumental" could be interpreted as informational, but Bell's presentation does not permit the inclusion of this parameter at all. I believe that these interactional dynamics should be distinguished from social context dynamics. Within this larger context, it becomes clear that Biber's Dimension I (informational–involved) is not the simple dichotomous continuum proposed by Biber, but is of necessity relatively simple at one end (informational) and rather complex at the other (involved), with a whole gamut of inter-personal-dynamic options. To illustrate the fact that all these primitives influence speech, and should be incorporated separately, I now turn to data which require the isolation of all these parameters.

3   Prosodic variation on negatives as evidence of style primitives

It is my own style analysis of both morphological and "ideational" prosodic variation that has revealed to me the limitations of Bell's analysis: Yaeger-Dror (1985, 1996a, b, 1997) analyzed the use of focal accent in sentences with *not*-negation (Tottie 1991), comparing a number of discourse settings. The evidence presented here concerns one intonational ideational selection variable: prosodic variation on *not*-negation, as in (1).

(1)   I *do not* want to go. [Hypothetical example]

That sentence can be varied in many ways: The negative can be reduced to (1r):[6]

(1r)   I *don't* want to go.

or it can be highlighted prosodically by making the vowel longer, and the pitch and amplitude prominent relative to other words, as in (1f):

(1f)   I do **no:t** want to go.

In (1f) the prominence is marked in the transcription by boldface. In (2), which occurred in a political debate, *not* was actually quite prominent pro-

---

[6] Where an example number followed by "r" is reduced, and one followed by "f" is full, or unreduced.

sodically. Theoretically, prosodic prominence is "continuous" – that is, the more emphatic the negative, the more the pitch will be prominent, deviating from the neutral sentence contour. However, to date only the likelihood of prosodic prominence has been measured, and it was found that the more informational the situation, the more likely prominence was to occur. The more interactive and social the situation, the less likely prominence was to occur.

(2)   An' roughly twenny-five percent **_don't_** wanna state holiday
       (MacNeill/Lehrer debate: Mecham)

American English reading prosody for sentences, prose passages, National Public Radio "news-speak," didactic presentations, political debates, group therapy sessions, dinner parties, and telephone conversations were all compared and a number of apparent 'primitives' were isolated.

In English, *not*-negation is both a dialect and pragmatic variable, and pragmatic/ideational and dialectal issues are not always simple to tease apart. Studies by Hazen (1996) and Biber (1988) clarify that contraction of negatives is a dialect variable in both America and England; Bell (1984) and others have shown that dialect style manipulates contraction, and that newspapers which are audience-designed for a more 'popular' audience are more likely to permit contractions than those designed for a more middle-class audience. Biber also concludes that register is relevant – with more planned or informational negatives being less likely to be contracted. Yaeger-Dror (1997) shows how closely contraction (dialect style) and reduction (ideational selection) are inter-related, and how both vary with register. To date, for English data, the following register dimensions appear most critical.

The INFORMATION–INTERACTION axis. While negatives carry critical information, and should be "stressed," and lengthened, they can also show disagreement, which may lead to their being reduced to mitigate that disagreement (Yaeger-Dror 1985). Analysis of contraction and prosodic variation (on the negative) both support the hypothesis that – at least in English – the more informational the register, the less likely the vowel is to be contracted (Yaeger-Dror 1997), and the more likely prosodic prominence is to be permitted (Yaeger-Dror 1985, 1996a). These two forms of acoustic prominence permit the listener readier access to the semantic information. Even when a speaker is obliged by a script to permit contraction of *not*, prominence is maintained if the focus is on speech, or on information retrieval, as in read isolated sentences (O'Shaughnessy and Allen 1983), or National Public Radio news broadcasts, which had pitch prominence on almost 100 percent of negatives (Hirschberg 1990).

On the other hand, the more interactional the social situation, the more likely it is that a range of other factors will come into play, and influence both *not*-contraction and -reduction. The more socially accommodative/convergent the situation, the more frequent contraction will be, and the less likely prosodic prominence is to occur (at least in English), even if no disagreement is being expressed: *not* was much less likely to be prominent in a didactic workshop where both information retrieval and interactional factors are relevant (20 percent) or even in read dialogue or informational prose passages, where the interactional component is artificial (20–50 percent), and *not* was generally contracted (Yaeger-Dror 1997). In an interactive situation, the less convergent the audience design situation or "frame," the more likely prominence is to occur. Table 10.2 presents the percentages for prosodically prominent *not* or modal+*n't* in specific social situations.[7]

FRAME. Specific frames can alter the percentages: conversations have below 20 percent prominence even on informative negatives, and below 5 percent on disagreements (not to mention that more than 90 percent of the negatives are contracted). Political debates, which are framed as being "about" disagreement, have much higher prominence percentages, and lower contraction rates.

FOOTING counts, since within a given frame, those who see themselves as ratified to disagree (like political debaters) focus more on negatives than those who don't (like moderators). A moderator's footing is supposed to be supportive, while the debaters' footing is to emphasize differences. Not surprisingly, in the Mecham/Babbitt debate, the moderator (MacNeil) only used prominence on supportive negatives. Similarly, within a therapy frame, therapists, even more than moderators, must shuffle into a supportive footing, with no confrontational negatives prosodically prominent, while teenaged group therapy patients use prominence 20 percent of remedial turns (Yaeger-Dror 1985). Even fictive footing is important: in read dialogue, polite interactions feature low focus on disagreement, while the children's-literature disagreements (studied from Cleary's *Ramona the Pest*) permit prominence on negatives.

In short, many of the primitives we have considered are relevant to a study of prosodic variation within a given dialect, just as they would be for a study of dialect style; they reflect audience, referee and ideational design characteristics, and are quantitatively analyzable. Prosodic and morphological information reveal common trends for pragmatic (interactive) variables leading me to propose that more pragmatic variables should be studied, and that they may well reveal different – and more nuanced – register variation even than low level phonetic variables like (wh) in New

---

[7] For discussion of methodology and greater analytical detail, see the papers cited.

Table 10.2. *Percentage of* not *prosodically prominent in various English corpora*

Corpus	Verb + *not*	
	Informational	Disagreement
Polite conversations		
Schegloff and Jefferson (1968), TG	18	0
Schegloff and Jefferson (1972), CH-4	13	2.3
Adult literature		
Keillor (1985), *Lake Wobegon Days*	49	33.3
Tyler (1988), *Breathing Lessons*	25	17
Children's literature		
Cleary (1968), *Ramona the Pest*	46.8	60
Debate		
Mecham	—	64.8
Babbitt	—	84.6

Zealand, or (ahr) in Cardiff or the American South West (Labov, Yaeger, and Steiner 1972, Yaeger, 1974).

4   Conclusion

The task set for the workshop was to determine style primitives, so that we can effectively consider the importance of style, or register, in any corpus. With that accomplished, we could determine the relative importance of different dimensions relative to a specific linguistic variable (e.g., (*wh*) or (*r*) variation), or perhaps to a whole conglomerate of variables (e.g., chain shifting, or prosodic preferences).

Although we expected to find little overlap in our understandings of style variation, Bell's and Coupland's papers showed a greater degree of agreement than had been expected. Among the primitives agreed upon were those referred to as referee design (identity) and audience design (relational), but while many studies permit the quantitative analysis of both, none permits us to distinguish between them without careful qualitative analysis. Other variables, like topic, purpose, and setting, were regarded by some as primitives, and by others as metaphoric – or parasitic on the primitives. Although most studies used dialect style variables for the analysis of style, in section 3 I found data which combined both morphological and prosodic variation, which provides a broader palette of variation. The reduction of *not* in English was found to vary radically with different dialect and ideational register parameters. The conclusion drawn from preliminary analysis is that morphology ([modal+]*not*) and prosody (the continuum from extreme prominence to reduction of *not*) work in tandem, and that both dialect style and ideational selection can be simultaneously relevant to a given analysis. Preliminary analysis of *not* reveals that several other register variables must be incorporated into the analysis, and that it is premature to distinguish among these variables by concluding that some are truly primitive while others are "metaphorical." I have suggested that we consider experimenting with a larger set of variables that can be combined in various ways, and that we only eliminate them (or define them as "parasitic") after further study. Bell (1984, this volume) has presented us with a challenge to determine a workable body of style primitives, but only extensive research in a range of different cultural and social situations, and with the careful attention to detail that his work exemplifies, will determine what the optimal primitives will be.

11 Language, situation, and the relational self: theorizing dialect-style in sociolinguistics[1]

Nikolas Coupland

It is difficult to assess the place of "style" in sociolinguistics. On the one hand, style is everything and everywhere – to the extent that we define styles as context-related varieties, and contextuality as the rationale for sociolinguistics. At this level of generalization, it would seem futile to try to theorize style, since a theory of style would be a theory of everything. On the other hand, style was operationalized as a single quantifiable dimension of sociolinguistic variation in Labovian surveys, and it is still with this focus that sociolinguists tend to address the issue of stylistic variation. From this standpoint, style may not have appeared to merit theorizing; it was (and for many still is) a patterning principle in numerical arrays, an axis on a graph. Sociolinguists have found the consequences of stylistic mapping to be informative, but style itself has needed no more explanatory effort than, at one time, did class or sex or age, as correlates of or as supposed determinants of language variation.

Sociolinguistic critiques of the Labovian conception of style surfaced in the 1970s and 1980s (e.g. Coupland 1980, Cheshire 1982, Bell 1984, Milroy 1987), in many cases voicing dissatisfaction with Labov's claim that stylistic variation was organized according to the degree of attention speakers pay to their own speech. Others wanted to establish social psychological and in particular motivational processes as a basis for understanding style-shifting (Giles 1970, Coupland 1984, 1985). Giles and his colleagues (see Giles and Powesland 1975) were developing a generalized dynamic model of social (inter-personal and inter-group) relations, speech accommodation theory, which offered one coherent way of theorizing style-shifting. Bell (1984) reworked the central claim of accommodation theory in his audience design model – the first systematic sociolinguistic account of style since Labov's seminal (1972) formulation.

More recently, some particular studies (Preston 1991, Yaeger-Dror 1991, Finegan and Biber 1994, Rickford and McNair-Knox 1994) and one

[1] I am grateful to Adam Jaworski, Allan Bell, and Justine Coupland for detailed comments on an earlier version of this text.

integrative collection (Biber and Finegan 1994) have produced new data and explicitly revived the theoretical debate about how style should be conceptualized within sociolinguistics. In most cases, these studies operate within the general parameters for style analysis established by Labov (not least in that they generally accept style to be "a dimension"), and in many respects take Bell's audience design framework as a departure point. This renewed attention to the "neglected dimension" of style (Bell 1994) is very welcome. On the other hand, these studies reconfirm the quantitative, variationist, unidimensional approach to style, leaving it conceptually isolated from other important theoretical traditions in sociolinguistics, let alone the wider analysis of human communication and social interaction.

Finegan and Biber are certainly right in claiming that sociolinguistics has lacked an integrated theory to locate its analyses of style. But their view of what such a theory should be, and even of what the *scope* of a relevant theory should be, is controversial. In this paper, I attempt a reappraisal, specifically *outside* of Labov's initial two-dimensional and quantitative model of sociolinguistic variation. My contention is that sociolinguistic approaches to style can and should engage with current social theorizing about language, discourse, social relationships and selfhood, rather than be contained within one corner (variationist, descriptive, distributional) of one disciplinary treatment (linguistics) of language. To some extent, then, the paper is about the theoretical limitations inherent in an autonomous sociolinguistics.

The main argument is this:

Style needs to be located within a model of human communicative purposes, practices and achievements, and as one aspect of the manipulation of semiotic resources in social contexts. In talking about style we need to distinguish variation in "dialect style" from variation within and across ways of speaking. Nevertheless, interpretations of style at the level of dialect variation must cross-refer to stylistic processes at other levels. Our theoretical understanding of style in general, and our interpretations of stylistic performance in particular instances, should not be limited by any single empirical or interpretive procedure. A more broadly conceived "dialect stylistics" can explore the role of style in projecting speakers' often-complex identities and in defining social relationships and other configurations of context. This is a perspective that allows sociolinguistics to engage with recent inter-disciplinary literatures on selfhood, social relationships, and discourse.

I shall elaborate on this conception and try to integrate existing sociolinguistic approaches to style within it, as far as proves possible. But the essence of my argument is to *challenge* many of the assumptions that underlie the best-established sociolinguistic approaches to style. Although the paper will not treat each of them in turn, they are listed here to help organize the discussion. They are the assumptions that:

1. to study variation in dialect style variables is an adequate representation of sociolinguistic style variation in general;
2. style varies independently of other domains of socially meaningful variation (e.g. referential meanings, pragmatic function, ways of speaking);
3. style is a situational correlate, rather than an active, motivated, symbolic process;
4. stylistic variants are semantically equivalent;
5. dialect style is one-dimensional:
   a. situationally, in that we will detect stylistic difference by looking at the same individual's (or groups of individuals') deployment of dialectal variables across situations that are ordered according to one underlying criterion (e.g. formality);
   b. linguistically, in that all style-shifts will be either toward or away from an identifiable linguistic level or norm, e.g. a standard variety;
   c. psychologically, in that linear shifts relate to one scaleable intra-personal variable, such as "attention to speech";
6. what is interesting and socially interpretable in relation to dialect style is exclusively variation, rather than styles in the context of their use;
7. for stylistic variation to be meaningful, we have to detect variation across stylistic "levels," defined as bands of relative frequencies of occurrence;
8. dialect style is a characteristic of the spoken text;
9. dialect style acts as a constraint on recipients' attributions of a speaker's social group membership (a middle-class speaker speaking casually, versus a working-class speaker speaking carefully); it has no implications for selves or selfhood;
10. dialect styles index personal and contextual attributes; they do not service local communicative intents.

After reappraising and challenging these assumptions, I shall briefly refer back to an earlier empirical study of my own to illustrate lines of interpretation that the broader perspective allows.

1   "Functional" variation

Sociolinguistics often appears to be the domain of language studies that is uncontroversially concerned with language as social action. Its guiding principles (communicative competence, socially constituted linguistics, contextualization, variationism, as these were formulated in the work of Hymes, Labov, Gumperz, and others) all point to a resolutely functional approach: not the narrow functionalism of speech act theory; rather the analysis of language varieties in the articulation of communicative purposes, practices and effects in social and cultural contexts. The foundation studies of sociolinguistics were concerned with "social meanings," although these were sometimes taken to be implied in the facts of variation. "Social meanings" have been studied in the sociolinguistics of personal or group relationships (the encoding of power/status/prestige and solidarity/intimacy) and of personal and social identification (the sociolinguistic expression of allegiances and antipathies). There is also a strong tradition which researches the social meanings of linguistic styles empirically – the "language attitudes" studies of social psychologists (cf. Ryan and Giles 1982, Giles and Coupland 1991).

At the same time, sociolinguistics has only occasionally defined its interests *explicitly* in terms of the analysis of communicative purposes (Hymes 1972 is an important exception). When sociolinguistics *has* foregrounded communicative purposes, "social" and "referential" purposes have sometimes been represented as two orthogonal dimensions underpinning all communicative acts. Holmes (1990:254), for example, models interaction as a vertical scale of "referential content" (100 percent–0 percent) intersected by a relational dimension labeled "solidarity–distance." Other influential treatments model social meanings as multidimensional, as in Brown and Levinson's (1987) specification of solidarity and distance as social factors mediating facework and politeness. But sociolinguistic models, particularly in the variationist tradition, have generally by-passed considerations of purpose and even of function, preferring to demonstrate the predictable links between language usage and social structural configurations.

Communication science, on the other hand, has frequently emphasized three core dimensions of communicative purposes, often distinguishing instrumental, relational, and identity goals (Craig 1986, Tracy 1991). Many different research paradigms in communication have addressed the ways in which interactants organize their exchanges in relation to *multiple*, simultaneously salient, goals, which may at times be conflictual amongst themselves (e.g. Bavelas et al. 1990), and as much emergent in interaction as preformed (Tracy and Coupland 1990). For the analysis of style, this general perspective, and questions of identity in particular, have a natural significance. In fact, a dominant emphasis in literary stylistics has been to interpret style as the expression of individuality and as the textual locus for an individual author's creative involvement with readers. Sociolinguists' willingness to ignore these traditional emphases in the study of style is part of a wider pattern of underplaying communicative goals, the functional complexity of language in use, and issues of identity and selfhood in general.

Style has generally been recognized as the dimension of intra-personal variation, somehow linked to variation in situational context. It would therefore seem appropriate to seek to explain its functioning partly in terms of individuals' social motivations and projected outcomes, however difficult this is in methodological terms. The case that language needs to be seen as a determinant of social situation just as much as conditioned by it has been argued in very many places (e.g. Brown and Fraser 1979, Giles and Coupland 1991, Schegloff 1994), and it again follows that we have to consider style as situational *achievement*, and as the fulfillment of communicative purposes (whether consciously or non-consciously represented) in relation to those social situations.

2   Dialect styles and ways of speaking

Where, in terms of linguistic levels, would we expect to find stylistic variables functioning in the service of communicators' strategic purposes? The variationist paradigm in sociolinguistics has considered style in terms of phonological, and sometimes morphosyntactic and lexical, variation. But within this range it has been overwhelmingly concerned with features from the repertoire of dialect (and mainly "accent") features. To be clear about this rather obvious point, the sociolinguistic analysis of style has been almost exclusively the top-down surveying of contextual variation in features ("sociolinguistic variables") that simultaneously characterize social and regional dialects. Those features that have been examined for their potential to vary "stylistically" have been those known (or expected) to vary in "social" dimensions – features which are diagnostic of social (usually status-related) differentiation in communities. The study of style has therefore tended to be linked firmly to, in fact embedded within, the study of dialect differentiation. But however we delimit "style," its remit extends well beyond dialect. Variation in forms of address, politeness, conversational dominance, lexical formality, communicative key, self-disclosiveness, and so on is uncontroversial ground for the study of style, but not of dialect style.

So it is reasonable to recognize two distinctions: firstly between variation in what we can call "dialect style" (stylistic variation in respect of variable features associated semiotically within "social" or socioeconomic class differentiation and attribution within sociolinguistic communities) and variation in "expressive" or "attitudinal" *style* (e.g. those prosodic and paralinguistic variables which are not indexically linked to social group membership);[2] and secondly between the above and Hymes's broader sense

---

[2] Jaworski points out (in a personal note) that there are predictable areas of overlap between dialect style and non-dialect style, for example in the feasibility of identifying "standard" forms of address or politeness which may co-occur with dialect standardness. At the same time, I would not see the likelihood of overlap as vitiating the dialect style versus non-dialect style distinction itself.

of the word "style," more commonly labelled "ways of speaking." Ways of speaking include style choices which are patterns of ideational selection – what we choose to mean, to whom, when, and where. Hymes argued for a sense of the term "style" that is "non-protean" (1974:434): simply "a way or mode of doing something," suggesting that a speech community should initially be viewed as comprising a set of styles – "the linguistic means that actually obtain in a community." Hymes goes on to characterize styles as reflecting personal choice, including choices which are motivated by the full range of semantic/pragmatic concerns: "Persons are recognized to choose among styles themselves, and the choices to have social meaning. (This is the vantage point from which a variety of phenomena treated separately under headings such as bilingualism, diglossia, standard and non-standard speech, and the like, can be integrated" (Hymes 1974:434–5). Dialect styles and ways of speaking are therefore distinguished in that, with dialect style, we are considering semiotic variants that do not themselves distinguish referential (or "ideational" in the Hallidayan sense) meanings, although they may of course "colour" these meanings in socially important ways. Ways of speaking are by definition patterns of ideational selection.

Returning to our earlier discussion of clusters of communicative purposes, we can now say that dialect style operates primarily in the expression of *identity and relational goals*; ways of speaking operate in relation to all three main constellations of communicative goals: instrumental, identity, and relational goals. From an entropic viewpoint, we might say that dialect style features are well suited to articulating identity and relational goals because they are "free" from the semiotic "burden" of articulating ideational meanings. That is, dialect style features bear their social meanings indexically more than referentially, as Labov and others have explained.

But it would be misleading to overemphasize this distinction. One element of sociolinguists' theorizing of dialect style to date has been the argument that stylistic variants (and indeed all sociolinguistic variants) are "equivalent." Lavandera (1978) points out that a sameness requirement underpins the establishment of sociolinguistic variables, and that the requirement is met in the case of phonological (and therefore "accent") variants by their *referential* sameness. But this methodological consideration has obscured the potential for dialect style variants to be *ideologically nonequivalent*. Dialect style variants may be alternative ways of achieving the same reference, but it does not follow that they are alternative ways of "saying" or "meaning" "the same thing."

Lee (1992), for example, asks "whether the differences between linguistic [dialect] varieties – specifically between standard and non-standard varieties – is simply a matter of superficial formal contrasts, or whether there are more important differences having to do with the kinds of meanings expressible in different varieties" (p. 165). He goes on to argue that "It is, of course, a commonplace that there are marked ideological differences associated with the use of a standard or a non-standard variety" which are "oriented towards different meaning potentials" (*ibid.*). Lee's position is that we can give a better account of the social significance of dialect-styles if we see them as "associated with different ways of speaking, different meaning orientations, different discourses" (p. 166). Milroy and Milroy appear to acknowledge the same point in saying that "relatively low level linguistic elements . . . [are] intertwined quite inextricably with social distinctions of various kinds important in the community" (1985:96).

As Hymes has implied, there is no reason to segregate the analysis of dialect style from that of ways of speaking in general. In semiotic terms, dialect styles are a subset of a community's culturally imbued ways of speaking and need to be analyzed in relation to other (non-dialectal) dimensions of cultural meaning. This is how, as social actors, we experience dialect styles and how we draw social inferences from their use. Dialect styles become meaningful for our self-identities and our relationships through the ways in which they cross-refer to other symbolic processes in discourse.

3   The illusion of non-motivated style-shifting

The dominant orientation to style (which has been fitfully challenged but as yet unconvincingly so – because of the intuitive strength and demonstrable empirical success of the original insights in Labov's work) has been a distributional one. That is, we have approached the analysis of style with the same perspectival and epistemological set that we have taken into the analysis of community stratification. There is no place for communicative purposes in this epistemology. A method which predetermines categories called "social contexts" and which then examines the aggregated scores speakers achieve on sociolinguistic indices across them *asks* only very limited questions about stylistic variation (Coupland 1980, 1984, Bell 1984). And the "success" of the answers (finding regular patterns of co-variation of "style" and context) seemed to warrant having asked those, and only those, questions.

But what is appropriate for surveying the aggregate behaviors of communities and their subgroups is not necessarily appropriate for the unraveling of contextual variation through style-shifting. When it comes to social stratification by class, gender, or age, individuals do not have the answers; the patterns that matter operate beyond the scope of the individual case. But when we come to the analysis of style, we see individuals interacting within their own space, time, and relational contexts. We can of course seek to generalize about "what most people stylistically do," and the results are informative and important. But this exercise is reductionist in that it rules out any possible interpretation of the *local* intra- and inter-personal processes which are style's domain.

It is necessarily true of all survey designs that group means obscure what is happening in local instances. But studies of community stratification are established at a level of generality that makes aggregation appropriate and necessary for them. The basic problematic of style, on the other hand, is inherently established at a local level which makes aggregation inappropriate, just as it would be inappropriate, say, to interpret musical performance through an aggregation of pitch or amplitude levels across performers and instances. What we have come to think of as the "two basic dimensions" of sociolinguistic variation – the social and the stylistic (Labov), or the dialectal and the diatopic (Halliday) – relate to two different domains of sociolinguistic process (organized, group-relevant diversity, versus contingent, individual-relevant diversity), and to two different modes of sociolinguistic understanding (generalization, versus specification). They are made to appear as two dimensions of the same planar surface purely as an artifact of the reporting exercise, by constituting them as apparently equivalent physical dimensions in graphs and tables. These, in turn, are made possible by having constructed categories of "situations" (casual, formal, reading, etc.) in the same manner as social categories such as class, sex, or age groups. (Sociological accounts of the theoretical limitations and the practical implications of establishing *social* categories in this way are themselves relevant to this discussion, but I shall not pursue them here.)[3]

4   The quantitative, distributional approach

Mapping stylistic variation as a single dimension cross-cutting a status dimension of dialect variation has enshrined many of the key assumptions about style that appear in the numbered list, above. This is a clear case where methodological convenience has curtailed theoretical elaboration,

---

[3] The disciplinary location of sociolinguistics is an interesting contextual issue here too. Sociolinguistics has traditionally been populated by people trained in the humanities, and many of us were not aware (I, at least, was not aware) of the dangers involved in bolting on some social insight to our linguistic understandings. We were probably reassured by statements that sociolinguistics (and especially "sociolinguistics proper"; Trudgill 1978) was really the right way of doing linguistics all along. In the grid-irons of Labovian numerical tables there was the possibility that we might have done our duty by sociology (cf. Williams 1992). In that context, it is particularly ironic that the traditional concerns of the humanities with "style" as a tenuous and elusive facet of language in action were ignored. But in the other direction too, sociolinguists were not often inclined to map their findings onto social theoretic concerns, because they did not appear to be necessary concerns in the climate of autonomous sociolinguistics.

even in the face of contrary evidence. Recent discussions about dialect style in sociolinguistics, although projected as revisions of current theory, actually reaffirm it.

If style is to be understood as intra- and inter-personally motivated, we cannot theorize style outside the realm of discursive social action. In proposing the audience design perspective on style, Bell (1984) proposed a "style axiom" to the effect that "Variation on the style dimension within the speech of a single speaker derives from and echoes the variation which exists between speakers on the 'social' dimension" (p. 151). This is, in the first place, an inductive generalization about the *extents* of "social" and "stylistic" variation as captured by the principal survey studies. In very many cases, the maximal range of variation quantified along the "style" axis is smaller than that along the "status" axis. Preston (1991) confirms the validity of this distributional observation through re-examining several VARBRUL studies. He then adds the specification that what he calls the "variation space" for style is also "contained within that of the social dimension" (p. 35).

But at the same time, Bell's axiom proposes an explanation of how dialect styles become socially meaningful. The primary repertoire (in the sense of Giles and Powesland 1975) of variable forms available to any one speaker is likely to be limited to those forms that have achieved their semiotic value through being distributed unevenly across status groups within the community. Bell's maxim therefore refers to the social *semiosis* of dialect style, and specifically to the semiotic origins of dialect style variation. In arguing that style variation "derives from" social variation, Bell is claiming that it is the social meanings that attach to dialect variants through their social status distribution within communities that makes them available for stylistic signification. (I have put this case in my own work; Gee [1990] and Milroy and Milroy [1985], as quoted above, also take this stance.)

However, Preston's VARBRUL analyses do not address these concerns. Preston's observations are based solely on distributional evidence from sociolinguistic surveys and the case he argues about "derivation" offers no explanations at the level of social semiosis. In his "status axiom," Preston makes the interesting further claim that "Variation on the 'status' dimension derives from and echoes the variation which exists within the 'linguistic' dimension" (p. 36). By this he means that the maximal extent of status-linked variation in the community as a whole is contained within the "variation space made available by the surrounding linguistic contexts" (p. 37). Preston therefore argues that there is a distributional "nesting" of sociolinguistic dimensions, linguistic–social–stylistic, that we should expect to find with variables that are not undergoing rapid change within communities (p. 46).

The relevant point for the moment is that Preston's arguments lead to predictive claims at the level of sociolinguistic distribution, but they do not take us any further towards *explaining* dialect style in use. At the end of the (1991) paper, however, Preston does speculate about a psychological model of dialect style production that would be consistent with his distributional claims (see also Preston 1989). That model characterizes sociolinguistic variables operating as probabilistically weighted "unfair coins" being "flipped" and "landing" as the realization of particular variant forms. So, "STATUS items are those permanent or long-term factors which are pre-loaded on these unfair coins, but STYLISTIC ones are read from the immediate environment and are volatile" (1991:52). Preston suggests that the stylistic "factor" operates (as in Labov's original conception) as a continuum "presumably something like LEAST-MONITORED to MOST-MONITORED" (*ibid.*). It is interesting to notice how Preston's model perpetuates the assumptions listed earlier. Stylistic choice is modeled mechanistically – as a set of output probabilities in speech conditioned by "social circumstances," including "stylistic" ones, which act as "filters." The model reifies as psychological processes "factors" which are, from another point of view, artifactual products of a specific and limited descriptive methodology.

Finegan and Biber (1994) entertain an alternative perspective on style which I cannot consider in detail here. Basically, they argue that because it is functionally motivated, register variation is basic in a community; that is, the contrary claim to Bell's style axiom. They contend that different social groups within a community will generally employ different registers, so that register variation somehow underpins social differentiation. More particularly, different registers have different "preferences" for either a "clarity mandate" (be clear) or for an "ease mandate" (be quick and easy). This is then taken to explain why varieties associated with high-status groups are (Finegan and Biber claim) those whose variant preferences orient to the clarity mandate, and vice versa.

Preston (1991) and Bell (1995) have debated Finegan and Biber's claims in detail. I would simply add that Finegan and Biber's approach is interesting in that it starts from a desire to understand sociolinguistic variation in functional terms. However, their claims about form–function correspondences seem overstated. Variants associated with low status groups and "informal" registers are not always the same ones. Also, less standard variants do not uniformly follow the ease mandate. As Ochs observes in relation to her Samoan data, "nonprestige variants are not always less complex than the variant captured in the [formal] informant session" (1988:37), and many other distributional findings challenge Finegan and

Biber's position.[4] The limitation of Finegan and Biber's position, as it appears to me, is its faith, once again, in a unidimensional motivating principle – in attempting to explain stylistic choice only in relation to an elaboration/simplicity criterion. Even if their claims about class, style, and elaboration were correct empirical generalizations (and there are clear counterexamples), they would have no resources to interpret stylistic variation to which elaboration/simplicity is irrelevant. Their model does not allow for the unique indexical properties of dialect style variables as I have sought to describe them.

5   Bakhtin and a dynamic sociolinguistics

Duranti and Goodwin (1992) begin their introductory essay in *Rethinking Context* as follows: "When we look at the work done within the last twenty years on the relation between language and context . . . we can see a trend toward increasingly more interactive and dialogically conceived notions of contextually situated talk" (Duranti and Goodwin (1992:1). Macaulay (1991:5–6) quotes Glassie (1982:5) to the effect that "What matters is not what chances to surround performance in the real world, but what effectively surrounds performance in the mind and influences the creation of texts." These comments are indicative of a rather general reappraisal of the theoretical importance of context in sociolinguistics, and the growing belief that sociolinguistics must account for the social organization of meanings through interactive discourses.

This emphasis has led over the last decade to a reconsideration of Bakhtin/Volosinov's theoretical writings (Volosinov 1973, Bakhtin 1981, Shuklan 1988, Emerson and Holquist 1992), on occasions quite explicitly connected with sociolinguistics (White 1984, Macaulay 1987, 1991). Bakhtin's work is suggestive, and somehow emancipatory, in relation to current sociolinguistic discussions of style. As White shows, the concepts of *sociolect* and *register* were used by Bakhtin to explore his central concept of *heteroglossia*: "There is interwoven with . . . generic stratification of language a *professional* stratification of language, in the broad sense of the

---

[4] Ochs cites tense–aspect structures in Samoan as an instance and refers to nominalization as a feature of informal discourse there. Other instances include postvocalic /l/ as a low-prestige feature in Bristol (UK) and the fact that postvocalic /r/ is high-status in some (USA) communities and low-status in others (UK); /e/ versus /ei/ (e.g. in *made/maid*) is a regularly available contrast in south-Wales "non-standard" English where the "standard" variety has /ei/; similarly, reduction to schwa is a pervasive feature of "standard" English unstressed vowel pronunciation, but not of "non-standard" Welsh English; many non-standard pronominal and adverbial variables are morphosyntactically complex relative to their standard equivalents (e.g. *you/youse* in north-east England; *where/where to* (in constructions such as *where to is it?*), *here/by here* in Cardiff).

term "professional," the language of the lawyer, the doctor, the business-man, the policeman, the public education teacher and so forth, and these sometimes coincide with, and sometimes depart from, the stratification into genres" (Bakhtin 1981 [translation]:289). "At any given moment of its his-torical existence language is heteroglot from top to bottom: it represents the coexistence of socio-ideological contradictions between the present and the past, between different epochs of the past, between different socio-ideolog-ical groups in the present, between tendencies, schools, circles and so forth all given in bodily form" (p. 291). But it is the relationships among sociol-ects and registers that are, for present purposes, most interesting in Bakhtin. White assesses this as follows:

Bakhtin considers the formal linguistic markers of register indissociable from the *intentional* dimension of its meaning. To study only the formal linguistic features of different registers without understanding how they appropriate, possess and dispos-sess language of specific concrete meanings, is to produce a mere catalogue of dead forms. Every register is a typification, a *style*, the bearer of specific sociocultural *intentions*; at the same time register is the bearer of self-referential *identity* which we recognize as such. Registers cannot help advertising themselves. We recognize them as pertaining to certain groups and certain social activities, hence as the registration of historical and social *distinctions* – not least power relations and hierarchies. (White 1984:124; emphasis added)

Key elements of this view of style are semiosis, identification, intention-ality, multidimensionality and conflict. Individual stylistic configurations are seen as necessarily espousing ideologies and sociocultural positions that have implications for the identities of their proponents. For Bakhtin, styles are conflict-oriented in the ways that social discourses are for critical lin-guists (Hodge and Kress 1988, Fairclough 1991, 1994, Fowler 1991, Lee, 1992). "Heteroglossia" is the struggle – of people through language – to maintain, assume, or subvert positions and control. Developing this view, however, Bakhtin claims that styles are never internally uniform, since "the word in language is half someone else's" (p. 293). All discourse "lives on the boundary between its own context and another, alien context" (p. 284; White 1984:126). Bakhtin conjures an image of the semiotic value of styles being subtly redefined in on-going interaction, attracting and resisting new connotations and allegiances.

This perspective sets a novel agenda for sociolinguistic investigations of style. Ochs, for example, takes up Bakhtin's notion of *ventriloquation* – speakers articulating meanings through others' voices. As she writes, "accounts of whose message and whose intentions are being communicated become highly textured, incorporating not only the speaker/writer but a range of social identities and relations" (Ochs 1988:20). The notion of ven-triloquation is highly appropriate in the context of dialect style variation, since dialect styles are defined through their semiotic potential to express "social" (regional, ethnic, class) and "personal" significances (personality traits and other individual differences). Ventriloquation is not to be confused with either imitation or quotation, although dialect representation via each of these means is not at all an insignificant dimension of dialect style (see Preston 1989 and Macaulay 1991; Speidel and Nelson [1989] give a useful overview of the nature and functioning of imitation).

6   Variable dialect personas and style

Bakhtin's perspective, motivational as it is, is still text-focused. He argues that styles or registers are socially indexical and that heteroglossic conflicts are conflicts among styles, and only indirectly among people. But we now need to return to the argument that sociolinguistics needs to incorporate a perspective on motivated communicative achievements. In researching language it is all too easy to invest language itself with affective and relational potential in the ways we refer to it. We talk of "powerful or solidary language," although it is people in their relationships who are powerful or solidary. When we talk of language change, it is people whose language use shifts in relation to their changing social and personal aspirations (Trudgill 1986).

Similarly, stylistic variation needs to be seen as person variation. When we converge stylistically to an interlocutor, we may gloss this as the reduction of (socio)linguistic dissimilarities, which it *is* under linguists' analytic microscopes. But from the perspective of the social actor, what is being reduced is the cultural and social divide between identities, the social personas they can project through their stylistic selections. Style, and in particular dialect style, can therefore be construed as a special case of the presentation of self, within particular relational contexts – articulating relational goals and identity goals. Speech accommodation theory (Giles and Powesland 1975, Giles, Coupland, and Coupland 1991, see Coupland 1996, for a review) has come closest to representing stylistic choice in this way, and makes specific reference to clusters of social motivations for, and consequences of, stylistic choice. But it too has understated the identificational processes in which dialect style is involved.

The view of style as persona management has received some support within the writings of critical linguists and critical theorists. Fowler (1977), for example, uses the notion of "mind-style" to express how value-judgments and "an impression of a world-view" (p. 76) are necessarily represented in all manner of social texts:

language constrains us to assume a style which announces our membership of a certain communicative group: this is the *sociolinguistic* dimension of discourse. Choices of sentence-structure and vocabulary act as indicators of the nature and structure of the social group within which we are communicating: semi-permanently, in the case of our socio-economic class or geographical origin, and temporarily, in response to the shifting communicative roles which we adopt on different occasions of language usage. (p. 77)

This is a rather informal gloss of variationism, and Fowler is seeking to draw on sociolinguistics for the purposes of literary criticism. But in its literary applications, variation becomes much more highly textured. Fowler's mind-styles are voicing conventions through which, in literary works, an author can project a diversity of individual world-views indexically, through linguistic representations of characters' values and belief-systems. Sociolinguistics can borrow back this awareness of how multiply textured styles (or "mind-styles") can be creatively constituted in social texts for its interpretations of dialect style variation.

How do we know that dialect styles carry these identity formatting potentials within them? When social psychologists have attended to the "social meanings" of dialect styles, they have typically presented fragments of (genuine or mimicked) spoken dialect performances to groups of listeners who have then "assessed" them, using Likert-type rating scales. Notice here that we again tend to talk of "the social meanings of styles," though in empirical studies it has only ever made sense to ask listeners for their judgments of *people* engaged in certain speaking activities. It is at the level of the person – an individual's personal and social identity – that our social judgments of speech styles reside. As experienced and acculturated sociolinguistic practitioners, everyday people may be able to abstract from this routine level of person-judging to rank "dialects" simply from their identifying label (cf. Giles 1970, Coupland, Williams, and Garrett 1994), but people's dialect performances are the basis of sociolinguistic semiosis.

Theoretical benefits follow from this perspective. First, we no longer have to contrast the "social" and the "situational" as independent dimensions of sociolinguistic variation. Dialect style as persona management captures how individuals, within and across speaking situations, manipulate the conventionalized social meanings of dialect varieties – the individual through the social. But it is the same process of dialectal self-projection that explains the effect of dialect stratification when the speech of social groups is aggregated in sociolinguistic surveys. Individuals within what we conventionally recognize to be meaningful social categories enact dialect personas with sufficient uniformity for survey researchers to detect numerical patterns of stratification. This allows us to recognize the correctness of Halliday's original argument (1978) that dialectal and diatopic variation are two sides of the same coin. It is in relation to group norms that stylistic variation becomes meaningful; it is through individual stylistic choices that group norms are produced and reproduced.

Dialect style as persona presumes that style variation will be inherently *multi*dimensional. From this perspective, there is no reason, other than analytic convenience, to limit our empirical studies of stylistic variation to single dimensions. We noted earlier that we have tended to accept the "naturalness" of the unidimensional view. On the other hand, in an earlier study (Coupland 1985, one aspect of which I shall briefly reconsider at the end of this paper) I suggested that one subset of phonological variables in a Cardiff DJ's broadcast talk variably projects an image of personal competence/incompetence, e.g. for humorous effect, while another set projects degrees of community affiliation. Similarly, in introducing her Samoan data, Ochs (1988) challenges "the assumption that communities have only one type of prestige variant, whereas many communities have a prestige variant, say, for Western-related activities (such as formal schooling, urban business, Western religions) and one or more prestige variants for traditional activities (such as formal meetings, rites of passage and other ceremonies)" (p. 37).

But who we can dialectally *be* is not constrained to the dimensions that are socially diagnostic within any one community. Giles and Powesland (1975) distinguished styles which operate within a speaker's primary versus secondary repertoires, where the term primary relates to the resources normally available within the local community. Secondary repertoires are made use of in mimicry or verbal play. Similarly, Bell's (1984) notion of "initiative" style-shifting recognizes the general category of creative, repertoire-expanding dialect style-shifts. Rampton (1991) explores the social functioning of "stylised Asian English," as a self-handicapping and self-parodying strategy in UK school contexts. In fact, stylization is a useful notion in that it refutes the implicit assumption that style variation must be mundane and non-strategic. Wolfowitz (1981:249) talks of "virtuoso performances" in her analysis of stylistic choice in Suriname Javanese, which suggests there can be an in-built self-critiquing function in style-choice, such that we can recognize more/less adequate performances, whatever their success in conveying social categorizations. This again casts stylistic variation as a dialogic process, with style-choices open to complex negotiation, inferencing and interpretation. In Suriname, Wolfowitz suggests, "The stylization of 'as-if' closeness is itself a kind of distance marker" (1981, p. 80). Also, "to labor at cultivating the best British accent is somewhat to invalidate the performance, since the essential stylistic message has to do with 'breeding'. To cultivate proper Javanese, on the other hand, is regarded as a life's work and is respected as such" (pp. 237–8).

Similarly, Eastman and Stein (1993) seek to formalize the notion of "language display," being how, through language (and, in their research, through lexical choice in particular), "members of one group lay claim to attributes associated with another, conveying messages of social, professional, and ethnic identity" (p. 187). Their analysis follows on from Goffman's (1959:242) assumption that "When an individual appears before others, he knowingly and unwittingly projects a definition of a situation, of which a conception of himself is an important part." Eastman and Stein argue that we should understand the objective of display more in relation to the ingroup than to the outgroup: "the displayer's intention is not to negotiate a definition of self as a member of another speech community but to be seen as an individual with attributes associated with that community of speakers" (p. 188). This reading dislocates "language display" from other interpretations of related phenomena. For example, speech accommodation theory specifies effects that linguistic convergence, maintenance, or divergence are likely to have on the recipient's perceptions – of the speaker and of the speaker/hearer relationship. And these effects depend on perceived degrees of similarity/dissimilarity between the speaker's accommodated style and the listener's own style. Eastman and Stein's perspective is similar, to the extent that the listener's perceptions are still likely to be involved, but as perceptions of the speaker in relation to all manner of potential reference groups (cf. Bell's [1984] notion of "referee design").

But it is equally likely that the designing of acts of linguistic display would be geared to the speaker's *self*-perceptions, projecting various versions of his or her social and personal identity, with different degrees of confidence and plausibility. Since we are continual, if often rather unsuccessful, reflexive monitors of our own self-projections, it is also necessary to theorize display as potentially a self-directed sociolinguistic activity. In just the way that we might admit to designing our dress and appearance for our own benefit (albeit monitored through the perceptions of others), so we can think of our speech-style choices as being oriented to our own self-evaluations.

The theoretical question raised by established sociolinguistic terminology is where to locate a distinction between "responsive" and "initiative" style-shifting, and the similar distinction between "situational" and "metaphorical" code-switching (Blom and Gumperz 1972). The distinctions are useful in that they draw attention to degrees of predictability within patterns of stylistic variation, since "responsive" and "situational" shifts are those in which output styles are likely to be adjudged "appropriate" or unmarked according to community norms. However, we lose the value of a human motivational perspective if we explain these shifts as the use of styles which are (mysteriously) "conditioned by the situation." From a self-identity perspective, shifts that are "appropriate" are nevertheless creative in the sense that speakers opt to operate communicatively within normative bounds. All dialect style usage is, to that extent, metaphorical and creative, but we sometimes opt to invoke personas whose metaphorical associations are predictable and so "appropriate" to particular social circumstances.

Style as self-identity also gives us a more mediated view of what has been called "topic" versus "addressee" effects. It has been possible to identify dialect style variation which co-occurs with variation in topic, channel, or participation (Coupland 1980, Bell 1984), and co-occurrence has been taken to be adequately explanatory. The notion of "addressee-registers" (babytalk, foreigner talk, elderspeak, etc.) has been canonized in sociolinguistics. But what can be said to underlie addressee-related shifts in dialect style? In the terminology of communication accommodation theory (Giles, Coupland, and Coupland, 1991), speech convergence or the "reduction of linguistic dissimilarities" between speakers has very regularly been shown to reflect the goals of "promoting social approval" and "promoting communication efficiency." "Divergence" has been shown to relate to the goal of "promoting intergroup distinctiveness." Each of these formats, which are conventional within studies of linguistic accommodation, specifies identity and relational goals. If we accommodate to achieve social approval, it is through projecting a version of our self-identity which is somehow "consistent with" an interlocutor's. And note that "designing a persona for an audience," in Bell's terms, need not be a matter of reducing dissimilarities between participants' speech characteristics. It could be offering a compatible or complementary persona. Promoting distinctiveness at the level of the social group will often entail projecting a self which is aligned with some group outside of the recipient's own. Promoting efficiency (and "effectiveness" seems to be the intended sense) is a goal more obviously located at the level of the relationship, although with clear implications of a speaker wanting to appear "pro-communicative."

In these ways, addressee-related style-shifts are again better explained as strategies in the arena of persona management. The shift of emphasis is a subtle one – from recognizing "accommodated styles" to recognizing speakers as "being accommodative" – from text to the relational self. Interpretations in terms of self-identity motives are entirely consistent with findings that we have generally represented as audience effects. In what Bell calls audience design, we can more precisely claim that speakers are projecting self-identities that are, to varying degrees and along possibly multiple dimensions, attuned to the preferences and ideological predispositions of audience members.

There are subtly novel issues here that sociolinguistics can research. For example, a local radio broadcaster may achieve a degree of solidarity with a community audience not so much because the broadcaster's dialect style, at some point and in some respect, "resembles their own" but rather because "solidarity" might be analyzable as a complex of inferential processes whereby listeners reconstruct social and personal images, of and "through" a speaker, which carry familiar or inclusive cultural echoes, in some specific domain of experience, and against a specific backdrop of cultural experiences and assumptions. If so, dialect style should be treated, analytically, as a repository of cultural indices, mediated by individual performance. Its salience will be located not within any aggregated "level" or "range" of dialect variants, but in the placement of individual or specifically grouped dialect features relative to other culturally signifying linguistic and discursive forms – dialect styles operating within ways of speaking.

The reading of dialect styles, or dialect-inferencing, needs to be modeled as a core aspect of both the production and reception of dialect styles (although variationist sociolinguistics has largely ignored issues of recipiency). "Listening to" dialect-performance is done from specifiable but predictably variable social, cultural, and ideological positions. We may orient to newsreading, for example, as "local community members," or as "observers of global affairs," bringing different priorities to bear on different sequences of talk or on different communicative purposes. Dialect-recipiency is therefore the negotiated evaluation of a speaker's projected persona relative to the local contextualization of talk, but also relative to listeners' personal experiences and normative expectations. So, degrees of similarity between a newsreader's dialect style and our own styles as individual listeners are only the most tenuous index of a global outcome that we label "solidarity" or "distance." In general, we need to find the empirical means of locating stylistic inquiry in the domain of strategic, discursive interaction.

7   Identity, the self, and interaction

These ideas connect to a remarkably consensual debate within current sociological and social psychological theory. Giddens (1991), for example, conceptualizes the self as a "reflexive project," cumulatively formed through social interaction in diverse settings. In this sense, Giddens argues that "autobiography . . . in the broad sense of an interpretative self-history produced by the individual . . . is actually at the core of self-identity in the modern world. Like any other formalised narrative, it is something that has to be worked at, and calls for creative input as a matter of course" (p. 76). This view is strongly echoed in the contemporary writings of Shotter, Gergen, Harre, and others (see Coupland and Nussbaum 1993, for a selective review). The phrase "the relational self" captures something of this shared view that we can only understand self-identity in an interactive and sociolinguistic sense.

The argument is a particular interpretation of the general case argued by

G. H. Mead, who saw the creation of the self as embedded in the sharing of experiences:

What the individual does is to indicate what the important characters in a co-operative process are. He indicates this to other members of the community; but . . . especially in the case of vocal gestures, he indicates it to himself as to others; and just insofar as he does indicate it to himself as to others, he tends to call out in himself the same attitude as in others. (p. 104)

Sociolinguists have been receptive to the view that, through language use, we all "have," or perhaps "betray," *multiple* identities (cf. Fishman, 1977). But we have not generally entertained the idea that people's identities are *embodied* sociolinguistically. Giddens argues that what he calls "the fragmentation of experience" (1991:189) is a far greater challenge to the self in late or "high" modernity than was previously the case. The modern world of shrinking distances and pervasive telecommunications offers us far more differentiated possibilities of self-definition and actualization. On the other hand, the notion of the self cannot live with too grossly compartmentalized identities. There is a tension between homogeneity and heterogeneity of self-enactment.

All self-development depends on the mustering of appropriate responses to others; an individual who has to be "different" from all others has no chance of reflexively developing a coherent self-identity. Excessive individuation has connections to conceptions of grandiosity. The individual is unable to discover a self-identity "sober" enough to conform to the expectations of others in his social milieu. (Giddens 1991:200–1)

The reflexive project of self-identity management therefore becomes a set of "active processes of temporal control and active interaction on which the integration of the self's narrative depends" (p. 77). Interaction is the forum not only for representing and realizing the self, but for rendering the self coherent. And the narrative of self-identity, Giddens argues (p. 185) is "inherently fragile." "A self-identity has to be created and more or less continually reordered against the backdrop of shifting experiences of day-to-day life and the fragmenting tendencies of modern institutions" (p. 186). This means that self-identity management depends on a fusion of both internal and external (contextual) processes. It is precisely Giddens' thesis that the "external" processes impinging on the self are less constraining in late or "high" modernity than in traditional cultural contexts. Class- or generation-based identity probabilities are far less rigid in the modern world than in traditional times. On the other hand, it is necessarily the case that the self is reflexively organized in relation to social exchanges:

Lacking external referents supplied by others [in traditional social orders], the life-span again emerges as a trajectory which relates above all to the individual's projects and plans. Others always figure in such life-planning, of course, from the members of the family of orientation to subsequent familial partners, children, friends, colleagues and acquaintances. New spheres of intimacy with some such others become crucial elements of frameworks of trust developed by the individual. But these have to be mobilised through the reflexive ordering of the lifespan as a discrete and internally referential phenomenon. (pp. 147–8)

The relevance of this perspective for sociolinguistic analyses of style is that, as speakers who are obliged to speak in more or less socially identifiable dialect styles, we inevitably project versions of our selves continually and in all contexts. Mead tended to understate the interpretive gap between our own and others' processing of our community-relevant (e.g. dialect) performances, and, as Labov insists, our degrees of attentiveness to our own speech. Mead also tended to suggest a closure and automaticity in the self-constitution process (which Giddens is at pains to correct).

Yet to speak "in" a dialect is very much to speak "through" a dialect, and so to endorse (perhaps fleetingly and inconsistently) a perspective that is inevitably heard to represent a "mind-style," a particular social formation. To speak through a particular dialect is to offer the interpretation of speaking from a particular cultural and social position, and against the background of a more or less predictable set of understandings and presuppositions. As social encounters become increasingly transdialectal and of course international through shared language codes, the cultural and ideological loading of dialect styles will arguably be of greater and greater significance.

8   A brief illustration

In 1985 I developed a case-study focusing on the stylistic creativity of a local radio disc jockey (DJ), Frank Hennessy (FH). FH is a "broad-accented" speaker of the Cardiff English dialect who is well known in the community not only as a radio presenter but also as an entertainer, folk-singer/song-writer, social commentator, and humorist. His popular image is built around his affiliation to and promotion of local Cardiff culture and folk-lore, in large measure through his dialect. For many, he typifies the non-standard Cardiff voice, perhaps even the stereotypical Cardiff "mind-style" – nostalgia for dockland streets and pubs, a systematic ambivalence to "Welshness," a sharp, wry humour and a reverence for the local beers, in particular "Brain's Dark Ale." In general, his show is a celebration of ingroup regional solidarity.

Extract 1 is a transcript of a continuous sequence from the radio show, interspersed by the playing of a record (the Checkmates' "Proud Mary") at line 5. The extract ends when another record is cued and played.

Extract 1

(A 152–181)

1 dear Frank   would you please give a mention on your birthday spot for our brother whose birthday is on the
                                                                              0   0

2 second of June well that was yesterday wasn't it so it's a happy birthday to (name) and lots of love from your
                                         0   1 0 0   0

3 sisters (names) and Mum of course   and also from all your family   his name is (name) and he lives at Seven Oaks
          0 1 0   1   0   1   1

4 Road   Ely in Cardiff   happy birthday (name) (cues record)   here's the Checkmates   Proud Mary   yeah
    1   3   0   0   1   2   0

5 (record plays and fades) oh good music there   the Checkmates and Proud Mary   and the wall of sound there
                                                                     2   1   2   1

6 of Phil Spector   unmistakable of course   they sound as if they going bananas don't they   talk about
                                                     2   1   4   1   2

7 bananas   we got Bananarama coming up next   but it's time to limber up this Sunday with the Margaret Morris
    4   4   03   1   0 0 1   1   1   0

8 Movement Special   that's a special day of exercise and dance at the National Sports Centre for Wales   it
         0   0   2   3   0

9 started about an hour ago at ten o'clock and it goes until five o'clock this afternoon   now the Margaret
    2   2 1   2   1   1   2   3   2   0

10   Margaret Morris Movement is a unique form of recreative movement   and it's um   well it's a system of
        1   1   0   0   0

11 exercise   which achieves physical fitness   but it's also capable of developing creative and aesthetic qualities which
     2   0 1 (R)   1   0

12 make it exceptional   in physical education and training   are you with me   ah   'cause I'm totally confused
     0   0   (R)   2 11

13   anyway it's equally suitable for men and women of all ages as well as children   even the kids can join in with
            0

14 this   and er the muscular control and coordination make it an excellent preparation for all sporting and athletic
                          1   1   0   0   1   0

15 activities   now all sessions today are absolutely free   so if the weather's a little bit gone against you and you
                                      (R)   1

16 fancy   well not running round in the rain   but er you fancy doing a bit of exercise it's all on at the National
                0   1 02   0   0   1   1   2 1

17 Sports Centre for Wales   that's at Pontcanna of course   started an hour ago you can go any time up until
                                0   0(I)   3   1   1   1   2

18 about five o'clock this evening   so there we are   as I said   Bananarama   here they are   with a
     2   2   1   4   2   0 04   4

19 little touch of (cues record) Rough Justice   I'll have to get me right arm in training you know   the pints
                                                  (R) 1   1 2 4   1   1   2

20 are getting heavier ((have)) you noticed that   or is it me getting weaker   have to drink six halfs instead of
(R)   1   1 0   1   1   1 1   1   1 4

21 me three usual darkies   ah (record)
                     4

The extract conveys something of the ingroup framing of the show. Many correspondents are regular contributors and are therefore to an extent radio personalities in their own right alongside Frank. Some open their letters with even more familiar forms of address than the "dear Frank" instance in the extract – "[h]ello, Franky Boy," "hi, hi Frank," "[h]ow's things, Our Kid." The show often carries announcements of local events, such as the Margaret Morris Movement Special introduced at line 7 of the extract. Other instances include a quiz feature which asks listeners to supply the original name of Wimbourne Street in "lovely old Splott" (a long-established working-class Cardiff city district) and the names of six paddle-steamers which operated in the Bristol Channel after the Second World War.

We need to recognize that, in a crucial sense, the show is *constituted dialectally*. Cardiff dialect is not merely an incidental characteristic of FH's own speech; it permeates much of the performance and imbues it with a regional significance. The radio show in fact has the informal title *"Hark, Hark, the Lark"* and is introduced and punctuated by a distinctive jingle – a whimsical, sung fanfare of the words *"Hark, hark the lark in Cardiff Arms Park"* with the characteristically Cardiff raised, fronted quality of /a:/ predominating throughout. FH perpetuates this phonological theme in his own "catch phrases," such as *it's remarkable, well there we are*, and *that's half tidy*. Notice how the extract ends with a list of phono-opportunities for [ae:] in highly prominent positions during the final three lines of transcript: *arm, halfs* (meaning "halves" or "half-pints"), and *darkies* ("pints of Dark Ale").

Correspondents often make their own contribution to this dialectal theme, sometimes consciously ending their letters with an opportunity for FH to produce a broad Cardiff variant of the (a:) variable – for example, *yours through a glass darkly* (Cardiff English does not regularly distinguish short from long /a/ and both can be realized with the stereotyped [ae] quality), *signed Prince of Darkness* (both these are again oblique references to Dark Ale), *don't forget Derby day*, or simply the words *ta* ("thank you") or *tarra* ("goodbye"). This single phonological variable, then, is a highly productive focus for the symbolic expression of shared Cardiff provenance and accompanying attitudes and allegiances. Each possible realization of a salient Cardiff English pronunciation feature is underlined, and a number below the line shows how standard or non-standard each realization is. In all cases, higher scores represent variants furthest from the supposed standard variety, which is taken to be Received Pronunciation (RP) and which is scored 0 (for a more detailed discussion of these variables and the dialect as a whole, see Coupland 1988):

> (h) 1 represents /h/ -less onset to a following vowel (so-called "aitch-dropped" realizations) in word-initial environments, where RP has /h/ as strong voiceless onset.
>
> (ng) 1 is alveolar rather than velar realization, in word-final verbal progressive -*ing* contexts.
>
> (r) is a single-tapped variant, as opposed to the standard post-alveolar continuant and its own variants, such as voiced or devoiced fricatives following plosives.
>
> (C cluster)1 is marked when an alveolar voiceless plosive is elided

in "simplifying" a specific type of consonant cluster: (i) continuant cluster + /t/, followed by a word with an initial consonant other than /y/ or /h/; (ii) the contracted negative "not" followed by a word with an initial consonant; (iii) word-final /t/ plus /s/ clusters formed by the reduction of "is" or "has."

(intervoc t)1 is a voiced or tapped allophone, occurring intervocalically, between unstressed syllables or following a stressed syllable, usually across a word boundary.

(ai)2 and (au)2 mark fully centralized start-points of these glides, with variants scored 1 where there is a lesser degree of centralization.

(ou)1 denotes variants with retracted start-points, which may also be monophthongal. As noted above, (a:) variants are scored progressively higher, from 0, which denotes a form as retracted as in RP, maximally open, through progressively fronter positions 1 and 2 to 3, which is maximally fronted, to 4 which is still fully front but also raised, in the area of [ae:].

With data like these, it seems possible and potentially productive to distinguish different communicative functions or modes of discourse within the show. We can see, even in the one extract, how FH's performance involves him in reading listeners' letters (lines 1–4), making public announcements (presumably based on prepared written sources, e.g. the Margaret Morris episode), introducing music-recordings (e.g. *here's the Checkmates Proud Mary*, line 3) and being funny (e.g. *I'll have to get me right arm in training you know*, line 19). Some generalizations can be made on this basis, although there would be no firm empirical basis for establishing categories of "function" secure enough to allow for quantification. For example, when FH talks about Cardiff people and events there seems to be a tendency for him to use more locally signifying variants of the variables marked in the transcript, e.g. on one occasion referring to a Cardiff-born singer:

"there you *a*re good old Cardiff TV st*a*r Shakin' Stevens dr*i*ving *h*imself crazy"

But similarly, quite consistent Cardiff pronunciations are used when FH makes joking references to his own incompetence. FH uses more standard pronunciations in connection with structuring and publicizing the show, when "competence" and "expertise" become more salient aspects of his identity:

"we've got for the ne*x*t two h*ou*rs s*o* stay with me until two o'clock"

"Frank *H*ennessy *h*ere on CBC two two one metres medium wave and n*i*nety-six VHF in ster*e*o"

But he does not use standard forms for all the variables on such occasions: those that are "corrected" are generally stigmatized features in social dialect terms (such as "*h*-dropping"). Specifically Cardiff features such as (a:) tend to remain in their local ("non-standard") form.

On the other hand, there are boundary problems inherent in such an approach. Does the verbal link between the playing of the two records in the extract (*they sound as if they going bananas don't they*, line 6) function primarily as humor – and a phono-opportunity for (a:) – or as the intro-duction of music-recordings? FH's announcement of the dance event is interspersed with humorous metadiscursive commentary on the announcement itself (*are you with me ah 'cause I'm totally confused*, line 12). It also shows elements of spontaneous ad-libbing (*now all sessions today are absolutely free so if the weather's a little bit gone against you and you fancy well not running round in the rain . . .*). Any text-based typology, assigning utterances to contextual or functional types, is therefore impre-cise. Although it allows us to produce some interesting general correlations between stylistic "levels" and contexts, the approach does not ultimately appear to do justice to the moment-to-moment creativity of FH's own per-formance.

This is so for at least three reasons. Firstly, Frank is not in fact limited to the alternation between more and less standard realizations of Cardiff English. Sometimes he uses features from other dialects. He adopts (what are, to British ears) "American" features to introduce some songs, including the *yeah* at the end of line 4 of the extract and, perhaps surprisingly, the title of the Bananarama song in line 18 (Bananarama are a British singing-group). Occasionally there are south-west-of-England dialect features, e.g. in connection with a mention of Dorsetshire; and Cockney features to introduce a song by Joe Brown and His Bruvvers.

Second, a correlational account cannot capture the inter-play between style, content, and key. Some of the dialect mimicry is playful, as in the case of American features parodying slick DJ patter. Again, the "social meaning" of broad Cardiff dialect seems different depending on whether the ideational focus of the talk is Frank himself (in which case it often conveys humor through self-deprecation) or cultural history (in which case it conjures social solidarity and a sense of community).

But thirdly and crucially, there is the theoretical consideration that the various configurations of "context" do not exist independently of FH's speech forms. It is often the case that we can only identify a "contextual type" *by virtue of* the stylistic attributes of FH's speech. He is the orches-trator of contexts, and this removes the empirical basis that justifies corre-lation. I referred above to FH's "performance" in the DJ role. FH is clearly a media "performer" in the specific sense of seeking to entertain and develop his media persona(s) with a degree of self-consciousness and overt planning and scripting. Variation in his speech and in particular his dialect should therefore be said to be not only styled but stylized (notwith-standing the problem of distinguishing these concepts, as discussed above). But "performance" is also the appropriate term because of Frank's stylistic creativity. His styles are not situational reflexes. They are ways of subtly activating multiple simultaneous dimensions of meaning potential.

In this case, more than merely representing a speech community (Cardiff), dialect opens up a range of potential personal and social iden-tities for FH, and diverse bases on which he can relate to his audience. Through stylistic choices in dialect, he can project, but then momentarily undermine, his "ethnic Cardiff" persona with a pastiche of the slick American DJ (*yeah*). Conversely, he can undermine his "DJ" projection with a strongly dialectized admission of personal incompetence (*I'll have to get me right arm in training*). He can manufacture the persona of the com-petent public announcer, then parody this role (and the announced event?) both referentially and through a dialect switch. Cardiff English is not merely "Frank's voice" but one of many culturally loaded voices that FH, and presumably his audience too, can manipulate for relational and other interactional purposes.

9   Retrospective

The significance of this brief illustration is not that it establishes the valid-ity of an analytic approach. On the contrary, this paper has constituted an appeal for *less* faith in an established method and in aggregated data. It is rather that the data appear to demand a far broader, more flexible, interpre-tive, and ethnographic apparatus to capture the stylistic processes at work. Those processes seem not to be monologic (Bakhtin wrote of "such *fictions* as 'the listener'" [Emerson and Holquist 1981:68]). In his style-choices, the DJ (again in Bakhtin's words) "presupposes not only the existence of the language system he is using, but also the existence of preceding utterances – his own and others' – with which his given utterance enters into one kind of relation or another (builds on them, polemicizes with them, or simply pre-sumes that they are already known to the listener)" (p. 69).

Dialect varieties, as a special case of what Bakhtin calls "utterances," are indeed "the drive belts from the history of society to the history of lan-guage" (p. 65), constitutive of a "language collective" (p. 68) replete with social and cultural echoes, associations, and "dialogic reverberations" (p. 94). "Our speech . . . is filled with others' words, varying degrees of other-ness and varying degrees of 'our-own-ness'" which "carry with them their own evaluative tone, which we assimilate, rework and reaccentuate" (p. 89). The "Hark hark" analysis is well summarized as FH borrowing, reworking, and reaccentuating dialect styles, creatively and multidimensionally. "The utterance," as Bakhtin writes, "is filled with *dialogic overtones*, and they must be taken into account in order to understand fully the style of the utterance" (p. 92).

12   Couplandia and beyond[1]

Howard Giles

Coupland's chapter – the distillation of known years of academic angst – represents a bold forge into new territories. It is a provocative and welcome challenge, and particularly with its appeal to structuration theory and "personhood." In what follows, and in the spirit of the inter-disciplinary ethos of this volume, I shall suggest ways in which the directions he proposes can be enriched by sociopsychological research and theory.

1   The multiplicities of styles and contexts

A prime concern of Coupland's is our overconcentration on uni–multidimensional approaches to style. He proposes that we need to focus upon more than one continuum of style, that is, beyond formality–informality. I agree that we need a more eclectic framework which encompasses a wider range of contextual definitions. Some years ago, we examined the work of social psychologists who claimed to have discovered a finite number of the ways in which individuals define situations in their minds' eyes (Giles and Hewstone 1982); in other words, how speaker–hearers carve up contexts psychologically and subjectively. Not surprisingly, perceived formality–informality was an important one of these; yet not the only one. At that time, we further suggested that an array of inter-individual variability in stylistic behaviors might be accounted for by moving away from objective definitions of contextual formality (e.g., where, and what, the context was, who was involved) to how speakers themselves defined the situations they were in. Indeed, what is a serious, formal topic for some, could be an utterly trivial irrelevance for others. Computing averages of how people's styles in taken-for-granted situations of formality–informality – as occurs in most quantitative, sociolinguistic surveys (as Coupland implies) – does "box away" intriguing variability that should, instead, be investigated. As a kind of compromise to traditional work, Giles and Hewstone argued that we need to

[1] Although this should not in any sense be taken to imply that Coupland would share my views herein, I am grateful to him for very useful and constructive comments on an earlier draft of this paper.

access more of our participants' own "situational construals" rather than relying on extant classifications of them by external (albeit often participating) researchers. Of course, not infrequently there is isomorphism between interviewees' construals and our own scientific judgments. Other times too, situational construals can be in profound contrast to the latter, but interviewees, nonetheless, conform behaviorally (for reasons of social desirability or evaluative apprehension) to our prevailing expectations of formality–informality. Yet critically, participants' situational construals and researcher classifications may not be congruent and the former can be powerful determinants of style variation. And, of course, contextual definitions can change radically many times during the course of an interaction and in ways that are reflected in style-shifts other than those mandated.

Such individual differences in situational definitions notwithstanding, and as alluded to above, our more "subjective" approach also highlighted dimensions of context other than formality–informality which could promote under-explored styles: cooperative–competitive; relaxed–tense; task-oriented–socioemotional; and group–person-oriented styles. Given Coupland's focus on multiple identities through style changes – as with his Cardiff DJ data – and recent work on language attitudes (e.g., Zahn and Hopper 1985), we can add at least one further dimension of style: its dynamism. Thus the social psychology of situations – admittedly in Western societies for the most part – implicates a range of potential style dimensions hitherto neglected. This can move us ahead conceptually, assist in our unveiling the cognitive work our informants engage in, and account for variability in our informants' sociolinguistic behaviors. Given Coupland's (and others') emphasis on the fact that language also *defines* – as well as is responsive to – situations, it is worth noting that perceived shifts in such styles (particularly from high-power others) will signal to interactants that the very context itself has changed or is open for renegotiation and, from our point of view, in *predictable* ways (see Giles and Hewstone 1982). Discourse sometimes allows us to look for understandings of what the nature of the situation is as well as our role and social identities in it – and it is to the latter construct that I now turn.

In parallel with social psychologists heralding situational definitions over objective taxonomies of context, they would also wish to focus more on subjective definitions of social group memberships. In other words, rather than allocate informants to socioeconomic, gender, ethnic, and so forth, categories based on external criteria, we advocate investigating the situated salience of the various social identities (Giles 1978). As an example, Allan Bell (chapter 9 in this volume) highlights the value of examining "ingroupedness" of style by arguing that his respondents' gender or ethnicity (Maori or European) could be marked in style-shifts. While this is clearly important, our perspective would have this taken further, and encourage that we empirically demonstrate *how* our interviewees' (and interviewers') situational definitions became more or less gendered and ethnically salient. With due appreciation of some limitations to this technique, this can be accomplished by requiring our participants to honestly reconstruct their ideas and feelings immediately after a recording session and whilst revisiting their remarks over the audio- or videotape.

Turning to another facet of unidimensionality, Coupland suggests we need to acknowledge that more than one image can be projected in a short time-frame. His Cardiff DJ provides fine examples of this. However, many of the instances of so-implied changes in style are extremely brief – for instance, (the American) "yeah." If I interject a "su:re" into my discourse in Santa Barbara, it might convey the impression of a different style that could be *accessed* further; that said, this usually causes a smile from recipient colleagues because they know it cannot actually be sustained authentically beyond this! Hence, is this one utterance – given I immediately and predictably have to resort back to British English – a shift in style – as *perceived* by my audience? I suggest not, although I am well prepared to appreciate that it *could* be. Yet this has not been demonstrated to my satisfaction at this moment. Indeed, I think that the Cardiff DJ's appeal to different dialectal forms is not so much a manifestation of separate, recurring shifts in style *per se* but, rather, an indication that his unique skill in targeting varied groups which the audience recognizes (and for which he, after-all, has been hired) is, itself, the very content of *his* radio style, or stylization. It would be interesting to ask listeners to note down, as they listen to him, when he *does* change style to their ears. I would anticipate that there might be far fewer subjective classifications of shifts than Coupland contends.[2]

This is not to acknowledge that shifts in one mere word pronunciation cannot be enormously socially significant. Indeed, the literature on linguistic shibboleths (Hopper 1986) demonstrates that a single, unintended intrusion of an ingroup (e.g., ethnic, socioeconomic status) speech marker into one's talk – which is otherwise authentically convergent on an outgroup – can induce the latter to avidly question your social authenticity. In situations of intense inter-group conflict (e.g., Northern Ireland), such miscarried group-presentations (see below) can sometimes be attributed with ultimate malevolent intent and lead to disastrous consequences for the "deceiver." I would prefer to see such a complex process of recategorization (along with its social meanings) as qualitatively very different from style-shifting (often-times deliberately encoded for instrumental gain).

---

[2] That said, one must also be open to the possibility – no less theoretically interesting – that certain listeners might hear even more shifts than analyzed as such (see Coupland 1980).

This also begs the question of what **is** a style change? Can we recognize one as such, and if so, what are our criteria? Coupland starts his paper by saying that "style" could, actually, be "everything and anything"; and here he is, sadly, on target. In line with the foregoing, I am disappointed by our lack of a **subjective** operationalization of style change. This can become even more potent when we confidently hear a shift in style that has not actually been enacted at all. We have (as have others) a number of instances of this in our data. For instance, we have shown that when another threatens our sense of ethnic identity, then we will hear that person diverge away from us into an outgroup accent – even when such linguistic differentiation was, actually, never activated (Bourhis et al. 1979). Indeed, our perceptions of, and labels for, speech style – and intra-individual variations of it – are subject to our social expectations and contextual knowledge. As another kind of illustration, my son's same hybrid linguistic behavior is attributed as resolutely "English" in California, but resoundingly "American" in Britain. And one basic premise of accommodation theory is that people converge towards, and diverge away from, where they *believe* target others are – and less so than where they can be measured objectively as residing linguistically (Thakerar, Giles, and Cheshire 1982). Hence, any operationalization of style change needs to take into account the fact that the perception of style variation can be as much a social attribution as a linguistic reality.

In sum, I resonate to Coupland's plea for us to become more multidimensional in our examination of style and variations in it. I would recommend that we expend some energies after how our informants define the situations they are in and the social identities activated as well as pursue what constitutes style variation subjectively for speakers and hearers.

2   The multiplicity of identities and goals

Coupland, in tandem, underscores the need for a shift of focus from mere addressee responsiveness to "identity management," and particularly as it relates to "self-evaluation." I have had some sympathy with this approach since appreciating the richness of his travel agent data some years back (Coupland 1984). Consequently, we invoked Baumeister's (1998) theory of self-presentation so as to redefine certain "accommodative shifts" as mere artifacts (Giles and Street 1985). Put another way, a person may wish to project an image – say, an assertive impression of status and dynamism – irrespective (and even uncaringly or unwittingly) of the sociolinguistic characteristics of their recipient. Given an equally assertive and prestigious receiver, this could be analyzed – and even interpreted by the latter – as convergence. However, when the hearer's style is more submissive, non-standard, and lethargic, that same behavior can be coded as divergence.

Hence, such image projections can come about without any concern for a recipient's style. In this way, the monitoring or not of *another*'s style might be an important theoretical complement to the "attention to one's own speech" mechanism.

Nonetheless, I underscore Coupland's point here. I think we need to take on board when addressivity is high–low, and orthogonally when, and which kind of self-presentation is high for both speakers and hearers. That said, I am interested in the focus on "self" in self-evaluation – for three reasons. First, Coupland's insight into self-evaluation will find further substance in current theories of self and identity (see Baumeister 1995). Space dictates only two exemplars here. For instance, self-affirmation theory suggests that people will seek alternative dimensions of self-worth when any facet of their identity is threatened (Spencer, Josephs, and Steele 1993). Hence, if you cannot succeed in sounding "proper" or highly educated, then you might diverge to a non-standard variety – not as a group differentiating tactic *per se* – but rather to affirm that you are a friendly, sociable person who is a fine reflection of the neighborhood community. Relatedly, self-identification theory (Schlenker 1986) proposes that people do not attempt to project the ideal image they would wish to – as this could be decoded and discredited as ingenuous (as can be the case with regard to certain kinds of hypercorrection; see Giles and Williams 1992). Hence, people often portray the most *plausible* impression they can. Bell (this volume) estimates that speakers use only 67 percent of their repertoire in stylistic variation, and this could be accounted for from Schlenker's position. Hence, a speaker might think "OK, I know I can't be accepted as a plausible ingrouper, however, I'm not the hick you might think I am either!" and, therefore, con-verge partially rather than fully (see Street 1982).

Second, the cultural bias on *self*-evaluation, *self*-presentation, *self*-image, and the like might be a curiosity – or even luxury – in some collectiv-istic cultures in South America and Asia. The focus on ingroup (family, community, etc.) values as over-riding individual concerns and liberties in such societies (Yum 1988) may make "group images" and "group-presenta-tions" a more viable, theoretical target for study. More generally though, I have urged the need to promote further the distinction between "self-" and "group-presentations." Interpretively for decoders and recipients, the social attribution could be critical. Understanding that someone is diverging their style away because of **me** as a discrete (perhaps even as an undesirable) *indi-vidual* has very different consequences for "me" than my attributing this as a distancing from one of my group memberships (e.g., as British); in this latter regard, I might be incurring rationale wrath for the ills of my colonial forefathers. I might be more empathic to this particular group-oriented divergence, but more disturbed by any individual-oriented tactic.

When discussing the need for us to take on board these issues, Coupland makes a few critical asides about communication accommodation theory (CAT). While I can accept that recent versions might require elaboration or clarification in some respects, I feel a few responses are necessary here. He claims that the construct of "identification" is not sufficiently highlighted in the theory. I have to contest this as many years ago we wrote that "convergence is a strategy of *identification* with the speech patterns of an individual *internal* to the social interaction, whereas speech divergence may be regarded as a strategy of *identification* with regard to the linguistic norms of some reference group *external* to the immediate situation" (Giles and Powesland 1975:156). Importantly, this notion of external identification aligns well – if not embraces – Bell's notion of "referee design" (this volume). Turning to another facet of unidimensionality, Coupland, rightly, underscores the need to acknowledge more than one communicative goal in any social encounter. However, again, accommodation theory does subscribe to the multiple goals of convergence or divergence of styles – some cognitive, and others more affective that we called "identity maintenance" (see Giles, Scherer, and Taylor 1979). For instance, and as an example of the former, I now will say, "Ask Barb about this" (with due attention to the postvocalic /r/) – because, otherwise, **Bob** will be approached instead! I intend no change in my persona by this sudden shift, my goal is mere communicative efficiency. For sure, there are many complex communicative goals of style-shifting yet to be articulated. Indeed, I often-times converge to a local dialect in California (say, in talking to a waitperson or student) merely to assume cultural anonymity, and thereby avoid constant questions about my assumed vacationing, geographical origins, immigrant status, or visiting professorial position.

3   Whither then now?

One can ask: has Coupland's zeal then gone a little too far? In some ways, perhaps so. He encourages that we have "less faith" in a Labovian tradition. However, I feel unclear about his rhetorical positioning on this. By this, does he mean we should subordinate the impact of the Labovian approach and the attending focus on attention to speech? I would feel uncomfortable if this was so and – in the highly constructive spirit of Bell's epilogue to this volume – feel we need to understand when one process is operating and when it is theoretically less relevant. After all, we do attend acutely to our own communications on many occasions but, on others, sudden group-presentation needs can over-ride self-monitoring. That said, it is important to recognize that "attention to speech" is not *always* associated with a prestige dialect and formal contexts; reading isolated words with non-standard,

Maori pronunciations, or my invoking the notion of imbibing the "Prince of Darkness," can make one profoundly self-aware. Similarly, we should not be too hasty in dismissing quantitative inclinations as it is feasible to accommodate all manner of methodological diversity in pursuit of common theoretical objectives (see Roger and Bull 1988).

But, maybe Coupland is not really proposing hegemony. If so, then we need to acknowledge a theoretical system that begins to embrace, and integrate, these and other processes. Yet while Coupland calls on us to envision new horizons, I find it a little too deconstructive for my own tastes currently. What do I do with it now? Most of us can produce case-study data that does not conform with our theoretical ideals; indeed, Bell (this volume) admits just this at one juncture when discussing his data. How will my, and your, studies change as a consequence of his treatise? How, if at all, can our recommendations for applied practice (as Fishman [1995] might now ask) change too? Although Coupland's primarily reactive stance is legitimate enough epistemologically, has he actually gone far enough to suggest concrete alternatives or complements? Hence, maybe ironically, we ought to venture further than Coupland demands.

Two issues come to mind here. First, perhaps we think too narrowly about style changes – as dichotomous on some occasions and continuous on others. Currently, I am working on law-enforcement–community interactions. Put glibly and briefly, an accommodating police officer can be a dysfunctional, and even dead, one under certain, life-threatening circumstances. Nonetheless, in this profession, great value is placed on sociolinguistic flexibility and accommodative practices to the extent that police officers should show caring, empathy, and respect, but also induce compliance and express their authority. Many are hired, in part, for having these two styles, but they tend to use them bidialectally as either/ors. Far fewer can manage the situatedly necessary *transitional* shifts between them. Out-of-the-blue shifts towards empathy can be interpreted by community recipients as patronizing, while sudden shifts to assertiveness can signal unintended hostility. In either case, the consequences can be harmful or brutal, and sometimes needlessly so. The officer who can feedback the need for a shift from addressivity to group-presentation and back again – to escalate and de-escalate – may be one who appears less in court, is involved in less violence, has fewer complaints lodged against him or her, and so forth.

The second issue dove-tails this. Much of our past focus on mechanisms has been cognitive, namely, attention to one's speech. However, it is – as psychology attested long ago – difficult to disentangle affective from cognitive processes (Zajonc 1980). Indeed, Labov (1984) has also considered relationships between cognitive and emotive facets of sociolinguistic usage.

In any case, different situations are not only marked by different cognitive appraisals – as I started out saying in this critique (e.g., co-operative–competitive) – but are complexly linked to various emotive associations of pleasantness and arousal. Of course, changes in felt emotions and moods can similarly change our understanding of what kinds of situation we are in, and this also allows us to craft our styles so as to change the emotive tone of these very same situations too. In other words, if an aroused police officer can, successfully, become more accommodating to an equally aroused civilian, the latter can then have his or her emotional tone changed or defused accordingly, and at an optimal, more comfortable, rate. Shame, pride, hate, sexual interest, guilt, and so forth are all concomitants of different style changes. (Indeed, the, sometimes strategic, attributional ambiguity attending shifts from formal to informal style [i.e., is he giving me a come-on? or trying to be humorous? or becoming more understanding of me? or just being plain more relaxed? or whatever] implicate different emotional states.) My earlier example of avoiding a negative emotional state such as frustration or irritation by my adopting an American brogue, suggests that I am attending to my speech so as to maintain an *affective* equilibrium. Communicatively competent speakers are those who, amongst other things, adapt to their listeners (e.g. Wiemann 1977) – optimal accommodators, in CAT terms. Inter-personal communication theory suggests that satisfying conversations are, after-all, those that are basically "enjoyable" (Hecht 1978). Hence, focusing our attention on affective factors and how we can change – by stimulation or defusion – the emotional tones of another is probably the device by which many style-shifts come about. Doubtless, a successful, everyday-invoker of narratives is one who is a fluid style-shifter. Interestingly, there are a number of inter-personal communication frameworks (that space precludes discussion of) that focus on emotion – namely, discrepancy-arousal (Cappella and Greene 1982), anxiety–uncertainty management (Gudykunst 1995), expectancy-violation (Burgoon 1995) theories – that would provide useful fodder in these regards.

Bell (this volume) opened his chapter by stating that **the** sociolinguist's core (in some ways, sociopsychological) question about style is: "*Why* did *this speaker* say it *this way* on this *occasion?*" To enhance our theoretical vitality, I think we need to engage many more fundamental questions as well. For example, and in tandem with the above, I contend we need to address:

2. What is a useful operationalization of "style"? Can, for instance, hearers interpret single utterances as a style-shift?

3. In what ways do speaker–hearer's subjective cognitive *and* emotional assessments of a situation affect their style choices, *and* vice-versa? Does the

recent explosion of the use of mediated forms of communication in the West at least – for home as well as organizational use – suggest new parameters? In other words, while we deal with problems of "depersonalized" styles in inter-group communication (e.g. overaccommodating elderly people, foreigner talk), will we have to attend to *hyper*personalized styles on the internet to foster certain kinds of more intimate contact after repeated log-ons? Will email provide us with qualitatively different situational and affective definitions – and hence new kinds of style variation as a consequence?

4. How are shifts managed, and with what variable social consequences?

5. Have people expectations about the range of styles available in their settings, organization, community, etc., violations from (or markedness of) which, in positive *and* negative directions, have social consequences?

6. Can we have a single theory that is adequate? Or do we need an assortment of mini-theories to address specific kinds of outcomes, motives, and performances? Can we not agree to cohese CAT (and its satellite models) with relevant aspects of audience and referee design so as to avoid cross-disciplinary redundancies?

7. How do people come to be effective style-shifters/accommodators or *not*, and in what way is this correlated with communicative competence and social skill? Is having the repertoire sufficient?

8. In what ways do style-shifts service other longer-term, even sociodevelopmental, functions? Trudgill (1986) discussed the relationship between accommodative practices and dialect shifts, and this moves us away from the contextual immediacy of Bell's core question to perhaps even, ultimately, a systems approach. For instance, are my not-so-subtle, brief American aberrations (alluded to earlier) one trajectory towards (desired) linguistic assimilation? Is the variable feedback I receive in this process a strategic training ground towards this end – and/or am I slowly acclimatizing my audience by the increasing frequency of these vocal aberrations to a gentle but full shift in their direction ultimately? Does my increasing comfort in engaging this have anything to do with my discomfort at being sociolinguistically distant from my Californian-sounding son with whom I am spending more and more time? The pursuit of long-term communicative goals by cross-contextual style variation over time is an interesting direction to address.

Visions of the future and new eras sometimes come from strange beginnings. As a fellow Welshperson with Coupland, I take some pride – and afford much gratitude to – his not only elevating my local, non-standard (Cardiff) dialect to one of academic significance, but for making it the basis, in some ways, for a radical rethink of core processes in our inter-discipline. The "Prince of Darkness" becomes the Prince of Light.

13 Style and stylizing from the perspective of a non-autonomous sociolinguistics

John R. Rickford

Coupland's paper – one of the most innovative and thought-provoking contributions in this volume – essentially consists of three parts: (1) a critique of quantitative sociolinguistic approaches to the analysis of style; (2) a proposal for a new approach in which dialect style as a marker of identity takes center stage, informed by goal-orientation and other concerns from communication theory; (3) an extract from a radio broadcast by a Welsh DJ, illustrating the new approach. I'll comment on each of these components in turn.

1   The critique of quantitative approaches to style

Coupland's critique of quantitative approaches to style ranges further and cuts deeper than the earlier, largely methodological, critiques that he cites. His is more conceptual, concerned with the underlying assumptions of quantitative stylistics (so to speak), which he lists as ten numbered points and elaborates on in subsequent sections. I won't repeat or comment on all of his points, but the overall thrust of the critique – directed at "the theoretical limitations inherent in an *autonomous* sociolinguistics" (emphasis added) – is one that I endorse, and have voiced before. For instance, to adequately account for the quantitative distributions by social class that we observe in local surveys of language use, we need to turn to sociological and anthropological models of social stratification and life mode, but these are quite unfamiliar to the average sociolinguist (Rickford 1986, Williams 1992, Milroy and Milroy 1992). And I agree with Coupland that the study of style can be enriched by drawing on the theory of communication studies and other fields. As sociolinguists and linguistic anthropologists, we cannot fully understand the cultural, ideological, social, political, psychological, and communicative underpinnings and ramifications of language data by making up *ad hoc* explanations of our own. We need to familiarize ourselves with, draw on and contribute to the theoretical, conceptual, and methodological issues and approaches in related fields. The need to reach beyond language to social theory becomes more imperative as we seek to move from descriptive or observational adequacy to explanatory adequacy.

Some of the specific assumptions that Coupland singles out are worth noting. The first, that "variation in dialect style variables is an adequate representation of sociolinguistic style variation in general," is certainly limiting, but its limitation has long been recognized. For instance, in his first major essay on the analysis of style, Labov (1972a [1966]:97) noted that:

> It is not contended that Style A [essentially = "casual"] and Style B [esentially = "careful"] are natural units of stylistic variation: rather they are formal divisions of the continuum set up for the purposes of this study, which has the purpose of measuring phonological variation along the stylistic axis. The discovery of natural breaks in the range of stylistic phenomena would have to follow a very different procedure.

Labov's conception was that identifying breaks in the continuum of the sociolinguistic interview was a valuable element of variation theory or socially "realistic" sociolinguistics (Labov 1972b:184; Hymes 1972a), which shared goals with "mainstream" linguistics (e.g. understanding the form and evolution of linguistic rules). One might question this view, by suggesting that even a socially realistic sociolinguistics would be better off if it conceptualized style in a broader sense. For instance, the social motivations for and embedding of language change might be better understood if we considered "style" in the broader sense of the presentation of self in everyday settings. (Cf. Eckert in this volume and 2000.) But the limitations of thinking of style only in terms of phonological and grammatical dialect features are even more evident in a "socially constituted" sociolinguistics of the kind proposed by Hymes (ibid.) and endorsed by Coupland – one in which social function rather than linguistic form is paramount. Some aspects of "style" that are potentially significant in a socially constituted sociolinguistics – e.g. lexical variation, address terms, and the different speech events in which individuals and groups engage – may be of rather less interest for those engaged in socially realistic sociolinguistics. Assumptions about what counts as relevant and how to study it depend significantly on what the enterprise or goal of sociolinguistics is. Labovian, Hymesian, and Couplandian conceptions of this are different. In discussing how to study style, we should not assume that we are now all united on what the goal or enterprise is, any more than we were a quarter of a century ago.

The third assumption identified by Coupland – that style is "a situational correlate, rather than an active, motivated, symbolic process," is one that I agree is deserving of critique, although I would add that substantive demonstrations of style-shifting as "an active motivated process" are less frequent than rhetorical endorsements of its importance. We particularly need empirical research on what aspects of speakers' styles are predictable from the sociocultural contexts of their "performance," and/or in line with exist-ing theory, and what are not. For instance, in Rickford and McNair-Knox's (1994) study of addressee- and topic-influenced style-shift, we found several instances in which Foxy's style-shifting between interviews III and IV was directly in line with Bell's audience design principles, given addressee and other differences between these two contexts. But Foxy's low use of key vernacular variables in interview II, where the addressees were both African American and familiar, as they were in interview IV, was con-trary to prediction. And while we cited some potential contributory factors for this result, we concluded that:

> our purpose is NOT to explain away the unusualness of interview II or to view it as aberrant. . . . While addressee variables do set up some valid expectations about the kind of language that Foxy (or anyone else) might use, we have to allow for the use of style as a resource and strategy, as an interactive and dynamic process . . .

At the same time, an approach that assumed that EVERYTHING in the realm of style was individually variable and dynamic and that NOTHING was regular or predictable would be as inadequate as an approach that pre-dicted the reverse. Judith Irvine's valid point (in chapter 1 of this volume) that style is about distinctiveness depends in part on understanding what is non-distinctive or predictable (or unmarked, in the related framework of Sankoff 1980).

I am ambivalent about the fifth assumption Coupland critiques – that style is one-dimensional. I have no problem with lambasting unidimen-sionality in the situational and linguistic sense – that relevant situations and variables can always be ordered according to one criterion, like for-mality, or standardness. But I have reservations about outright rejection of unidimensionality in the psychological sense – "that linear shifts relate to one scaleable intra-personal variable, such as 'attention to speech'." While attention to speech does not strike me as ultimately likely to be the "right" unidimensional model, the unidimensional audience design approach of Allan Bell, whom Coupland cites with approval throughout his paper, still strikes me as very promising. Multidimensional models (like those of Hymes 1972b and Preston 1986) will always be able to account for a wider variety of styles than unidimensional models, but they share the potential danger of never being able to be proven wrong. As Rickford and McNair-Knox (1994:241) note, Bell's (1984) model makes a series of specific, empirically falsifiable claims, and provides an integrative and predictive approach which sociolinguistics in general could benefit from.

Models with fewer variables are also more tractable than models with many, perhaps unlimited, variables, and they provide more ready explanations for how speakers come to acquire and control style-shifting. (Compare similar discussion of unidimensional versus multidimensional approaches to creole continua, in Rickford 1987:22–30.) It may be useful to push a unidimensional approach as far as it can go, modifying and extending it with additional factors and variables only where necessary. Or at least one might recognize that while no single underlying dimension may be capable of accounting for **all** aspects of stylistic variation, some may be more important (accounting for **most** of the variance) than others, requiring us to regard them as primary, and others as secondary, tertiary, and so on. Moreover, while we have been pursuing unidimensional approaches to style in a "universal" sense – as if attention, or audience or register – were the key covariable world-wide – what is stylistically significant may differ from one community to another, and ethnographic approaches will be necessary to reveal that. Hymes (1972b:66) seems to have anticipated both of these ideas with his concept of "hierarchies of precedence among components": "When individual societies have been well analyzed, hierarchies of precedence among components will very likely appear and be found to differ from case to case . . . For one group, rules of speaking will be heavily bound to setting; for another primarily to participants; for a third, perhaps, to topic." The fact that Hymes did this in the very article in which he outlined his multidimensional "components" model shows us that we should not consider multidimensional and unidimensional models as irreconcilable. Finally, I should add that despite his embrace of multidimensionality, Coupland comes close to embracing "identity" as a new "unidimensional" variable governing style. We should recall his critique that no one stylistic co-variable will suffice.

The danger of not heeding one's own admonitions is even greater when one looks carefully at Coupland's critiques of assumptions 7 and 9 – that only "relative frequencies of occurrence" are relevant in the study of style, and that styles are relevant only at the level of social groups, not individuals. Clearly language styles are identifiable and distinguishable by more than frequencies, but there is some danger, as one reads Coupland, that we might be tempted to eschew frequency considerations altogether, and **that**, I think, would be a retrograde step. Ditto for eschewing group styles – what it is like to sound "Black," or like a "Jet," or like a "burnout" – in favor of studying individuals alone. Group styles and individual styles are both realities, and each can help us to understand the other. I take Coupland's overall point to be that we should **not** restrict ourselves to the confines of any one approach, and I therefore oppose any suggestion that we rule out a potentially or demonstrably useful approach, even when the suggestion is implicit rather than explicit, and comes from Coupland himself.

2   Coupland's new approach to style

The new approach to the analysis of style that Coupland proposes involves several key elements, including: (1) considering style in relation to human communicative purposes and practices; (2) distinguishing "dialect style" from variation in "ways of speaking" more generally; (3) exploring how style projects speakers' identities and defines social relations.

In relation to the first element, Coupland excoriates sociolinguistics for its general neglect of communicative purpose, contrasting this with communication science, where purpose is theoretically and analytically central and where a distinction between instrumental, relational, and identity goals is commonly made. Unfortunately, perhaps because the distinction is so commonplace to him as a communication scientist, he does not define these terms; I was left to track them down (via Tracy 1991:4) to their source in Clark and Delia (1979:200):

(1) overtly *instrumental* [or *task*] objectives, in which a response is required from one's listener(s) related to a specfic obstacle or problem defining the task of the communicative situation, (2) *inter-personal* [or *relational*] objectives, involving the establishment or maintenance of a relationship with the other(s), and (3) *identity* [or *self-presentational*] objectives, in which there is management of the communicative situation to the end of presenting a desired self image for the speaker and creating or maintaining a particular sense of self for the other(s). (Emphasis and bracketed material added)

This conception of communicative goals is indeed rare in (quantitative) sociolinguistics, but I found it almost immediately useful. Soon after reading Clark and Delia, I used it to reflect analytically on an interaction I had at an Automatic Teller Machine (ATM) outside a bank. I had just gone to the walk-up ATM to withdraw some money, but it had no cash. As I was leaving on my bike, I noticed a woman standing outside her car completing a transaction at a second, drive-up ATM nearby. This was a holiday; the bank was closed, and we were the only people around. I wanted to find out whether this second ATM had cash (instrumental or task goal), so I called out to the woman to ask whether it did. But to "justify" this opening conversational move with a complete stranger, and to allay any fears she might have that I was a potential robber and she a potential victim (relational and identity goals), I said and did several things. I prefaced my request for information with the "explanation" that the "walk-up" machine had no cash, perhaps because so many people had been using it over the long holiday break (an explanation with which she expressed agreement). While waiting to use the drive-up machine, I maintained a good distance away from her, taking out my own wallet and ATM card quite conspicuously to establish my legitimacy as a bank customer. I did not move closer to the ATM until she had completed her transaction, stepped back into her car, closed the door, and begun to drive off. And, most importantly for the analysis of style, I used a very standard, polite register throughout the brief verbal exchange, attempting to portray myself as an educated, co-operative, upstanding community member.

While the analysis of goals along these and similar lines could be quite revealing for sociolinguistics, it is not without its complications. One source of complexity, discussed in the introduction to one of the references cited by Coupland (Tracy 1991) is that goals can be numerous, difficult to define, and impossible to link to discourse in any transparent, one-to-one relationship. A second complication, explored in another of Coupland's references (Craig 1986) is that goals can be distinguished in several other ways: as *functional* (in relation to outcomes describable by an external observer) versus *intentional* (existing in the mind of the speaker); as *positive* (directly causing behavior) versus *dialectical* (more loosely related to behavior, as with "happiness" or "success"); or as *formal* (having to do with official, conventionally expected, goals) versus *strategic* (having to do with what individual participants try to get out of the interaction for their personal goals). This last distinction seems virtually identical to one drawn by Hymes (1972b:61) between purposes conceived as "conventionally recognized and expected outcomes" (like the Venezuelan Waiwai's use of the *oho* chant to help accomplish a wedding contract), and purposes that represent the individual "goals" of participants (the Waiwai father-in-law and son-in-law, Hymes notes, have opposing goals in negotiating the wedding contract). Apart from this single instance, much of the theoretical complexity introduced by communication scientists over more than two decades of discussing "goals" will be new to us. We will have a lot of catching up to do, but it seems worthwhile.

In relation to the second element in Coupland's new approach – the distinction between "dialect style" and other "ways of speaking" – I have more questions and reservations. Dialect style involves phonological, grammatical, and lexical variables of the type traditionally associated with regional and social "dialects": (*-ing*), multiple negation, *soda* versus *pop*, and so on. This is distinguished on the one hand from expressive or attitudinal styles, like prosodic variables that are **not** linked to social groups, and, on the other, from "ways of speaking" in the broader sense delineated by Hymes. But I could not understand the sense in which ways of speaking distinguish ideational meanings while dialect styles do not, nor in which ways of speaking include instrumental goals, while dialect styles do not. After a close reading of Hymes (1974) I see both ways of speaking and dialect styles as capable of fulfilling all of the three basic goal types (instrumental, relational, and identity goals), and as equally capable of expressing ideological and "socio-symbolic" (Fischer 1958) shades of meaning. Overall, I agree with Coupland that "it would be misleading to overemphasize this distinction" – insofar as address terms, politeness, taciturnity, and other "ways of speaking" that are not traditionally associated with dialect style are indisputably aspects of "style." But having said this, I am not clear why we want to make or maintain the distinction in the first place. If the argument is that only dialect style features are associated with regional and social dialects, that is only because of our theoretical tunnel vision, for we have sufficient empirical evidence that regions and social groups **are** distinguished by forms of address, politeness patterns, and so on. And the fact of the matter is that when we assess the "styles" of people we hear, we generally attend, not just to the one or two dialect style variables on which sociolinguists tend to focus, but to a whole combination of co-occurrent features (Ervin-Tripp 1972), including forms of address, volume, volubility, and other elements typically excluded from dialect style.

Mention of how we "assess" styles reminds me of one aspect of Coupland's proposal that I really liked – his call for attention to neglected issues of style-reading and recipiency. Whites who talk Black might be perceived quite differently by Whites than they are by Blacks, for instance, and more generally, would-be convergers might be perceived quite differently by different social groups and individuals, but we do not completely understand the constraining factors, even after a quarter century of Accommodation Theory. Speaking more generally, we might ask: to what extent does competence in the interpretation of styles and speech-varieties extend beyond the boundaries of "the speech community" (that most controversial of objects)? Here, for instance, is an example of student chapel assistant Darron Johnson reading a biblical text (Luke 23:42–3) with a stylized laugh and repetition in the middle, in the course of an African American Sunday morning service in King's Memorial Church at Morehouse College, Atlanta, Georgia on February 11, 1996:

(1)   "And he said unto Jesus, 'Lord, remember me when thou comest into thy kingdom.' And Jesus said unto him, 'Verily I say unto thee, Today shalt thou be with me in paradise.'" *Huh huh, let me, let me read that again*: "'Verily I say unto thee – verily I say unto thee – Today shalt thou be with me in paradise.'"

I presume that many speakers of English, and of other languages worldwide, will understand that repetition of this type provides an emphasis or underscoring of a key point. But they will probably not know how pervasive textual repetition is in bible-reading and sermonizing in the Black church, nor how often preachers break out of their sermons and readings temporarily to alert their congregations to the significance of what they're doing: "'Watch this,' they'll say, or 'Follow me close, now.'" (Rickford and Rickford 2000:52). Nor will they know that a stylized laugh like Darron's is frequently used to suggest the speaker's delight with the content or the situation he or she is describing, its effect partly deriving from its similarity to the emphatic *huh* or *hunh-hunh* that Black preachers use at the end of breath groups as an energizing punctuation, as in this example (ibid:47):

> You wouldn't be here today, *hunh-hunh-hunh*,
> Hadn't God comforted you, *hunh-hunh-hunh* . . .

These elements, more or less unique to the Black worship tradition, allow Black congregants who hear Darron Johnson's short laugh, interpolation, and repetition to read and relish a little more of its ambience than outsiders to the community and to this tradition might.

Similarly, in the illustrations to be discussed in the next section, some aspects of what Cardiff radio personality FH does stylistically are uninterpretable to me without Coupland's guidance, just as what some of what Guyanese radio personality WM does are uninterpretable to him without my guidance. But some of their style-shifts are noticeable/receivable by both of us, without community-specific knowledge, since some aspects of style are projectable/sendable across speech community boundaries. What is local and what is general (one dare not say global or universal with this aspect of language use) in the production and interpretation of style remains to be specified, as it has for other aspects of language variation like *t,d* deletion (Kiparsky 1972).

The final element of Coupland's new approach is its focus on style as a marker of *identity*, or the presentation of self. This is an increasingly popular approach to style (its popularity partly due to Coupland's formulation), and one on which I myself have drawn in discussing the vernacular usage of African Americans, particularly teenagers (Rickford 1992, Rickford and Rickford 2000:chapter 12). I am surprised by the absence of any reference to the very relevant work of Le Page and Tabouret-Keller (1985) on language and ethnic identity, however, especially since Coupland seems to draw on similar notions of "projection." One respect in which the Le Page/Tabouret-Keller model might be useful is in reminding us that there are **limits** to the extent to which individuals can consciously adapt their style to project a certain persona or to identify with a particular group (see their constraints or riders – including adequate access to the group – on pp. 182 ff). Identity management and shift through style-selection and -shifting is not endless or unlimited. A more general concern I have is that we may be in danger of seeing **identity** as the only or primary factor affecting style, and of forgetting the role that other factors like purpose, audience, topic, and so on, play in effecting style-shift even when identity is held constant. To repeat the point made earlier: Let's not enshrine a new kind of unidimensionality while advocating multidimensionality, and let's not be limited by any one approach.

3   Coupland's illustration: excerpt from a Cardiff disc-jockey

With his closing discussion of the excerpt from a recording of a Cardiff radio disc-jockey (DJ), FH, Coupland nicely illustrates some of the principles and points raised earlier in the paper. There is, for instance, the strategic repeated use that FH makes in his radio broadcast of "phono-opportunities" for the use of salient Cardiff variables, like /a:/; we can probably all think of similar examples from the speech communities we have come into contact with. I cite a similar example from Wordsworth McAndrew, below, and Penny Eckert cites one from her work with pre-adolescents in San Jose in chapter 7 of this volume. All of these examples suggest that speakers are more aware of dialect features, and more capable of employing and exploiting them creatively, than we normally give them credit for. In FH's case, even the "shift" to standard forms when the projection of "competence" and "expertise" are in order is not total – regional Cardiff features are retained, while socially stigmatized features are "corrected."

Overall, the complexity of what FH is doing is emphasized: he is varying not only regionally and socially marked Cardiff features, but drawing also on American, south-west-of-England and Cockney features; the projection of various "personas" and identities is paramount, but (and this is reassuring), the relevance of content and key is also clear. And the "contexts" in which his speech forms are "set" do not pre-exist, but are to some extent created and constituted by the speech forms themselves. FH is not merely "using" a style, but "styling" or "stylizing." In words that are themselves well stylized, Coupland closes his "illustration" by observing that "Cardiff English is not merely 'Frank's voice' but one of many culturally loaded voices that FH, and presumably his audience too, can manipulate for relational and other interactional purposes."

I do have a couple of questions about the generalizability of this example to everyday conversation, but let me first cite a very similar example that I recorded in Guyana, South America. The radio personality in this case, Wordsworth McAndrew [WM] is a well-known local folklorist and defender/champion of "Creole" (versus English) language and culture. His program is called "What else?" – and like FM's "Hark, Hark, the Lark" title, it provides a ready (and frequently exploited) phono-opportunity for WM to use the highly marked low unrounded Creole /aa/ rather than the rounded English /ɔ:/. Although the title does not occur in the brief extract given below, "walk," pronounced as /waak/ in the closing lines of the extract, provides a similar opportunity.

Like FH, WM performs a number of different communicative functions within his show, and his style varies – sometimes subtly, sometimes dramatically – between them. The segments in which he "structures" the show, reminding the radio audience of the overall theme for the evening ("You're listenin', of course, to a program of 'Congo Songs'") or making a transition to the playing of the next song ("Right now, here's one of those 'Yamapeleh' or 'Gumbo' songs") are more formal, and show a higher incidence of English rather than Creole variants. The English copula is present ("You*'re* listenin' "), and two of the only three voiced inter-dental fricatives in the extract ("*the* drums," "*those* 'Yamapeleh' . . . songs") occur in these segments. As with FH, the move towards the standard is not complete, but it is noticeable, and it can be interpreted as a display of "expertise" in the performance of the "announcement" responsibilities all radio talk shows must fulfill.

In the segments in which WM revels in the kind of material unique to his Creole-oriented show, however – when he projects the persona of talking informally with an old friend about ring dances or the risqué song about a woman who arranges a tryst with her boyfriend's friend – in these the Creole elements are deliberately foregrounded. The preverbal copula is dropped ("dey Ø enjoyin' "), although, as in AAVE, the prenominal copula is more resilient ("Dey are men"), and all the phonological Creole variants are implemented (*d*ey, enjoyi*n,' A*n, cent*uh*'). The shift is especially marked in the final paragraph, where the basilectal or deep-Creole morphosyntax and lexicon of the Congo song's words ("*Waak a* side-line . . . *koonomoonoo gat 'e* fevah, . . . leh me wound *am*") spill over into the text introducing them like a warm infusion. Note the pronominal and phonological shift from *his girlfriend* to *e' frien*, and from morphologically marked (*felt, decided*) to unmarked past tense verbs (*waak, go, fin' out, call*).

(1)   **Wordsworth McAndrew** (Radio Program, GBS, Guyana, July 31, 1977; 047 – 60)

[As previous song ends.] Yeah, de story of de "dance-man." You're listenin', of course, to a program of "Congo Songs," done by the Annandale Sout' End group – ah – featuring guest leader CZ, on the drums, EG, and – ah – helpin' to sing, a whole bunch of women: LF, FJ, EC, IG, BE, HT, ITA, LC and LK.

Well, fuh de nex' couple of minutes, we want to – look at a slightly different kind of song, not de specific folksong with de specific explanations [i.e. not from the genre represented by the previous song], but – ah – songs da[t] are more or less – ah – how dey call dem in de Congo world, they call dem "Yamapeleh," or "Gumbo." Dat is, songs dey play when dey Ø enjoyin' demselves, in de ring, wid de drum in de middle, an' de women goin' out to de centuh to dance, wid de men, or widout de men if dey are men. An' if dey are no men, well of course, de women go out alone. An' dey'll – very special kind of Congo dance, which you'll have to see – ah – to understand.

Right now, here's one of those"Yamapaleh" or "Gumbo" songs I told you 'bout. It's an interesting one. It's in Creolese [local name for Guyanese Creole] of course, a slight – ah – African flavor to it. It's about a man who had a girl-frien', an' dis night – ah – *his* girlfriend felt – ahm – a little risqué – in which she *felt* like doin' someting wicked. An', dis man had a man-friend, an' de man-friend *decided* to *walk* de side-line [i.e. dam next to wide side-line canal in cane fields] so "*e* frien' wouldn' see '*e* goin." [So 'e] *waak* de side-line, an "*e go* to visit de girl. Den de man *fin' out*, an' so 'e *call* on *his* people [at] home to "bring a cutlass, leh me woun' *am*." [ie., "bring a machete let me wound him."] So de song says – ah – "*Waak* a side-line, my Cungo / koonomoonoo gat 'e fevah, my Cungo / Bring a cutlass, leh me wound *am*!" [i.e., "Walk on the side line, my Congo / the cuckold is hot and angry ("has his fever"), my Congo / Bring a machete, let me wound him!"]

Song begins: "Oh, *waak* a side-line, my Cungo . . ."

My point in introducing WM's excerpt is to reinforce the point of Coupland's illustration with FH. If we merely took their recordings, threw them in with socially similar individuals, and produced an aggregated analysis of the frequencies with which they used selected variables in different contexts, we would have missed something of the subtlety and complexity of what each is doing, moment by moment, in and through their varying "styles."

It occurs to me, however, that some verbal (and non-verbal) performances – especially those that involve radio broadcasts, large audiences, and public occasions **are** more stylized than others. And that people in such situations **are** trying more consciously than most of us may do in everyday life, to project personas of various types. I am reminded of the grandiloquent, tightly synchronized, but multifaceted bow that a steel band with about thirty members performed at a huge outdoor competition in Guyana several years ago. The stylization was distinctive, elaborate, and successful, eliciting oohs and aahs of appreciation from the audience and putting them in a positive mind-set towards the band even before they played their first note. There are undoubtedly parallels to this kind of stylization in one-on-one conversation, but the opportunities and possibilities for it seem to increase as audience size grows.

This raises the larger question of whether we can generalize as easily from broadcast styles to everyday spoken styles as the discussions in Coupland's paper for this volume, and in Bell (1984) would suggest. Like the excerpt from WM, their examples are insightful and revealing, but there may be limits on the applicability of data from these sources to everyday conversation. An interesting exercise would be to compare the radio styles of FH or WM with their styles in recorded interviews and everyday conversation in a wide range of contexts. Would they show the same range of features and personas? Or would their "on air" performances stand out as something quite distinct?

Another question is whether FH would agree with Coupland's analysis of what he's doing in the extract he cites, or whether WM would agree with my analysis of what he's doing in the extract I cite. As one turns (rightly so) to ethnographic approaches, and to questions of agency and purpose that go beyond statistical distributions, it seems important to arrive at interpretations that accord with or at least relate to those of local insiders and performers. In my dissertation work in Guyana (Rickford 1979), I didn't ask people to interpret their stylistic behavior in specific contexts as recorded and analyzed by me, but I did ask them about the appropriate contexts, in general, for the use of English and Creole. Audience considerations turned out to be very salient for them, as against topic, setting, or any of the many other dimensions an observer might have proposed, and it was important for me to take that into account in the analysis. But this then raises another question – of the extent to which speakers have any better access to intuitions about their *styles* than they do about other aspects of their linguistic behavior. Craig (1986:261) points out that speakers sometimes deny having any goals in informal conversation, although this is contestable, and that their accounts of their goals can be vague, inarticulate, even "demonstrably wrong." This is not sufficient reason to ignore such self-reports, but it does indicate that the process is neither straightforward nor easy.

That is probably a good note on which to conclude. What Coupland offers us is a sharp critique of some of the ways in which sociolinguistics has approached the study of style, and a vivifying vision of an alternative approach that draws on speech communication theory and discourse analysis and places the speaker, projecting his or her identities, at the center. The approach is not without its questions and difficulties, but the vision, the argumentation, and the illustrations are compelling enough to encourage us to follow. It would indeed be interesting if it were style (rather than social class or other constructs with more obvious social science connections) that finally led us most resolutely beyond autonomous sociolinguistics.

Part 4

Functionally motivated situational variation

14 Register variation and social dialect variation: the Register Axiom[1]

Edward Finegan and Douglas Biber

1 Introduction

Studies of synchronic linguistic variation have examined three principal kinds of correlates:
- the linguistic environment of the variable
- the social characteristics of the speaker
- the situation of use

Among features of the linguistic environment that have been correlated with phonological variation are the character of the following segment and the morphological status of the variable segment. Among the social dimensions with which linguistic variation has been correlated are gender, ethnicity, and socioeconomic status; and among the situational features are addressee, topic, opportunity for careful production, degree of shared context, and formality, the last often associated with "style."

A bounty of studies has investigated correlative variation between formality and socioeconomic status. Studies of communities in New York City, Norwich, Montreal, Detroit, and elsewhere gave rise to what was regarded as the "classic sociolinguistic finding" – namely, that "if a feature is found to be more common in the lower classes than in the upper classes, it will also be more common in the less formal than the most formal styles" (Romaine 1980:228). There has, however, been relatively little effort at explaining the relationships among the different kinds of variation – for example, between variation associated with situation of use and variation associated with the social characteristics of speakers. It is true, of course, that variable rule analyses incorporate both internal (i.e. linguistic) and external (e.g. social group and situational) variables into their representations, but they assume an

[1] As well as noting a continuing debt to those whose comments and help we acknowledge in Finegan and Biber (1994), we wish to express our appreciation to the participants at the Workshop on Style held at Stanford University and particularly to its organizers John Rickford and Penelope Eckert. Lesley Milroy deserves a special word of thanks for her thoughtful comments on our hypothesis. Dennis Preston and Allan Bell prove perennially provocative, and we appreciate their intellectual sparring.

Table 14.1. *Comparison of four models of sociolinguistic variation*

	Primary variation	Explanation
Bell	Dialect (inter-speaker)	No
Preston	Linguistic (internal)	No
Kroch	(Dialect)	Yes
Finegan and Biber	Register (intra-speaker)	Yes

independent contribution of individual constraints and thus do not directly address the relationships among different kinds of variation. In fact, no model has attempted to incorporate all that is known about variation, and the absence of a full model is not surprising, given the complexity and inter-dependence of factors underlying language variation.

Moreover, studies of register variation and style are under-represented in the sociolinguistics literature, although Rickford and McNair-Knox (1994:265) have noted that "style is too central to the methodological and theoretical concerns of our subfield for us to neglect it any longer." It is essential in pursuing such methodological and theoretical concerns to seek multivariate explanations, for enough is now known about language varia-tion to confirm that no single dimension can adequately explain it.

Concerning relationships among linguistic, social dialect, and stylistic variation, several partial models have been proposed that attempt to relate one kind of variation to at least one other kind. As a backdrop to our dis-cussion of an alternative proposal we review several of these models, recog-nizing that our sketches do not adequately represent the original richness of the proposals or substitute for first-hand acquaintance with them. The models of Bell (1984), Preston (1991), and Finegan and Biber (1989, 1994) are alike in that each posits one of the three kinds of variation as funda-mental and defines primary and secondary patterns by deriving one or another kind from the fundamental one. But these three models also differ among themselves in two important respects: (1) each posits a different kind of variation as primary; and (2) only one of the models takes the par-ticular distributions of its primary variation as requiring explanation. Also discussed here, though only briefly, is Kroch's (1978) model, which does attempt to explain patterns of social dialect variation but does not attempt to relate dialect variation to style.

Table 14.1 provides a summary of these four models. It indicates that Bell, Preston, and Finegan and Biber designate different kinds of variation as primary and that Bell and Preston offer no explanation for the patterns they take to be fundamental. By contrast, our model offers an explanation for the kind of variation that we posit as fundamental. Kroch addresses only social dialect variation and is not strictly comparable in his approach (hence "Dialect" appears in parentheses in table 14.1); his significance in this context is that, like us, he takes patterns of social dialect variation as calling for explanation. We should note that in Kroch's view are echoes of Labov's (1965, 1972) description of the mechanism of linguistic change.

In the remainder of section 1, we briefly describe the models of sociolinguistic variation proposed by Bell and Preston and outline an alternative proposal. In section 2 we offer four observations about sociolinguistic variation and explore logical explanations of the "classic sociolinguistic finding." In section 3 we recapitulate the model of sociolinguistic variation proposed in Finegan and Biber (1994) and show how that model explains the classic sociolinguistic finding. In section 4 we report new findings of social dialect variation in the British National Corpus that call into question fundamental aspects of Bell's and Preston's models. In section 5 we take up three topics: the systematic patterns of social dialect variation; the relationship between internal and external constraints on variation; and Bell's prediction that style variation presupposes social variation. Then we propose the Register Axiom as a substitute for the "classic sociolinguistic finding." Section 6 addresses the importance of incorporating a wide range of registers into studies of sociolinguistic variation.

1.1   Two models of sociolinguistic variation: Bell and Preston

The heart of Bell's model is captured by his "Style Axiom" (1984:151):

Variation on the style dimension within the speech of a single speaker derives from and echoes the variation which exists between speakers on the "social" dimension.

Bell's highly regarded model of audience design takes social dialect variation as fundamental and style variation as derivative. He argues that speakers accommodate their speech to that of their addressee and audience, thus creating patterns of style variation that reflect patterns of social dialects. In his analysis, patterns of social dialect variation go unremarked.

Bell (1984:151) sees "the nature of the interrelation between the two dimensions [as] more than an interrelation. It is . . . a cause-and-effect relationship" that holds for an individual speaker shifting from style to style so as "to sound like another speaker." He claims that "the significance of interspeaker [i.e., dialect] differences originates in the social evaluation of speakers who use a given linguistic feature." (To accommodate a number of acknowledged counterexamples to his model, he proposes "initiative design" as an alternative motivation for style variation.)

Bell's model (1984:151–2) makes three assumptions:

1. social dialect variation is primary
2. the patterns of social dialect variation do not require explanation
3. style variation presupposes social dialect variation

From these assumptions he concludes that "some linguistic variables will have both social and style variation, some only social variation, but none style variation only." In section 5.3, we offer counterevidence to the validity of this point.

Preston (1991) agrees with Bell in deriving style variation from what he calls status variation, but he posits internally constrained linguistic variation as primary, with "status" (including social dialect) variation secondary and style variation tertiary. Essentially, the grounding for Preston's model is the claim that for any variable feature the range of variation correlated with strictly linguistic constraints completely encompasses the range of variation that can be correlated with speaker status; in turn, then, the range of variation correlated with speaker status completely encompasses the range of variation correlated with style. Following Bell, the logic of Preston's grounding is simply that reflected variation must be narrower in range than what it reflects. (In Bell's [1984:153] metaphor, "As is the habit of mirrors, the reflection is less distinct than the original.") Pivotal to Preston's model are the putative patterns of inclusion, although numerous exceptions to the generalizations about such inclusionary patterns exist, as both Preston and Bell acknowledge.

While Bell's model leaves a gap by not undertaking an explanation for the patterns of dialect variation, Preston's model leaves two gaps: by not explaining why linguistic variation patterns as it does and by not asking how dialect patterns come to reflect linguistic variation or why they should. In Preston's model, the putative inclusion of each kind of variation within the range of another kind sufficiently demonstrates both a hierarchical ranking and a derivation. In other words, his model does not address the actuation problem (why variation is initiated) with respect to either the primary or secondary patterns. Principally from the putative patterns of inclusion, Preston infers that status variation must reflect linguistic variation, while concurring with Bell's view that style variation reflects status variation as a consequence of behavioral accommodation.

1.2   A theory of social dialect variation: Kroch

In an analysis that focuses exclusively on social dialects and is therefore related to the present discussion in limited ways, Kroch (1978; Kroch and Small 1978) describes certain systematic patterns of social dialect variation, proposing that they arise because higher status groups resist the "normal processes of phonetic conditioning" that characterize the speech of non-elite social groups. Kroch takes the patterns of social dialect variation as calling for explanation, and the one he offers differs sharply from the widely held view that "each group models its formal style on the speech behavior of those groups one or two steps above it in the social scale" (Labov 1969:23–4). In highlighting the critical importance to variation theory of explaining dialect patterns, Kroch addresses a central puzzle for sociolinguistic theory, and one to which we return below.

1.3   A communicative-function view of register and social dialect

In our communicative-function model of variation, we use the term "registers" to represent language varieties characteristic of particular situations of use. In this we follow Halliday (1978), Crystal and Davy (1969) and others (see Biber 1994). We construe "situation of use" broadly. Register includes not only the spoken varieties associated with situational "formality" and "informality" and often designated "styles" but other spoken and written varieties as well. Speech is the obvious primary mode, but, unlike many others, we posit a relationship among spoken and written varieties of language in literate societies, a relationship that is complex and not fully understood. We take it as self-evident that writing is an important and influential mode of expression, a legitimate linguistic channel supporting important registers in a community's linguistic repertoire and deserving of sociolinguistic study not only as a potentially significant interactant with the forms of spoken language but also as a major mode of discourse worthy of sociolinguistic analysis in its own right. No one would quarrel with the observation that one's internal lexicon can be substantially influenced by what one reads, and we think it equally plausible that grammar and perhaps even phonology could likewise be influenced. Sociolinguists have rightly criticized intuitional grammarians for sometimes confounding writing and speaking; and by focusing on actual speech sociolinguists have uncovered a great deal about language variation that might otherwise have remained obscure. In Western societies and many others, however, the repertoire of a speech community typically includes a wide range of both written and spoken registers, and sociolinguistics must recognize this rich range of registers in a community's repertoire if the patterns of linguistic variation in those communities are to be explained. Sociolinguistics cannot continue to exclude written registers from its purview and hope to describe the language variation of literate communities adequately. (We return to this point in section 6.)

We use "situation of use" or "situation" as shorthand designators for those facets of a communicative situation that may systematically affect the shape of linguistic expression in that situation. Besides mode (speaking and writing), situation of use includes setting, relative status of interlocutors, degree of familiarity with and shared background information among interlocutors, topic, purpose, availability of extra-linguistic channels as cues to interpretation, and other factors (cf. Biber 1994). Whether all parameters of situational variation have been identified we cannot say, nor to what extent all relevant parameters of variation can be reduced to a set of underlying dimensions. Many communicative situations are dynamic and subject to alteration in the course of interaction.

We take it as axiomatic that any linguistic feature can serve communicative and indexical functions, and that such features are conventional to greater or lesser degrees and serve communicative and indexical functions to greater or lesser degrees. In personal letters, for example, one would count as highly conventionalized a salutation like "Dear Chris" and a closing like "Sincerely yours." Among highly conventionalized features of fairy tales, one would count the opening "Once upon a time," and of weddings the pivotal performative "I now pronounce you husband and wife." One can readily imagine alternative salutations, closings, and pronouncements for the same communicative functions, and one can imagine circumstances in which the conventionalized expressions serve other functions (for example, as illustrations in the present paragraph). However, such expressions identify the named situations so saliently that they can be viewed as primarily conventionalized situational indices, irrespective of whatever else they may communicate or effectuate in the speech situation.

We can illustrate with a functional example. Texts exhibiting frequent nouns differ from texts exhibiting frequent pronouns in that the pronominal texts are characteristically more highly contextualized than the nominal ones, that is they rely on context to a greater degree. This is so much the case that a high frequency of pronouns can serve to index "colloquial" texts – and they do so not by convention, but by the fact that the functional role of pronouns in highly contextualized situations characteristically produces more frequent pronouns. Similarly, certain features of social dialects operate as indicators of social identity while at the same time serving as integral elements of speakers' grammatical or lexical systems. Salient indicators of regional and social identity are abundant, and whether or not they fall within the scope of grammatical or lexical patterns is not in question; the point is that certain features index social identity irrespective of other functions they serve in a given communicative situation. By contrast, most linguistic features do *not* achieve sufficient salience to index either speaker or situational identity, though the feature may be correlated with one or the other. For example, the frequency of relative clause types and other particular aspects of relative clauses have been shown to correlate with social groups (Kroch and Hindle 1982; Macaulay

1991:62–9), but that frequency is not sufficiently salient for relative clauses to index social identity. By contrast, the (th) and (dh) variables in New York City English have been shown to be indicators of social group identity (Labov 1966).

Relying on the findings reported in Biber (1988), we demonstrated in earlier work (Finegan and Biber 1989, 1994) and illustrate below in sections 3 and 3.1 that the distribution of certain linguistic features across registers exhibits patterns that can be explained by their communicative functions and the communicative situation in which they occur. Focusing on a subset of features defining Biber's (1988) Dimension 1 (the textual dimension representing "Involved versus Informational Production"), we indicated that such features are "of a particular kind, namely those that are *variable* within their communities across both social groups and situations of use, representing degrees of economy or elaboration" (1994:334). Economy variants contain less phonological content and often have wider semantic scope. Such variants are sometimes characterized as "condensed" or "abbreviated." In exploiting condensed variants, interlocutors typically must rely more on surrounding text and situational context as well as on shared background information to assist them in interpreting expression. "Elaboration" is the term we use to characterize expressions of greater explicitness, as with more frequent occurrences of prepositional phrases and relative clauses, and of nouns instead of third-person pronouns. Economy and elaboration are complementary functional parameters, and the distribution of certain linguistic features across registers can be explained by reference to them. Of course, other functional parameters also govern the distribution of features; economy – elaboration is merely one among several.

For features of the particular kind whose distributions across registers and dialects show the classic sociolinguistic pattern, we hypothesized that register variation is fundamental. We further hypothesized that frequency distributions across socioeconomic status groups reflect the differential access of those groups to the full range of situations of use. Because not all speakers have equal access to the full range particularly of literate registers, praxis in those registers is also not distributed equally. We believe that certain features of social dialect arise from this differential access to the full range of registers among social groups. The notion that access to particular ranges of use influences linguistic expression has been recognized by many researchers. We cited several sociolinguists in support of this observation, among them Heath (1986), Hymes (1973), Kay (1977), and Gumperz (1964).

Details of our model are presented in section 3. Before turning to that, we re-examine the "classic sociolinguistic finding."

2   Four observations and the "classic sociolinguistic finding"

Four observations about systematic patterns of register variation and social dialect variation are sufficiently well established in the literature to warrant attention in all proposed models of sociolinguistic variation. We list them below; the contents and the analysis follow closely our earlier discussion (Finegan and Biber 1994:317 ff.).

> **Four observations related to the classic sociolinguistic finding**
> A. The same linguistic features often serve as markers of social group and social situation.
> B. The distribution of such features across social dialects and registers (or "styles") is typically parallel, with variants that occur more frequently in less "formal" situations also occurring more frequently among lower-ranked social groups, and with variants that occur more frequently in more "formal" situations occurring more frequently among higher-ranked social groups.
> C. For many of these features, the distribution across situations is systematic, with more "formal" or more "literate" situations typically exhibiting a more frequent use of explicit and elaborated variants, in contrast with less "formal" or more "oral" situations typically exhibiting a more frequent use of economy variants.
> D. The distribution of these features across social dialects within a community is systematic, with higher-ranked social groups exhibiting more frequent use of elaborated and explicit variants and lower-ranked groups exhibiting more frequent use of economy variants.

Labov (1969:22–3) has called observation A "remarkable." Observations A and B combined have been such commonplace findings of sociolinguistic investigation that they have been said to constitute "the classic sociolinguistic finding." Observation C has been identified and illustrated by functional grammarians and documented in detail in a multidimensional framework by Biber (1988, 1995). Observation D underlies Kroch's theory of social dialect variation and has been noted by others, most recently Chambers (1995:230–53), who extends Kroch's observations on phonology to include morphology. It is important to note that the communities in which this pattern has been uncovered are principally North and Latin American and Western European urban communities, a fact that constrains the generalizability of observations B and D and a matter to which we return in section 5.1.

2.1   Logical explanations for the classic sociolinguistic finding

The classic sociolinguistic finding has at least four possible explanations, given below.

Four explanations for the classic sociolinguistic finding
1. Rather than being "remarkable," as Labov claims, the parallel pattern between social group and social situation is merely coincidental and needs no explanation. (In this case, figures, tables, and graphs linking social dialect and stylistic variation are misleading in that they implicitly suggest a relationship.)
2. Patterns of style and patterns of dialect are independent of one another, but both derive from an independent third pattern or set of principles. (In this case, only the third pattern would require an independent explanation, along with an explanation for its reflection in social dialect and style.)
3. The patterns of style reflect patterns of dialect variation. (In this case, the patterns of dialect variation would require independent explanation, as would their reflection in style.)
4. Dialect patterns reflect style variation. (This is our view, and in this case the patterns of style variation would require an independent explanation, as would their reflection in social dialect.)

Explanations 2, 3, and 4 have two aspects. First, the basic pattern would need to be explained: why are features of the primary pattern distributed as they are? Second, the link between primary and derived pattern must be explained: what links the secondary pattern to the basic pattern? As to explanation 1 we are unaware that any sociolinguist explicitly subscribes to it, and the raison d'etre of this volume contravenes its plausibility; we have nothing further to say of it. To our knowledge, explanation 2 has also not been fully and explicitly invoked, although it is not implausible. In fact, Preston's model falls partly under the logic of explanation 2 in that he takes patterns of social dialect and style to derive from patterns of inherent linguistic variation. Like Bell, Preston (1991:36) derives style variation from social dialect variation, but he goes even further by deriving social dialect variation (included within his "status variation") from linguistic variation: "Variation on the 'status' dimension derives from and echoes the variation which exists within the 'linguistic' dimension." Preston does not offer an independent explanation for the linguistic patterns or for their reflection in social dialect.

Bell's model falls within explanation 3, wherein style is taken to reflect dialect variation. Bell explicitly addresses the relationship between dialect and style by hypothesizing that patterns of style derive from and reflect patterns of social dialect. The logic of this explanation requires that patterns of social dialect variation can be explained, but Bell does not comment on the character of social dialect patterns. He has commented elsewhere that "the consensus of sociolinguistic findings is that the identity function of language is basic and all-pervasive,"[2] but this comment does not directly provide an independent explanation for the observed patterns of dialect variation. The claim that dialect features are basically identity markers leaves their particular distributional patterns unaddressed. The question for sociolinguistics is not whether particular groups claim certain linguistic features as identity markers but rather, as Kroch asks, why the markers pattern as they do with respect to those of other social groups. Bell's model could explain observations A and B on page 242, but it is not clear how it could explain observations C and D. The logic of explanation 3 requires that the patterns of dialect variation be explained, along with their reflection in style.[3]

As to explanation 4, it is our contention that, leaving aside highly conventionalized features of identity, many patterns of register variation can be explained by reference to the communicative functions of particular features across situations of use, and we hypothesize that social dialect patterns for those features derive from a combination of (a) their communicatively motivated distributions across registers; and (b) the differential access of social groups to praxis in those registers. In section 3 we recapitulate the argument.

3   Recapitulation of the communicative-function argument

In 1994 we highlighted the three kinds of variation customarily identified by sociolinguists and introduced a fourth kind into the equation. The three customary kinds are linguistic, social, and registral (or style) variation. The fourth kind is functional variation. We described three parameters of the communicative situation in an effort to explain the variation of linguistic features across contextually situated texts, that is, across registers. For illustration we selected the situational parameters of *planning*, *purpose*, and *shared context*. Variation in frequency of linguistic features in texts produced along these parameters we call register variation, and we tie it directly to functional considerations. We did not explicitly relate functional

---

[2] Bell (1995:268) offers citations to neither the putative consensus nor the putative minority positions, but earlier he had acknowledged that "No satisfying explanation has yet been advanced for the existence of indicators" (Bell 1984:152).

[3] In contrast to Bell's model, Kroch's theory addresses the systematic nature of variation across social groups (limiting his scope however to phonological variation). Kroch hypothesizes that speakers of the prestige dialect exert energy to resist "normal processes of phonetic conditioning" that are not resisted by non-elite speakers. His observation that certain features by which the dialects of socially stratified groups differ from one another represent greater and lesser realizations of the "normal processes of phonetic conditioning" is important. Because Kroch does not address the relationship between style and social dialect variation, his theory does not fall within the purview of our logical possibilities.

considerations to linguistic variation and said little about linguistic variation at all. Linguistic variation and functional variation appear to be intertwined in ways that are still little understood. It seems likely, for example, that considerable linguistic variation having to do with ease of articulation and with "natural generative phonology" can be related to the production mandate "Be quick and easy" (cf. the natural generative phonology of Stampe 1969). Likewise, variable linguistic constraints may be related to the mandate "Be clear" (see Slobin 1979:243). For example, consonant cluster simplification has been linked to syllabic stress and morphemic distinctness, matters amenable to functional explanations and constrained in part by competition between the competing mandates. Clarity typically calls for elaborated expression; ease typically calls for economical expression. When we look at linguistic variation across registers and across social groups, the functional task of certain linguistic features appears to play a significant role in their frequency of occurrence. (See also Yaeger-Dror 1997.)

Using Biber's (1988) findings, we showed in Finegan and Biber (1994) that patterns of register variation can be systematically explained by reference to three communicative parameters of the situation of use. We based our discussion on two observations:

- the distributional patterns of many features across situations can be shown to have motivation in the communicative functions of the features and the character of the communicative situation
- these features function in comparable ways for different social groups in a speech community

In sections 3.1–3.4 below, we argue that, for the kinds of features we have examined, their systematic distribution across social groups reflects the access of those groups to situations of use and to the registers that favor those features. This is particularly true of access to spoken and written literate registers, which in the societies that have been the focus of most sociolinguistic inquiry has been the social groups at the upper end of the socioeconomic scale. In section 3.1 we demonstrate the systematic patterns of register variation along three situational parameters and explain those patterns with reference to the communicative function of the features. Section 3.2 briefly rehearses the published findings of social dialect variation that illustrate the systematic distribution of economy and elaboration features across social groups. Section 3.3 addresses the implications of these two independent sets of findings and concludes that the distribution of certain features across social groups derives from the differential access of the groups to situations of use that favor elaboration or economy features. In particular, we believe that access to literate registers promotes a more frequent use of elaboration features. Section 3.4 clarifies several points of the communicative-function model.

3.1   The evidence from patterns of register variation

From Biber's (1988) Dimension 1, we selected four linguistic features that represent "economy" and three that represent "elaboration." The features of economy are contractions, THAT omission, pro-verb DO, and pronoun IT. Contractions are shortened word forms, typically containing apostrophes in written form to represent omitted sounds/letters, as in *won't, he's,* and *she'll.* Contractions are straightforward examples of expressive economy, most closely associated with phonology but covering written and spoken registers alike. THAT omission refers to the absence of the subordinator in sentences such as *She says she wants to win* as compared with *She says that she wants to win.* Both are grammatical; we take the former to represent a syntactically more economical expression than the latter. (This feature does not include omitted relative pronouns.) Pro-verb DO refers principally to uses of DO as a substitute for an entire phrase or clause, as in *Yes, he did*; in other words, excluding its use as an auxiliary with a main verb. The third measure of economy is the pronoun IT, a very generalized pronoun that can refer to an extremely wide range of objects and concepts and can serve as an anaphor for noun phrases or entire clauses.

The features of elaboration are attributive adjectives, prepositional phrases, and type/token ratio. Attributive adjectives are constituents of a noun phrase, serving to modify the noun, as with *tall ships* or *her stoic character*; excluded from this category are predicative adjectives (*She was stoic*). Prepositional phrases represent elaboration in that they serve as frames for speakers and writers to elaborate on the semantic content of a proposition, as shown in these examples:
• The Indian prime minister announced that government scientists had conducted underground atomic tests.
• *In a news conference in New Delhi on Monday*, the Indian prime minister announced that government scientists had conducted underground atomic tests *in June in a desert laboratory* about 300 miles *from the capital.*
The six prepositional phrases in the second example add specific information – the circumstances of the announcement as to time, date, and place and details of the tests as to time and location.

The third feature representing elaboration is type/token ratio, which represents the proportion of different words in a sample of text. The measure is typically based on the first four hundred words of a text; we illustrate the calculation with the six-word sentence *The cat sat on the mat.* Because the six word tokens include five different words (i.e. types), the sentence has a type/token ratio of 5/6. Type/token ratio is a direct measure of lexical diversity, a recognized measure of lexical elaboration, and is usually given as a decimal – in this case 0.83.

We demonstrated how the distribution of these features in strategically chosen pairs of registers varies systematically with the relative force of the two production "mandates" characterized by Slobin (1979) as clarity ("Be clear") and ease ("Be quick and easy").[4] In general, the clarity mandate urges specificity of expression, and specificity generally entails elaboration. The clarity mandate thus favors addressees, whose task is to interpret expression within context. On the other hand, speakers and writers are favored by the ease mandate, with its invitation to condensation and the consequent tendency to homonymy and generality of meaning.[5] (For further discussion of elaboration and economy, see section 4.) We focused on three aspects of the communicative situation: planning, purpose, and degree of shared context. Each represents a parameter along which different types of function can vary, and such functional variation correlates with the kind of linguistic variation that interests sociolinguists. Although we did not extend our discussion beyond those situational parameters, we recognize that other functional parameters may influence patterns of linguistic variation across registers.

The registers that we compared are some of those that form the basis for Biber's (1988) study of speech and writing. From the London Lund Corpus (Svartvik 1990) come Public speeches, Conversations, and Interviews. From the Lancaster–Oslo/Bergen Corpus (Johansson and Hofland 1989, Johansson, Leech, and Goodluck 1978) come Academic prose, General fiction, and Press reportage. The Personal letters register comes from a supplemental corpus collected by Biber (1988:66).

3.1.1 The planning parameter First, considering opportunities for careful production, we described the distribution of the seven features in Public speeches and Academic prose. These registers are informational in purpose and addressed to relatively large, non-interactive audiences, but they differ from one another with respect to opportunity for careful production. We reported the frequencies of the features per thousand words as given in table 14.2. The table shows that the features representing economy are more frequent in the on-line production of Public speeches than in the more

---

[4] While Grice's maxims are not culturally universal in any straightforward fashion, it is nevertheless worthwhile noting that Slobin's mandates can be viewed as related to the maxim of quantity and the maxim of clarity.

[5] Arguments for the relationship between condensed expression and generality or between elaboration and clarity do not need to be made here. It is well established that shorter words tend to be more frequent and to have greater semantic scope and that longer words are less common and tend to have narrower, or more specific, semantic content. Of course, there is inter-dependence among size of phonemic inventory, range of phonotactic constraints, and length of words needed to express any set of culturally defined referents. It is also axiomatic that features such as personal pronouns or pro-verbs designate a potentially wide range of referents, which could be made more specific by the use of full noun phrases or lexical verbs typically containing more phonological content than the equivalent pronoun or pro-verb.

Table 14.2. *Influence of production circumstances on the distribution of features in two registers (per thousand words)*

A. *Economy Features*

	Contractions	THAT *Omission*	*Pro-verb* DO	*Pronoun* IT
Public speeches	13.3	1.9	2.4	8.9
Academic prose	0.1	0.4	0.7	5.9

B. *Elaboration Features*

	Attributive Adjectives	*Prepositional Phrases*	*Type/Token Ratio*
Public speeches	48.9	112.6	49.0
Academic prose	76.9	139.5	50.6

planned register of Academic prose, while the features representing elaboration are more frequent in the planned texts of Academic prose than in the Public speeches. Planning permits speakers and writers to anticipate the needs of hearers and readers more readily and to provide a greater degree of explicit expression than can ordinarily be accomplished in situations with less opportunity for careful production. As Joseph (1987:36) notes: "The existence of the visual channel . . . provides a mechanism for virtues such as clarity to be perceived, measured, increased, planned in a conscious way."

3.1.2 The purpose parameter Purpose is a widely recognized parameter of the communicative situation. To highlight its influence on linguistic variation, we report the frequencies of seven features in Conversations and Interviews. Both these registers are produced on-line and face to face, with interaction possible between the interlocutors. A difference is that Conversation typically serves affective and involved purposes (with participants concerned about inter-personal relationships as well as informational exchange), whereas Interviews are largely informational and only secondarily inter-personal. Table 14.3, presenting frequencies per thousand words for the same linguistic features examined in table 14.2, shows that the four economy features occur more frequently in Conversations than in Interviews, while the three elaboration features are more frequent in Interviews than in Conversations. Given the differing purposes of the registers and the communicative functions of the features, this distribution is not surprising.

3.1.3 Parameter of shared context Degree of shared context is also widely seen as a significant aspect of a communicative situation. At one extreme, intimate interlocutors can speak to one another face to face – that is, simultaneously and in the same location – thus sharing maximal physical context

Table 14.3. *Influence of purpose on distribution of features in two registers (per thousand words)*

A. Economy Features

	Contractions	THAT *Omission*	*Pro-verb* DO	*Pronoun* IT
Conversations	46.2	9.6	9.0	20.0
Interviews	25.4	4.3	4.6	11.9

B. Elaboration Features

	Attributive Adjectives	*Prepositional Phrases*	*Type/Token Ratio*
Conversations	40.8	85.0	46.1
Interviews	55.3	108.0	48.4

Table 14.4. *Influence of shared context on distribution of features in two registers (per thousand words)*

A. Economy Features

	Contractions	THAT *Omission*	*Pro-verb* DO	*Pronoun* IT
Interviews	25.4	4.3	4.6	11.9
Public speeches	13.3	1.9	2.4	8.9

B. Elaboration Features

	Attributive Adjectives	*Prepositional Phrases*	*Type/Token Ratio*
Interviews	55.3	108.0	48.4
Public speeches	48.9	112.6	49.0

as well as background knowledge. At the other extreme, sharing minimal context, interlocutors separated in time and place and with no personal knowledge of one another can communicate through writing.

To represent registers at the situational poles of shared context, we contrast Interviews and Public speeches. Both are produced on-line and have an informational purpose. Both interviewer and the interviewee are acquainted with the interview topic, and they may know one another personally. They also share the time and place during the interview and can interact linguistically and gesturally. In contrast, producers of Public speeches typically do not know the members of their audience and have very limited interaction with them. As shown in table 14.4, these differences in the communicative situation are associated with differences in the frequency of linguistic features. The four economy features are more frequent in Interviews than in Public speeches, while among the elaboration

Table 14.5. *Overview of situational variation (per thousand words)*

A. *Economy Features*

	Contractions	THAT *Omission*	*Pro-verb* DO	*Pronoun* IT
Written				
Personal letters	22.2	12.8	4.3	11.0
General fiction	11.2	3.0	3.3	11.5
Press reportage	1.8	2.0	1.3	5.8
Academic prose	0.1	0.4	0.7	5.9
Spoken				
Conversations	46.2	9.6	9.0	20.0
Interviews	25.4	4.3	4.6	11.9
Public speeches	13.3	1.9	2.4	8.9

B. *Elaboration Features*

	Attributive Adjectives	*Prepositional Phrases*	*Type/Token Ratio*
Written			
Personal letters	44.2	72.0	52.5
General fiction	50.7	92.8	52.7
Press reportage	64.5	116.6	55.3
Academic prose	76.9	139.5	50.6
Spoken			
Conversations	40.8	85.0	46.1
Interviews	55.3	108.0	48.4
Public speeches	48.9	112.6	49.0

features prepositional phrases are more frequent and the type/token ratio higher in Public speeches than in Interviews. As it happens, attributive adjectives are more frequent in Interviews than in Public speeches, a reflection of the conflict between the promotion of economy by on-line production constraints and shared context competing with the promotion of elaboration by the informational purpose of Interviews.

3.1.4 Summary and extension of situational parameters These three situational parameters (opportunity for careful production, purpose, and degree of shared context) are intertwined, and they combine to produce degrees of preference for clarity or for ease. An overview of situational variation, displaying frequencies of the four economy features and the three elaboration features across several written and spoken registers, is shown in table 14.5.

Table 14.5 highlights the systematic distribution of these representative features across registers. Conversation has the highest frequency of economy features among the spoken registers, while Personal letters exhibit the highest frequency of them among the written registers. By contrast, Public speeches among spoken registers and Academic prose among written registers have the fewest economy features, as one would predict given their respective production circumstances, purposes, and degrees of shared context. As expected, the findings are reversed for the elaboration features. Among the written registers, Personal letters have the least frequent elaboration features and the most frequent economy features, while among the spoken registers, Conversation has the most frequent economy features and fewest elaboration features, as one would predict, given the respective production circumstances and the nature of the two mandates.

On the basis of that analysis, it would appear that the distribution of such features across situations of use is communicatively motivated and systematic. Simply put, there is evidence that for many linguistic features the application of the clarity and ease mandates explains their distribution across registers. We conclude that much linguistic variation across registers can be explained by systematic analysis of salient communicative parameters. Of course, other parameters of the communicative situation can influence the occurrence of these and other features.

3.2   The evidence from patterns of social dialect

In Finegan and Biber (1994:326–35), we described the findings of a score of investigations evidencing patterned distribution of features across socially ranked groups speaking half a dozen languages in a dozen communities. In eighteen tables we reproduced findings from sociolinguistic investigations of American English, English English, Scottish English, and Welsh English, of Canadian and Continental French, of Latin American Spanish, of Brazilian Portuguese, and of Flemish. Our examples included phonological, lexical, syntactic, and discourse variables. All the features in the tables can be interpreted as representing either economy or elaboration.

Overall, the distribution of features that can be interpreted as honoring the ease mandate was progressively more frequent in groups of lower status, while features that can be interpreted as honoring the clarity mandate were progressively more frequent in groups of higher status. As these studies are generally familiar to variationists, there is no need to review them here in detail, but tables 14.6a and 14.6b summarize those findings.

3.3   Implications of register and social dialect patterns

From these independent sets of register analyses and social dialect analyses we draw these conclusions:

Table 14.6a. *Distribution of economy features, showing more frequent use in lower social status groups for four languages*

Investigator	Feature	Social status Higher	Lower
English			
Wolfram 1969 (Detroit)	consonant cluster reduction	less	more
Wolfram 1969 (Detroit)	postvocalic /r/ omission	less	more
Labov 1966 (NYC)	postvocalic /r/ omission	less	more
Trudgill 1974 (Norwich)	/h-/ omission	less	more
Petyt 1980 (West Yorkshire)	/h-/ omission	less	more
Trudgill 1974 (Norwich)	third-singular present omission	less	more
Wolfram 1969 (Detroit)	third-singular present omission	less	more
Wolfram 1969 (Detroit)	noun plural omission	less	more
Wolfram 1969 (Detroit)	possessive omission	less	more
Wolfram 1969 (Detroit)	zero copula	less	more
Macaulay 1991 (Ayr)	subject relative omission	less	more
French			
Kemp, Pupier, and Yaeger 1980 (Montreal)	consonant cluster reduction	less	more
Sankoff and Cedergren 1971 (Montreal)	/l-, -l/ omission	less	more
Poplack and Walker 1986 (Ottawa-Hull)	/l-, -l/ omission	less	more
Ashby 1981	ne . . . pas → pas	less	more
Diller 1980	ne . . . pas → pas	less	more
Lindenfeld 1969	ne . . . pas → pas	less	more
Brazilian Portuguese			
Guy and Braga 1976	plural morpheme omission	less	more
Scherre 1981	plural morpheme omission	less	more
Spanish			
Cedergren 1970; 1973 (Panama)	/r/ → . . . → Ø	less	more
Cedergren 1970; 1973 (Panama)	para → pa	less	more
Cedergren 1970; 1973 (Panama)	esta → ta	less	more
Cedergren 1970; 1973 (Panama)	[s] → [h] → Ø	less	more
Terrell 1981 (Argentina)	/s/ omission	less	more

Note:
Third-singular present = third person singular present tense marker; subject relative = relative pronoun functioning as subject of its clause.

Table 14.6b. *Distribution of elaboration features, showing more frequent use in higher social status groups for two languages*

		Social status	
Investigator	Feature	Higher	Lower
English			
Kroch and Hindle 1982 (Philadelphia)	relative clause	more	less
Macaulay 1991 (Ayr)	non-restrictive relative clause	more	less
Macaulay 1991 (Ayr)	WH relative markers	more	less
Macaulay 1991 (Ayr)	lexical variety	more	less
Williams and Naremore 1969 (Detroit)	verb elaboration	more	less
Williams and Naremore 1969 (Detroit)	subject nominal elaboration	more	less
Coupland 1983 (Cardiff)	transition boundary	more	less
Coupland 1983 (Cardiff)	role identification marker	more	less
Coupland 1983 (Cardiff)	closing marker	more	less
Coupland 1983 (Cardiff)	purpose marker	more	less
Flemish			
Van den Broeck 1977 (Maaseik)	length of T-units	more	less

Note:
T-unit = one independent clause with its dependent clauses.

- Functional associations of many linguistic features lend ready interpretation to the patterns of distribution across situations of use among spoken and written registers.
- By contrast, nothing that we know about dialect variation or the character of variable linguistic features adequately explains why their distributions should be systematically patterned across social groups in the ways that they are.
- The distribution of the features across registers follows essentially the same pattern for speakers of all socially ranked groups, a phenomenon amenable to explanation by application of the clarity and ease mandates in the production of spoken and written registers in particular situations of use. We infer that register variation for these features reflects a communicative competence shared among social groups as a tailored response to the competing production mandates in different situations of use.
- The explanation for the patterned distribution of the relevant features across social dialects lies in differential access to the full range of registral praxis among socially ranked groups and, in particular, differential access to "literate" registers. The mechanisms underlying the transfer from access to situations and registers to frequency differences across social dialects in vernacular speech remain unknown but seem to lie in praxis.

The gap in knowledge as to how praxis translates into patterns of social dialect characterizes knowledge of dialect acquisition (particularly of quantifiably variable dialects); it is not unique to our model.[6] Dialect acquisition is inadequately researched, though our hypothesis is compatible with recent views. In the words of Labov (1994:583), "The actual evidence of language learning . . . shows that children do match in their production the frequency of the variables in their environment" (cf. also Chambers 1992, 1995). The relationship between praxis across registers and the formation of social dialects is a critical matter for future research.

3.4   Clarification of the communicative-function model

Our 1994 paper did not sufficiently emphasize certain important points. Here we endeavor to be explicit about matters that remained implicit in our earlier discussion.

- Nothing in our model should suggest that "working class speakers are more 'limited' in their expressive resources than middle class speakers."[7] Our model expressly assumes *equivalent* grammatical competencies among all social groups. It focuses on patterns of linguistic usage, distinguishing among social groups only in their access to and praxis in different kinds of communicative situations.
- Nothing in our model entails that each linguistic feature has a unique communicative function or must play only one role in any communicative situation. It is well known that linguistic features can play multiple roles simultaneously. The features we have investigated often have other communicative functions, which may interact with the ones we have identified.
- Nothing in our model would prohibit a particular linguistic variant from serving solely or primarily as an indicator of identity. Millennia before the inception of sociolinguistics, pronunciations of "shibboleth" distinguished Gileadites from Ephraimites in an eloquent Old Testament emblem of the identifying function of linguistic variables. We would not claim that all social dialect differences are communicatively motivated any more than we would claim regional differences to be so motivated.
- Nothing in our model entails that each function motivating the distribution of a given feature in one speech community must also motivate its distribution in another. Whereas basic communicative functions of such

---

[6] Though her thrust differs from ours, Romaine's (1994:84) statement that "What we see reflected in sociolinguistic patterns is the uneven distribution of access to the standard variety" points in the same direction as our hypothesis with respect to the relationship between access to registers and acquisition of sociolinguistic patterns.

[7] See the NSF proposal for the workshop on which the present volume is based. In that proposal, this characterization ambiguously refers to Bernstein's (1971) and our (1994) models.

features as pronouns and prepositions will be alike across communities, we recognize that identity features associated especially with particular lexical and phonological forms can readily differ from group to group.[8]

• Nothing in our model entails that a linguistic feature whose communicative functions explain its distribution across registers will necessarily be distributed differentially across dialects. On the contrary – in contrast to Bell and Preston – we claim that the influence of situational factors may be so strong as to limit dialect variability for some registral features. But our model does predict that a feature with a functional distribution across registers and a distribution across socially ranked dialects within a community will pattern in ways that reflect the access of speakers to praxis in those communicative situations, with their associated registers. (This does not mean that features will be distributed along a continuum from lowest to highest social-status group. The fundamental distribution is governed by access to registers, as we discuss in section 5.5 below.)

Our investigations over the past decade have repeatedly proved that explanations for language variation must be sought along multiple dimensions and that co-occurrence patterns of features in registers and dialects are critical to uncovering underlying patterns. The findings of our previous investigations have consistently shown that unidimensional analyses are inadequate to the task of understanding the complexities of linguistic variation. (See Finegan and Biber 1986, our earliest joint paper, presented at the 1983 NWAV meeting, and the detailed analyses presented in Biber 1985, 1986, 1988, 1995 and Biber and Finegan 1989.) To the extent that our model has relied on an overarching parameter of economy versus elaboration, it is a partial model that captures the relationship between interspeaker and intra-speaker variation for a particular kind of feature.

More fundamentally, by examining three situational parameters (purpose, planning, shared context), each with measurable effect on the distribution

---

[8] Nothing in our model should invite or would permit comparing a feature *across* different speech communities. The social variation that we reported reflects differences *within* speech communities. We do not contrast the distribution of features in the French of Montreal and Lyons nor the English of Norwich and New York City. Our model does not entail – as Bell (1995:268) apparently believed it would – that the preferred American terms *elevator* and *apartment* have a higher social ranking than the British synonyms *lift* and *flat*. It does not make claims about the distribution of features *across* regions but about their distribution *within* a speech community. Speech communities are properly and traditionally the domain of sociolinguistic investigation.

So far as we know, *elevator* and *lift* are not alternative lexical expressions in any speech community, and to suggest a contrast between (shorter) British *lift* and American (longer) *elevator* (or the reverse: American *hood* with British *bonnet*) is to misconstrue what we were attempting to describe and explain. We have said plainly enough: "We reiterate that the features investigated here are of a particular kind, namely those that are *variable* within their communities across both social groups and situations of use, representing degrees of economy or elaboration" (Finegan and Biber 1994:334).

of features across registers, we have shown the importance of analysis along multiple situational parameters. The analyses help explain the distribution of features across social dialect and register in the classic sociolinguistic pattern. Other features may call for explanation by appeal to different parameters of the communicative situation.

We think it is clear that communicative functions underlie register variation for certain grammatical and lexical features. It is also widely recognized that differential access to praxis can profoundly influence the speech patterns of social groups.[9] Heath (1986:156) puts it tidily: "The greater the opportunities for experiencing language use across a variety of contexts, the greater the linguistic repertoire the children . . . will learn." Kay (1977:31) had earlier made a similar point: "When a society develops writing and differentiates into social classes, literate persons will usually have more occasion to speak explicitly and will tend to develop a speech style more attuned to explicit, technical, context-independent messages." Other factors may contribute to the distribution of certain features, and identity functions may be sufficiently strong for phonological variables to supersede the social dialect pattern expected on the basis of communicative functions.

4   Social dialect variation in the British National Corpus

In our earlier paper (Finegan and Biber 1994), we relied on published findings to characterize patterns of social dialect variation. Since then we have explored register and social dialect variation in the British National Corpus (BNC). Among a range of spoken and written registers, the BNC includes spontaneous conversation recorded by about a hundred speakers of English who tape recorded their own ordinary interactions over the course of several days. The sample is broadly representative of ages, regions, and social status in Britain. The taped conversations were transcribed, and demographic information about the speakers is coded in the corpus.

Five socially ranked groups are represented among the recorder-carriers in the BNC, and their spontaneous conversations with interlocutors comprise several million words of transcribed speech. In our analysis here, we limit ourselves to conversations produced by the carriers of tape recorders, whose social status is known; the frequency counts in table 14.7 are based on nearly a thousand conversations. We have reduced the five socially stratified groups identified by compilers of the BNC to three groups, ranked from highest to lowest and identified as: A/B, C, and D/E.

---

[9] In Finegan and Biber (1994), we cite half a dozen distinguished sociolinguists to that effect; and we could easily have doubled or even tripled the number of citations.

Table 14.7. *Number of*
conversations and number of
words in three ranked groups of
speakers of British English

	Conversations	Words
A/B	189	427,000
C	621	1,264,000
D/E	158	444,000
TOTAL	968	2,135,000

Table 14.7 indicates the number of conversations and the number of words for each social group.

As with the register variation described in section 3.1 above, we examined features that could be interpreted as representing either economy or elaboration of expression and whose distribution across registers was known to be systematic (Biber 1988). As before, economy variants are more condensed than possible alternatives (they contain less phonological content and typically have wider semantic scope), and in exploiting them, interlocutors must rely to a greater extent on surrounding text and context, as well as shared background information, to help in the interpretation of expression. In this sense, third-person pronouns are more economical than nouns (though, in context, not necessarily less communicative): *he* more economical than *Tony Blair* or *that really popular bloke*, *she* more economical than *the Duchess of York*, and *it* more economical than *Carlsberg, desiccant silica-gel, your video remote control*, or *the house my grandfather lived in a hundred years ago*. Likewise, contractions such as *won't, he'll*, and *it's* are more economical than *will not* and *he will/he shall* and *it is/it has*. (Note too the tendency for contractions to increase the likelihood of homonymy and alternative semantic readings; for example, *it's* is the condensed form of both *it is* and *it has*.) We took third-person singular *do* as in *it don't matter* to represent economy in that the alternative expression *doesn't* has more phonological content. (Note that a paradigm distinguishing third-person singular *does* from all other person/number items is less simple, and perhaps less economical, than one with a single form throughout, but this represents a different view of economy from the one our model has employed.) Finally, as a feature of syntactic economy, we examined omission of subordinator *that* (not relative *that*), as in *I think Ø he said Ø he was covered actually.* We take the absence of *that* to be less expressive and more economical than its presence insofar as the subordinator explicitly signals the onset of the subordinate clause.

Table 14.8. *Frequency of five economy features and seven elaboration features in the conversations of three socially ranked groups in Britain (per thousand words)*

	A/B	C	D/E
Economy features			
*third-person pronouns	98.7	103.5	103.8
*third-singular DO	0.1	0.3	0.3
contractions	61.7	63.4	63.4
subordinator THAT omission	10.2	10.3	9.9
pro-verb DO	3.0	3.3	2.9
Elaboration features			
*relative clauses	1.2	1.1	0.9
type/token ratio	44.8	44.7	44.1
subordinators and conjuncts	16.8	16.6	15.7
phrasal AND	1.5	1.3	1.3
word length	3.6	3.6	3.6
prepositional phrases	63.0	63.2	61.9
nouns	141	141	140

Note:
Asterisks mark features whose mean frequency differences across groups are statistically significant at $p < .05$.

"Elaboration" is the term we use to characterize expressions of greater explicitness, as with more frequent versus less frequent occurrences of prepositional phrases and relative clauses. Subordinators and conjuncts are taken as exemplars of expressed (rather than contextually implied) relationships among clauses. Word length and type/token ratio are taken respectively as indices of potential and actual lexical variety, and lexical variety is an index of specificity. Although not all these features are orthodox sociolinguistic variables, several have been investigated, as with relative clauses by Van den Broeck (1977), Kroch and Hindle (1982), and Macaulay (1991), lexical variety by Macaulay (1991), and miscellaneous discourse features, akin to conjuncts and subordinators, by Coupland (1983).

The linguistic features investigated are listed below:

Economy features
- third-person pronouns: *she, him, it,* etc.
- contractions: *innit, cos, can't, I'm,* etc.
- third-person singular *do: it do, it don't, s/he don't,* etc.

- subordinator THAT omission
- pro-verb DO

Elaboration features
- type/token ratio
- relative clauses
- subordinators and conjuncts
- phrasal AND
- prepositional phrases
- word length (measured in letters per word)
- nouns

Table 14.8 provides the frequency per thousand words of these twelve features in the conversations of three ranked social groups. Two of the economy features follow the familiar pattern of higher frequency in lower-status groups: third-person pronouns and third-singular DO. Three others show no statistically significant differences among the three groups: contractions, subordinator THAT omission, and pro-verb DO. As to the elaboration features, only relative clauses follow the familiar pattern of greater frequency in higher-status groups. Type/token ratio, subordinators and conjunctions, and phrasal AND have distributions across status groups that do not differ significantly, and word length is static across the three groups. Given their distribution across registers (cf. Biber 1988), the statistically significant distributions across status groups occur in patterns that are consonant with our model. In other words, for features that have communicatively based register distributions, higher-status groups in Britain exhibit more frequent occurrences of elaboration features and less frequent occurrences of economy features, while lower-status groups in Britain exhibit less frequent elaboration features and more frequent economy features.

This analysis of the BNC shows two things. First, the distribution of several seldom-studied features across registers is paralleled by their distribution across social dialects, as with third-person pronouns, third-singular DO, and relative clauses. Second, several features highlighted in table 14.5 and earlier shown (Biber 1988) to be distributed across registers are *not* distributed differentially across social dialects. This second finding provides counterevidence to the prediction made by Bell and endorsed by Preston that style variation presupposes dialect variation. Clearly, for some features register variation occurs *without* dialect variation. Readers should note that the terms *style* and *register*, while united in their focus on situational varieties, differ in scope. In usage among sociolinguists, *style* is typically limited to a certain range of spoken varieties such as those encountered in sociolinguistic interviews, while *register* encompasses all spoken and written situational varieties. If Bell and Preston intend to limit their prediction to the range of styles represented in sociolinguistic interviews, it is a less interesting prediction than one that would include a representative range of registers in the everyday life of a speech community. We return to this point in section 5.3.

5   Discussion

In preceding sections of this chapter, we have rehearsed the findings and claims of our 1994 paper and in section 4 reported new findings from the BNC. Below, in section 5.4, we briefly examine the findings reported by Irvine (1990 and this volume) and offer a modification of the classic sociolinguistic finding. Leading up to that, three points warrant further discussion:
• the systematic patterns of social dialect variation
• the relationship between internal and external constraints on variation
• Bell's prediction that style variation presupposes social variation

5.1   Interpreting the patterns of social dialect variation

Sociolinguists have shown legitimate sensitivity about interpreting overall patterns of variation across social groups. Many investigators leave the patterns unremarked, in part because interpretations of social dialect patterns in the past have sometimes prompted judgments that disparage speakers of some dialects. Still worse, judgments have been associated with interpretations involving linguistic "deficits." As a result of such ill-founded and discriminatory inferences and conclusions by observers, the dialect patterns themselves have often been ignored and sometimes denied by sociolinguists – the researchers best suited to preventing misleading interpretations. As we pointed out in discussing logically possible explanations for the classic sociolinguistic finding, dialect patterns are systematic in complex ways that should be addressed if sociolinguists are to achieve explanatory models of linguistic variation. Given adequate understanding and sound explanation, there is reason to hope that the interpretations will not entail negative judgments of any social group.

Among linguists who have offered interpretations of the systematic patterns of social dialect variation are Kroch (1978) and Chambers (1995). As noted above, Kroch hypothesized that for ideological reasons speakers of the prestige dialect exert energy to resist "normal processes of phonetic conditioning" that non-elite speakers do not resist. Our model offers a different explanation for the patterns of social dialect. Recently, Chambers (1995) has offered still other reasons. What is noteworthy is that some variationists have tried to explain the patterns of social dialect variation, whereas others deny their existence. The issue must be addressed openly for further progress to be made.[10]

5.2   The relationship between internal and external constraints

In our 1994 paper, we briefly addressed the relationship between internal and external constraints. We begin here with an observation by Wolfram (1995:99):

> In the examination of variation, including situationally sensitive variation, there is an important aspect of systematic variation that is inherently linguistic in nature. Qualitatively, linguistic options are parametrically limited; quantitatively, there are independent linguistic factors that constrain variation in an important way. Ultimately, a sociolinguistic theory cannot ignore the linguistic side of the equation, and any attempt to answer the fundamental *actuation* (i.e., why is variation initiated to begin with) and *embedding* (i.e., how is variation instantiated) riddles of sociolinguistics must consider both **external**, or social, and **internal**, or linguistic, constraints in tandem. (boldface added; italics in original)

We concur with Wolfram that analysis of register and social dialect variation must take account of relevant linguistic constraints. We would go further and claim a relationship between "internal" constraints and the situational constraints that we have focused on. We remain convinced that, like registral variation, linguistic constraints will eventually prove to have communicative underpinnings in many cases.

In relating the communicative functions served by linguistic features to salient parameters of the communicative situation, we are addressing linguistic constraints. Research into the relationship between linguistic and functional distributions is increasing, and it appears that internal constraints on variation are often allied with communicative function. For example, the behavior of features sensitive to linguistic constraints coincides with behavior motivated by the conflict between the clarity and ease mandates, although there are certainly other parameters of the

---

[10] Chambers (1995:250) writes this:

> In the last thirty years of sociolinguistic research, we have come to understand how variables function in vernacular and standard dialects. It may be possible now to go beyond that and ask why. Why do certain variables recur in dialects around the world? Why is it these particular variables, not others, that persist? Why are they constrained in almost exactly the same ways in different, widely separated communities? Why are they embedded so similarly in the social strata?
>
> This vast, virtually unexplored area lies at the very root of our discipline. There exists a cluster of linguistic variables, both phonological and grammatical, with certain privileges of occurrence in child language, creoles, traditional and mainstream vernaculars. They are visible partly by their suppression in the standard dialect. Whether these can be reconciled in an integrated, coherent theory remains to be seen, but it is a necessary pursuit . . . because it lies at the very foundation of linguistic variation.

situation that need eventually to be included in an overall theory of variation.[11]

To exemplify the influence of linguistic factors on the occurrence of particular variants and to highlight the intertwined relationships among registral and linguistic constraints, we briefly examine subordinator THAT omission in three registers of the BNC: Conversation, Fiction, and News. In the BNC, the most frequent verbs governing THAT clauses are THINK and SAY, and all three registers show higher frequencies of subordinator THAT omission after these verbs than after others. Likewise, in all three registers, omission of THAT is promoted by:
- co-referential subjects in the matrix and subordinate clauses
- pronominal subjects in the subordinate clause

Features that promote retention of THAT include:
- conjoined THAT clauses
- passive voice main verbs
- an intervening NP between the matrix verb and the subordinate clause

Significantly, the very features that promote omission of subordinator THAT are themselves most common in Conversation (matrix verbs THINK and SAY, co-referential subjects, pronominal subjects). By contrast, features promoting THAT retention are least common in Conversation and most common in News (conjoined THAT clauses, passive voice matrix verbs, NPs intervening between matrix verb and subordinate clause). These patterns demonstrate a complex inter-play among the linguistic features governing subordinator THAT omission and retention, with the conditioning environments themselves distributed differentially across situations of use and thus across registers (Biber et al. 1999, section 9.2.9).

As a result, registers have their own norms of use, and those norms work to strengthen or weaken the influence of the linguistic factors governing the feature. In conversation, omission of subordinator THAT is the norm; consequently, the factors promoting omission are less influential in that register than in others. By contrast, in a register in which THAT retention is the norm, the linguistic features promoting omission are strongly influential. In sum, when a linguistic variant is not the norm in a particular register, the linguistic factors favoring the variant are most influential; but when a

---

[11] We think it promising that Preston's model places status variation within linguistic variation. To the extent that our model derives social dialect variation from register variation and systematically links register variation to communicative function, we see linguistic variation and register variation as intertwined. It would not surprise us, then, if Preston's status variation ordinarily fell within what we might call "linguistic/functional" variation. On the other hand, the evidence will not sustain a generalization that encompasses register variation within status variation. Nor can we identify any theoretical reason to expect that it should.

variant is the norm in a particular register, the factors favoring it are significantly less strong.[12]

5.3   The claim that style variation presupposes social variation

Bell (1984:151) predicts that "If style variation derives from social variation . . . we can expect that, qualitatively, some linguistic variables will have both social and style variation, some only social variation, but none style variation only – because style presupposes the social." When tested against the findings in our study of the BNC, the general validity of this claim is thrown into doubt. If style variation derives from and is encompassed within social dialect variation, we would expect significant variation across the status groups represented in the BNC for all the features in table 14.8, given that they are known to vary across registers (cf. Biber 1988). That is not, however, what we find. Instead, the distributions across social groups for nine of the twelve features exhibit no statistically significant variation. Below are listed the nine features that do not show statistically significant variation across the three ranked social groups.

Features showing no significant differences in frequency across three social groups
- contractions
- subordinator THAT omission
- pro-verb DO
- type/token ratio
- subordinators and conjuncts
- phrasal AND
- word length
- prepositional phrases
- nouns

To be sure, not all these features are orthodox sociolinguistic variables, but two of them (contractions and subordinator THAT omission) fit even the narrowest definition of sociolinguistic variable, while the others are indicative of wide patterns of feature distribution across registers and social groups. Besides contractions and subordinator THAT omission, the others are types of variables that would be useful to examine in variation studies more broadly representative than what can be realized in a sociolinguistic

---

[12] For example, with *think* or *say* verbs, subordinator *that* omission is greater than 90 percent in Conversation but only slightly greater than 50 percent in News. With other matrix verbs, the range of difference between Conversation and News is about 50 percent (with about 70 percent omission in Conversation and 20 percent in News). Likewise, with pronominal subjects in the subordinate clause, Conversation has almost 90 percent omission, while News has about 40 percent. (For details, see Biber et al. 1999.)

interview. In any case, these nine features and a wide range of others call for reassessment of the claim that style variation presupposes social dialect variation. That claim appears to be false, and therefore the Style Axiom at the base of Bell's and Preston's models is also in doubt.

5.4   A proposed revision to the classic sociolinguistic finding

The classic sociolinguistic finding (Romaine 1980:228) noted the correlated distribution of sociolinguistic features across styles and socioeconomic classes. That pattern characterized much of the sociolinguistic research that quantified variables across social groups and styles, and conventional wisdom held that groups modeled their speech on that of higher-ranked groups: "each group models its formal style on the speech behavior of those groups one or two steps above it in the social scale" (Labov 1969:23–4).

Recent investigation of speech communities outside the urban centers of America and Western Europe calls into question the generalizability of the classic sociolinguistic finding. For example, among the Wolof of Senegal are two classes – higher-ranking speakers of "noble speech" and lower-ranking speakers of "griot speech." According to Irvine (1990), noble speech is characterized by several features of condensation and a more infrequent use of certain elaboration features: focus markers, spatial deictics and determinants, modifiers, reduplicated forms, semantically neutral noun class markers, class markers, incomplete or inconsistent concord, and incomplete sentence structures. By contrast, the speech of the lower-ranked griots exhibits more frequent use of focus markers, spatial deictics, modifiers, morphological reduplication, class markers, complete and consistent concord, and verb–complement constructions that often convey details of sound and motion. Table 1.4 in Irvine (chapter 1 of this volume) displays her comparison of style contrasts in Wolof morphology and syntax.

What the Wolof data appear to illustrate is that in some speech communities lower-status social groups show a more frequent use of elaborated features and a less frequent use of condensed features than higher-ranking social groups. For the Wolof, lower-ranking griots show strikingly more elaborated and less condensed forms than the higher-ranking nobles. This finding contradicts the classic sociolinguistic finding but is what one would expect if the distribution of linguistic features in social groups reflected access to and praxis in the wider range of register, including more "literate" registers. Among the Wolof, it is the griots who have the task of articulating what the nobles wish to communicate publicly. In other words, the lower-ranked griots have access to the wider repertoire of registers and, in particular, to those registers that require greater explicitness and rely less on shared context. From the Wolof situation it becomes even clearer that it is not social status that determines whether the realizations of one's variable language features are more or less elaborated; rather, it is the range of registers that one has access to and utilizes. The classic sociolinguistic finding links language use in formal situations to higher-ranked groups and language use in casual situations to lower-ranked groups; those links appear to be artifacts of the distribution of communicative tasks in Western urban areas, where the higher-ranked groups have greater access to the literate (i.e., context independent) registers, whether spoken or written.[13]

As a substitute for the classic sociolinguistic finding, which correlates linguistic features of upper socioeconomic status groups with more formal situations and of lower socioeconomic status groups with less formal situations, we propose the Register Axiom:

> *The Register Axiom*
> If a linguistic feature is distributed across social groups and
> communicative situations or registers, then the social groups with greater
> access to the situations and registers in which the features occur more
> frequently will exhibit more frequent use of those features in their social
> dialects.

In particular, access to literate registers influences the character of social dialects with respect to features that represent elaboration, while lack of access to literate registers increases the occurrence of economy features.

6   Conclusion

We have described two recent proposals for integrating social dialect constraints and register constraints, including Preston's proposal for relating those kinds of variation to linguistic constraints. We have also rehearsed the patterns of register variation laid out in Finegan and Biber (1994) and repeated the arguments that led to our formulating a communicative-function model linking patterns of register variation to patterns of dialect variation. After addressing certain issues related to our 1994 paper, we presented new data on social dialect variation in the BNC. Those data demonstrate that a number of features not previously known to vary across

---

[13] The work of James Milroy and Lesley Milroy in Belfast has documented that the distribution of vowels across social groups is not linear (cf. Milroy 1982, 1991). Unlike the findings of Labov in New York City, where social groups can be aligned according to rank in their realization of both consonantal and vocalic variables, English speakers in Belfast cannot be aligned along a continuous line. Instead, a zigzag pattern characterizes the realization of vowels. We have not focused on vowels in our analysis or in formulating our model; we have concentrated principally on grammatical and lexical matters. We acknowledge here the valuable work of the Milroys in highlighting the non-universality of the linear patterns that underlay the classic sociolinguistic finding.

socioeconomic status groups follow patterns predicted by our model. We also presented counterevidence to the claim by Bell and Preston that features distributed across register must first be distributed across social dialects; that counterevidence calls into question any claim that style variation derives from status variation. Finally, we offered the Register Axiom as a substitute for the classic sociolinguistic finding.

In conclusion we reiterate a point concerning the potential influence of "literate" registers on the character of social dialect variation and the importance of including "literate" registers in sociolinguistic modeling. A notable distinction between our research efforts over the past decade and those of many others (though by no means all) in the variationist community is our systematic inclusion of written registers, along with spoken ones, as objects of analysis. More commonly, variationists exclude writing and concentrate on speech or even solely on the sociolinguistic interview. Immensely valuable as it has been, the sociolinguistic interview represents an extremely narrow range even of spoken registers and sometimes includes a somewhat artificial band of written registers (for example, reading passages and word lists). Obviously, face-to-face spoken registers are developmentally primary and written registers secondary, and our "way of doing linguistics" emphatically does *not* imply "the primacy of literacy over orality," as Bell (1995:267) wrongly claimed it does. Rather, our research is designed to explore a larger range of registers than many sociolinguists have hitherto investigated so as to uncover the relationships among spoken and written registers. We take the widest range of spoken registers as the object of sociolinguistic inquiry, including sermons and public speeches, as well as face-to-face and telephone conversation. While much remains unknown about patterns of variation in speech across registers, that is not sufficient reason to be ostrich-like with respect to written registers, especially given that we know so little about the mutual influence of written and spoken registers in a sociolinguistic context. The range of registers open to study in the sociolinguistic interview is patently inadequate to represent the range of variation in a community.

Little theoretical or empirical reason exists to cause suspicion that written registers are produced by a different grammar from the one that governs spoken registers. We think it more likely that written registers have their linguistic characteristics as a consequence of differences along the same situational parameters as other forms of linguistic expression. Those parameters would include audience, topic, purpose, setting, opportunity for planning, and assessment of interlocutor's shared background information. From our point of view, the social and psychological underpinnings of written registers are, with the exception of visual versus acoustic mode, no different in kind from those of spoken language (though they may differ in degree). Because the linguistic relationship between speech and writing is an empirical question that calls for further investigation, it is unfortunate that literate registers have been neglected in sociolinguistics. "Literate" cannot be altogether equated with "written" nor "oral" with "spoken." In Biber (1988) and in Finegan and Biber (1994), we distinguished "literate" from written and "oral" from spoken. We conclude here by reciting that discussion.[14]

The literature on variation demonstrates that the distribution of linguistic features across communicative situations cannot be adequately characterized by reference to a single dimension (such as casual/formal; written/spoken; or attention paid to speech); rather, a multidimensional framework is needed (see Hymes 1973, Biber 1988). It is nevertheless convenient to use the shorthand terms *literate* and *oral* to represent a number of independent dimensions of situational and linguistic variation. In these terms, a variety can be called *literate* to the extent that it has the situational and linguistic characteristics associated with stereotypical writing; a variety can be called *oral* to the extent that it has the situational and linguistic characteristics stereotypically associated with speech. Stereotypically literate varieties such as academic prose arise in circumstances characterized by careful production, informational purposes, and relatively little shared context between interlocutors. Stereotypical oral varieties such as conversation arise in situations characterized by on-line production, involved purposes, shared contexts, and extensive interaction. Naturally, most registers fall between these stereotyped extremes. (Finegan and Biber 1994:326)

As sociolinguistics broadens the range of registers falling within its purview and as the inadequacy of unidimensional analyses becomes more widely understood, we would hope that an enriched understanding of language variation will accommodate the wide range of influences that govern sociolinguistic variation.

---

[14] In his review of our edited volume, *Sociolinguistic Perspectives on Register* (Biber and Finegan 1994), Bell (1995) makes the following comment: "B&F's way of doing linguistics implies the primacy of literacy over orality. Languages which lack a certain range of registers appear as 'undeveloped,' especially when the register continuum is often classified in terms of literate vs. oral." The inverted commas around *undeveloped* presumably serve a function other than direct quotation, as *undeveloped* is not a term of our theory nor a word we would use in this connection. (By definition, a language that lacks writing lacks written registers, but it need not lack "literate" registers. On the other hand, we do not exclude the possibility that written registers may promote the development of certain linguistic features.) It is also not our perception that languages lacking certain registers appear grammatically undeveloped. Biber (1995) explores patterns of register variation across several languages, including Korean, Somali, and Nukulaelae Tuvaluan; some of the research Biber reports is based on dissertations written at the University of Southern California over the past decade or so, and it represents serious grappling by the respective researchers with the relationships among registers, and in some cases the development of registers, in languages and cultures that they knew extremely well.

15   Conversation, spoken language, and social identity

Lesley Milroy

1   Introduction

The general research agenda of Biber and Finegan is to develop a unified theory of style and register which cuts across speech and writing and incorporates work from different subdisciplines, chiefly Hallidayan register studies and quantitative sociolinguistics. In reading Biber and Finegan's (1996) formulation of their position, and indeed in rereading Biber and Finegan (1994), I experienced many disparate kinds of reaction to their work. Consequently, I had difficulty organizing this critique, and the structure of what follows may reflect this. The analysis presented strikes me as so wideranging and diffuse that it is hard to know where to begin. I shall comment in this introductory section first on some general issues, and then move on to more specific points.

Central concepts such as style, register, function, economy, elaboration, clarity, present many conceptual and terminological problems and sometimes seem to suffer from vagueness of definition and fluctuation in their reference even when the authors attempt to define them. This is partly because their analysis covers an immense amount of research territory, different parts of which are occupied by scholars working in different traditions. I therefore begin by querying whether a single model which is as wide as this one attempts to be is desirable or feasible. However, while I find this strategy of building an overarching top-down type of model which incorporates research carried out under different types of agenda quite problematic, some of the assertions which Finegan and Biber present as fundamental principles are reasonable. For example, they point out that differential access by social groups to communicative praxis and to literacy practices are central to an account of differentiated linguistic repertoires. In fact, sociolinguistically sensitive work on language acquisition carried out in Britain suggests that this is so: Gordon Wells carried out a survey in Bristol (Wells 1985), and found that rate and sequence in acquisition of a range of features did not vary according to social class. However, as soon as he introduced formal testing procedures the predictable social class difference appeared. Variable class-related literacy practices by parents seem to be related to this result; many middle class parents read to their children while on the whole working class parents did not. Also suggestive is work by Tizard and Hughes (1984). They examined in detail the communicative behavior of middle class and working class girls who had just begun to attend nursery school (three years old). They found little difference in the way the children developed spoken language at home in conversational contexts, but big differences emerged even at this early age when the children were introduced to more institutionally marked and literacy related discourse types, i.e. were requested by the teacher to respond to questions about stories and activities. This effect of writing upon speech is quite well known and examined in detail by a number of scholars, although because of the theoretical purpose of the field (i.e to model processes of linguistic change) it is typically not emphasized by quantitative sociolinguists.

Finegan and Biber suggest that the regular patterning of "registral features" across social dialects thus has a functional explanation. The word "function" is used in a number of different senses in linguistics and there is often slippage between these senses. For example, the way Poplack uses it in her 1980 study of variable plural marking in Spanish is quite different from the way Finegan and Biber use it; they think of function more broadly as contextually situated "communicative work" rather than fulfilling a role in the language system such as plural- or case-marking. "The distributional patterns of many features across situations can be shown to have motivations in the communicative functions of the features and the character of the communicative situation" (Biber and Finegan 1996:10). This broader definition of function allows consideration for example of deictic or anaphoric expressions such as pronouns versus full NPs; prepositional phrases such as "in the house," "across the street," versus pro-forms such as "here" or "there"; the grammatical characteristics of sentences in legal documents etc. which take the form they do for clear communicative reasons, to avoid ambiguity which could give rise to endless legal wrangling. In a parallel way features such as pronouns and pro-forms appear regularly in spoken language because the relevant features of context are available for interpretation. These are the types of registral features which Finegan and Biber have considered and whose social class distribution they have related to differences in access and praxis. However, they include also social function in their definition of function, that is the capacity of an element such as a nonstandard verb form to indicate social category membership. They call this "identity function," but this kind of function is something quite different from the "communicative function" discussed above and their use of these two senses of function is, as I will argue below, one point at which terminological slippage occurs, despite attempts at definition.

One general point of great importance (the implications to be picked up shortly) is that conversation needs to be distinguished from other spoken styles. For it is plain that differential access to literacy will feed back into many varieties of spoken language, particularly those used in institutional or work discourse, which are demonstrably parasitic on the written language. However, it is an open question just how far this is true of the casual peer conversation of speakers of any social class.

Having raised some general issues, I now deal with more specific points as follows: developing an account of the notion of "function"; defining features which occur across registers; and distinguishing "communicative" features from "identity" features; some problems with the ideas of elaboration and economy; the production mandates of ease and clarity; and finally some general conclusions which arise from these more specific comments.

2   Developing an account of function

A more thorough exploration of the notion of function which enables the development of its explanatory potential is required. Much relevant analysis is already available. An initial prerequisite to this discussion is a distinction between the structure of casual conversation – defined here rather narrowly as interactive discourse where no participant overtly controls rights to speak – and other spoken styles. These latter embrace different types of institutional and transactional discourse and are arguably quite different from conversation in their basic organization, such differences deriving from function in a sense which is similar to that defined as communicative function by Finegan and Biber. However, the functional pressures which give rise to structural features of conversation are rather specific to that genre in that they spring from its unplanned, interactive, and competitive character. Such features are structuring of utterances by clause-like chunks rather than sentences, lack of recognizable canonical sentences, repetitions and overlaps, interactive mode of specifying reference. These issues are dealt with from a great number of different angles; for example by Heath (1985), Brown and Yule (1983), Ochs (1979), Levinson (1983). Since everyday unplanned interactive discourse is not easily understood in terms of standard linguistic descriptors (and this is the crucial point), it needs to be considered separately if it is incorporated into an overall account of register. Finegan and Biber mention the "situational parameters" of planning, shared context, and purpose as being relevant to their account of function, and obviously they are; but they do not say precisely how (I shall suggest below that in conversation the creation of shared context is achieved in a very complex way which is not parallel to the way this parameter operates in other genres). This distinction I am suggesting is parallel to the major distinction between planned and unplanned discourse described by Ochs which is surely fundamental to any functional account of registral variation. In subsequent comments I suggest that not only the notion of function but also many of the other concepts which Finegan and Biber introduce need to be analyzed much more carefully.

3   Defining features which occur across registers

The features which are examined with respect to their variation across registers are not always clearly defined and are of many different kinds (see Biber and Finegan 1996:18). *Don't* is primarily a spoken language feature; THAT deletion is more difficult. It may also be reasonably described as embodying a spoken/written contrast where its function is to introduce nominal clauses ("he knew that/Ø Peter had arrived"). Relative clauses present a different problem (the apples that/which/Ø I bought were delicious). Here, the most formal variant favored in written styles is *which*, followed by *that*, while zero is the least formal variant. However, these forms are distributed regionally as well as socially. Moreover there are complex contextual constraints on *that/which* deletion (as reported by Harris 1993, Miller 1993, Henry 1995; see also example (1) below where a relative pronoun in subject position is deleted). Similar comments might be made about the pronoun *it*; are we looking at tokens of deictic/anaphoric/dummy subject or extraposed *it*? Following the principle of endweight this latter function is much more likely to occur in spoken language, for quite different reasons from other occurrences of *it*. These issues need to be addressed if we are to *interpret* the distributions which show up in Finegan and Biber's cross register analysis, as opposed to simply noting their existence.

Another question which arises is the motivation of Finegan and Biber for selecting these features and not others. For example, what is the rationale for considering prepositional phrases as an elaborating feature? The same questions might be asked with respect to the different cocktail of features extracted from the British National Corpus. And the use of relative clauses as an elaboration feature raises the issue of what counts as a relative clause: how are such clauses identified? For example, all of their following candidate relative clause structures occur in non-standard English, but it is not clear whether such structures are counted as such by Finegan and Biber:

(1)   They're still building them high rise flats # *are going up all over the place*
(2)   There's only one of us #*been on a chopper before*
(3)   The boy *as I asked*...
(4)   The girl *what's coming over*

Thus, problems arise with respect not only to function but also identification of features.

A minimum requirement arising from this discussion is to discriminate different types of features; features that can be specified *on a clearly principled basis* as doing some kind of specifiable communicative work (like full NPs rather than pronouns) need to be distinguished from socially symbolic features, described by Finegan and Biber as "indicators of identity." I'll comment now on the distinction between these two types of feature.

4   Identity features versus communicative features

Finegan and Biber make the point that nothing in their model prohibits a particular variant from serving primarily or solely as an indicator of identity (this volume). However, the implication of this observation needs to be taken further and some attempt made to distinguish classic sociolinguistic variables (i.e. indicators of identity) from communicatively functional variables. However, in their taxonomy of *elaboration* features versus *economy* features, Finegan and Biber consider distributions of pronouns (for example) which have a relatively clear functional motivation in their relation to shared context, along with forms like *she don't/doesn't* which are chiefly socially symbolic. Similar comments can be made about multiple negatives which usually do the same referential job as single negatives; the function of this variable is chiefly socially indexical. Indeed most types of phonological and morphological variation seem to be similarly socially symbolic, as do variants which appear in conventionalized routines like address terms and terms of greeting and parting. These socially symbolic elements are the kind that sociolinguists study, and we can consider such variants as operating in a way which does not suggest that they are selected in accordance with their communicative function (like pronouns versus full NPs) in the sense defined by Finegan and Biber. Quantitative sociolinguists have tried to limit themselves to these for very good reasons. They saw it as crucial that variants of a variable were referentially equivalent and there was a long-running controversy during the 1970s on just this issue of where the sociolinguistic variable should stop. Thus, the standard sociolinguistic view of style, for sound reasons, encompasses these purely socially symbolic variables rather than the communicatively motivated registral features which Finegan and Biber incorporate.

A general point which needs to be made about these features is that we *know* the social origin and history of many of them and so can draw strong inferences about their sociolinguistic status. We know for example that multiple negation appeared in standard literary texts until the feature was proscribed in the eighteenth century by grammarians who used mathematical, logical, and other arguments to justify their dictats. We know that third person forms such as *don't/doesn't* have fluctuated historically in their social significance. We know that the contemporary social distribution of such symbolic forms is arbitrary, arising from prescriptive ipsedixitisms; for example, until the nineteenth century *dove* was common in educated written British English; now *dived* is the standard form there but is apparently stigmatized in the United States. We also know that there is a pattern of historical residue which often means that archaic forms which survive in remote dialect areas become stigmatized. There are many examples in our own work in the geographically peripheral cities of Belfast and Newcastle upon Tyne.

The reason for the social class distribution of many socially symbolic forms is thus quite transparent and it seems to to be relatively easy to construct an argument that their stylistic distribution derives historically from this class distribution. However, the nature of the relationship between social class and the registral distribution of functionally motivated features is quite different and the line of explanation followed by Finegan and Biber in this latter case (that of differential access by social groups to different registers) is reasonable and defensible. The conclusion is thus that different types of variable should be clearly distinguished, but failure to make this distinction means that they encounter difficulties when the need arises to separate them out in an ad hoc way, as they do several times. For example, it is difficult to find evidence to support their assertion that identity functions can supersede the expected distribution according to communicative function, **particularly in the case of grammatical and morphological variables** (1996:22). How does this square with the undoubted fact that many speakers (in Europe at least) use localized phonology which is clearly indexical of identity, but at the same time control the full registral range? There seems to be no clear case for expecting these identity variables to be distributed according to function; we are dealing with two distinctly different sets of elements.

5   The notions of elaboration and economy

As will become clear, the comments here are related to those in the previous section on the distinction between identity and communicative variables. The chief point is that unless their nature and domain is more precisely defined, the key notions of *elaboration* and *economy*, which are said to characterize formal versus informal registers, present numerous conceptual and definitional problems. To illustrate, let us look at the notion of *the referring expression*; many of the features which Finegan and Biber consider are tied up with the communicator's task of specifying and keeping track of referents in a discourse. One way of identifying a referent rather precisely is by using a relative clause, and *classical* relative clauses are associated chiefly with written and formal spoken language (but see Miller 1993 for problems of definition, and also (1)–(4) above). However, it by no means follows that referents are less elaborately and more economically specified in casual conversational speech where relative clauses are rare. Clark and Wilkes-Gibbs (1986) have looked in detail at how referents are identified in conversation and often this is extremely elaborate, involving various types of non-standard NP. We can see this if we look at a casual conversation. In (5) below (taken from Lesser and Milroy 1993:170) two young women are making strenuous attempts to identify two particular car parks in Manchester city centre. These are specified respectively as "The car park behind the Arndale Centre" and "that little multi-storey one," but only after a considerable amount of collaborative effort has been exended in identifying them.[1]

(5)
S: they wanted to go to this posh shopping center car park/takes you an
        hour an half to park up/whereas if you keep to back streets and just go
        and park/you know/ (.) gets in this one behind Hills/this multi-storey
        thing/ *oh god*
B: *oh that one/*
        the one behind the Arndale Centre =
S: I don't know what the hell it were/ (.) but it went up and up and up and
        up/and oh god/aren't they aren't they law(?)/I would never dream of
        parking in a place like that
B.   *wouldn't you/*I don't mind them
S: you know where I used to park/I don't know if it's still (.) /behind the
        Oyster Bar/(.) you know *that*
B: *that* little one=
S: = yeah
B: = that little multi-storey one=
S: = yeah/I always park there

Clark and Wilkes-Gibbs find that reference is achieved very much more economically once speakers have established common ground, and some of the messier ways of establishing common ground are very elaborate, involving many repetitions of the kind characteristic of casual conversation which are evident in (5); for example in her first turn S tries a number of different ways of clarifying the referent, but it is her interlocutor who uses these cues to offer a candidate referring expression at the point where S appears to have exhausted her descriptive resources. Thus, successful refer-

---

[1] Transcription conventions as follows:
    Italics: simultaneous speech; (.): micropause; /tone group boundary; =: latched utterances
    with no gap.

ence in this case is achieved collaboratively and not particularly economically. The point is that it is the common ground variable which is chiefly associated with economy of expression, not registral or stylistic variation, as Clark and Wilkes-Gibbs make clear. If we want to explain the distribution of registral features, these issues need to be taken on board. The point is that we cannot claim in any general way, as Finegan and Biber appear to do, that the features of informal spoken language are more economical than those of written language.

Also relevant here is the issue of different types of feature as discussed in section 4. A socially symbolic variable such as presence or absence of /r/ functions differently from alternative registral features such as noun phrases or relative clauses versus pronouns. The former is not directly related to the need to create common (referential) ground, while the latter is. Finegan and Biber cite the prestigious zero realization of /r/ in British English as one of a small number of exceptions to their generalization that high-status social dialects are more elaborated / less economical (1996:23) than low-status ones. In fact there are so many clear morphological and phonological exceptions that the generalization is meaningless; consider, for example, (6) below, which sets out four irregular verb paradigms in the dialect of Tyneside in the North East of England (for details see Beal 1993). Of these, *treat* resembles standard English with respect to the elaboration/economy variable in that it distinguishes only two forms (*treat/tret* versus *treat/ treated*). However, *swing* and *get* are more elaborate in that they make three distinctions as opposed to the two made by standard English, as is *put* where the two forms distinguished in Tyneside dialect correspond to standard English's single form.

(6)

Base	Past	Perfect Participle
treat	tret	tret
swing	swang	swung
get	got	getten
put	put	putten

In a discussion of this general issue, Harris (1993) has pointed out that notions of economy and simplicity in socially distributed language varieties tend to be a matter of swings and roundabouts: what you gain on one you lose on the other. Thus, Irish English has a simpler strong verb system than standard English but a much more elaborated and complex tense/aspect system.

Many counterexamples to claims of an association between economy and the language patterns characteristic of low-status social groups can be taken both from current sociolinguistic data and from historical data. The British aristocratic pronunciations ['wɛskit] and ['fɒrɪd] ('waistcoat', 'forehead') are still of higher status than the relatively recently introduced (and presumably less economical) spelling pronunciations [wɛɪsˈkaʊt] and [fɒəˈhɛd]. The extent to which these features have a distribution across registers is not at all clear, and I would repeat the point argued in section 4 that the distributions of socially symbolic and communicatively functional forms are so different that attempts to generalize across the two categories are doomed to failure.

There is also a different sense in which the elaboration/economy contrast can be interpreted. In Belfast it was noted that vernacular phonology was actually more elaborate in that there were a larger number of regularly conditioned allophones; the middle-class variety was simpler, as argued by J. Milroy (1982). The distribution of variants of /a/ in the speech of a middle class and a working class speaker is shown in table 15.1; the tendency of users of relatively standardized forms of the language to converge on a single variant, considerably reducing complex, regular, and contextually determined allophonic variation, has been confirmed across a larger sample of speakers and more generally in analyses of other vowels in the system (see L. Milroy 1987:127; J. Milroy 1982).

This pervasive and regularly replicated pattern is congruent with the observation that leveled or contact language varieties lose distinctions which are present in more peripheral and localized and often therefore less prestigious varieties; in other words, standard languages may be seen to exhibit some characteristics of contact varieties, as do other leveled varieties with a wide territorial spread (see further Milroy 1998). This is likely to mean that in the sense illustrated by the data in table 15.1 high-prestige dialects are actually more economical than low-prestige dialects. Now Finegan and Biber may wish to argue that this is not what they mean by "economy." However, that the pattern noted here is a regular one is relevant to an accurate specification of what might be meant by "economy" in the context of stylistic or registral variation.

6   The "ease" and "clarity" production mandates

These are presented by Finegan and Biber as two sometimes competing principles to which communicators are oriented, and again both need much more consideration and specification. Perhaps the clarity mandate seems obvious, since people need to be able to communicate; but sometimes interlocutors are strategically ambivalent and unclear as, for example, the work of Brown and Levinson (1987) shows. Many registers are characterized by indirectness. With respect to the ease mandate, Finegan and Biber mention Stampe's natural phonology and in fact there is a tradition of sociolinguistic work which follows through this idea and tries to distinguish "general" sociolinguistic variables from "connected speech processes" (Dressler and

Table 15.1. *Elaboration and economy: range for (a) a working class and (b) a middle class Belfast speaker*

(a)

	ε	æ	a	ä	ɑ	ɔ
bag	+					
back			+			
cap				+		
map					+	
passage					+	
cab						+
grass						+
bad						+
man						+
castle				+		
dabble				+		
passing						+

(b)

	ε	æ	a	ä	ɑ	ɔ
bag			+			
back			+			
cap			+			
map			+			
passage			+			
cab			+			
grass			+			
bad			+			
man			+			
castle			+			
dabble			+			
passing			+			

Wodak 1982, Kerswill 1987). In practice this distinction turned out to be difficult to maintain, and this kind of analysis seems in recent years not to have been pursued. The ease mandate is problematic for other reasons; there is a traditional assumption that the principle of least effort is constantly at odds with the need to communicate efficiently, and this has sometimes been said rather vaguely to account for linguistic change. While this idea has not been systematically developed, there does exist relevant, theoretically motivated and well-developed work along comparable but subtly different lines. Clark and Schaeffer developed the "principle of least *collaborative* effort" (my emphasis) to account for the way in which interlocutors collaborated in constructing conversational contributions. They argued that conversational contributions were structured in two parts, the presentation and the acceptance phase, and that the more carefully designed the presentation by speaker A the faster its acceptance by speaker B. However, sometimes the presentation is problematic, necessitating much repair work before acceptance is achieved. Thus the responsibility for a successful conversational contribution is shared. The point here is that this carefully developed model is relevant to Finegan and Biber's clarity and ease mandates, and could profitably be evaluated prior to the formulation of rather simpler but untested maxims. This issue again points up the need to distinguish interactive from monologic or written discourse, discussed earlier in this paper. Finegan and Biber attempt to relate the ease mandate to the interests of speakers and writers (who are presumed to prefer to expend minimum effort) and the clarity mandate to the interests of addressees and hearers in that they prefer specificity. This dichotomy may make sense for writers and readers who are not engaged in interactive discourse, but speakers and addressees are another matter. The work of Clark and Schaeffer suggests that since interlocutors work together in achieving successful communication, this kind of assumption is, for interactive discourse at least, entirely on the wrong track.

7   Conclusion

I can summarize this critique by making two major points. First, there already exists a body of well-developed research which is highly relevant to different parts of the Finegan and Biber analysis, and it should be taken into account with a view to refining key concepts in their framework. Second, in view of the heterogeneous character and mixed conceptual heritage of much of this work, I very much doubt whether a unitary model of the kind they propose is appropriate, at least in the first instance. The bolting together of quantitative sociolinguistics (with its strong theoretical focus on explaining linguistic change, rather than exhaustively describing patterns of variation) with a pretheoretical framework such as that provided by Hallidayan register studies is particularly problematic if the research goal of Finegan and Biber is to develop an interpretation of the patterns of distribution of registral variants, rather than a simple description of those patterns. To achieve such a goal, they might consider omitting socially symbolic stylistic variables from their analysis, and concentrate further on the registral component by including work such as that of Clark and his colleagues which can help them move towards such an interpretation.

16 Style and the psycholinguistics of sociolinguistics: the logical problem of language variation

Dennis R. Preston

I have argued (Preston 1991) that a "funnel" of influences characterizes variation. The parts and hierarchical relations outlined there are shown in figure 16.1. This figure expands on Bell's (1984) claim that stylistic variation "echoes" or "reflects" status variation by adding the notion that status variation reflects variation determined by linguistic factors. In each case, the reflection is less powerful than the original. Specifically, Bell's location of stylistic variation in social space is derived from accommodation theory – speakers assess the social identity of interlocutors and (when they want to "please" them) move in their direction linguistically. Since persons of different social status groups use different linguistic features (and/or the same features in different proportions), speakers make use of those differences in their stylistic variation, an adjustment which Bell calls "audience design."[1]

I provided empirical support for these claims in Preston 1991 through a review of a number of quantitative studies. In nearly all,[2] the range of variation explained is largest for an influencing linguistic factor and larger for at least one status factor than for the stylistic one. For example, in Rickford 1981, a study of vowel-laxing, a linguistic factor (pronoun identity) determines the largest variation space, ranging from one pronoun (/ju/ = "you") with a probability of .84 ("promoting" laxing) to another (/wi/ = "we") of .04 ("demoting" laxing), while status variation ranges from only .66 (lower status, promoting laxing) down to .34 (higher status, demoting laxing), and stylistic variation is least, ranging from .64 (informal style, promoting

---

[1] Bell does not say, however, why members of different status groups use different linguistic features in the first place. Perhaps he would agree with Bloomfield's notion of communicative networks – the more frequent the interaction among interlocutors, the more similar their varieties (and vice versa; 1933:46–7). Perhaps Bell would also approve of Kroch's (1978) claim that upper-status groups shun natural linguistic processes (or embrace unnatural ones), in their desire to avoid the practices of the "non-elite" (and make their own practices more "costly").

[2] In those cases in which this relationship among influences did not exist in the data sets surveyed, the focus of the investigation was either a highly stereotyped lexical feature (e.g., the pronoun *voçe* in Brazilian Portuguese) or a feature involved in rapid and dramatic change.

279

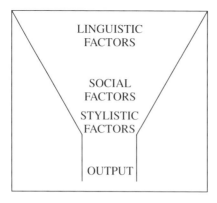

Figure 16.1 The "strength" of factors influencing variation (Preston 1991)

laxing) to .36 (impersonal style, demoting laxing).[3] (In fact, in this study, two other linguistic factors, pronoun function [.76 to .34] and phonological shape of the following segment [.70 to .34], also create variation spaces larger than that of the status dimension.)

Finegan and Biber (F&B) 1994 deny this hierarchical interpretation,[4] claiming that stylistic (or "registral" – their term) variation outweighs status (or "social dialect" or simply "dialect" in their work). They, too, appeal to empirical studies, citing evidence to show that certain features (namely those of linguistic elaboration) are more likely in literate registers, while other features (those of linguistic economy) are more likely in oral registers. F&B reason that economy is natural to certain registers (but not to social groups *per se*) and that certain registers are more likely to be learned by certain social groups (as a result of social practice within the speech community). F&B believe that this reasoning allows sociolinguists to locate the principal motivating factor for variation in the functionalist notion of communicative practice. The specific communicative mandates which they make use of are the competing ones of "be quick and easy"

---

[3] I cannot review the details of VARBRUL analysis here. It is a logistic regression program particularly well suited to the vagaries of natural data (e.g., paucal cells). The probabilistic scores may be interpreted by following a rule of thumb which states that scores over .50 "promote" the operation of a "rule" (i.e., the occurrence or non-occurrence of the feature) and those under .50 "demote" the operation. A relatively non-technical overview is available in Preston 1989; details are given in Sankoff 1978, and Young and Bayley 1996 is a thorough how-to.

[4] Finegan and Biber (1996:39) note, however, that they do not contest my claim that status and stylistic variation are both contained within linguistic variation, particularly if "linguistic" includes "communicative." Their problem is only with the superiority of the "social" over the "stylistic."

(which leads to economy) and "be clear" (which leads to elaboration) (Slobin 1979).

More recently, to provide an integrated or single-study approach to this problem, F&B have investigated a number of conversations from the British National Corpus (BNC), in which they evaluate the relationship between status (three social status groups) and form (i.e., economical versus elaborate). In an earlier study (1994), F&B showed that such forms were predictably distributed across various registers. Features such as planning (e.g., writing versus speech), informational purpose (e.g., interview versus conversation), and lack of shared knowledge (e.g., public speech versus interview) were shown to prefer elaborate rather than economical forms. In the BNC study, they note that only four of twelve such forms investigated show significant distribution for the three status groups.[5] From this (and earlier reviews of variation data), F&B conclude that register is more basic or powerful (i.e., a larger number of formal features are significantly distributed among registral variants than among social groups) and that differential access to various registers by social groups forms the basis of social dialect variation.

> The distribution of features across registers follows essentially the same pattern for all speakers of socially ranked groups, a phenomenon amenable to explanation by application of the clarity and ease mandates in the production of spoken and written registers in particular situations.
>
> Given a dialectally-independent communicative explanation for the distributional patterns of linguistic features across registers, it is plausible to infer that register variation reflects a fundamental communicative competence shared among social groups as tailored response to the competing production mandates in different situations of use.
>
> The explanation for the patterned distribution of the relevant features across social dialects lies in the differential access to the full range of registral praxis among socially ranked groups (in particular, differential access to "literate" registers). (Finegan and Biber 1996:20)

Why do Bell and I discover one set of relationships in surveying (and conducting) empirical work and F&B another? Perhaps a first step in making sense of this controversy lies in teasing out the boundaries of the concepts of status and style (or register). A beginning definition for stylistic differentiation for much sociolinguistic work is Labov's:

> But we find that *styles can be ranged along a single dimension, measured by the amount of attention paid to speech.* (Labov 1972:208; emphasis in the original)

Finegan and Biber have a radically more extensive definition than Labov's, cutting a wide swath of social and interactive concerns:

---

[5] Of the four which are significant, three are distributed in the predicted direction – i.e., the lower status groups make greater use of economical features.

In the communicative-function model of variation that we have been developing, we use the term "register" to represent language varieties characteristic of
particular situations of use, and we construe "situation of use" broadly. Register
includes not only the spoken varieties relating to "formality" and often designated
as "styles" but other spoken and written situational varieties as well.
    . . .
    Further, we take situation of use as a shorthand designator for those facets of a
communicative situation that may systematically affect the character of its linguistic
expression. Besides mode [i.e., writing versus speech], situation includes setting, relative status of interlocutors, degree of shared background information among
interlocutors, topic, purpose, availability of extra-linguistic channels as cues to
interpretation, and others. (1996:5; emphasis in the original)

Although Finegan and Biber's characterization seems all-inclusive, communicative function is its underlying rubric (as attention to speech is
Labov's and audience design is Bell's). Finegan and Biber do not attempt to
list all the factors which might influence language variation; they simply
sample the situational factors which they suspect will trigger the opposing
communicative mandates which they believe guide variety. Although they
list only mode, setting, relative status, shared information, topic, purpose,
and extra-linguistic channel cues, they obviously believe that, within such
parameters, they can show how these various characteristics of situations
of use are the determining factors of registers, which, due to their different
communicative functions, prefer economical or elaborate form. It is not
difficult to fill in the relationships they surely have in mind. As for mode,
writing involves register types which prefer elaboration, but speech involves
registers which prefer economy; as for setting, living rooms, playgrounds,
and bars involve registers which prefer economy, but board rooms,
churches, and schools involve registers which prefer elaboration, and so on.
In short, just as Labov surely believes that stylistic continuum positions
which can be correlated to attention to speech can also be reasonably correlated with such a range of situations of use, Finegan and Biber believe that
the structurally determined categories of elaborate and economical forms
can be correlated with registers which, in turn, can be correlated with a
range of situations of use.
    The components discussed so far (and others) are outlined in figures 16.2
and 16.3, putting what each position (i.e., Finegan and Biber's versus Bell's)
finds most significant in the middle of each diagram. In figure 16.2, Finegan
and Biber's scheme of things begins with structurally based "communicative mandates," which they link specifically to "Registers" (in turn, determined by situations of use) (Finegan and Biber[1]). The linkage is the first of
two main features for Finegan and Biber – elaborate linguistic structures
belong to literate situations of use; economical ones to oral ones.

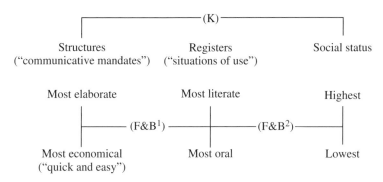

Figure 16.2 A Finegan and Biber model

The second link in figure 16.2 (Finegan and Biber[2]) represents Finegan and Biber's claim that different status groups have differential access to different registers (and, therefore, through the first link, to different structures). Lower-status groups have a more exclusive need for oral registers, so they make greater use of economical structures; higher-status groups have more need for literate registers, so they make greater use of elaborate ones. I have added a "K" (Kroch) factor to their model, for Finegan and Biber speak approvingly of Kroch's (1978) attempt to link status and structure directly (see note 1), although they are critical of it since it does not account for register.

To make figure 16.3 as comparable to figure 16.2 as possible, I have added a number of features not native to Bell's presentation. The representation begins with "Linguistic Factors," which I have claimed exert (except in unusual circumstances) the largest influences on variation (Preston 1991; hence "P," "Preston"). F&B make this feature a formal part of their model ("Structures" in figure 16.2), but, to my knowledge, Bell has not denied the "superiority" of linguistic to status factors, so it is added here. In addition, I have added the "K" factor, allowing that interpretation to serve as the link between structure and status (another link lacking in Bell's own characterization). Central to Bell's own claim, of course, is the "B" ("Bell") link between status and style, the latter deriving its (diminished) variable space from the former out of the speaker's desire to accommodate to the hearer (or to "imagined" hearers in what Bell calls "referee design," e.g., 1984). Finally, although Bell does not discuss it (and, in fact, calls it in his 1984 outline a "non-starter"), I have added to his model a Labovian ("L") link between style and structure, that of "attention-to-speech." Since Bell uses previous quantitative work in his 1984 review, he presumably is willing to make use of data acquired operationally from the stylistic continuum, and the increased attention required for processing some linguistic elements is, therefore, represented here.[6]

For general purposes of comparison, then, although a factor or connection has had to be added here and there, the two models deal with the same general categories, and it will require a more detailed analysis to determine why they result in different claims about the relative order or weight of influences on language variation.

Finegan and Biber's model requires the acceptance of some notions for both language and society which all may not be willing to accept. It is not altogether clear, for example, that an elaborate–economical scale can be devised for linguistic structures, particularly across modular components, for, as is well-known, so-called simplification in one component often triggers disaster in another, and it is often difficult to determine the overall simplicity or economy of far-reaching operations. For example, it would be difficult to claim whose version of embedded questions is more complex – AAVE's or Standard English's (SE's). In SE, auxiliary support disappears, so that *I know* + *Why did he leave?* becomes *I know why he left*. The string *why he left* is more economical from one point of view, for it does not require complex auxiliary support (and, in Finegan and Biber's surface approach is simply shorter), but the resulting AAVE construction (*I know why did he leave*) is more economical from an "operations" point of view, for one simply inserts the question form of a sentence as is.

Finegan and Biber note, however, that underlying economy (or grammatical simplicity) is not a part of their model (1996:23), so the search by Kroch and others (e.g., Chambers 1995) for more linguistically sensitive factors underlying variation is not a feature of F&B's work at all; they specifically note that their linguistic correlate to economical communicative function is purely surface economy (involving for word length, for example, such troublesome criteria as number of letters). Even surface notions of economy, however, can be slippery, as Chambers (1995) shows, not only for the ambiguity of economical or "easy" (as in "ease of articulation") but also for the difficulty in giving a principled account at, say, the phonetic level for the most economical form between a palatalized or non-palatalized one or a flapped or non-flapped one.

Finegan and Biber's use of the economy of linguistic form is related to a purely text-associated distribution. That is, they conduct an empirical (factor analytic) study of a number of linguistic features. When a number of

---

[6] I do not mean to suggest that Bell approves of the entire range of operational devices employed to acquire samples along the stylistic continuum. Following Milroy and Milroy 1977, for example, he notes that some tasks (especially literate ones) will produce stylistic performances which are extreme and should not be considered in evaluating his claims about audience design.

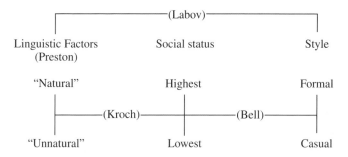

Figure 16.3 A Bell model

those features loads on a particular factor, that group is then related to a text type. Not surprisingly, the relatively abstract characteristics which might be associated with the text type end up being characteristics assigned to the linguistic elements of the group. Here is an example of this process from Biber 1988, which studies features in a wide variety of registral types. The following were found to load (positively) on "Factor Group #1":

private verbs, THAT deletion, contractions, present tense verbs, 2nd person pronouns, DO as pro-verb, analytic negation, demonstrative pronouns, general emphatics, 1st person pronouns, pronoun IT, BE as main verb, causative subordination, discourse, particles, indefinite pronouns, general hedges, amplifiers, sentence relatives, WH questions, possibility modals, non-phrasal coordination, WH clauses, final prepositions, adverbs, conditional subordination (p. 102)

Biber interprets these factors as follows:

All of them [i.e., the linguistic features which positively loaded on Factor Group #1, listed just above] can be associated in one way or another with an involved, non-informational focus, due to a primarily interactive or affective purpose and/or to highly constrained production circumstances. These features can be characterized as verbal, interactional, affective, fragmented, reduced in form, and generalized in content. (p. 105)

Biber then finds that this factor group correlates most highly with "telephone conversations" and "face-to-face conversations" and least well with "academic prose," "press reportage," and "official documents" (p. 128). Although it is interesting to find that this set of linguistic features correlates with the registral types investigated in such studies as Biber 1988, the characterization of the linguistic status of these elements, as cited above, is on much shakier ground, and I will return to the role of such linguistic features as these in the study of variation in general below.

The second concern with figures 16.2 and 16.3 has to do with social ordering and its connection to register (and, through it, to structure).

First, as work by Irvine (e.g., 1974) has shown, it is not the case that lowest-status speakers are necessarily those who observe the greatest clarity mandates. In Wolof society, for example, lower-status persons are typically those who speak with the greatest elaborateness, and highest-status speakers are considerably limited in their use of even fluent linguistic presentation. One may argue, however, that Wolof society is "peculiar" in this respect and that F&B's generalization is good but must be tempered by speech-community-by-speech-community investigations.

Second, Milroy (1996) convincingly identifies a number of linguistic features of lower-status varieties which are more "elaborate," but Finegan and Biber suggest that some such counterexamples (e.g., multiple negation) may result from their use as "identity features" rather than as ones which are primarily "communicatively functional" (Finegan and Biber 1996:23). If sociolinguistic variables as identity features involved only highly stereotypical and/or consciously monitored linguistic elements, then Finegan and Biber's treatment of them might be justified. Sociolinguistic work does identify a number of such high-profile features in individual constructions of identity. From Labov's work in Martha's Vineyard (1963) to Wolfram and Schilling-Estes' study of the "Ocracoke Brogue" (1995), it has been shown that such features may play an important role in the construction of local identity. In many more cases, however, sociolinguistic work shows that the construction of identity involves selection among features (and probabilities) from below the level of conscious awareness. In pioneering work in the Detroit suburbs, for example, Eckert (1988) shows that adolescents position themselves as "jocks" (school-oriented persons) or "burnouts" (street-oriented persons) by the direction they take in the movement of one part of the Northern Cities Vowel shift, a feature clearly below the conscious level of local (Detroit area) respondents (e.g., Preston 1996a). Similarly, Ito (1996) shows how a young woman from northern rural Michigan identifies herself as one who does not prefer the local area by adopting features of the same Northern Cities Vowel Shift much more rapidly than her age, status, and sex peers do, even those from farther south and from more urban areas, who, if such identity factors were not involved, could be expected to adopt such expanding urban forms earlier. Such uses of linguistic variables in the development of personal identities seem to be the rule (rather than the exception), and if the use of a linguistic variable for the purposes of identity construction is not accounted for in Finegan and Biber's treatment, then their formulation could hardly hope to have the considerable generality they claim for it.

Third, Finegan and Biber's notion of differential access as the principal source of dialect variation appears to be not significantly different from

Labov's characterization of the vernacular (e.g., 1972). It is, Labov claims, the first-learned, most deeply embedded speech variety and is, therefore, the most consistent or regular. The basic registers of the vernacular are clearly familial or inter-personal ones; therefore, all cases of more focused attention (and mandates for greater clarity) will correlate with less vernacular (and therefore more superficially embedded, less automatic, less well-learned) features. In short, all non-vernacular language behavior draws on less well-entrenched rules and is more likely to follow the clarity mandate, requiring greater attention.

If this reasoning is correct, then the communicative mandates of F&B provide an alternative view rather than a radical revision of the attention to speech continuum. The vernacular is the variety which encompasses those registers which demand the least attention to speech, for they are guided by the ease maxim (which entails economy of form) and are the very forms most deeply embedded in a speaker's life history of language acquisition and use. As speakers add to their vernacular, they do so only to make use of other registers. These "non-vernaculars," however, call up the communicative mandate of clarity, which not only demands elaborate formal realization but also requires performance of later-learned and more poorly controlled features. Both elaborateness and non-vernacular use, then, point to greater effort and attention to form,[7] and both Finegan and Biber and Labov, therefore, base stylistic variation on a psycholinguistic foundation. Some linguistic features are easier and/or more deeply embedded than others; they require less energy in performance, for they are inherently less difficult and/or better known.

For Finegan and Biber, however, differential access seems to predict a relatively complete acquisition of non-vernacular features by higher-status speakers. In contrast, Labov believes that all members of the speech community are less proficient in their non-vernaculars. Of course, those who are more regularly exposed to some non-vernaculars (and have greater need for them) would have more control over them, but Labov's perception of the acquisition of non-vernaculars seems less categorical than the picture for upper-status speakers proposed by F&B. To oversimplify, their partially opposing views might be represented in the following way:

---

[7] Labov does not intend for attention to speech to be equated with overt awareness of linguistic facts. This must be the case, for even respondents who are evidencing the influence of change from below (that is, change from below the level of conscious awareness, e.g., Labov 1972) do so with increasing frequency (generally for prestige forms) of variables in elicitation environments which trigger greater attention to speech (e.g., word lists and reading passages). Attention to speech must be, therefore, a global concern that does not require overt knowledge of a linguistic detail to be in effect. I review (in Preston 1996c) a number of different senses of awareness which may be applied to non-linguists' "cognitive attitudes" towards linguistic form.

		Vernacular	Non-vernacular
Finegan and Biber	Lower-status control	Complete	Incomplete
	Upper-status control	Complete	Complete
Labov	Lower-status control	Complete	Incomplete
	Upper-status control	Complete	Incomplete

Finegan and Biber go further, however, for they believe that the later acquisition of the non-vernacular registers by upper-status speakers even feeds back into their vernacular usage: "[E]ven their [i.e., higher status speakers'] conversational norms will come to reflect more frequent use of literate forms" (Finegan and Biber 1994:339).[8] Finegan and Biber raise doubts, therefore, about control of an original vernacular by upper-status speakers in general, and there may be an even greater contrast between their and Labov's view than that suggested in the outline given above:

		Vernacular	Non-vernacular
Finegan and Biber	Lower-status control	Complete	Incomplete
	Upper-status control	Incomplete	Complete
Labov	Lower-status control	Complete	Incomplete
	Upper-status control	Complete	Incomplete

The most important source of variation for Finegan and Biber comes from postvernacular language acquisition and is manifested in the lower-status speakers' lack of control over the registers which demand those structures. (They make little of the structures which are required by registers at less elaborate levels, ones, apparently, not under the control of upper-status speakers, although this fact would seem to follow from their reasoning.) If upper-status speakers lack systematicity in economical registers and lower-status speakers lack systematicity in elaborate ones, the variation which results should look like that in figure 16.4, which illustrates a lack of systematic or orderly variation in the elaborate (more formal) areas of lower-status use and, although Finegan and Biber do not discuss it, a similar pattern among upper-status speakers in their economical (or less formal) registers. The variation spaces between upper- and lower-status speakers at any point on the stylistic dimension is smaller than the variation along the entire range of the stylistic dimension for either lower- or upper-status speakers, suggesting, as Finegan and Biber would have it, that stylistic (or registral) variation is more powerful than status variation.

Figure 16.4 does not represent, however, the sort of variation which has

---

[8] On the other hand, Labov seems to suggest that one may "ruin" one's vernacular. "We have not encountered any nonstandard speakers who gained good control of a standard language, and still retained control of the nonstandard vernacular" (1972:215). This suggests that there are speakers with "new" (adult learned) vernaculars or, perhaps, speakers with no vernaculars at all.

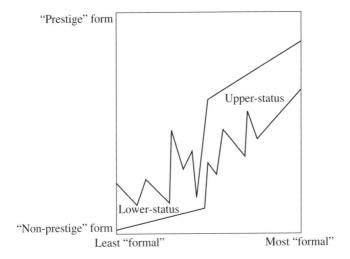

Figure 16.4 Hypothetical variation of upper- and lower-status groups alongside prestige (vertical) and stylistic (horizontal) dimensions

been uncovered in large numbers of sociolinguistic investigations (Preston 1991), although hypercorrection shows a certain lack of systematicity in the more formal registers by lower-middle- and/or upper-working-class speakers. Hypercorrection, however, is a special case of variation, one which usually suggests on-going linguistic change, specifically, change of the sort which has awakened public consciousness (e.g., Labov 1972: chapter 5). There are, however, numerous cases of stable variation (affecting all speakers in the speech community) in which regular, systematic variation occurs across the entire stylistic continuum. In short, all speakers display variation in their formal and casual registers, suggesting that systematic patterns of variation are not simply (or usually) the result of one group's failure to master the other's norms for the appropriate register.

In fact, if one follows the logical outcomes of F&B's proposal for variation, in which registral selection is the basis for most variation, why would lower-status speakers ever introduce any variation at all into their vernacular performances when they are clearly not using those registers which would require their poorly controlled non-vernacular systems? Similarly, why would upper-status speakers ever show variation in their non-vernaculars if their well-learned non-vernacular systems are the appropriate registral choice? Such intra-registral variation has been shown, however, in many studies.

With their focus on the acquisition of different structural properties of registers, F&B appear to revive the "Bickerton–Labov dispute," in which

Bickerton (e.g., 1971) finds (nearly) all variation to be a by-product of the choice among different grammars or "lects" (a finding which Chomsky supports even for stylistic variation, 1988:118), while Labov (e.g., 1969) finds a great deal of variation to be "inherent" (i.e., within a single grammar). If the several grammars of a speaker are all "fully formed," then one who moves back and forth among them is simply a "code-switcher" and selects according to the sorts of determining factors which have been outlined for code-choice. Roughly, they include, of course, not only F&B's idea that the choice of registers entails eventual code-selection (through the communicative mandates of ease and clarity) and Bell's idea that stylistic choices reflect the use of codes contributed by speakers from other social status groups, but also (at least) "identity expression" (e.g., Milroy 1980:115), "accommodation" (e.g., Giles and Powesland 1975:158), "speaker alignment" (e.g., Myers-Scotton 1993:113), "domain" (e.g., Fishman 1972:43), and "metaphoric (and situational) switching" (e.g., Blom and Gumperz 1972:425).

Although these various characterizations of the motivations for code choice all doubtless touch on reasonable explanations, none of them expresses a specific concern for the degree of knowledge of the code (or "grammar," as I prefer to call it), and, in fact, none specifically notes whether or not the choices of the speaker are ones which are made within the confines of one grammar (inherent variability) or across grammars (code choice). Interestingly, the idea that there are multiple grammars in one speaker allows for variation which not only occurs across grammars but also results from attempts to employ poorly formed grammars, perhaps the sort one has as a member of the speech community with limited access to some of its registers. If one selects a poorly formed grammar, then all the facts we have learned about second language acquisition may apply. Speakers may "overgeneralize," "transfer," "avoid," and so on.[9] One fact which may influence the interpretation of empirical counts of variation, therefore, might be the failure to identify the basic linguistic source of the variation itself – inherent, code-switched, or disfluent. Finegan and Biber certainly encourage us to look in the direction of the last.

An inspection of the sorts of elements which vary between economical and elaborate registers in Finegan and Biber's work shows, however, that the question of different grammars is not involved. Finegan and Biber surely do not want to claim that upper-status speakers have grammars which do not include fluent access to such features as private verbs, THAT

---

[9] The variationist enterprise is well-known in second language acquisition circles (see, for example Bayley and Preston 1996), but second language acquisition findings (whether from those of a variationist bent or not) have influenced the sociolinguistics enterprise only a little (but see Trudgill 1986).

deletion, contractions, present tense verbs, second person pronouns, DO as pro-verb, and so on, the features listed above from Biber's 1988 study for less elaborate registers. Similarly, they would surely not claim that lower-status speakers lack control over such linguistic features as conjuncts (e.g., "however"), agentless passives, adverbial past participial clauses, by-passives, past participial WHIZ deletions, other adverbial subordinators (e.g. "since," "while"), and predicative adjectives. Unlike the list given earlier, however, which included linguistic features which loaded on the most interpersonal registers (and, were, therefore, assumed to be most economical), these are the features which load onto a factor group which has the highest occurrence among the most impersonal or least interactive registers (e.g., academic prose and official documents) and are, presumably, those which would be classified as most elaborate (Biber 1988).

Such features are the text and information structure dependent elements of a language. As Finegan and Biber discover, they vary (in frequency) among text types (which have different requirements for the delivery of information). As such, they do not dramatically vary (if at all) across social status lines, for they are not determined by choices which are related to status. In the most extreme cases – when some text types are exclusively the domain of one status group or another, as in professional registers – grammatical elements might be more exclusive and actuate the "different grammars" interpretation, but this is hardly an important factor in the most general (conversational, narrative, transactional) registers of the speech community.

More importantly, such variables as those treated typically in Finegan and Biber's work do not meet the basic requirement for the study of variation – the choice of more than one semantically equivalent element in environments where all have a privilege of occurrence (e.g., Wolfram 1993). When Finegan and Biber show that particular texts are characterized by a high proportion of certain linguistic features, they do not carefully indicate the alternatives. In classic sociolinguistic work, the sort Bell and I refer to, an essential step is the characterization of the alternative forms of the variable, and in areas of syntax, this may be particularly difficult, as Labov (1978) has shown. F&B's work is not uninteresting; it answers questions about the selection of linguistic resources in the realization of different linguistic tasks, but it is an empirical question to determine whether or not speakers of different social status levels will employ different resources in realizing the same tasks, and Finegan and Biber do not really investigate this question. In their more recent work with the BNC, they claim that there is no significant variation in the implementation of some linguistic features across social status groups. The features they report on are the following:

ECONOMY FEATURES
3rd-person pronouns: *she, him, it,* etc.
contractions: *innit, cos, can't, I'm,* etc.
3rd-person singular DO: *it do, it don't, s/he don't,* etc.
THAT omission
pro-verb DO

ELABORATION FEATURES
type/token ratio
relative clauses
subordinators & conjuncts
phrasal AND
prepositional phrases
word length (measured in letters per word)
nouns
(Finegan and Biber 1996:26)

Finegan and Biber show that there is little social status variation among this group of variables and take this to be "counterevidence to the prediction made by Bell (and endorsed by Preston) that style variation presupposes dialect [i.e., status] variation" (1996:28). If we examine these features one by one, however, it is clear that most of them are not ones which would satisfy the definition of a variable.

(1) Third-person pronouns. The density of pronouns in texts has a tendency to be a fixed ratio (e.g., Givón 1983) according to information status. It is not clear, however, what the alternative to pronominalization is; if F&B mean for it to be a noun, then the appearance of the alternative would, in many cases, strike native speakers as odd, "ungrammatical" (or even linguistically perverse):

A: Did you see John yesterday?
B: Yes, I saw John.
A: What was John doing?
B: John was riding a bike.
A: Was John riding John's bike?
B: Yes, John was.
       etc. . .

Since we learn about texts (rather than social status) by investigating the density of an item which is not paired with a viable alternative (at least in many contexts), it is no small wonder that we learn more about texts than status. The fact that lower-social-status groups employ significantly more of this economy structure than the upper-status groups may simply have more to do with the specific information structures of the texts investigated and little to do with social status *per se.*

(2) Contractions. Contractions are classic sociolinguistic variables, but they do not contrast evenly (from a statistical point of view) with non-

contracted forms in all environments, and there are those in which contraction is impossible (*"Do you know where he's?"); therefore, a text-count of contraction in general cannot reveal the variable facts about it. It is not surprising, therefore, that this feature is not sensitive to social status, although it is odd to note that some relatively non-standard British English contractions (e.g., "innit" = "isn't it") are combined with standard ones (e.g., "he's," "I'm") in this count, a categorization feature which is sure to result in a demotion of whatever social-status distinctions did occur.

(3) Third-person singular DO. Not surprisingly, this feature shows significant social-status variation; it is one of only a few variables which Finegan and Biber study which would appear to be a classic sociolinguistic one (e.g., "he do" versus "he does"). Finegan and Biber's findings, however, simply reflect the very wide social-class stratification of third-person omission, known on both sides of the Atlantic. For Norwich, for example, Trudgill reports a range of third-person omission, from 0 percent in middle middle-class speakers to 97 percent in lower working-class speakers (1995:32), a wide variation space which Finegan and Biber do not show to be greater in register-induced performances.

(4) THAT omission. Although there may be subtle differences in meaning implied by THAT versus Ø (e.g., Bolinger 1972), it is a variable which shows no social-status distinctions in the sorts of texts Finegan and Biber examine. That is surely not a surprising feature of texts (or of languages in general), since such features may be so ubiquitous in certain texts that they do not figure in any other sort of variation at all. In Biber's 1988 study, for example, THAT omission was the second highest factor to load on the group which was eventually associated with conversational registers.

(5) Pro-verb DO. *Do* support is like pronominalization. It is a relatively predictable feature of texts, and one could devise a *"do-less"* sequence like the one given above which avoided the pronoun *he* which would be equally absurd. In short, the categorical envelope of variation is not well described here, and there are other factors (e.g., pleading *do* – *"Tell us a story." "No." "Oh do, do!"*) which would contribute to these counts in even more dramatic ways. Those facts aside, however, *do* support seems to be such an unremarkable feature of ordinary texts (with variation from one sort of text to another) that it is not surprising that it does not emerge as a social-status characteristic.

I will not review in detail the remaining factors which Finegan and Biber survey from the BNC for the "elaborate" side of their argument. Only one of them ("relative clause") shows significant distribution (more frequent for upper-status speakers) in the expected direction, and another ("noun," presumably elaborate in contrast with "pronoun," but see above) shows a significant status distribution in the "wrong" direction (i.e., greater frequency among lower-status speakers). Suffice it to say that these factors also fail to meet the criteria for sociolinguistic variables. Finegan and Biber specifically note, for example, that relative clauses are simply measured against "their absence" (1996:6). It is as difficult to prepare a principled list of alternates for "subordinators & conjuncts," "phrasal AND," and "prepositional phrases." They are all text-bound features of language use (as is "type/token ratio") and bear little (or no) relation to social status. That "word length" is not significant probably does have to do with the fact that conversational registers are investigated here, for I have no doubt that, in more impersonal registers, a greater word-length figure would be found for upper-status speakers – a result, one would think, simply of educational experiences.

Finegan and Biber do not find social status variation to be very important because they do not look at features which would support it; instead, they investigate the deployment strategies of linguistic units in texts, and, when they focus on conversation (rather than on academic or written texts), as they do in their BNC survey, they find little patterning across social classes. When they do include features which are especially sensitive to class (e.g., third-singular DO), they find, as one would expect, significant status distribution. When they find status distribution on a variable which is not treated in the classic sociolinguistic sense (by pairing it with a specific alternative or alternatives), their findings are very difficult to interpret (e.g., those for "relative clause").

It is not the case, however, that the deployment of ubiquitously known linguistic features will not differ for social-status groups within the same text. Kleiner (1996), for example, shows that middle-class speakers are much less inclined to use imperative constructions in direction-giving than are working-class speakers. This finding, interpreted by Kleiner to reflect on the different deployment of "politeness" strategies in public encounters by speakers of different social statuses, satisfies the classic techniques of sociolinguistic investigation by carefully identifying a variable (imperative versus non-imperative structures in direction-giving). F&B's investigation of text types does not, in general, set up these oppositions in this classic fashion.[10]

---

[10] Text counts like the ones F&B propose may reveal interesting differential patterns of use according to communicative or information structure, but I suspect they will be of a much more detailed sort. Alfaraz (1996), for example, shows that Cuban Spanish conversations exhibit considerably more overlap than European-American ones (in several varieties of North American English). That fact, however, has interesting repercussions in the organization of information structure. Since interlocutors "know" that the ends (and beginnings) of sentences will be overlapped, they move new information to a position different from that classically identified (i.e., "put new information last"). Such a conversational mandate will rather obviously have repercussions in the frequency of use of topicalization and focusing devices.

In conclusion, Finegan and Biber do not convincingly show that Bell and I are wrong about the sorts of features which have been the main focus of sociolinguistic research, and I personally doubt that they will be successful in encouraging most practicing sociolinguists to pay greater attention to the written end of the stylistic continuum in the search for the principal motivations for variation and change in the speech community, although none of us would discourage investigation in that direction.

But what of the positive effects?

First, Finegan and Biber's text-counts are interesting in their own right. They reveal a complex interaction of communicative devices and registral types, and, as I have suggested above, a promise for an even more careful study of the differential positions of social groups within such a framework. Although I believe their conclusions are not valid for general variation theory, due, primarily, to the basic formulation of the variables they study, I do not consider their work uninteresting at all. Although they play for a different team, they are in the same sport. I will show in greater detail below exactly what team I believe they play for.

Second, although they have not criticized my claim that linguistic influences are generally strongest in variation, F&B's work has in general prompted me to question more carefully why indeed that should be so and why social-status differences should derive from (and mirror) that fact. I take heart in the continued reworking of Kroch's position on the degree to which natural processes are eschewed by upper-status speakers, particularly the reformulation given in chapter 5 of Chambers 1995. If, in fact, it is the general case that upper-status speakers have more highly constrained rule systems (as a result of their opposition to natural processes), then it is a reasonable interpretation that this suppression of natural rules might usually manifest itself more weakly than the influence of the natural processes themselves. Even when a natural process is said to be a pattern of use strongly led by one social group, determining linguistic factors outweigh or are nearly as large as the social ones. Haeri (1994), for example, states that "Palatalization, perhaps more than any other aspect of the Cairene [Egyptian Arabic] phonology, distinguishes the speech of men and women" (p. 97). But her VARBRUL runs for "weak" palatalization of dental stops show a variation space for following environment which ranges from .69 (for glides) down to .12 (for non-mid and high front vowels). The gender space for the same variable is only .60 for women to .38 for men. Although VARBRUL runs are not done on style, it is clear that its effect is much weaker.[11]

---

[11] "Strong" palatalization (in which an affricate results) shows only a slightly greater envelope for gender (Haeri 1994:96–7), perhaps the beginnings of a gender-stereotyped form.

The implications for the funnel of figure 16.1 are clear. Natural processes carry the most weight in determining variation, although severe speech community stereotyping, particularly by association with a specific social group, may over-ride this generalization (e.g., Preston 1991). In cases where there is no such severe stereotyping, however, upper-status speakers maintain social position and identity linguistically by opposing such natural processes, creating a variation space which is powerful, but not so large as that created by the natural processes themselves. When the opposing influences of social groups and natural processes are in place, interaction among groups initiates the sort of stylistic variation which mirrors social status as outlined by Bell (1984).

In fact, such reasoning, at greater levels of specificity, has already been expressed in the variationist literature:

> PRINCIPLE OF PHONETIC IMPLAUSIBILITY: Constraints on variability may be altered in ways that violate the apparent phonetic naturalness of constraint hierarchies if:
>
> a.   there is a significant categorical shift in the status of the unit, such as a shift between peripheral and non-peripheral status for vowels
> b.   the change is taking place at a beginning or end point in the S-slope change curve, thus involving incipient or obsolescing forms
> c.   the change involves competing socially significant norms at a conscious level (Wolfram and Schilling-Estes 1995:713)

In (a), Wolfram and Schilling-Estes simply point to apparent violations, ones which fail to take into account the actual status of the variable under study. In (c) they reiterate what I say above about highly stereotyped features, but in (b) they point to unstable (unnatural) conditions which appear to be associated with acquisition and loss, an issue I turn to next.

A third positive effect of F&B's work, in my opinion, is their redirecting attention to the problem of inherent variability (one grammar), code-switching (multiple grammars), and, within the domain of the last, the possible choice of poorly formed grammars in an individual's linguistic repertoire. It is not enough, however, to suggest that the processes of first and second language acquisition (and pidgin–creole formation or historical change in general) are like those of variety acquisition, for to acknowledge this parallelism without incorporating it explicitly into the design of variation studies may lead to missed opportunities or, perhaps worse, misleading interpretations. What are some principled ways in which variationists may be able to characterize their data as stemming from choices within a single grammar, choices across grammars, and choices which entail the employment of poorly formed (emerging, fossilized, or dying) grammars? I offer three suggestions, beginning with the one I believe has been most often (though, unfortunately, not always) applied in variation studies.

(1) The evidence from variation and systematicity. Although not always phrased in theoretically specific terms, many patterns of systematic variation have been shown to point towards patterns of use which would seem to indicate one consistent grammar, in spite of considerable diversity among speakers. Labov's definition of the speech community itself relies on the notion of shared norms of interpretation (1972:158) but, more recently, assumes a "uniform structural base" (1989:2). In New York City, for example, even though some lower-status speakers have nearly categorical absence of non-prevocalic /r/ in their most casual styles and some upper-status speakers have nearly categorical presence of the same feature in their most formal ones, they are members of the same speech community (and, presumably, share a grammar) since they all share the belief that /r/ is more appropriate to more formal speech (and all increase its incidence in such performances) (Labov 1966). More recently, Guy (1991) has shown that a consistent, single grammar may show considerable variation within the framework of a specific theory (not entailing the positing of a separate grammar). Briefly, Guy shows that the frequencies of t/d deletion may be mathematically related to the levels of derivational history within the framework of lexical phonology. I know of no more elegant proof that single-grammar variation is not a tacked-on afterthought to the real business of linguistics.

Within constraints systems of variation studies, there are also indications that speakers may have different grammars, not variants of the same one. Guy's (1980) discussion of the different constraint orderings of "pause" (his "Q" factor for New York City and Philadelphia) was an early and dramatic illustration that such an ordering difference was a feature which "must be learned by children acquiring a dialect, and must be accounted for in the grammar of a dialect" (p. 28).

As already suggested, variationists have found unusual patterns (e.g., hypercorrection of third singular -s in Fasold 1972) to suggest that some members of the speech community control an emerging grammar less well than others, evidenced by the overuse of a particular variant, usually in more formal styles, and Wolfram and Schilling-Estes, cited above, note that the irregularity or unnaturalness of constraint orderings at either end of the typical S-curve of language change suggests that rules are incipient or obsolescing (hence, less well-formed).

In general, then, although perhaps not as often as one would like, practitioners of variationist linguistics have been careful to point out the implications for grammatical status as they emerge from quantitative research.

(2) The evidence from theoretical considerations. Less frequently, it has been argued that a speaker must be drawing on either different, the same, or deficient grammars due to underlying dependencies or implicational

patterns in rule systems. Of course, such claims are not related to the variationist enterprise unless quantitative data are used to assess them. Some of the more important work in this area has come from studies of substrate–superstrate influences in language contact, in which determining the contribution of a different grammar is an essential step. Harris (1991), for example, claims that Irish English is significantly different from other varieties of English (i.e., has a different grammar) due to the smaller number of constraints on elements in it which can be extracted in *it*-cleft constructions (e.g., *It's doing his lessons that Tim is, It's drunk he is*) (pp. 197–8). The constraints in Irish English turn out to be similar to those of constraints on the same structure in Irish.

Such cases are far from simple. Harris finds different grammars in this contact situation, but Kerswill finds that speech communities (at least emerging ones) may be based on superficial structural similarities which derive from different underlying grammars (1995:204). I suspect, however, that such different grammars will disappear in favor of a unified system in the acquisition of later generations, although I do not want to disregard the emergence of what may be an independent rule system in language-mixing (e.g., Bhatia and Ritchie 1996). That different grammatical inventories (even ones which lead, through contact, to similar surface phenomena) might be a short-term accompaniment to contact-induced change seems very reasonable, but it highlights the fluid relationships between and among the grammars of individuals in a rapidly changing speech community, not a long-term difference in underlying grammatical systems.[12]

In some cases, reasoning from a theoretical perspective shows that speakers may employ variable elements within the same grammatical format. Meechan and Foley (1994), show, for example, how variable agreement (*There is/are some people in the other room*) may result from an option in raising at the LF ("logical form") level for the postverbal NP; that is, a unified grammar is satisfied and all its other elements and relations may be kept in place (under certain conditions) whether an operation which would trigger agreement between *be* and the postverbal NP occurs or not. Unfortunately, even such sophisticated work as Meechan and Foley's usually requires some "tinkering" with the theoretical machinery, for even those systems which appear to be open to the ideas of internal (or inherent, single-grammar) variability (e.g., optimality theory) still seem to produce categorical results (Guy 1994).

Perhaps most problematic from a theoretical perspective is the idea that variation may arise from poorly formed grammars, and there may be

---

[12] Of course, there may be long-term underlying grammatical differences, particularly in the case of dramatic social separation. The long-standing argument about the grammatical status of AAVE focuses on just such a likelihood (e.g., *American Speech*, Spring 1987).

several senses in which the notion of a poorly formed grammar is a poorly formed concept. First, as first and second language acquisition specialists have shown, a child or inter-language grammar may be studied on the basis of its own internal structure, not simply as deficient in terms of the target. Second, it might be asserted that one either has (or does not have) a grammar. "Poorly formed," therefore, is a reference to accessibility, not to the shape of the grammar itself.

This first position is admirable for its Saussurian divorce of the synchronic and diachronic, but that is not always a desirable split, particularly when you have a pretty good idea of where you are going and would like to have a better idea of how you might get there. Although the targets of variety change might be less well-specified than those of second language acquisition, quantitative work often points rather conclusively to an eventual winner – which denies neither the possibility for stable variation nor dramatic reversals (as in, for example, "correction from above"). The study of the stages of a developing inter-dialect, therefore, ought to be more carefully articulated in terms of theoretical repercussions. When the alternative forms of a putative linguistic variable are actually the product of competing grammars, the path in the history of competing forms ought to manifest itself quite differently from the path of competing forms within the framework of inherent variability. Again, such studies are much more common in the framework of second language acquisition, where, for example, different settings within UG have been shown to be predictors of success rates in acquisition. For example, Flynn (1989) shows that the parametric setting of head-direction in L1 (Spanish "same" – Japanese "different") has a considerable influence on the acquisition of English relative clauses.

Second, grammars in flux may simply be there, but they may also have properties other than their accessibility. For example, they seem to be extremely open to change (or "permeable," as Adjémian 1976 suggests), and some research in second language acquisition suggests that grammars which even break universal principles may briefly arise (e.g., Klein 1995), strongly suggesting that "poorly formed" may be an important grammatical as well as access characterization.[13]

(3) The evidence from psycholinguistics: Psycholinguistic measures of underlying linguistic competence are not new; Fodor and Bever (1965) was the first in a series of experiments which set out to determine the degree to which one could isolate perceptual strategies which aid in associating lexical strings with their underlying structures (the so-called

---

[13] Acquisition of other varieties, even if only for reasons of social distinctiveness or the maintenance of gross stereotypes, hardly accommodative at all, is also common, and it is clear that the "grammars" thus acquired are often very faulty. See, for example, Preston 1992, Preston 1996c, and Niedzielski and Preston 1999.

"click" experiments). For the most part, however, variationist studies are based on empirical observations and/or elicitations (e.g., Wolfram and Fasold's 1974 discussion of "structural elicitation"), not experimental studies (except, of course, for studies of language attitudes). When respondent judgments have been used, they appear more often to serve the function of adding to the data pool of less frequently observed constructions (e.g., Butters' 1973 attempt by means of a rating scale to determine which multiple modal constructions were allowed in Southern US English).

Nevertheless, some work focuses (or can be interpreted to focus) on the question of one-or-many grammars. Labov et al. (1968) report on several "tasks," including repetition, in which respondents translate into their own variety forms said to them in another, suggesting that the other variety represents a grammar over which they have little (or no) control. Rickford (1987) reports on the use of grammar "correction" tests (in Guyanese Creole), compares the results of these tasks with data collected from spontaneous conversation, and evaluates (and urges) the use of intuitive as well as conversational data in the study of variation. Labov (1991) asks if positive *any more* (= "nowadays," e.g., *I'm really tired any more*) can be incorporated into a pan-lectal grammar of English. He concludes (p. 286) that it cannot, on the basis of questionnaire data which elicits respondents' semantic interpretations and grammaticality judgments of the construction rather than its use. Fasold (1994) used the Internet to solicit judgments concerning possible variation in the application of Binding Theory (to reflexives). Sells, Rickford, and Wasow (1996) rely on native speaker intuition as well as production data in their study of the syntax of negative inversion in AAVE. Preston (1996a) asks respondents to match words on the basis of "same" or "different" vowels according to their own pronunciation (following a method outlined by DiPaolo 1988) and shows that European-American and African-American respondents in southern Michigan apparently share a single, underlying phonological system (neither of which reflects any reorganization of the phonemic system as might be expected by the effects of the Northern Cities Chain Shift).

In general, however, the use of judgments in reaching conclusions about the underlying grammar (or grammars) of respondents has not been a major trend in variation studies. Once again, psycholinguistic concerns have been considerably more in evidence in second language acquisition. In fact, the use of grammaticality judgments to uncover underlying grammatical competence has become such a common feature in second language acquisition that an entire section of a recent anthology on research methodology in the field focuses on it (Tarone, Gass, and Cohen 1994: section III). Many of the second language acquisition findings have important implications for the assessment of grammatical competence, and, hence, might be applied to the determination of inherent variability or multiple grammars. Munnich, Flynn, and Martohardjono (1994) show, for example, that Japanese learners of English performed better on a grammaticality judgment test than on an elicited performance task for both grammatical and ungrammatical strings but that the imitation task provided interesting supplementary information which might have been masked by the judgment task's elicitation of more conscious knowledge.

More recently, reaction-time studies have been applied to second language acquisition data, which have clear implications for the study of grammatical competence in so-called monolinguals. Cook (1990), for example, measures comprehension time in investigating parameterized binding (as revealed in reflexives and pronouns) among native speakers of English and Romance-language, Norwegian, and Japanese learners of English, languages which have increasingly "distant" settings from English according to the Subset Principle (Wexler and Manzini 1987:61). It is shown, however, that the "relative processing difficulty of binding in different types of sentences in English is the same regardless of the L1 setting for the governing category parameter." Cook concludes that, in this case, neither L1 transfer nor the Subset Principle can account for the similarities since pronominals, which should have the opposite order of processing difficulty from the reflexives, show the same order.

It is not the case, therefore, that variationist linguistics and sister disciplines are without means of investigating the question of single, multiple, and weak grammars. Unfortunately, when major claims about theory based on differential access to grammars are made, however, we do not have a great deal of powerful evidence to use in evaluation, for variationist work in general has been weak in its uses of the reasonings and methodologies outlined just above. In fact, variationists have generally avoided even theoretical model-building in the psycholinguistic area (but see in Preston 1996b the most recent version of the psycholinguistic model of variation I introduced in Preston 1989). We are beholden, then, to Finegan and Biber for reminding us of this responsibility.

To conclude, let me try to characterize from a more general perspective why I believe Finegan and Biber made the error they did and why in some ways it is not an error at all. I will not focus on the fact that in some ways the difference between Bell's and Finegan and Biber's conclusions might simply have been the result of Finegan and Biber's failing to organize their variables in the classical variationist fashion, although I believe that is so. There is, however, another sense of Finegan and Biber's enterprise in which one could argue that their variables should not be organized in that way at all. I have already suggested that the sorts of variables they investigate are those which are sensitive to information structure and are much more likely,

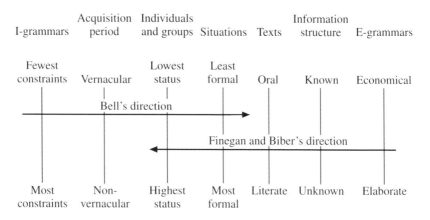

Figure 16.5 A general characterization of language variation factors

therefore, to be the product of text types and their information-structuring demands and (especially since they are often in complementary distribution with their alternatives or not specifically a member of a variable set at all) are not likely to be reflected in social structure.

In figure 16.5 I foolishly try to represent nearly all the concerns which I believe bear on this puzzle. From left to right, it features, first, a slot for "Grammar" (although from what I have said above it should be clear that multiple grammars, some of which might be poorly formed, may stand in that position). I build in Chamber's 1995 notion that the elements of a grammar may be ranked on the basis of their density of constraints, a notion not far, I believe, from Kroch's 1978 characterization of "natural processes." Second, I deal with the ambiguous notion *vernacular* in only one way – by reference to its status as the earliest learned and, therefore, the most deeply embedded and easily accessed of all the varieties speakers have at their command. I align all vernaculars with the fewest constraints in the grammatical column to the left. Third, I note that individuals and groups in the society are stratified, but I do not have room to include the rich ideological package of preferences, beliefs, and cultural practices that accompanies them, although, by excluding it, I do not mean to suggest that it does not play an important function in language choice. I consider it an integral component of individuals and groups. Fourth, when individuals interact, they produce culturally describable (and rankable) situations, some of which are very straightforward in their influence on the next (fifth) component – text choice, which, following Finegan and Biber, we might rank on the oral–literate scale. Texts (and positions in texts as well as subparts of them) have most to do with information structure, and I provide that in the next (sixth) component, again one which might be ranked on the basis of information status.

The last (seventh) component is a surprise; we are back at grammar (where we started), but the characteristics of grammar which are outlined here are those which connect to information structure, perhaps the elaborate versus economical cline Finegan and Biber use. So far as I know, grammarians of every ilk admit to the abstract structural characteristics of the far-left grammar and to the ability of the structural patterns of that far-left grammar to carry different instantiations of information in the far-right grammar – two sides of the same coin. Of course, functionalists see a one-to-one relationship between the two factors and many others do not, but those theoretical skirmishes need not concern us here. Both aspects of grammar exist; whether they map directly onto one another (or have a cause–effect relationship) is, luckily, not our problem.

It should now be obvious why Finegan and Biber and Bell discover different things (and why neither Bell nor Finegan and Biber object to my claim that linguistic factors have the greatest strength). Bell and I begin at the far-left grammar and move through presumptions about fluency to social status. As I suggest above, higher-status speakers may have better control over those least vernacular, more heavily constrained areas of the grammar, creating, in the social linguistic structure of the speech community, a variation space which is not as big as but reflects the linguistic constraints themselves (the explanatory dimension missing in my earlier characterizations of this relationship). Bell then points out that situations, which involve cross-status interaction in many cases, make use of accommodation to status norms to accomplish different degrees of formality (or "distance" as I prefer to call it, e.g., Preston 1986). Bell (and I) then peter out; we do not go on to consider the relationship of different kinds of interactions to different sorts of texts, although neither of us would deny the importance of the study of text types in the sociolinguistic enterprise.

Just where we give out, Finegan and Biber have run into us from the opposite direction. Their far-right grammar, however, has yielded an information-status rather than structural interpretation, one much more likely to have to do with the sorts of surface-oriented economical versus elaborate and interactional known versus unknown characteristics they find. These characteristics are the basics of their analysis and map directly onto text types, which, based in situations, they find to be the strongest elements influencing variation (outside of the communicative mandates of the grammar itself). From there, they move ever leftward to the individual, the last (and therefore weakest) element in their search for the influences on linguistic variables. I suspect that, for the sorts of variables they investigate, they are probably right.

This is not exactly the case of the blind scholars and the elephant. I believe Bell and I see the far-right grammar (and the other characteristics Finegan and Biber investigate) just as I am sure Finegan and Biber see the far-left and the factors we prefer. When we grabbed the grammar of the elephant, however, we felt the structural component and moved in the direction which that implied (fluencies, status variation, and subsequent social interaction factors). When Finegan and Biber grabbed the same elephant by its grammar, they felt instead its communicative potential and walked in the opposite direction. To their credit, they have walked a little farther around than Bell and I, for they at least got to people, and we fell well short of texts (and perhaps only implied situations).

In conclusion, I believe there is both style and substance in the difference Bell and I and Finegan and Biber find in the determining characteristics of linguistic variation. Bell and I proceed on the basis of the essential correctness of the Labovian sociolinguistic enterprise, including its specific characterization of the linguistic variable, one well suited to the structural interpretation of a grammar. We probably presume too much about interaction and too little about the importance of texts (especially along their oral–literate dimension), and probably way too little about the possibility for variation in the marshaling of information structure. Finegan and Biber are guilty as well, I believe, in confusing the variation of text-information structures with the sorts of structural variables which have been studied in most variationist work, and they brush aside the importance of structural differences too cavalierly, but they move a little farther around the elephant than Bell and I, and they bring the entire creature back to our attention.

References

INTRODUCTION

Baugh, John 1979. Linguistic Style Shifting in Black English. PhD thesis, University of Pennsylvania.

Bauman, Richard 1977. *Verbal Art as Performance*. Prospect Heights, IL: Waveland.

Bauman, Richard and Sherzer, Joel (eds.) 1974. *Explorations in the Ethnography of Speaking*. Cambridge: Cambridge University Press.

Bell, Allan 1977. The Language of Radio News in Auckland: a Sociolinguistic Study of Style, Audience and Subediting Variation. PhD thesis, University of Auckland.

1984. Language Style as Audience Design. *Language in Society* 13(2): 145–204.

Bernstein, B. 1971. *Class, Codes and Control*. London: Routledge.

Biber, Douglas and Finegan, Edward (eds.) 1994. *Sociolinguistic Perspectives on Register*. Oxford: Oxford University Press.

Bourdieu, Pierre 1982. *Ce que Parler Veut Dire: l'Economie des Echanges Linguistiques*. Paris: Fayard.

Briggs, Charles L. 1988. *Competence in Performance: the Creativity of Tradition in Mexicano Verbal Art*. Philadelphia: University of Pennsylvania Press.

Briggs, Charles L. and Bauman, Richard 1992. Genre, Intertextuality, and Social Power. *Journal of Linguistic Anthropology* 2(2): 131–72.

Bucholtz, Mary 1996. Geek the Girl: Language, Femininity and Female Nerds. In J. Ahlers, L. Bilmes, M. Chen, M. Oliver, N. Warner and S. Werhteim (eds.), *Gender and Belief Systems*, pp. 119–82. Berkeley: Berkeley Women and Language Group.

California Style Collective 1993. *Variation and Personal/Group Style*. Paper presented at the 21st Annual Conference on New Ways of Analyzing Variation in English. Ottawa: University of Ottawa.

Coupland, Nikolas 1980. Style-shifting in a Cardiff Work-setting. *Language in Society* 9(1): 1–12.

Eckert, Penelope 2000. *Linguistic Variation as Social Practice*. Oxford: Blackwell.

Eckert, Penelope and McConnell-Ginet, S. 1992. Think Practically and Look Locally: Language and Gender as Community-Based Practice. *Annual Review of Anthropology* 21: 461–90.

Ervin-Tripp, Susan M. 1972. On Sociolinguistic Rules: Alternation and Co-occurrence. In John J. Gumperz and Dell Hymes (eds.), *Directions in*

Sociolinguistics: the Ethnography of Communication, pp. 213–50. New York: Holt, Rinehart and Winston.

Finegan, Edward and Biber, Douglas 1994. Register and Social Dialect Variation: an Integrated Approach. In Douglas Biber and Edward Finegan (eds.), *Sociolinguistic Perspectives on Register*, pp. 315–47. Oxford: Oxford University Press.

Gal, Susan and Irvine, Judith T. 1997. The Boundaries of Languages and Disciplines: How Ideologies Construct Difference. *Social Research* 62: 967–1001.

Giles, Howard (ed.) 1984. *The Dynamics of Speech Accommodation*. Amsterdam: Mouton.

Giles, Howard, Coupland, Justine and Coupland, Nikolas 1991. *Contexts of Accommodation: Developments in Applied Sociolinguistics*. Cambridge: Cambridge University Press.

Giles, Howard and Powesland, Peter F. 1975. *Speech Style and Social Evaluation*. London: Academic Press.

Heath, Shirley Brice 1983. *Ways with Words*. Cambridge: Cambridge University Press.

Hindle, Donald M. 1979. The Social and Situational Conditioning of Phonetic Variation. PhD thesis, University of Pennsylvania.

Hymes, Dell 1964. Introduction: Toward Ethnographies of Communication. In John J. Gumperz and Dell Hymes (eds.), *The Ethnography of Communication*. *American Anthropologist* 66(6): 1–34.

    1972. Models of the Interaction of Language and Social Life. In John J. Gumperz and Dell Hymes (eds.), *The Ethnography of Communication*, pp. 35–71. New York: Holt, Rinehart and Winston.

Irvine, Judith T. 1979. Formality and Informality in Communicative Events. *American Anthropologist* 81: 773–90.

    1985. Status and Style in Language. In Judith Irvine (ed.), *Annual Review of Anthropology*, pp. 557–81. Mountain View, CA: Annual Reviews.

Kroch, Anthony S. 1978. Toward a Theory of Social Dialect Variation. *Language in Society* 7: 17–36.

Labov, William 1966. *The Social Stratification of English in New York City*. Washington, DC: Center for Applied Linguistics.

    1972. Hypercorrection by the Lower Middle Class as a Factor in Linguistic Change. In William Labov (ed.), *Sociolinguistic Patterns*, pp. 122–42. Philadelphia: University of Pennsylvania Press.

    1975. On the Use of the Present to Explain the Past. In Luigi Heilmann (ed.), *Proceedings of the 11th International Congress of Linguists*, pp. 825–51. Bologna: Mulino.

Milroy, Lesley 1987. *Observing and Analysing Natural Language*. Oxford: Blackwell.

Rickford, John R. 1979. Variation in a Creole Continuum: Quantitative and Implicational Approaches. PhD thesis, University of Pennsylvania.

Rickford, John R. and McNair-Knox, Faye 1994. Addressee- and Topic-influenced Style Shift: a Quantitative Sociolinguistic Study. In Douglas Biber and Edward Finegan (eds.), *Sociolinguistic Perspectives on Register*, pp. 235–76. Oxford: Oxford University Press.

Rickford, John R. and Rickford, Russell J. 2000. *Spoken Soul: the Story of Black English*. New York: John Wiley.
Van den Broeck, Jef 1977. Class Differences in Syntactic Complexity in the Flemish Town of Maaseik. *Language in Society* 6: 149–81.
Wolfram, Walt A. 1969. *A Sociolinguistic Description of Detroit Negro Speech*. Washington, DC: Center for Applied Linguistics.

1 "STYLE" AS DISTINCTIVENESS

Bourdieu, Pierre 1984[1979]. *Distinction*. Cambridge, MA: Harvard University Press.
　　1985. The Social Space and the Genesis of Groups. *Social Science Information* 24(2): 195–220.
Eagleton, Terry 1991. *Ideology: an Introduction*. London: Verso.
Errington, J. Joseph 1984. *Language and Social Change in Java*. Athens, OH: Ohio University Center for International Studies.
　　1988. *Structure and Style in Javanese*. Philadelphia: University of Pennsylvania Press.
Ervin-Tripp, Susan M. 1972. On Sociolinguistic Rules: Alternation and Co-occurrence. In John J. Gumperz and Dell Hymes (eds.), *Directions in Sociolinguistics: the Ethnography of Communication*, pp. 213–50. New York: Holt, Rinehart and Winston.
Ferguson, Charles A. 1994. Dialect, Register, and Genre: Working Assumptions about Conventionalization. In Douglas Biber and Edward Finegan (eds.), *Sociolinguistic Perspectives on Register*, pp. 15–30. Oxford: Oxford University Press.
Gal, Susan 1992. Dialect Variation and Language Ideology. Paper presented at the Annual Meeting of the American Anthropological Association, San Francisco.
Gal, Susan and Irvine, Judith T. 1995. The Boundaries of Languages and Disciplines: How Ideologies Construct Difference. *Social Research* 62(4): 967–1001.
Geertz, Clifford 1960. *The Religion of Java*. Chicago: University of Chicago Press.
Greenberg, Joseph 1960. Concluding Comments. In Thomas Sebeok (ed.), *Style in Language*, pp. 426–8. Cambridge, MA: MIT Press.
Gumperz, John J. 1968. The Speech Community. In David L. Sills (ed.), *International Encyclopedia of the Social Sciences*, vol. 9, pp. 381–6. London: Macmillan.
Halliday, Michael A. K. 1964. The Users and Uses of Language. In Michael A. K. Halliday, A. McIntosh and P. Strevens (eds.), *The Linguistic Sciences and Language Teaching*, pp. 75–110. London: Longman.
　　1976. Anti-languages. *American Anthropologist* 78: 570–84.
　　1978. *Language as Social Semiotic*. London: Edward Arnold.
Haynes, John 1995. *Style*. London and New York: Routledge.
Hebdige, Dick 1979. *Subculture: the Meaning of Style*. London and New York: Methuen.
Irvine, Judith T. 1978. Wolof Noun Classification: the Social Setting of Divergent Change. *Language in Society* 7: 37–64.

1989. When Talk isn't Cheap: Language and Political Economy. *American Ethnologist* 16(2):248–67.

1990. Registering Affect: Heteroglossia in the Linguistic Expression of Emotion. In Catherine A. Lutz and Leila Abu-Lughod (eds.), *Language and the Politics of Emotion*, pp. 126–61. Cambridge: Cambridge University Press.

Irvine, Judith T. and Gal, Susan 2000. Language Ideology and Linguistic Differentiation. In Paul Kroskrity (ed.), *Regimes of Language: Ideologies, Polities and Identities*, pp. 35–83. Santa Fe, NM: School of American Research.

Jakobson, Roman 1960. Closing Statement: Linguistics and Poetics. In Thomas Sebeok (ed.), *Style in Language*, pp. 350–77. Cambridge, MA: MIT Press.

Kroskrity, Paul, Schieffelin, Bambi B. and Woolard, Kathryn A. (eds.) 1992. *Language Ideologies*. Special issue, *Pragmatics* 2(3).

Kroskrity, Paul (ed.) 2000. *Language Ideologies: the Cultures of Language in Theory and Practice*. Santa Fe, NM: School of American Research.

Labov, William 1966. *The Social Stratification of English in New York City*. Washington, DC: Center for Applied Linguistics.

Sebeok, Thomas (ed.) 1960. *Style in Language*. Cambridge, MA: MIT Press.

Silverstein, Michael 1979. Language Structure and Linguistic Ideology. In R. Clyne, William F. Hanks and C. Hofbauer (eds.), *The Elements: a Parasession on Linguistic Units and Levels*, pp. 193–247. Chicago: Chicago Linguistics Society.

1992. The Uses and Utility of Ideology: some Reflections. In Paul Kroskrity, Bambi B. Schieffelin, and Kathryn A. Woolard (eds.), special issue on Language Ideologies. *Pragmatics* 2(3): 311–24.

Wolff, J. U. and Poedjosoedarmo, S. 1982. *Communicative Codes in Central Java*. Ithaca, NY: Cornell University Department of Asian Studies, Southeast Asia Program, data paper 116.

Woolard, Kathryn A. and Schieffelin, Bambi B. 1994. Language Ideology. *Annual Review of Anthropology* 23: 55–82.

2 VARIETY, STYLE-SHIFTING, AND IDEOLOGY

Andersen, E. S. 1990. *Speaking with Style: the Sociolinguistic Skills of Children*. London: Routledge.

Blom, Jan-Petter and Gumperz, John J. 1972. Social Meaning in Linguistic Structures. In John J. Gumperz and Dell Hymes (eds.), *Directions in Sociolinguistics: the Ethnography of Communication*, pp. 407–34. New York: Holt, Rinehart and Winston.

Butters, Ronald R. 1984. When is English "Black English Vernacular"? *Journal of English Linguistics* 17: 29–36.

Ervin, Susan 1964. Language and TAT Content in Bilinguals. *Journal of Abnormal and Social Psychology* 68: 500–7.

Farber, Jerry 1969. *The Student as Nigger: Essays and Stories*. North Hollywood: Contact. (Reprinted by Pocket Books, 1970.)

Fuller, Janet 1993. Hearing Between the Lines: Style Switching in a Courtroom Setting. *Pragmatics* 3: 29–44.

Gregory, Dick 1964. *Nigger*. New York: Pocket Books.

1971. (Richard Claxton Gregory) *No more Lies: the Myth and the Reality of American History*. New York: Harper and Row.

1976. *Up from Nigger*. New York: Stein and Day.

Gumperz, John J. 1982. *Discourse Strategies*. Cambridge: Cambridge University Press.

Gumperz, John J. and Berenz, N. 1993. Transcribing Conversational Exchanges. In Jane Edwards and Martin Lampert (eds.), *Talking Data: Transcription and Coding Methods for Language Research*, pp. 91–122. Hillsdale, NJ: Lawrence Erlbaum.

Heller, Monika 1992. The Politics of Codeswitching and Language Choice. *Journal of Multilingual and Multicultural Development* 13: 123–42.

Hill, Jane 1995. Junk Spanish, Covert Racism and the (Leaky) Boundary between Public and Private Spheres. *Pragmatics* 5: 204–12.

Jacquemet, M. 1996. *Credibility in Court: Communicative Practices in the Camorra Trials*. Cambridge: Cambridge University Press.

Jun, D. 1992. Bilingualism among Korean-Americans: on Factors Related to the Knowledge of Honorifics of the Korean Language. Honors thesis, University of California.

Kirshenblatt-Gimblett, Barbara 1972. Traditional Storytelling in the Toronto Jewish Community: a Study in Performance and Creativity in an Immigrant Culture. Unpublished dissertation, Department of Folklore, University of Indiana, Bloomington, IN.

Labov, William 1966. *The Social Stratification of English in New York City*. Washington, DC: Center for Applied Linguistics.

1980. Is there a Creole Speech Community? In A. Valdman and A. Highfield (eds.), *Theoretical Orientations in Creole Studies*, pp. 369–88. New York: Academic Press.

Lambert, Wallace E., Anisfeld, M. and Yeni-Komshian, Grace 1965. Evaluational Reactions of Jewish and Arab Adolescents to Dialect and Language Variations. *Journal of Personality and Social Psychology* 2: 84–90.

McClure, E. 1981. Formal and Functional Aspects of the Code Switched Discourse of Bilingual Children. In R. P. Duran, *Latino Language and Communicative Behavior*, pp. 69–94. Norwood, NJ: Ablex.

Mitchell-Kernan, Claudia 1971. Language Behavior in a Black Urban Community (Monographs of the Language-Behavior Research Laboratory 2). University of California, Berkeley.

1972. On the Status of Black English for Native Speakers: an Assessment of Attitudes and Values. In Courtney B. Cazden, Vera P. John and Dell Hymes (eds.), *Functions of Language in the Classroom*, pp. 195–210. Prospect Heights, IL: Waveland.

Myers-Scotton, Carol 1993. Common and Uncommon Ground: Social and Structural Factors in Codeswitching. *Language in Society* 22: 475–504.

Osgood, Charles E. 1960. The Cross-Cultural Generality of Visual–Verbal Synesthetic Tendencies. *Behavioral Science* 5: 146–69.

Poplack, Shana 1980. Sometimes I'll Start a Sentence in Spanish Y TERMINO EN ESPANOL: Toward a Typology of Code-switching. *Linguistics* 18: 581–618.

Rampton, Ben 1991. Interracial Panjabi in a British Adolescent Peer Group. *Language in Society* 20(3): 391–422.

Rickford, John R. and McNair-Knox, Faye 1994. Addressee- and Topic-influenced Style Shift: a Quantitative Sociolinguistic Study. In Douglas Biber and Edward

Finegan (eds.), *Sociolinguistic Perspectives on Register*, pp. 235–76. Oxford: Oxford University Press.

Sato, Charlene J. 1973. Another Look at Hawaian English. Unpublished paper for Rhetoric 152, University of California, Berkeley.

Shatz, Marilyn G. and Gelman, Rochel 1973. The Development of Communication Skills: Modifications in the Speech of Young Children as a Function of Listener. *Monographs of the Society for Research in Child Development* 38(152): 1–37.

Shuy, Roger W. 1980. Code Switching in *Lady Chatterley's Lover*. In M. W. S. De Silva (ed.), *Aspects of Linguistic Behavior: Festschrift for R. B. LePage*, pp. 223–40. York Papers in Linguistics 9. University of York.

Woolard, Kathryn A. 1987. Codeswitching and Comedy in Catalonia. *IPrA Papers in Pragmatics* 1(1): 106–22.

Woolard, Kathryn A. and Gahng, T.-J. 1990. Changing Language Policies and Attitudes in Autonomous Catalonia. *Language in Society* 19(3): 311–13.

3 THE ETHNOGRAPHY OF GENRE IN A MEXICAN MARKET

Abrahams, Roger D. 1981. Shouting Match at the Border: the Folklore of Display Events. In Richard Bauman and Roger D. Abrahams (eds.), *"And Other Neighborly Names": Social Image and Cultural Process in Texas Folklore,* pp. 303–21. Austin: University of Texas Press.

Bakhtin, Mikhail M. [1965]. *Rabelais and his World.* Trans. Hélène Iswolsky. Bloomington: Indiana University Press.

Bauman, Richard 1983. *Let your Words be Few: Symbolism of Speaking and Silence among Seventeenth-century Quakers.* Cambridge: Cambridge University Press.

1986. *Story, Performance, and Event: Contextual Studies of Oral Narrative.* Cambridge: Cambridge University Press.

Bauman, Richard and Briggs, Charles L. 1990. Poetics and Performance as Critical Perspectives on Language and Social Life. *Annual Review of Anthropology* 19: 59–88.

Biber, Douglas 1988. *Variation across Speech and Writing.* Cambridge: Cambridge University Press.

1994. An Analytical Framework for Register Studies. In Douglas Biber and Edward Finegan (eds.), *Sociolinguistic Perspectives on Register*, pp. 31–56. Oxford: Oxford University Press.

Biber, Douglas and Finegan, Edward 1989. Drift and the Evolution of English Style: a History of Three Genres. *Language* 65: 487–517.

(eds.) 1994. *Sociolinguistic Perspectives on Register.* Oxford: Oxford University Press.

Briggs, Charles L. and Richard Bauman 1992. Genre, Intertextuality, and Social Power. *Journal of Linguistic Anthropology* 2(2): 131–72.

Burke, Kenneth 1968[1931]. *Counter-statement.* Berkeley and Los Angeles: University of California Press.

Dargan, Amanda and Zeitlin, Steven 1983. American Talkers: Expressive Styles and Occupational Choice. *Journal of American Folklore* 96: 3–33.

Ervin-Tripp, Susan M. 1972. On Sociolinguistic Rules: Alternation and Co-occurrence. In John J. Gumperz and Dell Hymes (eds.), *Directions in*

Sociolinguistics: the Ethnography of Communication, pp. 213–50. New York: Holt, Rinehart and Winston.

Ferguson, Charles A. 1994. Dialect, Register, and Genre: Working Assumptions about Conventionalization. In Douglas Biber and Edward Finegan (eds.), *Sociolinguistic Perspectives on Register*, pp. 15–30. Oxford: Oxford University Press.

Flores Farfán, José Antonio 1984. *La interacción verbal de compra-venta en mercados otomíes*. Mexico City: Centro de Investigaciones y Estudios Superiores en Antropología Social.

Goffman, Erving 1974. *Frame Analysis*. New York: Harper and Row.

Graham, Joe 1981. The *caso*: an Emic Genre of Folk Narrative. In Richard Bauman and Roger D. Abrahams (eds.), *"And Other Neighborly Names": Social Process and Cultural Image in Texas Folklore*, pp. 11–43. Austin: University of Texas Press.

Hanks, William F. 1987. Discourse Genres in a Theory of Practice. *American Ethnologist* 14: 668–92.

Hymes, Dell 1989[1974]. Ways of Speaking. In Richard Bauman and Joel Sherzer (eds.), *Explorations in the Ethnography of Speaking*, 2nd edn., pp. 433–51. Cambridge: Cambridge University Press.

Kapchan, Deborah. 1993. Hybridization and the Marketplace: Emerging Paradigms in Folkloristics. *Western Folklore* 52: 303–26.

1995. Performance. *Journal of American Folklore* 108: 479–508.

Kuiper, Koenraad 1992. The Oral Tradition in Auction Speech. *American Speech* 67: 279–89.

Kuiper, Koenraad and Haggo, Douglas 1984. Livestock Auctions, Oral Poetry, and Ordinary Language. *Language in Society* 13: 205–34.

Lindenfeld, Jacqueline 1978. Communicative Patterns at French Marketplaces. *Semiotica* 23: 280–90.

1990. *Speech and Sociability at French Urban Marketplaces*. Amsterdam and Philadelphia: Benjamins.

Mitchell, T. F. 1957. The Language of Buying and Selling in Cyrenaica: a Situational Statement. *Hespéris* 44: 31–71.

Santamaría, Francisco J. 1983. *Diccionario de Mejicanismos*. Mexico City: Editorial Porrua.

Shesgreen, Sean (ed.) 1990. *The Criers and Hawkers of London: Engravings and Drawings by Marcellus Laroon*. Stanford: Stanford University Press.

4 THE QUESTION OF GENRE

Bakhtin, Mikhail M. 1986. *Speech Genres and other Essays*. Edited by M. Holmquist and C. Emerson, translated by V. McGee. Austin: University of Texas Press.

Bell, Allan 1984. Language Style as Audience Design. *Language in Society* 13(2): 145–204.

Biber, Douglas and Finegan, Edward (eds.) 1994. *Sociolinguistic Perspectives on Register*. Oxford: Oxford University Press.

Briggs, Charles and Bauman, Richard 1992. Genre, Intertextuality, and Social Power. *Journal of Linguistic Anthropology* 2(2): 131–72.

Brown, Gillian and Yule, George 1983. *Discourse Analysis*. Cambridge: Cambridge University Press.

Ferguson, Charles A. 1994. Dialect, Register, and Genre: Working Assumptions about Conventionalization. In Douglas Biber and Edward Finegan (eds.), *Sociolinguistic Perspectives on Register*, pp. 15–30. Oxford: Oxford University Press.

Goffman, Erving 1981. *Forms of Talk*. Philadelphia: University of Pennsylvania Press.

Gumperz, John J. 1982. *Discourse Strategies*. Cambridge: Cambridge University Press.

Hymes, Dell. 1974a. *Foundations in Sociolinguistics: an Ethnographic Approach*. Philadelphia: University of Pennsylvania Press.

   1974b. Ways of Speaking. In Richard Bauman and Joel Sherzer (eds.), *Explorations in the Ethnography of Speaking*, pp. 433–51. Cambridge: Cambridge University Press.

Ochs, Elinor, Smith, Ruth and Taylor, Carolyn 1996. Detective Stories at Dinnertime: Problem-solving Through Co-narration. In D. C. Brenneis and R. K. S. Macaulay (eds.), *The Matrix of Language*, pp. 39–55. Boulder: Westview.

Rickford, John R. and McNair-Knox, Faye 1993. Addressee- and Topic-influenced Style Shift: a Quantitative Sociolinguistic Study. In Douglas Biber and Edward Finegan (eds.), *Sociolinguistic Perspectives on Register*, pp. 235–76. Oxford: Oxford University Press.

Schiffrin, Deborah 1994. Making a List. *Discourse Processes* 17: 377–406.

Urban, Greg 1991. *A Discourse-Centered Approach to Culture: Native South American Myths and Rituals*. Austin: University of Texas Press.

5 THE ANATOMY OF STYLE-SHIFTING

Anshen, Frank 1969. Speech Variation among Negroes in a Small Southern Community. Dissertation, New York University.

Bell, Allan 1984. Language Style as Audience Design. *Language in Society* 13(2): 145–204.

Bortoni-Ricardo, Stella M. 1985. *The Urbanization of Rural Dialect Speakers: a Sociolinguistic Study in Brazil*. Cambridge: Cambridge University Press.

Coupland, Nikolas 1980. Style-shifting in a Cardiff Work-setting. *Language in Society* 9(1): 1–12.

Cukor-Avila, Patricia 1995. The Evolution of Rural AAVE in a Texas Community: an Ethnolinguistic Study. PhD dissertation, University of Michigan.

Douglas-Cowie, Ellen 1978. Linguistic Code-switching in a Northern Irish Village: Social Interaction and Social Ambition. In Peter Trudgill (ed.), *Sociolinguistic Patterns in British English*, pp. 37–51. London: Edwin Arnold.

Eisikovits, Edina 1981. Inner-Sydney English: an Investigation of Grammatical Variation in Adolescent Speech. Dissertation, University of Sydney.

Gumperz, John J. 1964. Linguistic and Social Interaction in Two Communities. In John J. Gumperz and Dell Hymes (eds.), *The Ethnography of Communication*. *American Anthropologist* 66(6): 137–53.

Guy, Gregory 1980. Variation in the Group and the Individual: the Case of Final

Stop Deletion. In William Labov (ed.), *Locating Language in Time and Space*, pp. 1–36. New York: Academic Press.

Hindle, Donald M. 1980. The Social and Structural Conditioning of Phonetic Variation. PhD thesis, University of Pennsylvania.

Joos, Martin 1961. *The Five Clocks*. New York: Harcourt, Brace and World.

Kenyon, John 1948. Cultural Levels and Functional Varieties of English. *College English* 10: 31–6. (Reprinted in Harold B. Allen (ed.), *Readings in Applied English Linguistics*. 2nd edn., pp. 294–302. New York: Appleton-Century-Crofts.)

Labov, William 1963. The Social Motivation of a Sound Change. *Word* 19: 273–309.

   1964. Stages in the Acquisition of Standard English. In Roger W. Shuy (ed.), *Social Dialects and Language Learning*, pp. 77–103. Champaign, IL: National Council of Teachers of English. (Reprinted in Harold B. Allen and Gary Underwood (eds.), *Readings in American Dialectology*, pp. 473–98. New York: Appleton-Century-Crofts, 1971.)

   1965. On the Mechanism of Linguistic Change. *Georgetown Monographs on Language and Linguistics* 18: 91–114. (Also in William Labov (ed.), *Sociolinguistic Patterns*, ch. 7. Philadelphia: University of Pennsylvania Press, 1972.)

   1966a. *The Social Stratification of English in New York City*. Washington, DC: Center for Applied Linguistics.

   1966b. Hypercorrection by the Lower Middle Class as a Factor in Linguistic Change. In William Bright (ed.), *Sociolinguistics*, pp. 84–113. The Hague: Mouton. (Also in William Labov (ed.), *Sociolinguistic Patterns*, pp. 122–42. Philadelphia: University of Pennsylvania Press, 1972.)

   1972. The Linguistic Consequences of Being a Lame. *Language in Society* 2: 81–115. (Also in William Labov, *Language in the Inner City: Studies in the Black English Vernacular*, pp. 255–97. Philadelphia: University of Pennsylvania Press, 1972.)

   1984. Field Methods of the Project on Linguistic Change and Variation. In John Baugh and Joel Sherzer (eds.), *Language in Use*, pp. 28–53. Englewood Cliffs: Prentice Hall.

   1993. The Unobservability of Structure. Paper given at 22nd Annual Conference on New Ways of Analyzing Variation in English, Ottawa.

Labov, William, Cohen, Paul, Robbins, Clarence and Lewis, J. 1968. A Study of the Non-standard English of Negro and Puerto Rican Speakers in New York City. *Cooperative Research Report 3288*, Vols. I and II. Philadelphia: US Regional Survey (Linguistics Laboratory, University of Pennsylvania).

Labov, William and Harris, Wendell A. 1986. De Facto Segregation of Black and White Vernaculars. In David Sankoff (ed.), *Diversity and Diachrony*, pp. 45–58. Philadelphia: Benjamins.

Modaressi-Tehrani, Yahya 1978. A Sociolinguistic Analysis of Modern Persian. Doctoral dissertation, University of Kansas.

Payne, Arvilla 1976. The Acquisition of the Phonological System of a Second Dialect. Dissertation, University of Pennsylvania.

Poplack, Shana 1978. On Dialect Acquisition and Communicative Competence: the Case of Puerto Rican Bilinguals. *Language in Society* 7: 89–104.

Preston, Dennis R. 1989. Style, Status, Change: Three Sociolinguistic Axioms.

Paper given at the 18th Annual Conference on New Ways of Analyzing Variation in English, Durham, NC.

Prince, Ellen F. 1987. Sarah Gorby, Yiddish Folksinger: a Case Study of Dialect Shift. Sociology of Jewish Languages. *International Journal of the Sociology of Language* 67: 83–116.

Roberts, Julia 1993. The Acquisition of Variable Rules: t,d Deletion and -ing Production in Preschool Children. Dissertation, University of Pennsylvania.

Trudgill, Peter 1974. *The Social Differentiation of English in Norwich.* Cambridge: Cambridge University Press.

Van den Broeck, Jef 1977. Class Differences in Syntactic Complexity in the Flemish Town of Maaseik. *Language in Society* 6: 149–82.

6   A DISSECTION OF STYLE-SHIFTING

Baugh, John 1983. *Black Street Speech: its History, Structure, and Survival.* Austin: University of Texas Press.

Bell, Allan 1984. Language Style as Audience Design. *Language in Society* 13(2): 145–204.

Chomsky, Noam and Halle, Morris 1968. *The Sound Patterns of English.* New York: Harper and Row.

Coupland, Nikolas 1980. Style-shifting in a Cardiff Work-setting. *Language in Society* 9(1): 1–12.

Ervin-Tripp, Susan M. 1972. On Sociolinguistic Rules: Alternation and Co-occurrence. In John J. Gumperz and Dell Hymes (eds.), *Directions in Sociolinguistics: the Ethnography of Communication,* pp. 213–50. New York: Holt, Rinehart and Winston.

Gal, Susan 1979. *Language Shift: Social Determinants of Linguistic Change in Bilingual Austria.* New York: Academic Press.

Giles, Howard and Powesland, Peter F. 1975. *Speech Style and Social Evaluation.* London: Academic Press.

Kozol, Jonathan 1991. *Savage Inequalities.* New York: Basic.

Labov, William 1966. *The Social Stratification of English in New York City.* Washington, DC: Center for Applied Linguistics.

  1972a. *Sociolinguistic Patterns.* Philadelphia: University of Pennsylvania Press.

  1972b. *Language in the Inner-City: Studies in the Black English Vernacular.* Philadelphia: University of Pennsylvania Press.

  1984. Field Methods of the Project on Linguistic Change and Variation. In John Baugh and Joel Sherzer (eds.), *Language in Use,* pp. 84–112. Englewood Cliffs, NJ: Prentice Hall.

Rickford, John R. 1997. Unequal Partnership: Sociolinguistics and the African American Speech Community. *Language in Society* 26: 161–97.

Trudgill, Peter 1981. Linguistic Accommodation: Sociolinguistic Observation on a Sociopsychological Theory. In D. S. Masek, R. A. Hendric and M. F. Miller (eds.), *Papers from the Parasession on Language and Behavior,* pp. 218–37. Chicago: Chicago Linguistic Society.

Walters, Keith 1987. Linguistic Variation and Change in Korba, a Small Tunisian Town. PhD thesis, University of Texas, Austin.

Wolfson, Nessa 1976. Speech Events and Natural Speech. *Language in Society* 5: 81–9.

7 STYLE AND SOCIAL MEANING

California Style Collective 1993. Personal and Group Style. Paper presented at 22nd Annual Conference on New Ways of Analyzing Variation in English, Ottawa.

Eckert, Penelope 1987. Relative Values of Opposing Variables. In Keith M. Denning, Sharon Inkelas, Faye McNair-Knox and John R. Rickford (eds.), *NWAV–XV at Stanford*, pp. 101–10. Department of Linguistics, Stanford University.

1996. (ay) goes to the city: Reminiscences of Martha's Vineyard. In John Baugh, C. Feagin, Gregory Guy and Deborah Schiffrin (eds.), *Towards a Social Science of Language: Festschrift for William Labov*, pp. 47–68. Amsterdam and Philadelphia: Benjamins.

2000. *Linguistic Variation as Social Practice*. Oxford: Blackwell.

Labov, William 1966. *Social Stratification of English in New York City*. Washington, DC: Center for Applied Linguistics.

Mendoza-Denton, Norma 1997. Chicana/Mexicana Identity and Linguistic Variation: an Ethnographic and Sociolinguistic Study of Gang Affiliation in an Urban High School. PhD thesis, Stanford University.

Schilling-Estes, Natalie 1998. Investigating "Self-conscious Speech": the Performance Register in Ocracoke English. *Language in Society* 27: 53–83.

8 ZEROING IN ON MULTIFUNCTIONALITY AND STYLE

Aijmer, Karin 1986. Why is *actually* so Popular in Spoken English? In Gunnel Tottie and Ingegard Bäcklund (eds.), *English in Speech and Writing: a Symposium*, pp. 119–29. Uppsala: Almqvist and Wiksell.

Baker, Philip and Syea, Anand (eds.) 1996. *Changing Meanings, Changing Functions: Paper Relating to Grammaticalization in Contact Languages*. London: University of Westminster Press.

Biber, Douglas and Finegan, Edward 1988. Adverbial Stance Types in English. *Discourse Processes* 11: 1–34.

Blakemore, Diane 1987. *Semantic Constraints on Relevance*. Oxford: Blackwell.

Blass, Regina 1990. *Relevance Relations in Discourse*. Cambridge: Cambridge University Press.

Boxer, Diana 1993. *Complaining and Commiserating: a Speech Act View of Solidarity in Spoken American English*. New York: Peter Lang.

Brinton, Laurel J. 1996. *Pragmatic Markers in English: Grammaticalization and Discourse Function*. Berlin: Mouton de Gruyter.

Bruyn, Adrienne 1995. *Grammaticalization in Creoles: the Development of Determiners and Relative Clauses in Sranan*. Amsterdam: Institute for Functional Research into Language and Language Use.

Bybee, Joan L. and Pagliuca, William 1987. The Evolution of Future Meaning. In Anna Giacalone Ramat, Onofrio Carruba and Giuliano Bernini (eds.), *Papers from the 7th International Conference on Historical Linguistics*, pp. 108–22. Amsterdam: Benjamins.

Chafe, Wallace 1986. Evidentiality in English Conversation and Academic Writing. In Wallace Chafe and Johanna Nichols (eds.), *Evidentiality: the Linguistic Coding of Epistemology*, pp. 261–72. Norwood, NJ: Ablex.

Dancygier, Barbara 1992. Two Metatextual Operators: Negation and Conditionality in English and Polish. In Laura A. Buszard-Welcher, Lionel Wee and William Weigel (eds.), *Proceedings of the Eighteenth Meeting of the Berkeley Linguistics Society*, pp. 61–75. Berkeley, CA: Berkeley Linguistics Society.

Dowty, David 1991. Thematic Proto-roles and Argument Selection. *Language* 67: 547–619.

Ducrot, Oswald 1980[1972]. *Dire et ne pas dire*, 2nd edn. Paris: Hermann.

Ernst, Thomas Byden 1984. *Toward an Integrated Theory of Adverb Position in English*. University of Indiana Linguistics Club.

Ferrara, Kathleen 1997. Form and Function of the Discourse Marker *anyway*: Implications for Discourse Analysis. *Linguistics* 35: 343–78.

Finegan, Edward and Biber, Douglas 1994. Register and Social Dialect Variation: an Integrated Approach. In Douglas Biber and Edward Finegan (eds.), *Sociolinguistic Perspectives on Register*, pp. 315–47. New York: Oxford University Press.

Fraser, Bruce 1988. Types of English Discourse Markers. *Acta Linguistica Hungarica* 38: 19–33.

Givón, Talmy 1979. *On Understanding Grammar*. New York: Academic Press.

Greenbaum, Sidney 1969. *Studies in English Adverbial Usage*. London: Longman.

Heine, Bernd, and Reh, Mechthild 1984. *Grammaticalization and Reanalysis in African Languages*. Hamburg: Helmut Buske.

Heine, Bernd, Claudi, Ulrike and Hünnemeyer, Friederike 1991. *Grammaticalization: a Conceptual Framework*. Chicago: University of Chicago Press.

Hopper, Paul J. and Traugott, Elizabeth Closs 1993. *Grammaticalization*. Cambridge: Cambridge University Press.

Horn, Laurence R. 1985. Metalinguistic Negation and Pragmatic Ambiguity. *Language* 61: 121–74.

Jackendoff, Ray 1972. *Semantic Interpretation in Generative Grammar*. Cambridge, MA: MIT Press.

Labov, William 1974. On the Use of the Present to Explain the Past. In Luigi Heilmann (ed.), *Proceedings of the 11th International Congress of Linguists*, pp. 825–52. Bologna: Mulino.

Lavandera, Beatriz 1978. Where Does the Sociolinguistic Variable Stop? *Language in Society* 7: 171–82.

Lehmann, Christian 1995[1982]. *Thoughts on Grammaticalization*. Munich: Lincom Europa. (Originally published as *Thoughts on Grammaticalization: a Programmatic Sketch*, vol. I (Arbeiten des Kölner Universalienprojekts 49). University of Cologne.)

Lightfoot, David 1991. *How to Set Parameters: Arguments from Language Change*. Cambridge, MA: MIT Press.

Lipari, Lisbeth 1996. Journalistic Authority: Textual Strategies of Legitimation. *Journalism and Mass Communication Quarterly* 73: 821–34.

Macaulay, Ronald K. S. 1995. The Adverbs of Authority. *English World-Wide* 16: 37–60.

Meillet, Antoine 1958[1912]. L'évolution des formes grammaticales. In *Linguistique historique et linguistique générale*, pp. 130–48. Paris: Champion. (Originally published in *Scientia* (Rivista di Scienza) 12(26): 6.)

Pagliuca, William (ed.) 1994. *Perspectives on Grammaticalization*. Amsterdam: Benjamins.

Pérez, Aveline 1990. Time in Motion: Grammaticalisation of the *be going to* Construction in English. *La Trobe University Working Papers in Linguistics* 3: 49–64.

Powell, Mava Jo 1992. The Systematic Development of Correlated Interpersonal and Metalinguistic Uses in Stance Adverbs. *Cognitive Linguistics* 3: 75–110.

Prince, Ellen F. 1987. Sarah Gorby, Yiddish Folksinger: a Case Study of Dialect Shift. *International Journal of the Sociology of Language* 67: 83–116.

Rickford, John R. 1992. Grammatical Variation and Divergence in Vernacular Black English. In Marinel Gerritsen and Dieter Stein (eds.), *Internal and External Factors in Syntactic Change*, pp. 175–200. Berlin: Mouton de Gruyter.

Roberts, Ian G. 1992/93. A Formal Account of Grammaticalization in the History of Romance Futures. *Folia Linguistica Historica* 13: 219–58.

Schiffrin, Deborah 1987. *Discourse Markers*. Cambridge: Cambridge University Press.

  1990. Between Text and Context: Deixis, Anaphora, and the Meaning of *then*. *Text* 10: 245–70.

Sweetser, Eve E. 1990. *From Etymology to Pragmatics: Metaphorical and Cultural Aspects of Semantic Structure*. Cambridge: Cambridge University Press.

Thompson, Sandra A. and Mulac, Anthony 1991. A Quantitative Perspective on the Grammaticization of Epistemic Parentheticals in English. In Traugott and Heine, pp. 313–29.

Traugott, Elizabeth Closs 1995. The Role of the Development of Discourse Markers in a Theory of Grammaticalization. Paper given at the 12th International Conference on Historical Linguistics, Manchester.

  in press. Constructions in Grammaticalization. In Brian Joseph and Richard Janda (eds.), *Handbook of Historical Linguistics*. Oxford: Blackwell.

Traugott, Elizabeth Closs and Heine, Bernd (eds.) 1991. *Approaches to Grammaticalization*, 2 vols. Amsterdam: Benjamins.

Weinreich, Uriel, Labov, William and Herzog, Marvin I. 1968. Empirical Foundations for a Theory of Language Change. In W. P. Lehmann and Y. Malkiel (eds.), *Directions for Historical Linguistics: a Symposium*, pp. 95–189. Austin: University of Texas Press.

9 BACK IN STYLE

Bakhtin, Mikhael M. 1981. *The Dialogic Imagination*, edited by M. Holquist, translated by C. Emerson and M. Holquist. Austin: University of Texas Press.

  1986. *Speech Genres and other Late Essays*. Austin: University of Texas Press.

Bell, Allan 1977. The Language of Radio News in Auckland: a Sociolinguistic Study of Style, Audience and Subediting Variation. PhD thesis, Auckland: University of Auckland.

  1984. Language Style as Audience Design. *Language in Society* 13(2): 145–204.

  1990. Audience and Referee Design in New Zealand Media Language. In Allan Bell and Janet Holmes (eds.), *New Zealand Ways of Speaking English*, pp. 165–94. Bristol: Multilingual Matters, and Wellington: Victoria University Press.

1991. Audience Accommodation in the Mass Media. In Howard Giles, Justine Coupland and Nikolas Coupland (eds.), *Contexts of Accommodation: Developments in Applied Sociolinguistics*, pp. 69–102. Cambridge: Cambridge University Press.

1992. Hit and Miss: Referee Design in the Dialects of New Zealand Television Advertisements. *Language and Communication* 12(3/4): 327–40.

1994. The Origins of Style. Paper presented to Workshop on Language Style and Attitudes, Sociolinguistics Symposium 10, Lancaster University.

1995. Review of Douglas Biber and Edward Finegan (eds), 1994: *Sociolinguistic Perspectives on Register. Language in Society* 24(2): 265–70.

Bell, Allan and Johnson, Gary 1997. Towards a Sociolinguistics of Style. *University of Pennsylvania Working Papers in Linguistics* 4(1): 1–21.

Biber, Douglas and Finegan, Edward (eds.), 1994. *Sociolinguistic Perspectives on Register*. Oxford: Oxford University Press.

Blom, Jan-Petter and Gumperz, John J. 1972. Social Meaning in Linguistic Structure: Code-switching in Norway. In John J. Gumperz and Dell Hymes (eds.), *Directions in Sociolinguistics: the Ethnography of Communication*, pp. 407–34. New York: Holt, Rinehart and Winston.

Brown, Penelope and Levinson, Stephen C. 1987. *Politeness: some Universals in Language Usage*, 2nd edn. Cambridge: Cambridge University Press.

Brown, Roger and Gilman, Albert 1960. The Pronouns of Power and Solidarity. In Thomas A. Sebeok (ed.), *Style in Language*, pp. 253–76. Cambridge, MA: MIT Press.

Clark, Herbert H. and Carlson, Thomas B. 1982. Hearers and Speech Acts. *Language* 58(2): 332–73.

Coupland, Nikolas 1980. Style-shifting in a Cardiff Work-setting. *Language in Society* 9(1): 1–12.

1984. Accommodation at Work: some Phonological Data and their Implications. *International Journal of the Sociology of Language* 46: 49–70.

1996. Hark, Hark the Lark: Multiple Voicing in DJ Talk. In David Graddol, Dick Leith and Joan Swann (eds.), *English: History, Diversity and Change*, pp. 325–30. Milton Keynes: Open University; London: Routledge.

Coupland, Nikolas, Coupland, Justine, Giles, Howard and Henwood, Karen 1988. Accommodating the Elderly: Invoking and Extending a Theory. *Language in Society* 17(1): 1–41.

Dorian, Nancy C. 1981. *Language Death: the Life Cycle of a Scottish Gaelic Dialect*. Philadelphia: University of Pennsylvania Press.

Douglas-Cowie, Elaine 1978. Linguistic Code-switching in a Northern Irish Village: Social Interaction and Social Ambition. In Peter Trudgill (ed.), *Sociolinguistic Patterns in British English*, pp. 37–51. London: Edward Arnold.

Duranti, Alessandro and Goodwin, Charles (eds.) 1992. *Rethinking Context: Language as an Interactive Phenomenon*. Cambridge: Cambridge University Press.

Ervin-Tripp, Susan M. 1972. On Sociolinguistic Rules: Alternation and Co-occurrence. In John J. Gumperz and Dell Hymes (eds.), *Directions in Sociolinguistics: the Ethnography of Communication*, pp. 213–50. New York: Holt, Rinehart and Winston.

Ferguson, Charles A. and Gumperz, John J. (eds.) 1960. *Linguistic Diversity in*

South Asia (*International Journal of American Linguistics* 26(3)). Bloomington: Indiana University Press.

Finegan, Edward and Biber, Douglas 1994. Register and Social Dialect Variation: an Integrated Approach. In Douglas Biber and Edward Finegan (eds.), *Sociolinguistic Perspectives on Register*, pp. 315–47. Oxford: Oxford University Press.

Fishman, Joshua A. 1972. Domains and the Relationship between Micro- and Macrosociolinguistics. In John J. Gumperz and Dell Hymes (eds.), *Directions in Sociolinguistics: the Ethnography of Communication*, pp. 235–53. New York: Holt, Rinehart and Winston.

Gal, Susan 1979. *Language Shift: Social Determinants of Linguistic Change in Bilingual Austria*. New York: Academic Press.

Giles, Howard and Powesland, Peter F. 1975. *Speech Style and Social Evaluation*. London: Academic Press.

Gumperz, John J. 1967. On the Linguistic Markers of Bilingual Communication. *Journal of Social Issues* 23(1): 48–57.

Holmes, Janet 1995. *Women, Men and Politeness*. London: Longman.

Holmes, Janet, Bell, Allan and Boyce, Mary 1991. *Variation and Change in New Zealand English: a Social Dialect Investigation* (Project report to the Foundation for Research, Science & Technology). Wellington: Victoria University, Linguistics Department.

Labov, William 1972. *Sociolinguistic Patterns*. Philadelphia: University of Pennsylvania Press.

1984. Field Methods of the Project on Linguistic Change and Variation. In John Baugh and Joel Sherzer (eds.), *Language in Use: Readings in Sociolinguistics*, pp. 28–53. Englewood Cliffs, NJ: Prentice-Hall.

Lambert, Wallace E. 1967. A Social Psychology of Bilingualism. *Journal of Social Issues* 23(2): 91–109.

Le Page, Robert B. 1980. Projection, Focussing, Diffusion. *York Papers in Linguistics* 9: 9–31.

McEntegart, Damian and Le Page, Robert B. 1982. An Appraisal of the Statistical Techniques used in the Sociolinguistic Survey of Multilingual Communities. In Suzanne Romaine (ed.), *Sociolinguistic Variation in Speech Communities*, pp. 105–24. London: Edward Arnold.

Meyerhoff, Miriam 1994. Sounds Pretty Ethnic, eh?: a Pragmatic Particle in New Zealand English. *Language in Society* 23(3): 367–88.

Myers-Scotton, Carol 1993. *Social Motivations for Code-switching: Evidence from Africa*. Oxford: Clarendon.

Preston, Dennis R. 1991. Sorting out the Variables in Sociolinguistic Theory. *American Speech* 66(1): 33–56.

Rampton, Ben 1995. *Crossing*. London: Longman.

Rickford, John R. and McNair-Knox, Faye 1994. Addressee- and Topic-influenced Style Shift: a Quantitative Sociolinguistic Study. In Douglas Biber and Edward Finegan (eds.), *Sociolinguistic Perspectives on Register*, pp. 235–76. Oxford: Oxford University Press.

Sacks, Harvey, Schegloff, Emanuel A. and Jefferson, Gail 1974. A Simplest Systematics for the Organization of Turn-taking for Conversation. *Language* 50: 696–735.

Schilling-Estes, Natalie 1998. Investigating "Self-conscious" Speech: the Performance Register in Ocracoke English. *Language in Society* 27(1): 53–83.

Te Taura Whiri i te Reo Maori/Maori Language Commission 1996. Ae Ranei, he Taonga tuku iho? National Maori Language Survey 1995: Provisional Findings. Wellington: Te Taura Whiri.

Thakerar, Jitendra N., Giles, Howard and Cheshire, Jenny 1982. Psychological and Linguistic Parameters of Speech Accommodation Theory. In Colin Fraser and Klaus R. Scherer (eds.), *Advances in the Social Psychology of Language*, pp. 205–55. Cambridge: Cambridge University Press.

Traugott, Elizabeth Closs and Romaine, Suzanne 1985. Some Questions for the Definition of "Style" in Sociohistorical Linguistics. *Folia Linguistica Historica* 6(1): 7–39.

Yaeger-Dror, Malcah 1991. Linguistic Evidence for Social Psychological Attitudes: Hyperaccommodation of (r) by Singers from a Mizrahi Background. *Language and Communication* 11(4): 309–31.

  1993. Linguistic Analysis of Dialect "Correction" and its Interaction with Cognitive Salience. *Language Variation and Change* 5(2): 189–224.

Youssef, Valerie 1993. Children's Linguistic Choices: Audience Design and Societal Norms. *Language in Society* 22(2): 257–74

10 PRIMITIVES OF A SYSTEM FOR "STYLE" AND "REGISTER"

Bell, Allan 1984. Language Style as Audience Design. *Language in Society* 13(2): 145–204.

  1991a. Audience Accommodation in the Mass Media. In Howard Giles, Justine Coupland and Nikolas Coupland (eds.), *Contexts of Accommodation: Developments in Applied Sociolinguistics*, pp. 69–102. Cambridge: Cambridge University Press.

  1991b. *Language in the News Media*. Oxford: Blackwell.

Ben Rafael, E. 1994. *Language Identity and Social Division: the Case of Israel*. Oxford: Clarendon; New York: Oxford University Press.

Biber, Douglas 1988. *Variation across Speech and Writing*. Cambridge: Cambridge University Press.

Biber, Douglas and Finegan, Edward (eds.) 1994. *Perspectives on Register: Situating Register Variation within Sociolinguistics*. Oxford: Oxford University Press.

Blom, Jan-Petter and Gumperz, John J. 1972. Social Meaning in Linguistic Structures. In John J. Gumperz and Dell Hymes (eds.), *Directions in Sociolinguistics: the Ethnography of Communication*, pp. 407–34. New York: Holt, Rinehart and Winston.

Brown, Penelope and Levinson, Stephen C. 1978. Universals of Language Usage: Politeness Phenomena. In E. Goody (ed.), *Questions and Politeness: Strategies in Social Interaction*, pp. 56–289. Cambridge: Cambridge University Press.

Brown, Roger and Gilman, Albert 1960. The Pronouns of Power and Solidarity. In Thomas Sebeok (ed.), *Style in Language*, pp. 253–76. Cambridge, MA: MIT Press.

Cheshire, Jenny 1982. *Variation in an English Dialect: a Sociolinguistic Study*. Cambridge: Cambridge University Press.

Cleary, B. 1968. *Ramona the Pest*. New York: Scholastic. (Read by Stockard Channing. Listening Library, 1990.)

Coupland, Nikolas 1984. Accommodation at Work. *International Journal of the Sociology of Language* 46: 49–70.

1985. "Hark, Hark the Lark": Social Motivations for Phonological Style-shifting. *Language and Communication* 5(3): 153–71.

1988. *Dialect in Use*. Cardiff: University of Wales Press.

Coupland, Nikolas and Giles, Howard (eds.) 1988. Communication Accommodation Theory: Recent Developments. Special issue of *Language and Communication* 9(3/4).

Eckert, Penelope 1989. *Jocks and Burnouts: Social Categories and Identity in the High School*. New York: Teachers" College Press.

Giles, Howard, Coupland, Justine and Coupland, Nikolas (eds.) 1991. *Contexts of Accommodation: Developments in Applied Sociolinguistics*. Cambridge: Cambridge University Press.

Giles, Howard and Coupland, Nikolas 1991. *Language: Contexts and Consequences*. Pacific Grove, CA: Brooks/Cole.

Goffman, Erving 1971. *Relations in Public*. New York: Harper and Row.

Hazen, Kirk 1996. Linguistic Preference and Prescriptive Dictum: on the Phonological and Morphological Justification of *ain't*. In Jennifer Arnold, Renee Blake, Brad Davidson, Scott Schwenter and Julie Solomon (eds.), *Sociolinguistic Variation: Data, Theory and Analysis*, pp. 101–12. Stanford: CSLI.

Hindle, Donald M. 1979. The Social and Situational Conditioning of Phonetic Variation. PhD thesis, University of Pennsylvania.

Hirschberg, J. 1990. Accent and Discourse Context: Assigning Pitch Accent in Synthetic Speech. *Proceedings of the Eighth National Conference on Artificial Intelligence*, vol. II, pp. 952–7. Cambridge, MA: MIT Press.

Keillor, Garrison. 1985. *Lake Wobegon Days*. New York: Penguin. (Read by Garrison Keillor, Minnesota Public Radio, 1986.)

Labov, William 1972. *Sociolinguistic Patterns*. Philadelphia: University of Pennsylvania Press.

Labov, William, Yaeger, Malcah and Steiner, R. 1972. *A Quantitative Study of Sound Change in Progress*. Philadelphia: US Regional Survey.

MacNeil, T. and Lehrer, J. 1988. MacNeil–Lehrer Report, broadcast on PBS. Debate between Bruce Babbitt and Evan Mecham.

Mendoza-Denton, Norma 1994. Multiple Membership and Stance Taking in Latina Adolescents' Conversation. Ms.

Ochs, Elinor 1992. Indexing Gender. In Alessandro Duranti and Charles Goodwin (eds.), *Rethinking Context*, pp. 336–58. Cambridge: Cambridge University Press.

O'Shaughnessy, D. and Allen, J. 1983. Linguistic Modality Effects on Fundamental Frequency. *Journal of the Acoustical Society of America* 74: 1155–71.

Papademetre, Leo 1994. Self-defined, Other-defined Cultural Identity: Logogenesis and Multiple-group Membership in a Greek Australian Sociolinguistic Community. *Journal of Multilingual and Multicultural Development* 15: 507–26.

Prince, Ellen F. 1987. Sara Gorby, Yiddish Folksinger: a Case Study of Dialect Shift. *International Journal of the Sociology of Language* 67: 83–116.

Rickford, John R. and McNair-Knox, Faye 1994. Addressee- and Topic-influenced Style Shift: a Quantitative Sociolinguistic Study. In Douglas Biber and Edward Finegan (eds.), *Perspectives on Register: Situating Register Variation within Sociolinguistics*, pp. 235–76. Oxford: Oxford University Press.

Sacks, Harvey 1992. *Harvey Sacks' Lectures on Conversation*, edited by Gail Jefferson, 2 vols. Oxford: Blackwell.

Sacks, Harvey and Jefferson, Gail 1964–65. "GTS-5"/Group Therapy Session #5, transcribed by Gail Jefferson.

Schegloff, Emmanuel and Jefferson, Gail 1968. "TG"/ "Two Girls," transcribed by Gail Jefferson.

  1972. "CH-4," transcribed by Gail Jefferson.

Schilling-Estes, Natalie 1998. Investigating "Self-conscious Speech": Performance Register in Ocracoke English. *Language in Society* 27: 53–83.

Tottie, Gunnel 1991. *Negation in English: a Study in Variation*. Cambridge: Cambridge University Press.

Trudgill, Peter 1972. Sex, Covert Prestige and Language Change in the Urban British English of Norwich. *Language in Society* 1: 179–96.

  1986. *Dialects in Contact*. Oxford: Blackwell.

Tyler, Anne 1988. *Breathing Lessons*. (Read by Jill Eikenberry, New York: Random House, 1990.)

Yaeger, Malcah 1974. Speaking Style: some Etic Realizations and their Significance. *Pennsylvania Working Papers on Linguistic Change and Variation* 1: 1.

Yaeger-Dror, Malcah 1985. Intonational Prominence on Negatives in English. *Language and Speech* 28: 197–230.

  1988. The Influence of Changing Group Vitality on Convergence toward a Dominant Norm. *Language and Communication* 8: 285–305.

  1991. Hypercorrection of (r) for Singers from a Mizrahi Background. *Language and Communication* 11(4): 309–31.

  1993. Linguistic Analysis of Dialect "Correction" and its Interaction with Cognitive Salience. *Language Variation and Change* 5: 189–224.

  1994. Linguistic Data Solving Social Psychological Questions: the Case for (resh) as a Measure of Ethnic Self-identification. *Israel Social Science Research* 9: 109–60.

  1996a. Register as a Variable in Prosodic Analysis: the Case of the English Negative. *Speech Communication* 19: 39–60.

  1996b. Intonation and Register Variation. In Jennifer Arnold, Renee Blake, Brad Davidson, Scott Schwenter and Julie Solomon (eds.), *Sociolinguistic Variation: Data, Theory and Analysis*, pp. 243–60. Stanford: CSLI.

  1997. Contraction of Negatives as Evidence of Variation in Register Specific Interactive Rules. *Language Variation and Change* 9: 1–38.

11 LANGUAGE, SITUATION, AND THE RELATIONAL SELF

Bakhtin, Mikhael M. 1981. *The Dialogic Imagination*, edited by M. Holquist, translated by C. Emerson and M. Holquist. Austin: University of Texas Press.

Bavelas, J. B., Black, A., Chovil, N. and Mullett, J. 1990. *Equivocal Communication*. Newbury Park: Sage.

Bell, Allan 1984. Language Style as Audience Design. *Language in Society* 13(2): 145–204.

    1994. Style: Still the Neglected Dimension? Paper presented at Sociolinguistics Symposium 10, Lancaster, April.

    1995. Review of Douglas Biber and Edward Finegan (eds.), *Sociolinguistic Perspectives on Register*, 1994. *Language in Society* 24(2): 265–70.

Biber, Douglas and Finegan, Edward (eds.) 1994. *Sociolinguistic Perspectives on Register*. Oxford: Oxford University Press.

Blom, Jan-Petter and Gumperz, John J. 1972. Social Meaning in Linguistic Structures: Code-switching in Norway. In John J. Gumperz and Dell Hymes (eds.), *Directions in Sociolinguistics: the Ethnography of Communication*, pp. 407–34. New York: Holt, Rinehart and Winston.

Brown, Penelope and Fraser, Colin 1979. Speech as a Marker of Situation. In Klaus R. Scherer and Howard Giles (eds.), *Social Markers in Speech*. Cambridge: Cambridge University Press.

Brown, Penelope and Levinson, Stephen C. 1987. *Politeness: some Universals in Language Usage*. Cambridge: Cambridge University Press.

Cheshire, Jenny 1982. *Variation in an English Dialect: a Sociolinguistic Study*. Cambridge: Cambridge University Press.

Coupland, Nikolas 1980. Style-shifting in a Cardiff Work-setting. *Language in Society* 9(1): 1–12.

    1984. Accommodation at Work: some Phonological Data and their Implications. *International Journal of the Sociology of Language* 46: 49–70.

    1985. "Hark, Hark the Lark": Social Motivations for Phonological Style-shifting. *Language and Communication* 5(3): 153–71.

    1988. *Dialect in Use*. Cardiff: University of Wales Press.

    1996. Accommodation Theory. In Jan Verscheuren, J-O. Ostman and Jan Blommaert (eds.), *Handbook of Pragmatics*, pp. 21–6. Amsterdam and Philadelphia: Benjamins.

Coupland, Nikolas and Nussbaum, J. (eds.) 1993. *Discourse and Lifespan Identity*. Newbury Park: Sage.

Coupland, Nikolas, Williams, A. and Garrett, P. 1994. The Social Meanings of Welsh English: Teachers' Stereotyped Judgements. *Journal of Multilingual and Multicultural Development* 15(6): 471–89.

Craig, Robert T. 1986. Goals in Discourse. In Donald G. Ellis and William A. Donohue (eds.), *Contemporary Issues in Language and Discourse Processes*. Hillsdale, NJ: Lawrence Erlbaum.

Duranti, Alessandro and Goodwin, Charles (eds.) 1992. *Rethinking Context: Language as an Interactive Phenomenon*, pp. 1–42. Cambridge: Cambridge University Press.

Eastman, C. M. and Stein, R. F. 1993. Language Display: Authenticating Claims to Social Identity. *Journal of Multilingual and Multicultural Development* 14(3): 187–202.

Emerson, C. and Holquist, M. (eds.) 1992. *M. M. Bakhtin: Speech Genres and Other Late Essays*. Austin: University of Texas Press.

Fairclough, Norman 1991. *Discourse and Social Change*. Cambridge: Polity.

    1994. *Critical Language Awareness*. London: Longman.

Finegan, Edward and Biber, Douglas 1994. Register and Social Dialect Variation:

an Integrated Approach. In Douglas Biber and Edward Finegan (eds.), *Sociolinguistic Perspectives on Register*, pp. 315–47. Oxford: Oxford University Press.

Fishman, Joshua A. 1977. Language and Ethnicity. In Howard Giles (ed.), *Language, Ethnicity and Intergroup Relations*, pp. 15–57. London: Academic Press.

Fowler, Roger 1977. *Linguistics and the Novel*. London: Methuen.

1991. *Language in the News*. London: Routledge.

Gee, James P. 1990. *Social Linguistics and Literacies: Ideology in Discourses*. London: Falmer.

Giddens, Anthony 1991. *Modernity and Self-Identity: Self and Society in the Late Modern Age*. Cambridge: Polity (in association with Basil Blackwell).

Giles, Howard 1970. Evaluative Reactions to Accents. *Educational Review* 22: 211–27.

Giles, Howard, Coupland, Justine and Coupland, Nikolas (eds.) 1991. *Contexts of Accommodation: Developments in Applied Sociolinguistics*. Cambridge: Cambridge University Press.

Giles, Howard and Coupland, Nikolas 1991. *Language: Contexts and Consequences*. London: Open University Press.

Giles, Howard and Powesland, Peter F. 1975. *Speech Style and Social Evaluation*. London: Academic Press.

Glassie, H. 1982. *Passing the Time in Ballymenone*. Philadelphia: University of Pennsylvania Press.

Goffman, Erving 1959. *The Presentation of Self in Everyday Life*. New York: Doubleday.

Halliday, Michael A. K. 1978. *Language as Social Semiotic*. London: Edward Arnold.

Hodge, R. and Kress, G. 1988. *Social Semiotics*. Cambridge: Polity.

Holmes, Janet 1990. Politeness Strategies in New Zealand Women's Speech. In Allan Bell and Janet Holmes (eds.), *New Zealand Ways of Speaking English*, pp. 252–75. Clevedon: Multilingual Matters.

Hymes, Dell 1972. Models of the Interaction of Language and Social Life. In John J. Gumperz and Dell Hymes (eds.), *Directions in Sociolinguistics: the Ethnography of Communication*, pp. 35–71. New York: Holt, Rinehart and Winston.

1974. Ways of Speaking. In Richard Bauman and Joel Sherzer (eds.), *Explorations in the Ethnography of Speaking*, pp. 433–51. Cambridge: Cambridge University Press.

Labov, William 1972. *Sociolinguistic Patterns*. Philadelphia: University of Pennsylvania Press.

Lavandera, Beatriz 1978. Where Does the Sociolinguistic Variable Stop? *Language in Society* 7(2): 171–82.

Lee, D. 1992. *Competing Discourses: Perspective and Ideology in Language*. London: Longman.

Macaulay, Ronald K. S. 1987. Polyphonic Monologues: Quoted Direct Speech in Oral Monologues. *IPrA Papers in Pragmatics* 1(2): 1–34.

1991. *Locating Dialect in Discourse: the Language of Honest Men and Bonnie Lasses in Ayr*. Oxford: Oxford University Press.

Mead, G. H. 1936. The Problem of Society: How we Become Selves. In M. H.

Moore (ed.), *Movements of Thought in the Nineteenth Century*, pp. 101–10. Los Angeles: University of California Press. (Reprinted in reduced form in Ben G. Blount (ed.), 1974, *Language, Culture and Society*, pp. 101–10. Cambridge, MA: Winthrop.)

Milroy, Lesley 1987. *Observing and Analysing Natural Language*. Oxford: Basil Blackwell.

Milroy, James and Milroy, Lesley 1985. *Authority in Language: Investigating Language Prescription and Standardisation*. London: Routledge and Kegan Paul.

Ochs, Elinor 1988. *Culture and Language Development*. Cambridge: Cambridge University Press.

Preston, Dennis R. 1989. *Perceptual Dialectology: Nonlinguists' Views of Areal Linguistics*. Dordrecht: Foris.

1991. Sorting out the Variables in Sociolinguistic Theory. *American Speech* 66: 33–56.

Rampton, Ben 1991. Interracial Panjabi in a British Adolescent Peer Group. *Language in Society* 20(3): 391–422.

Rickford, John and McNair-Knox, Faye 1994. Addressee- and Topic-influenced Style Shift: a Quantitative Sociolinguistic Study. In Douglas Biber and Edward Finegan (eds.), *Sociolinguistic Perspectives on Register*, pp. 235–76. Oxford: Oxford University Press.

Ryan, E. B. and Giles, Howard 1982. *Attitudes Towards Language Variation*. London: Edward Arnold.

Schegloff, Emanuel A. 1994. On Talk and its Institutional Occasions. In P. Drew and J. Heritage (eds.), *Talk at Work*, pp. 101–34. Cambridge: Cambridge University Press.

Shuklan, A. 1988. *Bakhtin School Papers*. Oxford: RPT.

Speidel, G. E. and Nelson, K. E. 1989. *The Many Faces of Imitation in Language Learning*. New York: Springer Verlag.

Tracy, Karen (ed.) 1991. *Understanding Face-to-Face Interaction: Issues Linking Goals and Discourse*. Hillsdale, NJ: Lawrence Erlbaum.

Tracy, Karen and Coupland, Nikolas (eds.) 1990. *Multiple Goals in Discourse*. Clevedon: Multilingual Matters.

Trudgill, Peter 1978. Introduction: Sociolinguistics and Sociolinguistics. In Peter Trudgill (ed.), *Sociolinguistic Patterns in British English*, pp. 1–18. London: Edward Arnold.

1986. *Dialects in Contact*. Oxford: Basil Blackwell.

Volosinov, Valentin Nikolaevic 1973. *Marxism and the Philosophy of Language*. Transl. Ladislav Matejka and I. R. Titunik. New York: Seminar. (First published 1929 and 1930.)

White, A. 1984. Bakhtin, Sociolinguistics and Deconstruction. In F. Gloversmith (ed.), *The Theory of Reading*, pp. 123–46. London: Harvester.

Williams, Glyn 1992. *Sociolinguistics: a Sociological Critique*. London and New York: Routledge.

Wolfowitz, C. 1991. *Language Style and Social Space: Stylistic Choice in Suriname Javanese*. Urbana and Chicago: University of Illinois Press.

Yaeger-Dror, Malcah 1991. Linguistic Evidence for Social Psychological Attitudes: Hyperaccommodation of (r) by Singers from a Mizrahi Background. *Language and Communication* 11(4): 309–31.

12 COUPLANDIA AND BEYOND

Baumeister, R. F. 1995. Self and Identity: an Introduction. In A. Tesser (ed.), *Advanced Social Psychology*, pp. 51–98. New York: McGraw Hill.

1998. The Self. In G. Lindzey, S. Fisk, and D. Gilbert (eds.), *Handbook of Social Psychology*, pp. 680–740. Reading, MA: Addison-Wesley.

Bourhis, R. Y., Giles, Howard, Leyens, J. P. and Tajfel, Henry 1979. Psycholinguistic Distinctiveness: Language Divergence in Belgium. In Howard Giles and R. N. St Clair (eds.), *Language and Social Psychology*, pp. 158–85. Oxford: Blackwell.

Burgoon, J. K. 1995. Cross-cultural and Intercultural Applications of Expectancy Violations Theory. In R. L. Wiseman (ed.), *Intercultural Communication Theories*, pp. 194–215. Thousand Oaks: Sage.

Cappella, J. N. and Greene, J. 1982. A Discrepancy-arousal Explanation of Mutual Influence in Expressive Behavior for Adult–Adult and Infant–Adult Interaction. *Communication Monographs* 49: 89–114.

Coupland, Nikolas 1980. Style-shifting in a Cardiff Work-setting. *Language in Society* 9(1): 1–12.

1984. Accommodation at Work: some Phonological Data and their Implications. *International Journal of the Sociology of Language* 46: 49–70.

1988. *Dialect in Use*. Cardiff: University of Wales Press.

Fishman, Joshua A. 1995. Good Conference in a Wicked World: on some Worrisome Problems in the Study of Language Maintenance and Language Shift. In W. Fase, K. Jaspaert and S. Kroon (eds.), *The State of Minority Languages*, pp. 311–17. Lisse: Swets and Zeitlinger.

Giles, Howard 1978. Linguistic Differentiation between Ethnic Groups. In Henry Tajfel (ed.), *Differentiation Between Social Groups*, pp. 361–93. London: Academic Press.

Giles, Howard and Hewstone, M. 1982. Cognitive Structures, Speech and Social Situations: Two Integrative Models. *Language Sciences* 4: 187–219.

Giles, Howard and Powesland, Peter F. 1975. *Speech Style and Social Evaluation*. London: Academic Press.

Giles, Howard, Scherer, Klaus R. and Taylor, D. M. 1979. Speech Markers in Social Interaction. In Klaus R. Scherer and Howard Giles (eds.), *Social Markers in Speech*, pp. 343–81. Cambridge: Cambridge University Press.

Giles, Howard and Street, R. 1985. Communicator Characteristics and Behavior. In M. L. Knapp and G. R. Miller (eds.), *Handbook of Interpersonal Communication*, pp. 205–61. Beverly Hills, CA: Sage.

Giles, Howard, and Williams, A. 1992. Accommodating Hypercorrection: a Communication Model. *Language and Communication* 12: 343–56.

Gudykunst, W. B. 1995. Anxiety/Uncertainty Management (AUM) Theory: Current Status. In R. L. Wiseman (ed.), *Intercultural Communication Theories*, pp. 8–58. Thousand Oaks: Sage.

Hecht, M. L. 1978. Toward a Conceptualization of Interpersonal Communication Satisfaction. *Quarterly Journal of Speech*, 64: 47–62.

Hopper, R. 1986. Speech Evaluation of Intergroup Dialect Differences: the Shibboleth Schema. In W. B. Gudykunst (ed.), *Intergroup Communication*, pp. 126–36. London: Edward Arnold.

Labov, William 1984. Intensity. In Deborah Schiffrin (ed.), *Meaning, Form, and Use in Context: Linguistic Applications*, pp. 43–70. Georgetown: Georgetown University Press.

Roger, D. and Bull, P. (eds.) 1988. *Conversation: an Interdisciplinary Perspective.* Clevedon: Multilingual Matters.

Schlenker, B. L. 1986. Self-identification: Toward an Integration of the Private and Public Self. In R. Baumeister (ed.), *Public Self and Private Self,* pp. 21–62. New York: Springer-Verlag.

Spencer, S. J., Josephs, R. A. and Steele, C. M. 1993. Low Self-esteem: the Uphill Struggle for Self-integrity. In R. F. Baumeister (ed.), *Self-Esteem: the Puzzle of Low Self-Regard*, pp. 21–36. New York: Plenum.

Street, R. L., Jr. 1982. Evaluation of Noncontent Speech Accommodation. *Language and Communication* 2: 13–31.

Thakerar, Jitendra N., Giles, Howard and Cheshire, Jenny 1982. Psychological and Linguistic Parameters of Speech Accommodation Theory. In Colin Fraser and Klaus R. Scherer (eds.), *Advances in the Social Psychology of Language*, pp. 205–55. Cambridge: Cambridge University Press.

Trudgill, Peter 1986. *Dialects in Contact.* Oxford: Blackwell.

Wiemann, J. M. 1977. Explication and Test of a Model of Communicative Competence. *Human Communication Research* 3: 195–213.

Yum, J. O. 1988. The Impact of Confucianism on Interpersonal Relationships and Communication Patterns in East Asia. *Communication Monographs* 55: 374–88.

Zahn, C. J. and Hopper, R. 1985. Measuring Language Attitudes: the Speech Evaluation Instrument. *Journal of Language and Social Psychology* 4: 113–23.

Zajonc, R. 1980. Feeling and Thinking: Preferences Need No Inferences. *American Psychologist* 35: 151–75.

13 STYLE AND STYLIZING FROM THE PERSPECTIVE OF A NON-AUTONOMOUS SOCIOLINGUISTICS

Bell, Allan 1984. Language Style as Audience Design. *Language in Society* 13(2): 145–204.

Clark, Ruth Anne, and Jesse G. Delia 1979. *Topoi* and Rhetorical Competence. *The Quarterly Journal of Speech* 65: 187–206.

Craig, Robert T. 1986. Goals in Discourse. In Donald G. Ellis and William A. Donohue (eds.), *Contemporary Issues in Language and Discourse Processes*, pp. 257–73. Hillsdale, NJ: Lawrence Erlbaum.

Eckert, Penelope 2000. *Linguistic Variation as Social Practice*. Oxford: Blackwell.

Ervin-Tripp, Susan M. 1972. On Sociolinguistic Rules: Alternation and Co-occurrence. In John J. Gumperz and Dell Hymes (eds.), *Directions in Sociolinguistics: the Ethnography of Communication*, pp. 213–50. New York: Holt, Rinehart and Winston.

Fischer, J. L. 1958. Social Influences on the Choice of a Linguistic Variant. *Word* 14: 47–56.

Hymes, Dell 1972a. The Scope of Sociolinguistics. In Roger W. Shuy (ed.), *Sociolinguistics: Current Trends and Prospects*, pp. 313–33 (Report of the 23rd annual round table on language and linguistics). Washington, DC: Georgetown University Press. (Reprinted in Hymes 1974: 193–209.)

1972b. Models of the Interaction of Language and Social Life. In John J. Gumperz and Dell Hymes (eds.), *Directions in Sociolinguistics: the Ethnography of Communication*, pp. 35–71. New York: Holt, Rinehart and Winston. (Reprinted in Hymes 1974: 29–66.)

1974. *Foundations in Sociolinguistics: an Ethnographic Approach.* Philadelphia: University of Pennsylvania.

Kiparsky, Paul 1972. Explanation in Phonology. In S. Peters (ed.), *Goals of Linguistic Theory*, pp. 189–227. Englewood Cliffs, NJ: Prentice Hall.

Labov, William 1972a. The Isolation of Contextual Styles. In William Labov, *Sociolinguistic Patterns*, pp. 70–109. Philadelphia: University of Pennsylvania Press.

1972b. The Study of Language in its Social Context. In William Labov, *Sociolinguistic Patterns*, pp. 183–259. Philadelphia: University of Pennsylvania.

Le Page, Robert B. and Tabouret-Keller, Andree 1985. *Acts of Identity: Creole-based Approaches to Language and Ethnicity.* Cambridge: Cambridge University Press.

Milroy, Lesley and Milroy, James 1992. Social Network and Social Class: Toward an Integrated Sociolinguistic Model. *Language in Society* 21(1): 1–26.

Preston, Dennis R. 1986. Fifty Some-odd Categories of Language Variation. *International Journal of the Sociology of Language* 57: 9–47.

Rickford, John R. 1979. Variation in a Creole Continuum: Quantitative and Implicational Approaches. PhD thesis, University of Pennsylvania.

1986. The Need for New Approaches to Social Class Analysis in Sociolinguistics. *Journal of Communication* 6: 215–21.

1987. *Dimensions of a Creole Continuum: History, Texts, and Linguistic Analysis of Guyanese Creole.* Stanford: Stanford University Press.

1992. Grammatical Variation and Divergence in Vernacular Black English. In Marinel Gerritsen and Dieter Stein (eds.), *Internal and External Factors in Syntactic Change*, pp. 175–200. The Hague: Mouton.

Rickford, John R. and McNair-Knox, Faye 1994. Addressee- and Topic-influenced Style Shift: a Quantitative Sociolinguistic Study. In Douglas Biber and Edward Finegan (eds.), *Sociolinguistic Perspectives on Register*, pp. 235–76. Oxford: Oxford University Press.

Rickford, John R. and Rickford, Russell J. 2000. *Spoken Soul: the Story of Black English.* New York: John Wiley.

Sankoff, Gillian 1980. *The Social Life of Language.* Philadelphia: University of Pennsylvania Press.

Tracy, Karen 1991. Introduction: Linking Communicator Goals with Discourse. In Karen Tracy (ed.), *Understanding Face-to-Face Interaction: Issues Linking Goals and Discourse*, pp. 1–17. Hillsdale, NJ: Lawrence Erlbaum.

Williams, Glyn 1992. *Sociolinguistics: a Sociological Critique.* London: Routledge.

14 REGISTER VARIATION AND SOCIAL DIALECT VARIATION

Ashby, William J. 1981. The Loss of the Negative Particle *ne* in French: a Syntactic Change in Progress. *Language* 57: 674–87.

Bell, Allan 1984. Language Style as Audience Design. *Language in Society* 13(2): 145–204.

1995. Review of Douglas Biber and Edward Finegan (eds.), *Sociolinguistic Perspectives on Register* (1994). *Language in Society* 24(2): 265–70.

Bernstein, B. 1971. *Class, Codes and Control*, vol. I. London: Routledge.

Biber, Douglas 1985. Investigating Macroscopic Textual Variation through Multi-feature/Multi-dimensional Analyses. *Linguistics* 23: 337–60.

1986. Spoken and Written Textual Dimensions in English: Resolving the Contradictory Findings. *Language* 62: 384–414.

1988. *Variation across Speech and Writing*. Cambridge: Cambridge University Press.

1994. An Analytical Framework for Register Studies. In Biber and Finegan, pp. 31–56.

1995. *Dimensions of Register Variation: a Cross-Linguistic Comparison*. Cambridge: Cambridge University Press.

Biber, Douglas, and Finegan, Edward 1989. Drift and the Evolution of English Style: a History of Three Genres. *Language* 65: 487–517.

(eds.) 1994. *Sociolinguistic Perspectives on Register*. Oxford: Oxford University Press.

Biber, Douglas, Johansson, Stig, Leech, Geoffrey N., Conrad, Susan and Finegan, Edward 1999. *The Longman Grammar of Spoken and Written English*. London: Longman.

Cedergren, Henrietta 1970. Patterns of Free Variation: the Language Variable. Ms.

1973. The Interplay of Social and Linguistic Factors in Panama. PhD thesis, Cornell University.

Chambers, J. K. 1992. Dialect Acquisition. *Language* 68: 673–705.

1995. *Sociolinguistic Theory*. Oxford: Blackwell.

Coupland, Nikolas 1983. Patterns of Encounter Management: Further Arguments for Discourse Variables. *Language in Society* 12: 459–76.

Crystal, David and Davy, Derek 1969. *Investigating English Style*. London: Longman.

Diller, Anne-Marie 1980. Subject NP Structure and Variable Constraints: the Case of *ne* Deletion. In Shuy and Shnukal, pp. 68–75.

Finegan, Edward and Biber, Douglas 1986. Toward a Unified Model of Sociolinguistic Prestige. In David Sankoff (ed.), *Diversity and Diachrony*, pp. 391–7. Amsterdam: Benjamins.

1989. Toward an Integrated Theory of Social Dialect Variation. Ms., Department of Linguistics, University of Southern California.

1994. Register and Social Dialect Variation: an Integrated Approach. In Biber and Finegan, pp. 315–47.

Givón, Talmy 1979. From Discourse to Syntax: Grammar as a Processing Strategy. In Talmy Givón (ed.), *Syntax and Semantics*, vol. XII: *Discourse and Syntax*, pp. 81–112. New York: Academic Press.

Gumperz, John J. 1964. Speech Variation and the Study of Indian Civilization. In Dell Hymes (ed.), *Language in Culture and Society*, pp. 416–28. New York: Harper and Row.

Guy, Gregory R. 1980. Variation in the Group and the Individual: the Case of Final Stop Deletion. In Labov, pp. 1–36.

Guy, Gregory and Braga, M. L. 1976. Number Concordance in Brazilian Portuguese. Paper presented at 5th Annual Conference on New Ways of Analyzing Variation in English, Washington, DC.

Halliday, Michael A. K. 1978. *Language as Social Semiotic: the Social Interpretation of Language and Meaning*. London: Edward Arnold.

Heath, Shirley Brice 1986. Sociocultural Contexts of Language Development. In Bilingual Education Office, California State Department of Education, *Beyond Language: Social and Cultural Factors in Schooling Language Minority Students*. Los Angeles: California State University, Los Angeles (Evaluation, Dissemination and Assessment Center).

Hymes, Dell 1973. Speech and Language: on the Origins and Foundations of Inequality Among Speakers. *Daedalus* 102: 59–85. (Reprinted in Einar Haugen and Morton Bloomfield (eds.), *Language as a Human Problem*, pp. 45–71. New York: Norton, 1974.)

Irvine, Judith T. 1990. Registering Affect: Heteroglossia in the Linguistic Expression of Emotion. In Catherine Lutz and Lila Abu-Lughod (eds.), *Language and the Politics of Emotion*, pp. 126–61. Cambridge: Cambridge University Press.

Johansson, Stig and Hofland, Knut 1989. *Frequency Analysis of English Vocabulary and Grammar: Based on the LOB Corpus*, 2 vols. Oxford: Clarendon.

Johansson, Stig, Leech, Geoffrey N. and Goodluck, Helen 1978. *Manual of Information to Accompany the Lancaster–Oslo/Bergen Corpus of British English, for Use with Digital Computers*. Oslo: Department of English, University of Oslo.

Joseph, John Earl 1987. *Eloquence and Power: the Rise of Language Standards and Standard Languages*. New York: Blackwell.

Kay, Paul 1977. Language Evolution and Speech Style. In Ben G. Blount and Mary Sanches (eds.), *Sociocultural Dimensions of Language Change*, pp. 21–33. New York: Academic Press.

Kemp, William, Pupier, Paul and Yaeger, Malcah 1980. A Linguistic and Social Description of Final Consonant Cluster Simplification in Montreal French. In Shuy and Shnukal, pp. 12–40.

Kroch, Anthony S. 1978. Toward a Theory of Social Dialect Variation. *Language in Society* 7: 17–36.

Kroch, Anthony S. and Hindle, Donald M. 1982. A Quantitative Study of the Syntax of Speech and Writing (Final report to the National Institute of Education. Grant no. G78–0169).

Kroch, Anthony S. and Small, Cathy 1978. Grammatical Ideology and its Effect on Speech. In David Sankoff (ed.), *Linguistic Variation: Models and Methods*, pp. 45–55. New York: Academic Press.

Labov, William 1965. On the Mechanism of Linguistic Change. *Georgetown Monographs on Language and Linguistics* 18: 91–114. (Reprinted in Labov 1972: 160–82.)

  1966. *The Social Stratification of English in New York City*. Washington, DC: Center for Applied Linguistics.

  1969. *The Study of Nonstandard English*. Champaign, IL: National Council of Teachers of English.

  1972. *Sociolinguistic Patterns*. Philadelphia: University of Pennsylvania Press.

  (ed.) 1980. *Locating Language in Time and Space*. New York: Academic Press.

1994. *Principles of Linguistic Change*, vol. I: *Internal Factors*. Oxford: Blackwell.

Lindenfeld, Jacqueline 1969. The Social Conditioning of Syntactic Variation in French. *American Anthropologist* 71: 890–8. (Reprinted in Joshua A. Fishman (ed.), *Advances in the Sociology of Language*, vol. II, pp. 84–113. The Hague: Mouton, 1972.)

Ma, Roxana and Herasimchuk, Eleanor 1968. The Linguistic Dimensions of a Bilingual Neighborhood. In Joshua A. Fishman, Roxana Ma and Robert Cooper (eds.), *Bilingualism in the Barrio*. Washington, DC: Office of Education.

Macaulay, Ronald K. S. 1991. *Locating Dialect in Discourse: the Language of Honest Men and Bonnie Lasses in Ayr*. Oxford: Oxford University Press.

Milroy, James 1982. Probing under the Tip of the Iceberg: Phonological "Normalization" and the Shape of Speech Communities. In Suzanne Romaine (ed.), *Sociolinguistic Variation in Speech Communities*, pp. 35–47. London: Edward Arnold.

1991. The Interpretation of Social Constraints on Variation in Belfast English. In Jenny Cheshire (ed.) *English Around the World: Sociolinguistic Perspectives*, pp. 75–85. Cambridge: Cambridge University Press.

Petyt, K. M. 1980. *The Study of Dialect*. London: Andre Deutsch.

Poplack, Shana 1980. The Notion of the Plural in Puerto Rican Spanish: Competing Constraints on (s) Deletion. In Labov, pp. 55–67.

Poplack, Shana and Walker, Douglas 1986. Going Through (*L*) in Canadian French. In David Sankoff, pp. 173–98.

Preston, Dennis R. 1991. Sorting Out the Variables in Sociolinguistic Theory. *American Speech* 66: 33–66.

Rickford, John R. and McNair-Knox, Faye 1994. Addressee- and Topic-influenced Style Shift: a Quantitative Sociolinguistic Study. In Biber and Finegan, pp. 235–76.

Romaine, Suzanne 1980. Stylistic Variation and Evaluative Reactions to Speech. *Language and Speech* 23: 213–32.

1994. *Language in Society: an Introduction to Sociolinguistics*. Oxford: Oxford University Press.

Sankoff, David (ed.) 1986. *Diversity and Diachrony*. Amsterdam: Benjamins.

Sankoff, Gillian and Cedergren, Henrietta 1971. Some Results of a Sociolinguistic Study of Montreal French. In Regna Darnell (ed.), *Linguistic Diversity in Canadian Society*, pp. 61–87. Edmonton: Linguistic Research.

(eds.) 1981. *Variation Omnibus*. Carbondale and Edmonton: Linguistic Research.

Scherre, Maria Marta Pereira 1981. La Variation de la Règle d'Accord du Nombre dans le Syntagme Nominal en Portugais. In Sankoff and Cedergren, pp. 125–33.

Scherre, Maria Marta Pereira and Naro, Anthony J. 1991. Marking in Discourse: "Birds of a Feather." *Language Variation and Change* 3: 23–32.

Shuy, Roger W. and Shnukal, Anna (eds.) 1980. *Language Use and the Uses of Language*. Washington, DC: Georgetown University Press.

Slobin, Dan I. 1979. *Psycholinguistics*, 2nd edn. Glenview, IL: Scott, Foresman.

Stampe, David 1969. The Acquisition of Phonetic Representation. *Papers from the Fifth Regional Meeting of the Chicago Linguistic Society*, pp. 443–54. Chicago: Department of Linguistics, University of Chicago.

Svartvik, Jan (ed.) 1990. *The London–Lund Corpus of Spoken English: Description and Research*. Lund: Lund University Press.

Terrell, Tracy D. 1981. Diachronic Reconstruction by Dialect Comparison of Variable Constraints. In Sankoff and Cedergren, pp. 115–24.

Trudgill, Peter 1974. *The Social Differentiation of English in Norwich*. Cambridge: Cambridge University Press.

Van den Broeck, Jef 1977. Class Differences in Syntactic Complexity in the Flemish Town of Maaseik. *Language in Society* 6: 149–81.

Williams, Frederick and Naremore, Rita C. 1969. Social Class Differences in Children's Syntactic Performance: a Quantitative Analysis of Field Study Data. *Journal of Speech and Hearing Research* 12: 778–93.

Wolfram, Walt A. 1969. *A Sociolinguistic Description of Detroit Negro Speech*. Washington, DC: Center for Applied Linguistics.

　　1995. Review of Douglas Biber and Edward Finegan (eds.), *Sociolinguistic Perspectives on Register* (1994). *Studies in Second Language Acquisition* 17(1): 98–9.

Yaeger-Dror, Malcah 1997. Contraction of Negatives as Evidence of Variance in Register-Specific Interactive Rules. *Language Variation and Change* 9: 1–36.

15 CONVERSATION, SPOKEN LANGUAGE, AND SOCIAL IDENTITY

Beal, J. 1993. The Grammar of Tyneside and Northumbrian English. In Milroy and Milroy, pp. 187–213.

Biber, Douglas and Finegan, Edward 1996. Register and Social Dialect Variation: a Reconsideration. Paper presented at the Style Workshop, Stanford University.

Brown, Gillian and Yule, George 1983. *Discourse Analysis*. Cambridge: Cambridge University Press.

Brown, Penelope and Lavinson, Stephen C. 1987. *Politeness: some Universals in Language Use*. Cambridge: Cambridge University Press.

Clark, Herbert H. and Schaeffer, E. F. 1989. Contributing to Discourse. *Cognitive Science* 259–94.

Clark, Herbert H. and Wilkes-Gibbs, D. 1986. Referring as a Collaborative Process. *Cognition* 22: 1–39.

Dressler, Wolfgang U. and Wodak, Ruth 1982. Sociophonological Methods in the Study of Sociolinguistic Variation in Viennese German. *Language in Society* 11(1): 339–70.

Edwards, V. 1993. The Grammar of Southern British English. In Milroy and Milroy, pp. 214–38.

Finegan, Edward and Biber, Douglas 1994. Register and Social Dialect Variation: an Integrated Approach. In Douglas Biber and Edward Finegan (eds.), *Sociolinguistic Perspectives on Register*, pp. 315–47. Oxford: Oxford University Press.

Harris, John 1993. The Grammar of Irish English. In Milroy and Milroy, pp. 139–86.

Heath, J. 1985. Discourse in the Field: Clause Structure in Ngandi. In Johanna Nichols and A. C. Woodbury (eds.), *Grammar Inside and Outside the Clause*, pp. 89–110. Cambridge: Cambridge University Press.

Henry, A. 1995. *Belfast English and Standard English: Dialect Variation and Parameter Setting*. Oxford: Oxford University Press.

Heritage, J. 1988. Current Developments in Conversation Analysis. In D. Roger and P. Bull (eds.), *Conversation*, pp. 21–47. Clevedon and Philadelphia: Multilingual Matters.

Kerswill, Paul 1987. Levels of Linguistic Variation in Durham. *Journal of Linguistics* 23: 25–49.

Lesser, R. and Milroy, Lesley 1993. *Linguistics and Aphasia: Psycholinguistic and Pragmatic Aspects of Intervention*. London: Longman.

Levinson, Stephen C. 1983. *Pragmatics*. Cambridge: Cambridge University Press.

Miller, J. 1993. The Grammar of Scottish English. In Milroy and Milroy, pp. 99–138.

Milroy, James 1982. Probing under the Tip of the Iceberg: Phonological "Normalization" and the Shape of Speech Communities. In Suzanne Romaine (ed.), *Sociolinguistic Variation in Speech Communities*, pp. 35–47. London: Arnold.

Milroy, James and Milroy, Lesley (eds.) 1993. *Real English: the Grammar of English Dialects of the British Isles*. London: Longman.

Milroy, Lesley 1987. *Observing and Analysing Natural Language*. Oxford: Blackwell.

1998. Gender, Social Class and Supralocal Norms: Dialect Leveling as Language Change. In Chalasani, Mani C., Grocer, Jennifer E. and Haney, Peter. J. (eds.), *Proceedings of the Fifth Annual Symposium about Language and Society*, pp. 38–49. University of Texas, Austin.

Ochs, Elinor 1979. Planned and Unplanned Discourse. In Talmy Givón (ed.), *Syntax and Semantics*, vol. XI, pp. 51–80. New York: Academic Press.

Poplack, Shana 1980. The Notion of the Plural in Puerto Rican Spanish: Competing Constraints on (s) Deletion. In William Labov (ed.), *Locating Language in Time and Space*, pp. 55–68. New York: Academic Press.

Tizard, B. and Hughes, M. 1984. *Young Children Learning at Home and at School*. London: Fontana.

Wells, G. 1985. *Language Development in the Preschool Years*. Cambridge: Cambridge University Press.

16 STYLE AND THE PSYCHOLINGUISTICS OF SOCIOLINGUISTICS

Adjémian, C. 1976. On the Nature of Interlanguage Systems. *Language Learning* 22: 297–320.

Alfaraz, Gabriela 1996. The Information-status of NPs in Overlapping Talk. 25th Annual Conference on New Ways of Analyzing Variation in English, Las Vegas.

Bayley, Robert and Preston, Dennis R. (eds.) 1996. *Second Language Variation and Linguistic Variation*. Amsterdam and Philadelphia: Benjamins.

Bell, Allan 1984. Style as Audience Design. *Language in Society* 13(2):145–204.

Bhatia, Tej K. and Ritchie, William C. 1996. Bilingual Language Mixing, Universal Grammar, and Second Language Acquisition. In William C. Ritchie and Tej K. Bhatia (eds.), *Handbook of Second Language Acquisition*, pp. 627–88. New York: Academic Press.

Biber, Douglas 1988. *Variation across Speech and Writing*. Cambridge: Cambridge University Press.

Bickerton, Derek 1971. Inherent Variability and Variable Rules. *Foundations of Language* 7: 457–92.

Blom, Jan-Petter and Gumperz, John J. 1972. Social Meaning in Linguistic Structure: Code-switching in Norway. In John J. Gumperz and Dell Hymes (eds.), *Directions in Sociolinguistics: the Ethnography of Communication*, pp. 407–34. New York: Holt, Rinehart and Winston.

Bloomfield, Leonard 1933. *Language*. New York: Holt, Rinehart and Winston.

Bolinger, Dwight 1972. *That's That*. The Hague: Mouton.

Butters, Ronald R. 1973. Acceptability Judgments for Double Modals in Southern Dialects. In Charles-J. N. Bailey and Roger W. Shuy (eds.), *New Ways of Analyzing Variation in English*, pp. 276–86. Washington, DC: Georgetown University Press.

Chambers, J. K. 1995. *Sociolinguistic Theory*. Oxford: Blackwell.

Chomsky, Noam 1988. *Language and Problems of Knowledge: the Managua Lectures*. Cambridge, MA: MIT Press.

Cook, Vivian J. 1990. Timed Comprehension of Binding in Advanced L2 Learners of English. *Language Learning* 40(4): 557–99.

DiPaolo, Marianna 1988. Pronunciation and Categorization in Sound Change. In Kathleen Ferrara, Becky Brown, Keith Walters, and John Baugh (eds.), *Linguistic Change and Contact*. Papers from the 16th Annual Conference on New Ways of Analyzing Variation in English, pp. 84–92. Department of Linguistics, University of Texas, Austin.

Eckert, Penelope 1988. Sound Change and Adolescent Social Structure. *Language in Society* 17: 183–207.

Fasold, Ralph W. 1972. Tense Marking in Black English. Arlington, VA: Center for Applied Linguistics.

1994. *The Distribution of Reflexives: Alternation, Violation, Variation*. Papers from the 23rd Annual Conference on New Ways of Analyzing Variation in English, Stanford.

Fasold, Ralph W., Bailey, Guy, Labov, William, Rickford, John R., Spears, Arthur K., Vaughn-Cooke, Fay Boyd, and Wolfram, Walt 1987. *Are Black and White Vernaculars Diverging?* Papers from the NWAVE–XIV Panel Discussion. *American Speech* 62(1): 3–80.

Finegan, Edward and Biber, Douglas 1994. Register and Social Dialect Variation: an Integrated Approach. In Douglas Biber and Edward Finegan (eds.), *Sociolinguistic Perspectives on Register*, pp. 315–47. Oxford: Oxford University Press.

1996. Register and Social Dialect Variation: a Reconsideration. NSF "Workshop on Style," Stanford University.

Fishman, Joshua A. 1972. *The Sociology of Language: an Interdisciplinary Social Science Approach to Language in Society*. Rowley, MA: Newbury House.

Flynn, Susan 1989. The Role of the Head-Initial/Head-Final Parameter in the Acquisition of English Relative Clauses by Adult Spanish and Japanese Speakers. In Susan M. Gass and Jaquelyn Schachter (eds.), *Linguistic Perspectives on Second Language Acquisition*, pp. 89–108. Cambridge: Cambridge University Press.

Fodor, Jerry A. and Bever, Thomas G. 1965. The Psychological Reality of Linguistic Segments. *Journal of Verbal Learning and Verbal Behavior* 4: 414–20.

Giles, Howard and Powesland, Peter F. 1975. *Speech Style and Social Evaluation.* London: Academic Press.

Givón, Talmy 1983. Topic Continuity in Discourse: an Introduction. In Talmy Givón (ed.), *Topic Continuity in Discourse: Quantified Cross-language Studies,* Typological Studies in Language 3, pp. 1–43. Amsterdam and Philadelphia: Benjamins.

Guy, Gregory R. 1980. Variation in the Group and the Individual: the Case of Final Stop Deletion. In William Labov (ed.), *Locating Language in Time and Space,* pp. 1–36. New York: Academic Press.

1991. Explanation in Variable Phonology: an Exponential Model of Morphological Constraints. *Language Variation and Change* 3(1): 1–22.

1994. Violable is Variable: Principles, Constraints, and Linguistic Variation. Paper from the 23rd Annual Conference on New Ways of Analyzing Variation, Stanford University.

Haeri, Niloofar 1994. The Linguistic Innovation of Women in Cairo. *Language Variation and Change* 6(1): 87–112.

Harris, John 1991. Conservatism Versus Substratal Transfer in Irish English. In Peter Trudgill and J. K. Chambers (eds.), *Dialects of English: Studies in Grammatical Variation,* pp. 191–212. London and New York: Longman.

Irvine, Judith T. 1974. Status Manipulation in the Wolof Greeting. In Richard Bauman and Joel Sherzer (eds.), *Explorations in the Ethnography of Speaking,* pp. 167–91. Cambridge: Cambridge University Press.

Ito, Rika 1996. The Northern Cities Shift in Northern Rural Michigan. Paper from the 25th Annual Conference on New Ways of Analyzing Variation in English, Las Vegas.

Kerswill, Paul 1995. Phonological Convergence in Dialect Contact: Evidence from Citation Forms. *Language Variation and Change* 7(2): 195–207.

Klein, Elaine C. 1995. Evidence for a "Wild" L2 Grammar: When PPs Rear their Empty Heads. *Applied Linguistics* 16(1): 87–117.

Kleiner, Brian 1996. Class Ethos and Politeness. *Journal of Language and Social Psychology* 15(2): 155–76.

Kroch, Anthony S. 1978. Toward a Theory of Social Dialect Variation. *Language in Society* 7(1): 17–36.

Labov, William 1963. The Social Motivation of a Sound Change. *Word* 19: 273–309.

1966. *The Social Stratification of English in New York City.* Washington, DC: Center for Applied Linguistics.

1969. Contraction, Deletion, and Inherent Variability of the English Copula. *Language* 45(4): 714–62.

1972. *Sociolinguistic Patterns.* Philadelphia: University of Pennsylvania Press.

1978. *Where Does the Linguistic Variable Stop? A Reply to Beatriz Lavandera* (Sociolinguistic Working Paper 44). Austin, TX: Southwest Educational Development Laboratory.

1989. Exact Description of the Speech Community: Short å in Philadelphia. In Ralph Fasold and Deborah Schiffrin (eds.), *Language Change and Variation,* pp. 1–57. Amsterdam: Benjamins.

1991. The Boundaries of a Grammar: Inter-dialectal Reactions to Ppositive *any more*. In Peter Trudgill and J. K. Chambers (eds.), *Dialects of English: Studies in Grammatical Variation*, pp. 273–88. London: Longman.

Labov, William, Cohen, Paul, Robbins, Clarence and Williams, John 1968. A Study of the Non-Standard English of Negro and Puerto Rican Speakers in New York City. USOE Final Report, Research Project No. 3288.

Meechan, Marjory and Foley, Michele 1994. On Resolving Disagreement: Linguistic Theory and Variation – *There's bridges. Language Variation and Change* 6(1): 63–85.

Milroy, Lesley 1980. *Language and Social Networks*. Oxford: Blackwell.

1996. Handout to accompany response to the presentation of Edward Finegan and Douglas Biber. NSF "Workshop on Style," Stanford University.

Milroy, Lesley and Milroy, James 1977. *Speech and Context in an Urban Setting* (Belfast Working Papers in Language and Linguistics 2). Ulster Polytechnic.

Munnich, Edward, Flynn, Suzanne and Martohardjono, Gita 1994. Elicited Imitation and Grammaticality Judgment Tasks: What they Measure and How they Relate to Each Other. In Elaine E. Tarone, Susan M. Gass and Andrew D. Cohen (eds.), *Research Methodology in Second Language Acquisition*, pp. 227–43. Hillsdale, NJ: Erlbaum.

Myers-Scotton, Carol 1993. *Social Motivations for Codeswitching*. Oxford: Oxford University Press.

Niedzielski, Nancy and Preston, Dennis R. 1999. *Folk Linguistics*. Trends in Linguistics: Studies in Monographs 122. Berlin: Mouton de Gruyter.

Preston, Dennis R. 1986. The Fifty Some-odd Categories of Language Variation. *International Journal of the Sociology of Language* 57: 9–47.

1989. *Sociolinguistics and Second Language Acquisition*. Oxford: Blackwell.

1991. Sorting out the Variables in Sociolinguistic Theory. *American Speech* 66: 33–56.

1992. Talking Black and Talking White: a Study in Variety Imitation. In Joan H. Hall, Nick Doane and Dick Ringler (eds.), *Old English and New: Studies in Language and Linguistics in Honor of Frederic G. Cassidy*, pp. 327–55 (Garland Reference Library of the Humanities 1652). New York and London: Garland.

1996a. The Northern Cities Chain Shift in your Mind. Paper from the 25th Annual Conference on New Ways of Analyzing Variation in English, Las Vegas.

1996b. Variationist Linguistics and Second Language Acquisition. In William C. Ritchie and Tej K. Bhatia (eds.), *Handbook of Second Language Acquisition*, pp. 229–65. New York: Academic Press.

1996c. Whaddayaknow: The Modes of Folk Linguistic Awareness. *Language Awareness* 5(1): 40–74.

Rickford, John R. 1981. A Variable Rule for a Creole Continuum. In David Sankoff and Henrietta Cedergren (eds.), *Variation Omnibus*, pp. 201–8. Edmonton: Linguistic Research.

1987. The Haves and Have Nots: Sociolinguistic Surveys and the Assessment of Speaker Competence. *Language in Society* 16(2): 149–77.

Sankoff, David (ed.) 1978. *Linguistic Variation: Models and Methods*. New York: Academic Press.

Sells, Peter, Rickford, John R. and Wasow, Thomas 1996. Variation in Negative

Inversion in AAVE: an Optimality Theoretic Approach. In Jennifer Arnold, Renée Blake, Brad Davidson, Scott Schwenter and Julie Solomon (eds.), *Sociolinguistic Variation: Data, Theory, and Analysis*, pp. 161–76 (Selected papers from 23rd Annual Conference on New Ways of Analyzing Variation in English, Stanford). Stanford: CSLI.

Slobin, Dan I. 1979[1971]. *Psycholinguistics*, 2nd edn. Glenview, IL: Scott, Foresman.

Tarone, Elaine E., Gass, Susan M. and Cohen, Andrew D. (eds.) 1994. *Research Methodology in Second Language Acquisition*. Hillsdale, NJ: Erlbaum.

Trudgill, Peter 1986. *Dialects in Contact*. Oxford: Blackwell.

1995[1974]. *Sociolinguistics: an Introduction to Language and Society* (New Edition). Harmondsworth, Middlesex: Penguin.

Wexler, Kenneth and Manzini, M. Rita 1987. Parameters and Learnability in Binding Theory. In Thomas Roeper and Edwin Williams (eds.), *Parameter Setting*, pp. 41–89. Dordrecht: Reidel.

Wolfram, Walt A. 1993. Identifying and Interpreting Variables. In Dennis R. Preston (ed.), *American Dialect Research*, pp. 193–221. Amsterdam: Benjamins.

Wolfram, Walt A. and Fasold, Ralph W. 1974. *The Study of Social Dialects in American English*. Englewood Cliffs, NJ: Prentice-Hall.

Wolfram, Walt A. and Schilling-Estes, Natalie 1995. Moribund Dialects and the Endangerment Canon: the Case of the Ocracoke Brogue. *Language* 71(4): 696–721.

Young, Richard and Bayley, Robert 1996. VARBRUL Analysis for Second Language Acquisition Research. In Robert Bayley and Dennis R. Preston (eds.), *Second Language Acquisition and Linguistic Variation*, pp. 253–306. Amsterdam: Benjamins.

Index